STAR WARS
THE MANDALORIAN
VISUAL GUIDE

WRITTEN BY **PABLO HIDALGO**

CROSS-SECTION ARTWORK BY **JOHN R. MULLANEY**

STAR WARS
THE MANDALORIAN
VISUAL GUIDE

WRITTEN BY **PABLO HIDALGO**

CROSS-SECTION ARTWORK BY **JOHN R. MULLANEY**

CONTENTS

Foreword 6
Introduction 8
Galaxy Map 10

PART I: A NEW COMPANION

The Mandalorian 16
Razor Crest 18
Inside the *Razor Crest* 20
Mando's Weapons 22
Pagodon 24
The Mythrol 26
Threats of the Ice 28
Nevarro 30
Greef Karga 32
The Safe House 34
Imperial Business 36
Nevarro Covert 38
The Armorer 40
The Armorer's Workshop 42
Arvala-7 44
Kuiil 46
Blurrgs 48
IG-11 50
Grogu 52
Offworld Jawas 54
Mudhorn 56
Paz Vizsla 58
Upgraded Armor 60
Sorgan 62
Sorgan Village 64
Cara Dune 66
Klatooinian Raiders 68
Riot Mar 70
Peli Motto 72
Peli's Droids 74

Toro Calican 76
Dewbacks 78
Fennec Shand 80
The Roost 82
Migs Mayfeld 84
Malk's Crew 86
Bothan-5 88
Bothan-5 Crew 90
Moff Gideon 92
The Darksaber 94
Outland TIE Fighter 96
Gideon's Assault 98
Underground Escape 100
Rising Phoenix 102

PART II: A NEW QUEST

Fight Night 106
Mos Pelgo 108
Cobb Vanth 110
Tuskens 112
Krayt Dragon 114
Frog Lady 116
Maldo Kreis 118
Alliance Veterans 120
Trask 122
High Seas Treachery 124
Bo-Katan Kryze 126
Bo-Katan's Unit 128
Imperial Target 130
Nevarro Revitalized 132
Imperial Base 134
Corvus 136
Rule of the Magistrate 138
Ahsoka Tano 140
Tython 142

Boba Fett	144
Boba Fett's Equipment	146
Boba Fett's Starship	148
Tython Assault	150
Morak	152
Morak Imperial Base	154
Preparing the Attack	156
Imperial Light Cruiser	158
Luke Skywalker	160

THE BOOK OF BOBA FETT

Glavis Ringworld	164
Mando's N-1 Starfighter	166
Inside Mando's N-1	168
Ossus	170
Battle of Mos Espa	172

PART III: A NEW HOME

The Covert Relocated	176
Return to Nevarro	178
Anzellan Droidsmiths	180
The Pirate King	182
Kalevala	184
R5-D4	186
Mandalore	188
Mythosaur	190
Intrigue on Coruscant	192
Learning the Way	194
Grogu's Past	196
Kelleran Beq	198
Rescuing Ragnar	200
IG-12	202
Adelphi	204
For Love or Money	206
Plazir-15	208
Shadow Council	210
Mandalorian Survivors	212
Moff Gideon's Forces	214
Confronting Gideon	216
Showdown on Mandalore	218
Nevarro Homestead	220

CODA: THE MANDALORIAN AND GROGU

Chasing the Remnant	222
Welcome to the Neighborhood	224
Republic Business	226
Index	228
Acknowledgments	232

FOREWORD

"The whole is greater than the sum of its parts" is a famous quote from Aristotle, and it's one that applies to storytelling and filmmaking, and especially to a galaxy far, far away.

It takes an army of talented artists to create a show like *The Mandalorian*. It all starts with story, and builds from there, both literally and figuratively. The story of Din Djarin is complicated and emotional, as is the story of Mandalore. The Mandalorian way of life is strict, with an honor-bound code, a deep lore, and an even deeper fanbase. The world-building around this mythology was first imagined by George Lucas, then expanded upon by Dave Filoni, Jon Favreau, and all of the amazing writers, directors, and artisans who have worked on *The Mandalorian*. As Din Djarin, I'm humbled to include myself in this company, and honored to help expand the storytelling of Mandalore, of Din, and, of course, of Grogu.

Fans might not realize all of the hard work, dedication, and little details that go into each and every episode of *The Mandalorian*, but they can catch a glimpse of that here, in this book. From the biggest details—like the *Razor Crest* itself—to the smallest—like Mando's Whispering Birds—this book shines a spotlight on the costumes, props, vehicles, and characters, and allows fans to go deeper into the storytelling of the show.

The Mandalorian wouldn't be what it is today without those fans, and a book like this is a way for them to experience the show—and all the hard work that goes into it—in an all-new way.

I hope you enjoy all of the little details and the sum of our parts.

After all, this is the Way.

PEDRO PASCAL
NOVEMBER 2025

INTRODUCTION

The worlds that the Mandalorian visits are full of dangerous surprises. They're a mix of shadowy taverns, wide-open horizons, sparsely settled frontier outposts, and colorful characters with checkered pasts. The galaxy is healing from the last great war, but many of its citizens are wondering how much time is left before the next one.

As the first-ever live-action *Star Wars* television series, *The Mandalorian* intricately weaves threads inspired by samurai and Western films, while also pulling in beloved elements from decades of *Star Wars* storytelling. It is a world of vivid detail as befits all *Star Wars* tales, and now it heads to the big screen where the franchise was born.

This book is a means of examining that detail and soaking in its surroundings. It's a showcase of the creative talents behind the series, placed in the context of the larger galaxy. There is much to learn in these pages, but there are some names and backgrounds that will remain unknown. There are secrets some will kill to protect. There are some masks that will never come off.

This is the Way.

GALAXY MAP

Reconstruction following the Galactic Civil War is slow-going and complex. The last great war prior to the Empire versus Rebellion conflict, known as the Clone Wars, was one of separatism. Worlds that were wary of Galactic Republic stewardship are even more suspicious of a nascent New Republic's promises of union. These doubts are exacerbated in the Outer Rim, which bore the brunt of disruption from warfare and has traditionally disdained the reach of central governments.

GALACTIC FACTIONS

THE NEW REPUBLIC
New Republic expansion was tempered and cautious, emphasizing egalitarianism and consensus among its member worlds. Many former Imperial territories were ceded to the new government by treaty, but vast swaths are only nominally held, with very little official presence.

IMPERIAL REMNANT
Debate continues whether the Imperial remnant is a singular scattered polity or a number of unrelated splintered factions. Warlords and opportunists seized control of local territories in the name of the Empire in the months after the Battle of Endor, requiring concerted efforts by the New Republic and other groups to quash and liberate the affected worlds.

MANDALORIANS
Mandalorians are a rare sight in the galaxy, yet a subject of growing folklore. Individual Mandalorians are still potent warriors, but as a people they are broken and diffuse—a shadow of their former greatness.

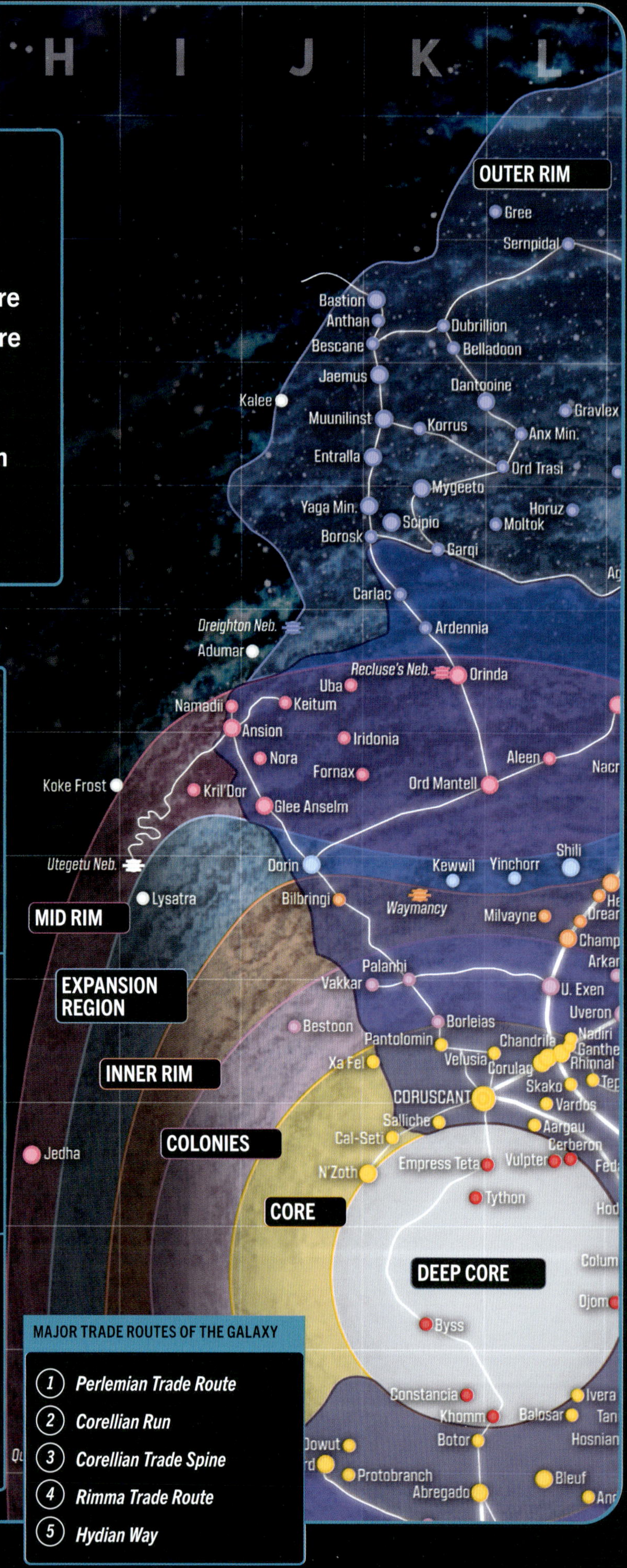

MAJOR TRADE ROUTES OF THE GALAXY
1. Perlemian Trade Route
2. Corellian Run
3. Corellian Trade Spine
4. Rimma Trade Route
5. Hydian Way

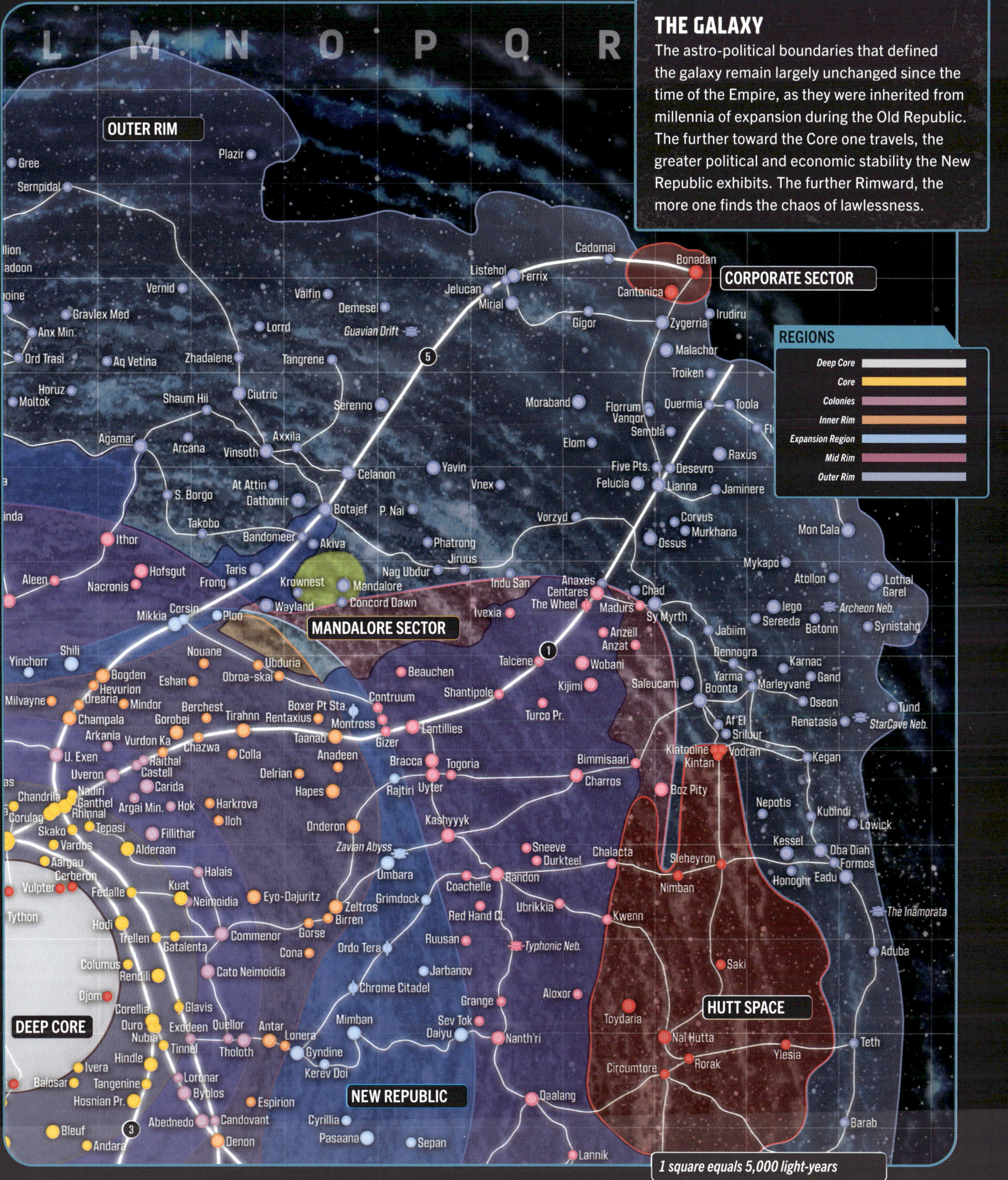

GALAXY MAP CONTINUED

MANDALORIAN HISTORY

ANCIENT ORIGINS
Early settlers to what would become Mandalorian space find tough worlds that force them to hone their survival skills. They discover the metal beskar and use it to forge armor and tame the monstrous wilderness.

REPUBLIC CONFLICT
Mandalorians refuse integration into the growing Republic. They see the expanding government as encroaching on their space, leading to conflict between the Republic—particularly the Jedi of the era—and the Mandalorians.

TARRE VIZSLA
In an attempt to cement a peace, Mandalorian Tarre Vizsla becomes a Jedi initiate. He crafts a Jedi weapon that combines aspects of both cultures: the Darksaber.

INTERNAL HOSTILITIES
Mandalorian space becomes a tinderbox of strife as individual houses and families vie for power. This culminates in a calamitous civil war that scorches the surface of their capital planet, Mandalore, forcing its people to live in hermetic domes.

NEW MANDALORIANS
In the aftermath of this destruction arises Duchess Satine Kryze of Kalevala, who proposes a new way forward that emphasizes peace. This era is marked by an undercurrent of resentment from restless warriors that form the Death Watch splinter faction.

CLONE WARS CHAOS
Death Watch, goaded by shadowy puppet masters, seizes power over Mandalore in a coup. The Republic avoids interceding due to Mandalore's neutrality in the Clone Wars. But in time, the Republic does enter the fray and is positioned to take stewardship of the world when the Empire arises.

IMPERIAL RULE AND GREAT PURGE
The Empire installs loyal Mandalorian governors. Attempts at internal rebellion trigger a brutal crackdown known as the Night of a Thousand Tears orchestrated by Moff Gideon. This prompts an exodus of refugees and a scattering of Mandalorians.

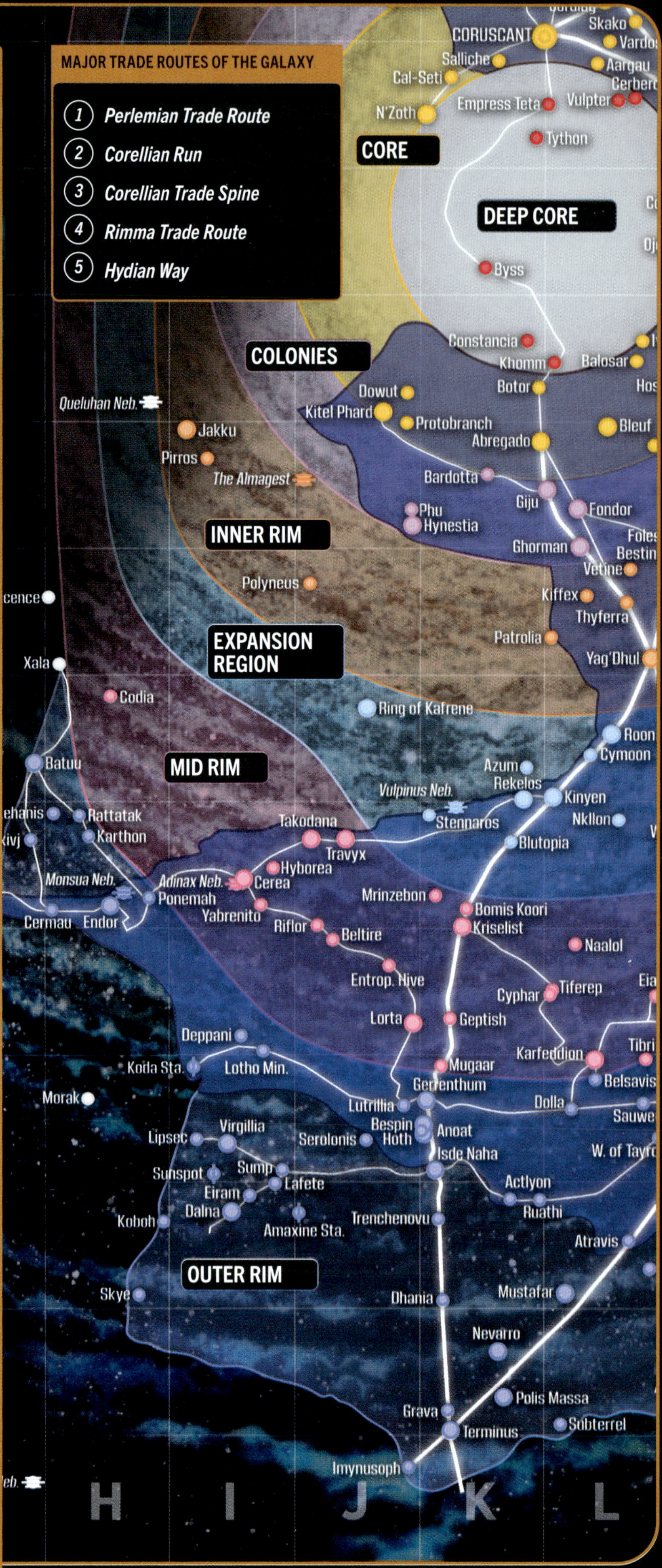

MAJOR TRADE ROUTES OF THE GALAXY

1. Perlemian Trade Route
2. Corellian Run
3. Corellian Trade Spine
4. Rimma Trade Route
5. Hydian Way

PART I:
A NEW COMPANION

Even in the most stable of times, bounty hunting is an unpredictable profession. As the New Republic struggles to bring peace and security to the galaxy, the limited reach of its control means denizens must find their own paths to justice. Bounty hunters fill that gap, pursuing fugitives for profit, and the mysterious Mandalorian earns a reputation for being a reliable tracker.

The economic and political uncertainties hit this ordinarily reliable trade. The Mandalorian's primary contact in the Bounty Hunters Guild, Greef Karga of Nevarro, has little in the ways of lucrative contracts, but there is an intriguing offer: a no-questions-asked assignment with a hefty payoff. Though Mando doesn't relish being hired by ex-Imperials, work is work. He signs on to track the mysterious "asset."

The asset—a wide-eyed Child with strange gifts and enigmatic origins—changes the Mandalorian's life, transforming the cold, solitary hunter into a compassionate guardian. Mando makes an enemy of the Bounty Hunters Guild for absconding with the Child and retreating further into the Outer Rim. As he outpaces other hunters, Mando makes new allies in his quest to keep the Child safe. With the number of trusted allies running low, Mando reaches out to outlaw partners from yesteryear, securing perilous work to keep covering his costs of living dangerously, and keeping ever on the move.

In time, Mando realizes he cannot keep running. His actions have focused Imperial attention on Nevarro and threaten the sanctity of the secret Mandalorian enclave there. The mastermind seeking the Child, Moff Gideon, appears from the shadows.

PART I: A NEW COMPANION

THE MANDALORIAN

Hidden behind patchwork armor and the distinctive T-visored helmet of his culture, the mysterious gunslinger known only as the Mandalorian completes jobs for the Bounty Hunters Guild in the Outer Rim. As his reputation spreads, there are very few tangible details about the warrior beyond his effectiveness. Since the Great Purge of Mandalore, his warrior culture is all but extinct. The few examples of its famed armor are more likely to be encountered in the collections and galleries of the rich and powerful than being worn by its people. The Mandalorian is a throwback, and rare enough that his moniker of "the Mandalorian" (or the less formal Mando) does sufficient work describing him.

The Mandalorian works alone, with his scant possessions and formidable arsenal kept aboard his ever-mobile home, the starship *Razor Crest*. He is a Bounty Hunters Guild member in good standing and has a lucrative working relationship with Guild agent Greef Karga. In exchange for bounties delivered, Mando earns money that he then distributes to a secret Mandalorian enclave on the planet Nevarro. There, a revered Armorer crafts new armor pieces for him, while channeling a portion of Mando's pay to the foundlings who need it most.

MYSTERIOUS PAST

The Mandalorian vows to keep his face and his past hidden. His real name is Din Djarin, and a tragic day during the Clone Wars on his homeworld of Aq Vetina still haunts him. It was the day his parents were killed by battle droid fire; the day he nearly met the same fate; the day Mandalorians came rocketing in to rescue him; the day he became a foundling. From that day onward, Din would follow the path of the Way, a Mandalorian system of beliefs.

Ion prod conductor tines

Leather bandolier with lower-grade power charges

Leg strap carries higher-grade power charges

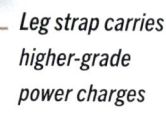

The Mandalorian takes cover as he tries to explain to destructive IG-11 that they are both fellow Guild members.

CURRENT ACQUISITIONS

The three bounties currently accounted for aboard the *Razor Crest*:

ROSH JOTH
Smuggler. Thief. Human male. Captain of *Heavy Dragon*. 4,000-credit capture alive.

SENNI RESEETA
Con artist. Human female. 8,000-credit capture alive.

CHIHDO
Smuggler. Rodian male. Weapons dealer. 3,000-credit capture alive.

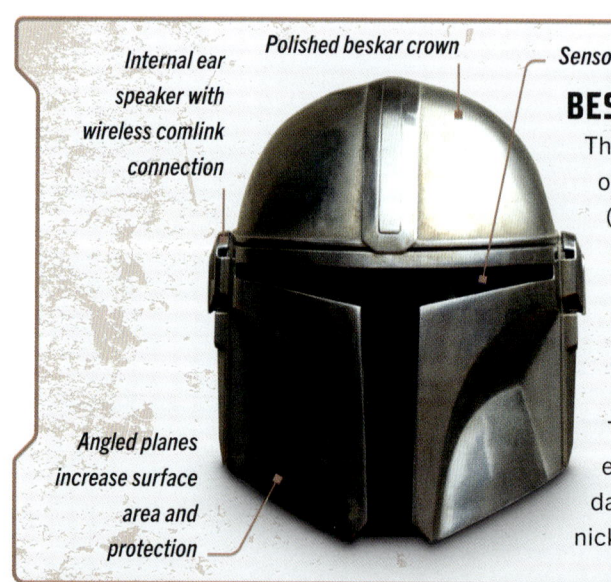

Internal ear speaker with wireless comlink connection

Polished beskar crown

Sensor-lined T-visor

Angled planes increase surface area and protection

BESKAR'GAM BUY'CE

The purest example of beskar armor on Mando's person is his helmet (or *buy'ce* in Mandalorian parlance). With a gleaming, unpainted finish, its surface most resembles the raw beskar ingots that are then forged by the Armorer. The helmet's T-visor is lined with advanced electronics that transform sensor data into information overlays nicknamed "Mandovision."

A WORK IN PROGRESS

The Mandalorian's patchwork appearance mirrors the attempts of his people to slowly, methodically rebuild. His armor is a mix of genuine Mandalorian parts and salvage—stopgap measures to cover any weaknesses while he earns enough credits to pay for replacement beskar pieces. As his success grows, so too does his resemblance to a traditional Mandalorian warrior.

"THIS IS THE WAY."
— THE MANDALORIAN

DATA FILE

SUBJECT The Mandalorian (real name Din Djarin)
HOMEWORLD Aq Vetina
SPECIES Human
AFFILIATION Bounty Hunters Guild; the Nevarro Mandalorian Covert
HEIGHT 1.8 m (5 ft 11 in)

Salvaged Imperial shoretrooper pauldron

Unarmored body parts protected by tough worker fatigues

Battered chest plate of impure beskar

Mandalorian gauntlets feature lightweight honeycomb construction to reduce encumbrance that might drag down reflexes in combat situations.

Utility belt holds spare ammo, explosives, and other equipment

Insulating gloves with sensory feedback to activate armor features

PART I: A NEW COMPANION
RAZOR CREST

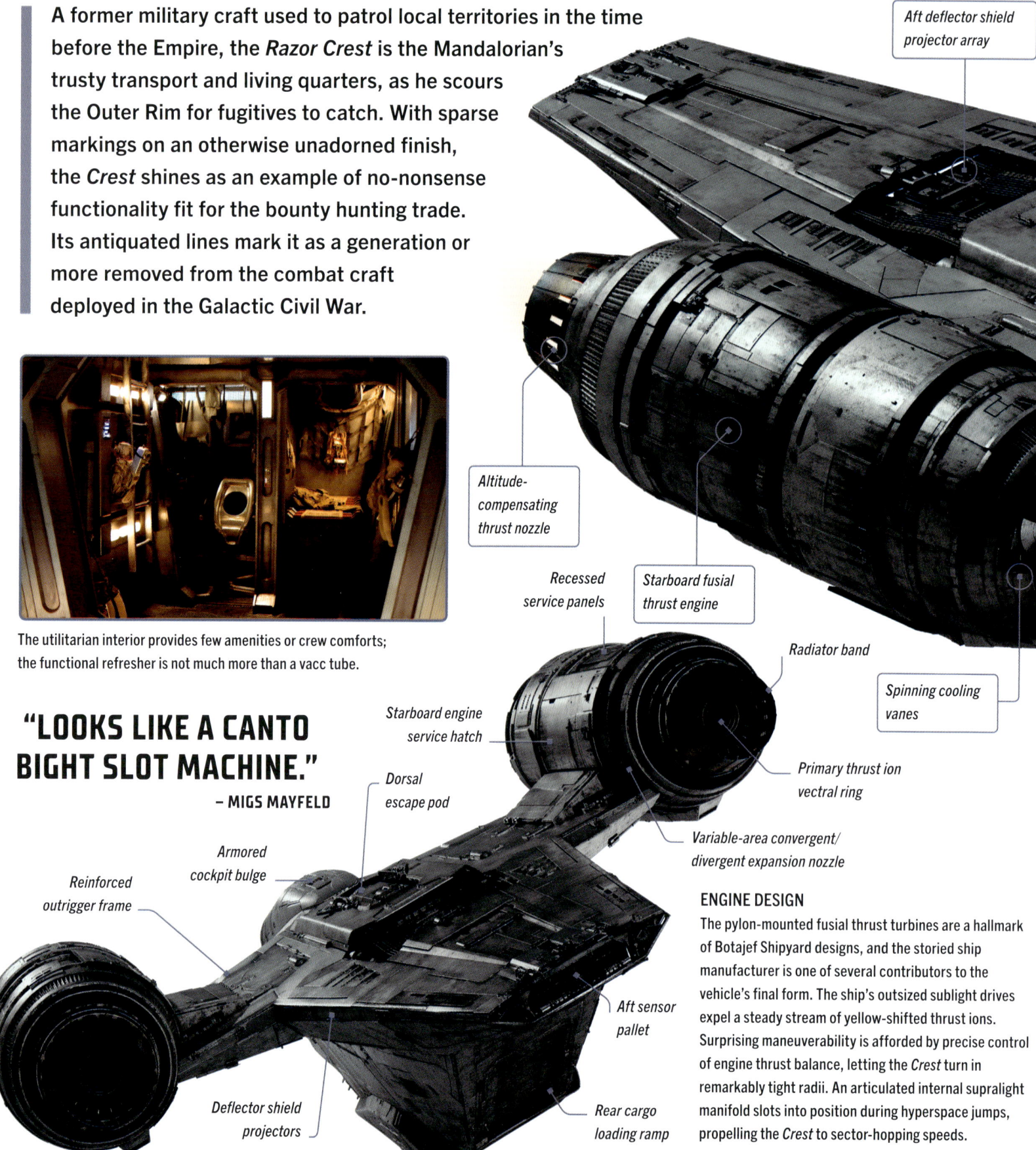

A former military craft used to patrol local territories in the time before the Empire, the *Razor Crest* is the Mandalorian's trusty transport and living quarters, as he scours the Outer Rim for fugitives to catch. With sparse markings on an otherwise unadorned finish, the *Crest* shines as an example of no-nonsense functionality fit for the bounty hunting trade. Its antiquated lines mark it as a generation or more removed from the combat craft deployed in the Galactic Civil War.

The utilitarian interior provides few amenities or crew comforts; the functional refresher is not much more than a vacc tube.

> "LOOKS LIKE A CANTO BIGHT SLOT MACHINE."
> – MIGS MAYFELD

Labels:
- Aft deflector shield projector array
- Altitude-compensating thrust nozzle
- Recessed service panels
- Starboard fusial thrust engine
- Radiator band
- Spinning cooling vanes
- Starboard engine service hatch
- Primary thrust ion vectral ring
- Dorsal escape pod
- Variable-area convergent/divergent expansion nozzle
- Armored cockpit bulge
- Reinforced outrigger frame
- Aft sensor pallet
- Deflector shield projectors
- Rear cargo loading ramp

ENGINE DESIGN
The pylon-mounted fusial thrust turbines are a hallmark of Botajef Shipyard designs, and the storied ship manufacturer is one of several contributors to the vehicle's final form. The ship's outsized sublight drives expel a steady stream of yellow-shifted thrust ions. Surprising maneuverability is afforded by precise control of engine thrust balance, letting the *Crest* turn in remarkably tight radii. An articulated internal supralight manifold slots into position during hyperspace jumps, propelling the *Crest* to sector-hopping speeds.

Port armored fuel tankage

Repulsorlift atmospheric drive adaptor

Reinforced transparisteel viewport

Heavy laser cannon barrel

Forward sensor and avionics bay

Heat-reflective reentry hull coating

Cannon heat dissipation shroud

CREST'S COCKPIT
The pilot's seat in the *Razor Crest* sits high within a wraparound viewport, granting the Mandalorian an exceptional field of vision beyond the ship's sensors. The other cockpit seats are intended for passengers rather than copilots, as everything required to fly the *Crest* can normally be handled by the pilot.

OFF THE GRID
During the time of the Empire, the Imperial Space Ministry kept transponder records of all licensed civilian starships in operation within its domain. The *Razor Crest* predates this mandate and is excepted from it by its military origins. Therefore, it broadcasts no such identification, making it a rare example of a civilian craft that can fly as a "ghost"—an anonymous craft whose business remains unknown. Though not specifically equipped for stealth operations, this feature does keep the *Razor Crest* unnoticed by the inattentive.

DATA FILE
MANUFACTURER Corellian Engineering Corporation (subsidiary: Belsmuth Consolidations Ltd.)

MODEL ST-70 M-111 Razor Crest series

TYPE Assault gunship

DIMENSIONS Height: 7.4 m (24 ft 3 in); width: 16.3 m (53 ft 6 in); length: 24.27 m (79 ft 8 in)

WEAPONS 2 forward Mk 3e/W heavy laser cannons

AFFILIATION Bounty Hunters Guild

PART I: A NEW COMPANION

INSIDE THE *RAZOR CREST*

The *Razor Crest*'s hold is indicative of its original design intent as a military craft. The barren interior could carry war materiel or hardened troops hanging onto cargo netting. In its current incarnation, Mando keeps the hold empty in anticipation of assignments that may lead to acquiring larger targets, more bounties than expected, or trappings such as speeders and speeder bikes. Access to the cockpit is via a ladder that extends up into the flight deck.

GUTTED ON ARVALA-7
Thieving Jawas in the hardened mud desert raid an unattended *Razor Crest*, stripping it of its vital components and rendering it a flightless wreck. Mando's first attempt to reclaim the parts—disintegrating a number of Jawas with his pulse rifle—fails, and he is forced to turn to a more diplomatic, transactional arrangement to reclaim his ship's innards.

EMERGENCY SYSTEMS
In case the *Razor Crest* suffers catastrophic failure, a single coffin-like escape pod sits between the engines along the spine of the ship. It is optimized for pilot access, sitting on the upper deck with the cockpit compartment. Once activated, the pod launches from the ailing *Crest*, fired free of any blast radius by compressed air.

- Articulated vent plates assist with maneuverability
- Atmospheric sampling sensors
- Cockpit access doors
- Scomp link socket
- Ladder to lower deck
- Toylike knob head
- Hyperdrive activation lever
- Targeting sensor array
- Avionics bay service hatch
- Lateral maneuverability pedals
- Cot/bunk
- Forward sensor units
- Calibrated mounting brace
- Vacc tube/refresher privy
- Armored heat dissipation shroud

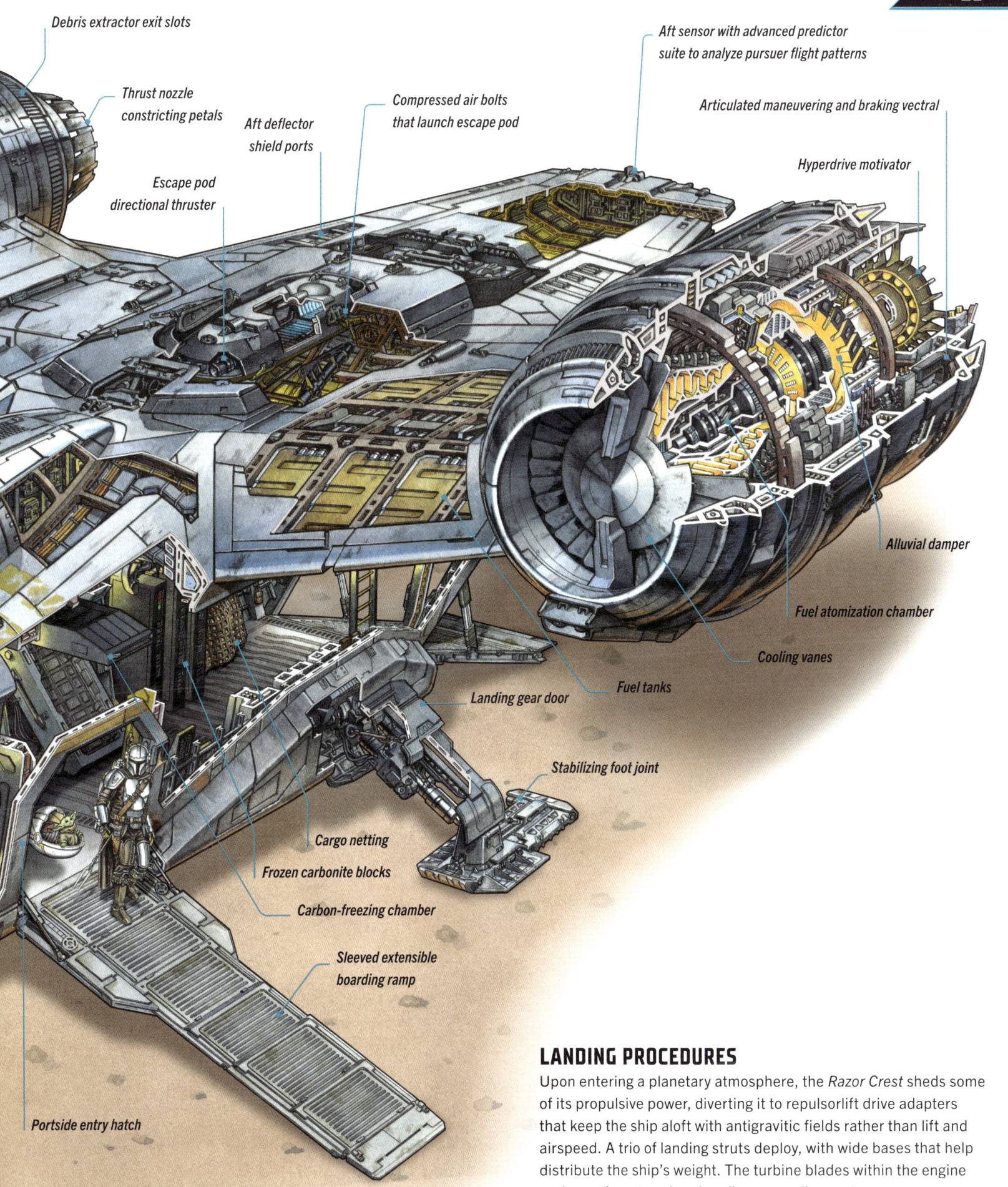

LANDING PROCEDURES

Upon entering a planetary atmosphere, the *Razor Crest* sheds some of its propulsive power, diverting it to repulsorlift drive adapters that keep the ship aloft with antigravitic fields rather than lift and airspeed. A trio of landing struts deploy, with wide bases that help distribute the ship's weight. The turbine blades within the engine pods continue to spin primarily as a cooling system.

PART I: A NEW COMPANION
MANDO'S WEAPONS

Success and survival in the bounty hunting business are dependent on well-maintained equipment and weaponry. The hunter that neglects them risks their life and livelihood. As a follower of the Way, Mando's affinity for his kit goes far deeper than just seeing it as tools of the trade. Mandalorians treat their armor and survival implements as sacred. Mando has a stock of preferred weapons in addition to a range of mission-specific gear he keeps stowed and ready should the need arise.

RAZOR CREST'S ARMORY
Kept within a sealed, double-doored compartment in the *Razor Crest* is Mando's expanded arsenal—an array of more than a dozen pistols, rifles, and explosive devices. Mando's more frequently used weapons are kept within reach. His Amban rifle, when on board the *Razor Crest*, is magnetically affixed to the bulkhead next to the cockpit door.

AMBAN RIFLE
Mando's long-range sniper rifle is as iconic as he is, and easily distinguished by a forked barrel that doubles as an ion prod electro-bayonet. The rifle can be classified as a disruptor because of its devastating firepower. One blast can disintegrate a humanoid-sized organic target. At full charge, the rifle drains a power cell per shot.

Power cell port hatch control

Release trigger

Removeable electroscope

Hardened construction so rifle can be used as melee staff

DATA FILE
MANUFACTURER	Amban Arms
WEAPON SYSTEM	Notimo-6 phase-pulse disruptor rifle
MASS	3.65 kg (8 lbs)
POWER SYSTEM	Proprietary Notimo-6 power cells
COOLING SYSTEM	Air-cooled with low rate of fire
AMMUNITION YIELD	1 power cell per disruptor round

Mando lines up a long-range shot on one of the Jawa scavengers who have stripped the *Razor Crest* on Arvala-7.

CUSTOM-MACHINED VIBROBLADE

MANDO'S GAUNTLETS

Gauntlets are a semi-standard piece of Mandalorian kit. In the conflict-ridden past, Mandalorians would load out their vambraces with defensive and offensive gear. The tradition continues, though more often than not the gauntlets are mismatched leftovers, as full suits of beskar armor are exceedingly rare. Mando's gauntlets are an 85 percent beskar blend.

Pinned by an angry blurrg, Mando tries to free his arm in order to roast the beast with his flame projector.

LEFT VAMBRACE

RIGHT VAMBRACE

Taking cover behind some debris, Mando picks his shots carefully with his trusty IB-94.

BLASTECH IB-94 BLASTER PISTOL

A contemporary of the DL-44 blaster pistol, the IB-94 proves less popular due to the constant upkeep it requires: cleaning its power contacts, filling its reactant gas, and lubricating its internal valves. Those who put in the effort find a reliable weapon with greater range and firepower than comparable pistols. Its limited run ensures the weapon's relative scarcity.

PART I: A NEW COMPANION

PAGODON

A briny ocean separates Pagodon's rocky surface from its icy shell, and within those waters lurks sea life vital to the planet's economy. A variety of cold-water fishes produce insulating oils through specialized glands, and these organs can be harvested for a number of medicinal and industrial purposes. Pagodon is remote enough not to have become subject to complete industrial exploitation, so intrepid trawlers and haulers carve out a dangerous living on the ice for the promise of big payouts.

The Mandalorian treads one of the boardwalks that provides a non-slippery surface and absorbs predator-luring vibrations along its desolate length.

Ferryman's Reach

Volcanic vents

Nightwood forests

Softer ice pack

DATA FILE

REGION Outer Rim

SECTOR Pelgrin

SYSTEM Pagodon

DIAMETER 5,149 km (3,200 miles)

TERRAIN Frozen oceans; little exposed land

MOONS 2

POPULATION No official census; estimated to be under 500,000

ICY ITEMS OF INTEREST

FERRYMAN'S REACH
Several collections of huts have sprung up to support the trawlers. They supply intrepid anglers and netters as they embark.

LANDING YARDS
Undifferentiated stretches of ice strong enough to support a starship are what pass as "ports" on this largely unsettled world.

THE BOARDWALKS
Equatorial timbers not only form the foundations of snow-deflecting domes, but also the walkways that connect them to tiny communities.

MOMONTH'S PUBLIC HOUSE
A heated structure serving drinks to trawlers and visitors, Momonth's has a pressure-sealed irising door to keep out the biting winds.

TRAWLER WISDOM
The orbital paths of Pagodon's moons churn the waters and shape the flow of ocean life. Smart trawlers know to consult tide charts and work out their hunting territories. Some of the more seasoned anglers rely on intuition instead, claiming an innate advantage from familiarity with the sea.

> "I'D STAY OFF THE ICE IF I WERE YOU!"
> – PYAN BOSEN

FACT FILE

SKINK PIT
Landed ships evacuating their gray holds of sludge and organic wastes risk attracting ravinaks on the prowl.

INCLEMENT CONDITIONS
Predator interest and ice density keep communities from growing too big, making Pagodon settlements appealing to those avoiding crowds.

Dleggman's Outfitters: seasonal fishing supply shack

Weather monitoring station and communications center

Abandoned dump shack, now a community junk pile

Ice pack varies from two to five meters thick

Detritus from gray holds

PART I: A NEW COMPANION

THE MYTHROL

Now a fugitive, the Mythrol was an accountant from the Nevarro magistrate's office who earned a bounty on his head for "creative bookkeeping" that enriched his coffers at his superior's expense. The Mythrol's skill in bureaucratic data-wrangling meant he was able to erase an extensive holotrail and wipe records of all traces of him. But not even this cunning malcontent can erase his chain code from within the records available to the Bounty Hunters Guild.

This chatty criminal is not much of a threat to the Mandalorian. His bounty includes no hazard rate multipliers or ammunition stipends. It is imperative that he is captured alive, so Mando tacks him onto a stint of hunts, which have already filled his cargo hold full of profitable acquisitions during his return to Nevarro. The Mythrol, not one for confrontation, attempts to talk his way out of capture. He does, after all, have access to further ill-gotten funds. Mando follows both his own code and that of the Bounty Hunters Guild, and will not be bribed.

COLD CONFRONTATION
The Mythrol's meek demeanor draws the ire of a trio of rowdy trawlers on Pagodon. They jokingly size up his piscine attributes, wondering aloud about the value of his glands. Though Mando springs to the Mythrol's aid, the act brings a different kind of trouble into the criminal's life.

> "LOOK, THERE MUST BE SOME MISTAKE. I CAN GET YOU MORE CREDITS."
> – MYTHROL TO MANDO

Mando shoves the Mythrol under the nozzles of aerosolized carbonite spray jets, which quickly coat the victim in the alloy.

CARBON-FREEZING TRANSPORTATION
Carbon-freezing is an increasingly popular means of restraining prisoners, made infamous by Jabba the Hutt's display of a carbon-frozen Han Solo in his throne room. What was once primarily an industrial gas containment system has been adapted to lock life-forms in stasis for easy delivery to the Bounty Hunters Guild.

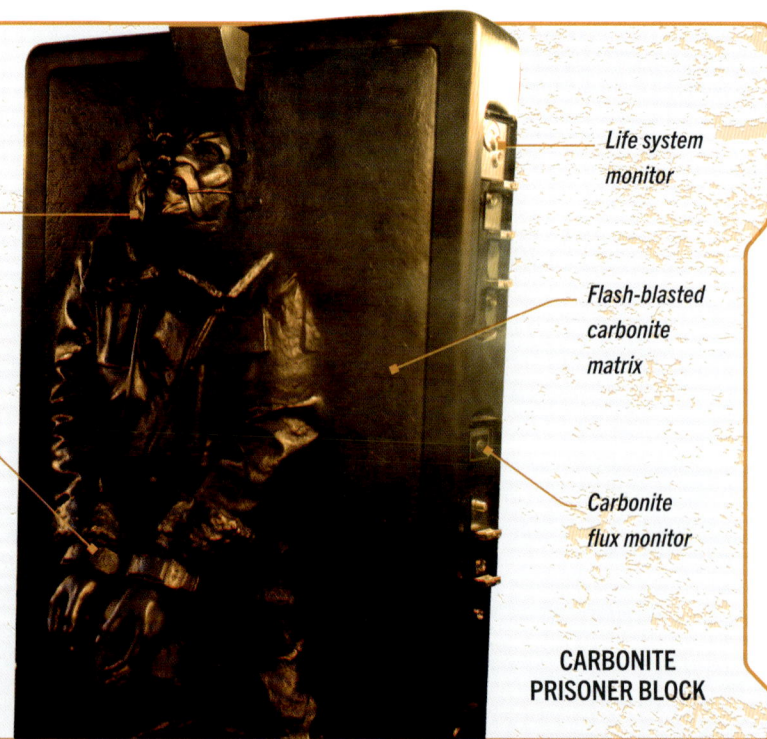

- Anguished grimace from frozen carbonite contact
- Binders made of carbonite alloy melt when block is thawed
- Life system monitor
- Flash-blasted carbonite matrix
- Carbonite flux monitor

CARBONITE PRISONER BLOCK

DATA FILE

SUBJECT "The Mythrol"
HOMEWORLD Nevarro (base of operations)
SPECIES Mythrol
AFFILIATION Fugitive
HEIGHT 1.73 m (5 ft 8 in)

AQUATIC HERITAGE
A Mythrol starts life as a water-based polliwog and becomes amphibious during their fledgling years. After a series of moltings, their vestigial fin webbing fades away, making their later years better suited for life on land.

Insulated qartuum-hide jumpsuit

Controls linked to his humidity vest

Electro-stun carbonite binders

Coin purse filled with high-denomination credits

Mando marches the Mythrol across the frozen boardwalk leading out of the fishing village, on the way to his waiting vessel.

PART I: A NEW COMPANION
THREATS OF THE ICE

Ferryman's Reach on Pagodon is a short speeder ride away from an area of ice set aside for ship landings. Misleadingly named the yards, it lacks any sort of docking amenities. Such items must be brought in from the Reach at hauling and rental cost. This minimalist approach is designed to confine business transactions to within the settlement. Though it is possible to walk to and from the yards, speeder travel is recommended to avoid numerous natural hazards.

> "I ASSURE YOU, THIS SPEEDER IS BRAND NEW. IT'S THE LATEST MODEL."
> – BARLIDAN

Polarized lenses reduce glare from ice

Perforated sheath protects trunk from frostbite

Truncated kloo horn modified for Kubaz embouchure

Barlidan sits on a storage box that conceals a heating generator.

The weather-beaten pilot holds it together better than his rickety speeder.

SPEEDER PILOT
Pursued by aggressive creditors, this weather-beaten man fled to Pagodon, where he saves what little he can from his job as a courier driver on the ice. He has absorbed the scant local folklore to engage his fares in small talk. He's been accused of being too chatty by more than one customer.

BARLIDAN
The ferryman Barlidan has an ear for droid languages, and he can mimic astromech binary with a simple kloo horn. Pagodon's lack of insects and its subzero temperatures make Barlidan pine for warmer worlds where such life is typically more abundant. Barlidan misses the sights, smells, and tastes of home.

RAVINAK

With powerful muscles concealed by a layer of insulating blubber, hungry ravinaks can propel themselves up through the ice to hunt prey on the surface.

- Cutting nodes weaken ice for breaching
- Sealing blowhole
- Powerful fore limbs
- Scutes dull and break off with age
- Forked tail
- Ground ravinak tusks are valued for purported healing qualities
- Hardened claws
- Muscular fluke builds impressive speed
- Repeated passes rubbing their dorsal spikes against the ice cover enable ravinaks to burst through to the surface.

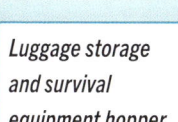

SECOND CHOICE SPEEDER

The Mandalorian rejects the first offered speeder due to his disdain for droids. He'd rather have an organic pilot. The Ferryman whistles up a clunker of a speeder, which arrives at the station belching smoke and shedding hatch covers. Despite its eyesore appearance, it proceeds across the ice smoothly.

The control cabin is kept simple and operational with the barest of upkeep. Some labels and gauges have faded or peeled away with age.

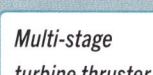

DATA FILE

MANUFACTURER	Mobquet Swoops and Speeders
MODEL	M-335
TYPE	Personal landspeeder
DIMENSIONS	Height: 1.19 m (3 ft 11 in); width: 3.16 m (10 ft 4 in); length: 6.06 m (19 ft 11 in)
SPEED	225 kph (139 mph)
WEAPONS	None
AFFILIATION	Independent

- Luggage storage and survival equipment hopper
- Multi-stage turbine thruster
- External heating bars mounted over grille

PART I: A NEW COMPANION

NEVARRO

A young planet gradually cooling off from an active volcanic phase, Nevarro is a sparsely populated world in the Outer Rim Territories that once boasted an Imperial presence. After the collapse of the Empire, the planet was downgraded from Imperial foothold to Imperial footnote, with most of its operatives seemingly fleeing—leaving a scant few behind in hiding. Underground, beneath the planet's hardened black crust, surviving Mandalorians have also made temporary homes for themselves.

> "THE SUN DROPS FAST ON NEVARRO."
> – GREEF KARGA

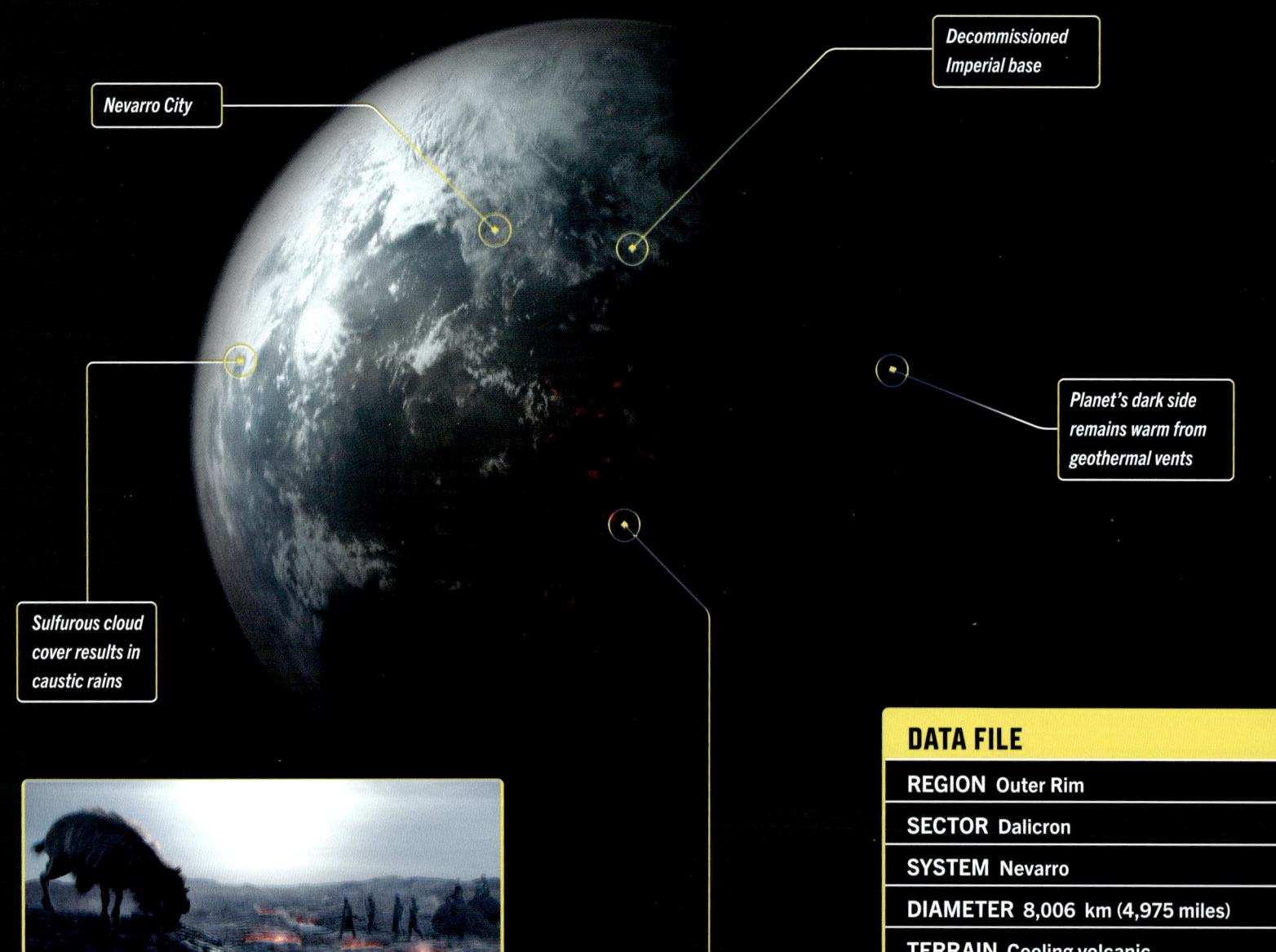

Nevarro City

Decommissioned Imperial base

Planet's dark side remains warm from geothermal vents

Sulfurous cloud cover results in caustic rains

Geologically active equatorial zone

Hungry qartuums can eat and metabolize a wide range of minerals. The shaggy hircine beasts are a source of tough but nutritious meat.

DATA FILE

REGION	Outer Rim
SECTOR	Dalicron
SYSTEM	Nevarro
DIAMETER	8,006 km (4,975 miles)
TERRAIN	Cooling volcanic
MOONS	None
POPULATION	4 million

AMID THE ASHES

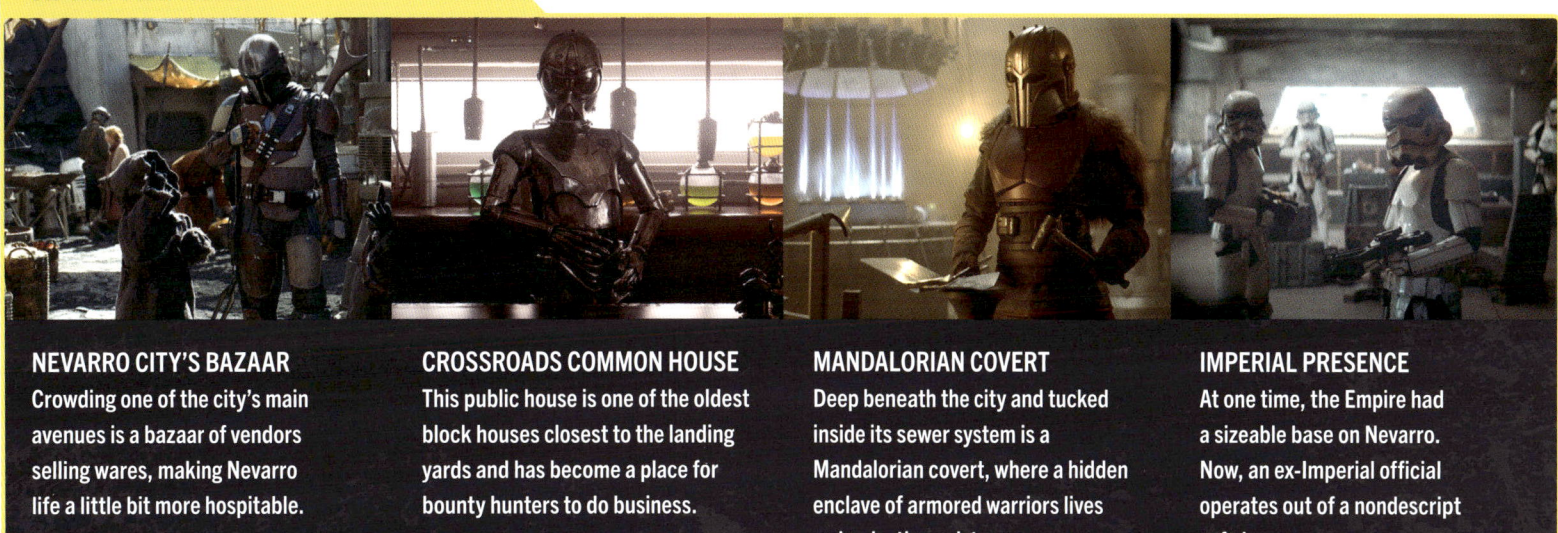

NEVARRO CITY'S BAZAAR
Crowding one of the city's main avenues is a bazaar of vendors selling wares, making Nevarro life a little bit more hospitable.

CROSSROADS COMMON HOUSE
This public house is one of the oldest block houses closest to the landing yards and has become a place for bounty hunters to do business.

MANDALORIAN COVERT
Deep beneath the city and tucked inside its sewer system is a Mandalorian covert, where a hidden enclave of armored warriors lives a clandestine existence.

IMPERIAL PRESENCE
At one time, the Empire had a sizeable base on Nevarro. Now, an ex-Imperial official operates out of a nondescript safe house.

NEVARRO CITY

Nevarro City grew up around the Bulloch lava-tube network. Porous rock keeps the tubes from collecting rain, thus creating a natural underground sewer system that was expanded and fortified along with the city. Most buildings are not freestanding, but rather brutalist tunnels cut from the rock, with avenue-facing facades being their main differentiating feature.

City gate once held a bell, long since vanished

When viewed from the surface, Nevarro City mostly disappears. Few structures extend far from the lava tubes.

Public house's communications antenna extends from lava tube

Livestock outfitters pen

Colorful awnings denote trade

PART I: A NEW COMPANION
GREEF KARGA

> The affable Greef Karga is a boisterous businessman who always wants things to go smoothly, but is experienced enough to prepare for the worst. It is a survival instinct vital to his role as local Bounty Hunters Guild boss on Nevarro. Karga works well with Mando and keeps the hunter supplied with bounties, often setting aside the most lucrative ones for his armored friend. That Mando reliably delivers means Karga can depend on his own percentages from these assignments.

It is Karga who connects Mando to the mysterious Imperial Client's bounty for the asset on Arvala-7. The Guild boss knows few details beyond that the Client is casting a wide net and hiring many hunters, but he bets correctly that Mando will be the one to succeed. Karga receives a few bars of Imperial-branded beskar bullion as his percentage.

What Greef doesn't count on is for Mando to break Guild code and steal back the asset from the Client after delivery and payment. This makes Mando an enemy of the Guild, and the two business partners find themselves pointing blasters at each other after an intense bounty hunter shootout.

Greef has a reserved table at the Nevarro Common House where he conducts business, out in the open where it's safest.

GREEF THE GUNSLINGER
Greef is quick on the draw, and his honed coordination lets him wield paired blaster pistols in combat. His skills are on display when Greef blasts fellow Guild hunters that were aiming to kill Mando. Having witnessed the abilities of the Child firsthand, and realizing that the unchecked Imperial presence on Nevarro is a threat to all, Karga proposes a deal to Mando—team up and eliminate the Client. It is Greef's hope that with the Imperial leadership on Nevarro destroyed, the stormtroopers will leave.

- Steely gaze tracks enemy movement
- Braced gunfighter stance
- Holster cut for fast draw
- Weight distributed evenly for balanced firing

TOOLS OF THE TRADE
The return of tracking fobs issued by authorized Guild agents is part of the proof required to secure payment. The compact short-range sensor unit keeps a computerized record of a target's biometric profile and legal chain code. Low bounties prevail as the uncertain galactic economy keeps clients from paying premium Guild rates.

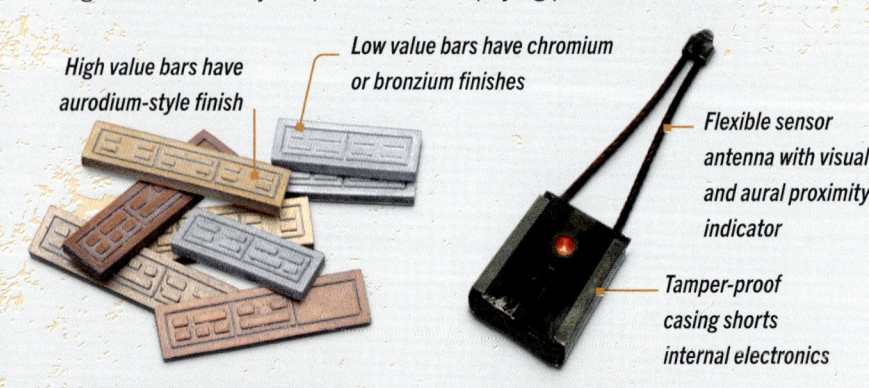

- High value bars have aurodium-style finish
- Low value bars have chromium or bronzium finishes
- Flexible sensor antenna with visual and aural proximity indicator
- Tamper-proof casing shorts internal electronics

PHYSICAL CREDIT INGOTS   **TRACKING FOB**

BOUNTY PUCKS
Guild bounties are contained within a holoprojector called a holopuck in the trade. The puck emits a profile holo of the target and a clear listing of the bounty value.

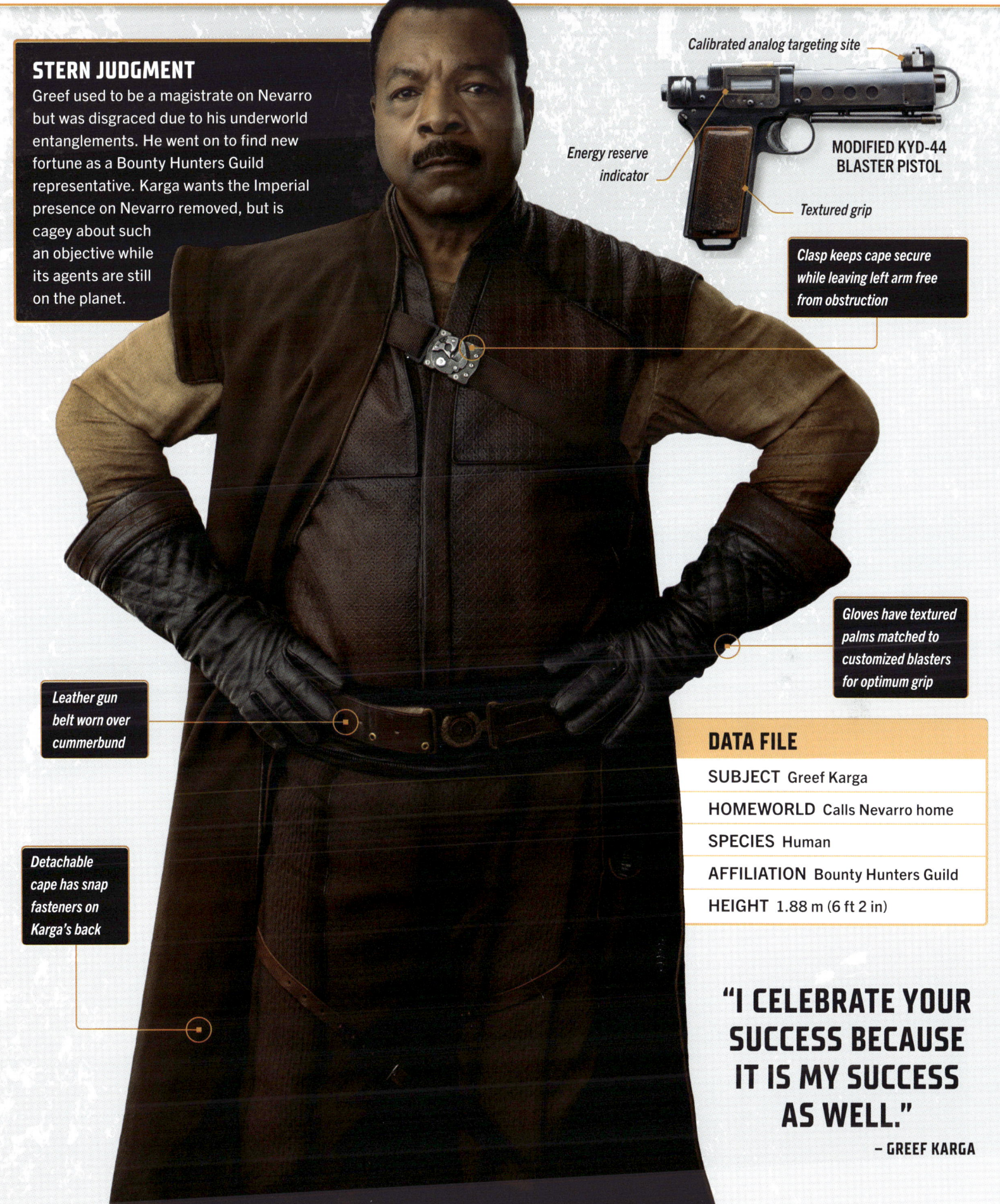

STERN JUDGMENT

Greef used to be a magistrate on Nevarro but was disgraced due to his underworld entanglements. He went on to find new fortune as a Bounty Hunters Guild representative. Karga wants the Imperial presence on Nevarro removed, but is cagey about such an objective while its agents are still on the planet.

Calibrated analog targeting site

Energy reserve indicator

MODIFIED KYD-44 BLASTER PISTOL

Textured grip

Clasp keeps cape secure while leaving left arm free from obstruction

Gloves have textured palms matched to customized blasters for optimum grip

Leather gun belt worn over cummerbund

Detachable cape has snap fasteners on Karga's back

DATA FILE

SUBJECT	Greef Karga
HOMEWORLD	Calls Nevarro home
SPECIES	Human
AFFILIATION	Bounty Hunters Guild
HEIGHT	1.88 m (6 ft 2 in)

> "I CELEBRATE YOUR SUCCESS BECAUSE IT IS MY SUCCESS AS WELL."
> – GREEF KARGA

PART I: A NEW COMPANION
THE SAFE HOUSE

The Empire has fallen. Where an Imperial outpost once held authority on Nevarro, it has since been seemingly abandoned, and the few remaining representatives of the august regime are in hiding. Nevarro remains apolitical, so any circumspection has more to do with keeping current activities away from the attention of the New Republic rather than keeping secrets from the locals themselves. Nevarro City's safe house is an old industrial blockhouse not far from the market. Its fortified door remains closed unless visitors are explicitly welcomed inside.

DATA FILE
- **SUBJECT** TK-7919
- **HOMEWORLD** Crondre
- **SPECIES** Human
- **AFFILIATION** Imperial remnant
- **HEIGHT** 1.8 m (6 ft)
- **AGE** 31 standard years

REMNANT STORMTROOPERS
The stormtroopers left to protect the Client at the safe house are a far cry from the gleaming parade that once marched on Empire Day. No longer equipped with a galaxy of resources, these troopers wear battered armor and wield worn weaponry. Less than a squad's worth of stormtroopers stand guard at the safe house. When the Mandalorian has reason to turn against his Imperial Client, he makes short work of them.

Plastoid pauldron

TK-4610
TK-4610 was part of an Imperial unit that pulled out of Hypori in the last weeks of the Galactic Civil War. Unwilling to be captured like the rest of his unit, TK-4610 fled to Nevarro.

Built-in Comtech Series IV comlink

Vocoder direct speaker

Plastoid breastplate

Energy ration on utility belt

BlasTech E-22 blaster rifle

Malfunctioning MFTAS targeting system

TK-6717
TK-6717 was a sentry stationed at the larger Nevarro base and was given orders to relocate on the pretense it was being abandoned. He is dedicated to protecting the Client.

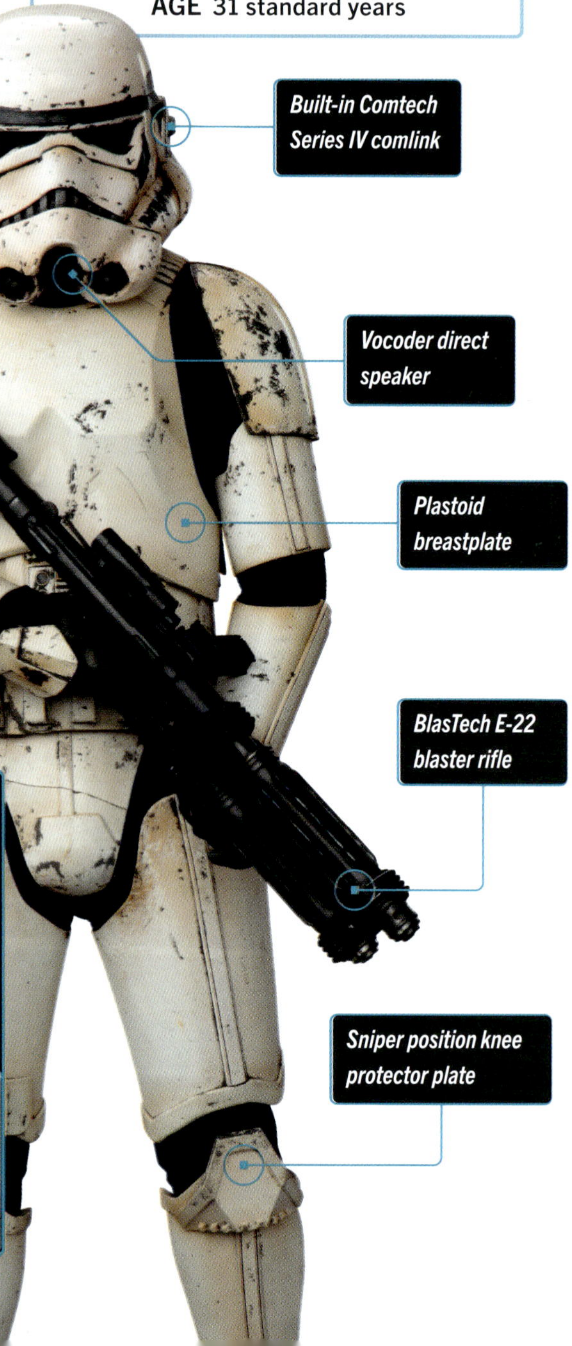

Sniper position knee protector plate

CENTRAL CHAMBER

The central chamber is used for conducting meetings with the Client. Four stormtroopers stand watch at strategic positions in case negotiations should sour. Though slatted windows allow natural light to pour in, their transparency is fogged to prevent spying. The Client, who insists on a civilized level of decorum, manages his transactions from behind a reinforced desk.

> "THE EMPIRE IS GONE, MANDO. ALL THAT ARE LEFT ARE MERCENARIES AND WARLORDS."
> – GREEF KARGA

The Client and Doctor Pershing are eager to carry on their work, though they remain tight-lipped as to what it entails.

Access to Imperial holdings in Nevarro City is controlled by a nonreplicable invitation chit that must be electronically scanned.

TT-87 GATEKEEPER DROID

Built into the main entry doorframe of the safe house is a TT-87 gatekeeper droid. The droid extends its photoreceptor on a mechanical stalk to examine visitors, looking specifically for an invitation chit. Based on this programming, it either summons security or an escort droid to lead the visitor inside.

Upon first doing business with the Client, the Mandalorian flashes a chit to the gatekeeper droid, who examines it multi-spectrally.

- Rotating iris assembly
- Multifaceted optical lens
- Sealing "lash" has electrostatic scrubber that cleans eye

PART I: A NEW COMPANION
IMPERIAL BUSINESS

Greef Karga's unusual lead on a deep-pocketed prospect brings Mando to an Imperial holdout and a Client with no name and an unusual request. The dignified official does not wear an officer's badge, yet has the air of a high rank. His quarry has no chain code; no holopuck projects the target's likeness. Instead, biometric data is loaded into a tracking fob, and positional data for the world of Arvala-7 is all Mando is given to work with.

The promised reward, an entire camtono of beskar, is too valuable to turn down. To begin with, the Client offers Mando two ingots of the rare metal, stamped with the Imperial sigil indicating their capture during the Great Purge, as a down payment. Mando sees this as no insult—their provenance matters little once it has been returned to Mandalorian hands.

What the Client intends to do with the asset is of no concern to Mando, as such an inquiry would break the code of discretion honored by the Bounty Hunters Guild. But once Mando meets his target on Arvala-7, everything begins to change.

The Client remains true to his word and hands over 18 ingots of pure beskar, despite their dubious origins.

IMPERIAL ACCOLADES
The Order of Six-Spoked Roundel was a highly regarded honor bestowed for meritorious service to the Empire. The medallion could only be awarded by one of the Grand Moffs or the Emperor himself.

Bardottan silk ribbon

Aurodium-cast Imperial sigil

THE CLIENT
Having lived through the glory of the Galactic Empire at its height, the Client now lives in the shadows of a broken galaxy. He laments the state of the New Republic and the chaos that spreads in the Outer Rim. The Client longs to see order return.

The asset's tracking fob

DOCTOR PENN PERSHING

An Imperial science officer working under the Client, Dr. Pershing seems most eager to get a hold of the asset and examine it thoroughly. Unlike the pragmatic Client, Pershing insists the asset be brought in alive. The doctor is skittish when it comes to conflict and confrontation and is uneasy around the Mandalorian.

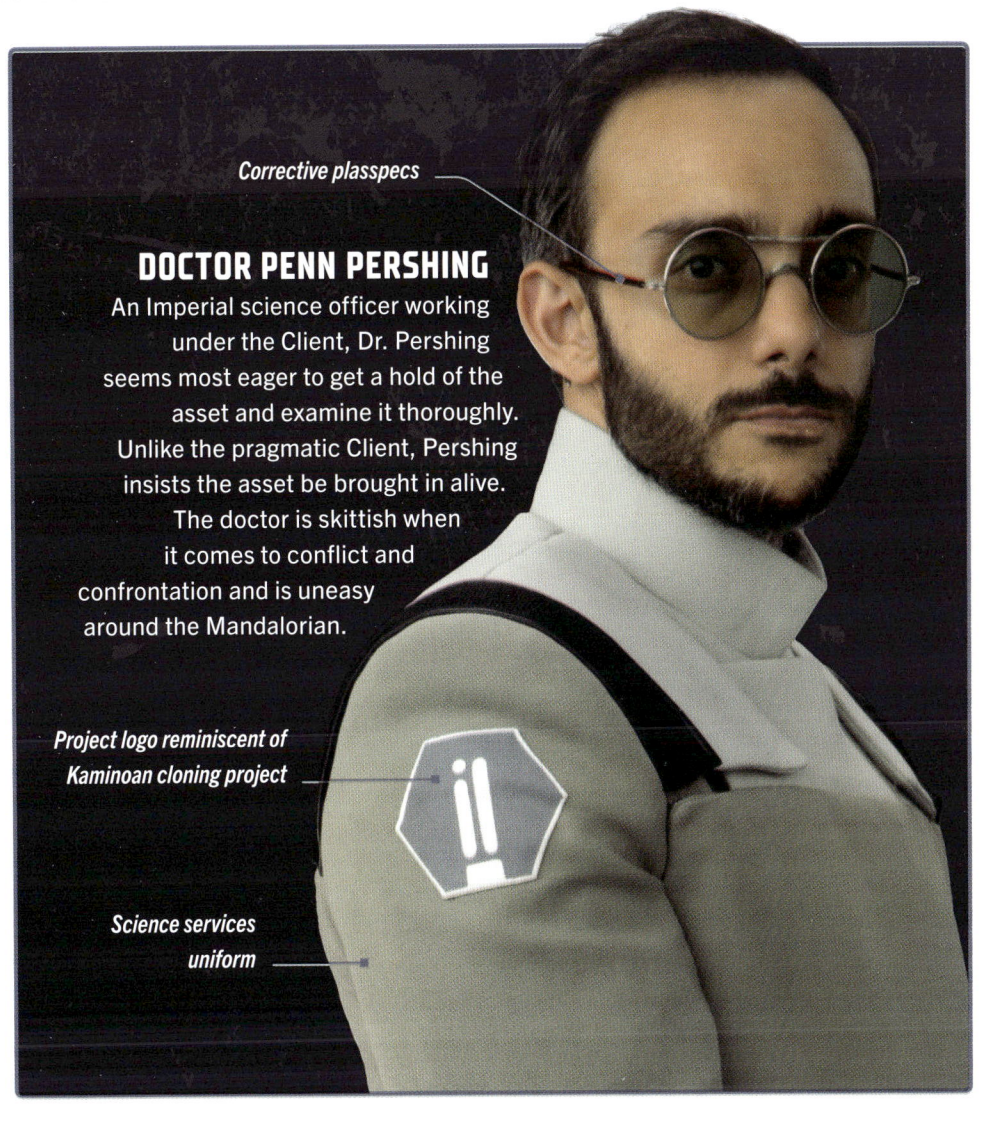

- Corrective plasspecs
- Project logo reminiscent of Kaminoan cloning project
- Science services uniform

INTERROGATOR DROID

Though known for their horrific use in intense interrogations, IT-O units are technically medical droids, albeit a perversion of their underlying function. They have sophisticated life-sign monitors and the means to inject medicine.

- Electroshock assembly
- Grasping claw

CAMTONO OF BESKAR

Camtonos are portable vaults for the storage and transportation of valuables. Sensor-shielded, vac-sealed, lightweight, and reinforced, a camtono offers security and privacy. Its simple electronics are not connected to any exterior network, making camtonos hard to slice. The Locris Syndicated Securities 3.8-liter capacity ICM-683 is a popular model found throughout the galaxy.

CAMTONO (CLOSED)
- Coding lock sequence button
- Carry handle
- Sealed plastoid doors
- Suspension field conductor pad

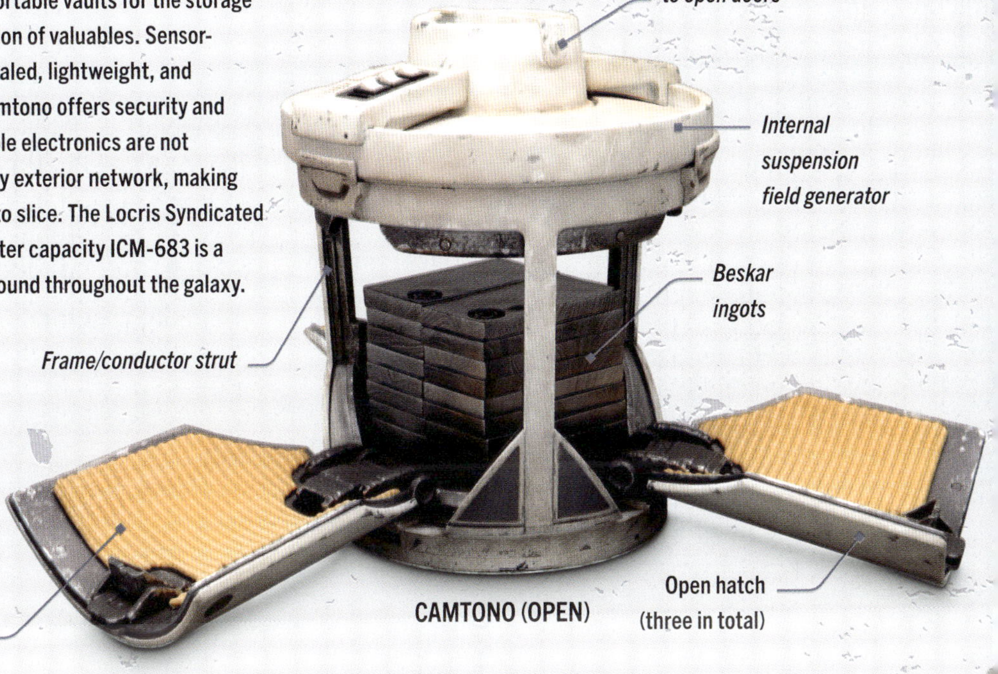

CAMTONO (OPEN)
- Carry handle twisted to open doors
- Internal suspension field generator
- Beskar ingots
- Frame/conductor strut
- Open hatch (three in total)

PART I: A NEW COMPANION

NEVARRO COVERT

Mandalorian history is marked by strife. Ironically, it did enjoy a respite from warfare during part of the Clone Wars. At this point, Mandalore was ruled by Duchess Satine Kryze, whose entrenched neutrality and pacifism provoked Death Watch, a violent sect that longed to return Mandalore to its more martial ways. Stoked by offworld agents, Mandalore fragmented into civil war. Armor and clan delineations grew in importance. Chaos rocked the glittering cities of the capital planet.

Following the Clone Wars, Mandalore was ruled by the Galactic Empire. The might of this regime proved to be a stabilizing influence, facilitated by collaborators on the planet. For a time, the Imperial occupation yielded peace. However, it was not to last, requiring an Imperial crackdown that has become known as the Great Purge, or the Night of a Thousand Tears. Refugees from Mandalorian territories were scattered. One particular group of exiles has set up a covert in the sewers beneath Nevarro.

Beneath Nevarro City, a Mandalorian plays cu'bikahd with a foundling as an exercise to teach history and strategy.

When Mando needs it most, the Mandalorians of his covert swoop in on jetpacks to assist, weapons blazing.

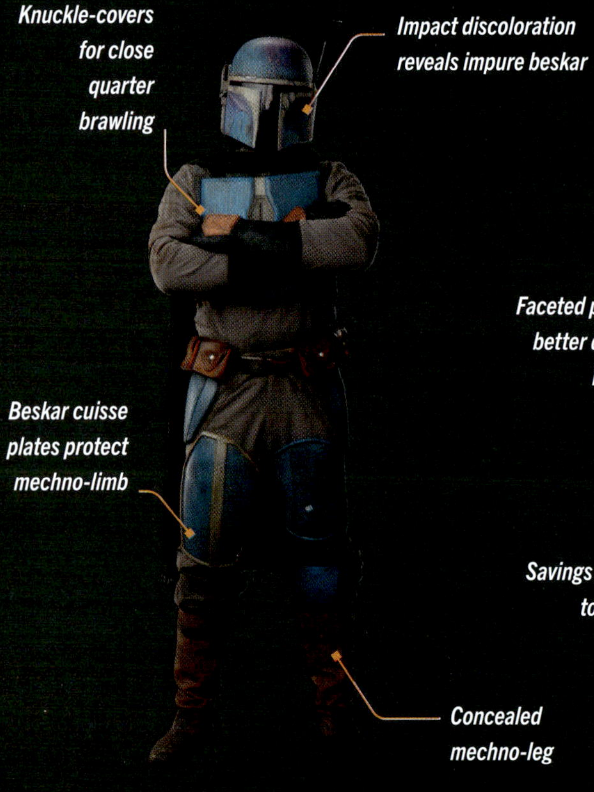

HEWITT DALA
- Knuckle-covers for close quarter brawling
- Beskar cuisse plates protect mechno-limb
- Concealed mechno-leg

EMAST KELBORN
- Impact discoloration reveals impure beskar
- Faceted plastron better deflects impacts
- Utility pouch
- Savings are devoted to completing leg armor

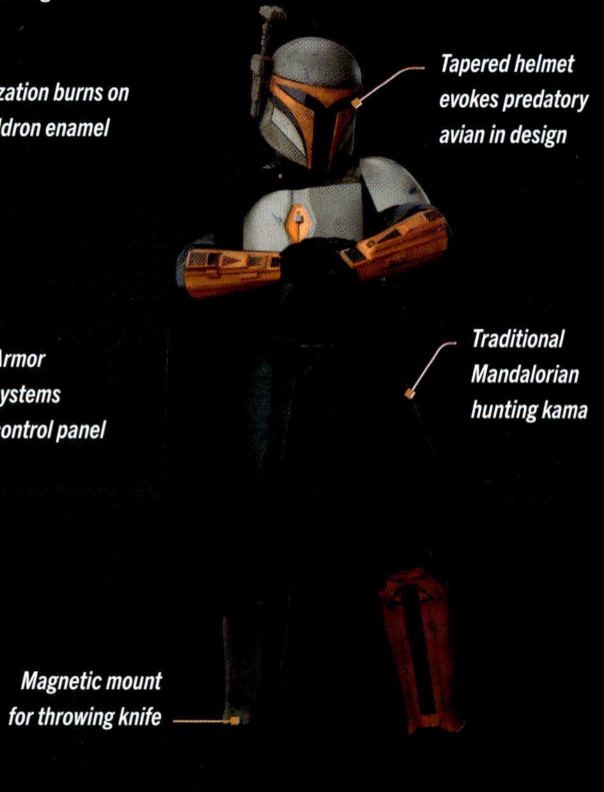

AMOT TENAU
- Ionization burns on pauldron enamel
- Armor systems control panel
- Tapered helmet evokes predatory avian in design
- Traditional Mandalorian hunting kama
- Magnetic mount for throwing knife

FOUNDLINGS

The future of Mandalore lies in the foundlings. Many are children rescued from warzones, who are now parentless due to the violence of enemies. Adherents of the Way bring the foundlings to coverts where they are adopted into clans. The children learn history and traditions, and will eventually earn the right to wear true beskar armor.

- Industrial helmet as a "starter"
- Breather attachment port
- Welder's visor
- Warm woolen jerkin

TABBER, MINO (SEATED), AND ZEM

- Death Watch shoulder pauldron
- Clan Bralor color
- Captured DL-17 blaster rifle
- Simplified EE-3 carbine rifle
- Sniper-plate knee armor
- Protective leg padding beneath pants
- Concealed expansion hollow for dart launchers

KORT BRALOR

- Painted jaig eyes symbol
- Sensor-baffling cape
- BlasTech EE-3 carbine rifle

PEN VARAD

- Cape can conceal armaments
- Blend of livery denotes multiple clan lineages
- Salvaged vambrace
- Heirloom cuirass

IDALIA DESTA

PART I: A NEW COMPANION

THE ARMORER

The Armorer is a rarified class in Mandalorian culture, predating even the rise of Mandalore the Great in its ancient history. Though Mandalorians have faced major societal upheaval over the centuries, the Armorer endures as a revered position. As long as beskar defines the strength of Mandalore, there is a need for skilled artisans to shape that steel into its strongest form.

So all-consuming is the esteemed station that personal identity, history, and even clan origins vanish under the mantle of Armorer. The Armorer who lives in the Mandalorian covert on Nevarro is known only as such—for she needs no other name.

Aside from her role in crafting armor, the Armorer offers wisdom and guidance to her fellow Mandalorian exiles. It is said that the patience, skill, intuition, and perseverance required to shape beskar gives an Armorer insight into what is required to live the Way to its fullest. Her products are not made to order. Instead, she judges what a Mandalorian postulant needs in both armor and a path in life to follow.

PLANISHING HAMMER
- Reinforced shaft
- Beskar-carbonite composite head

MAGNATONGS
- Boss hinge plate
- Reins built for safety distance

- Activator for micro-analysis sensors
- The Armorer wears minimal armor to ensure the beskar is distributed among others
- Mantle of thick winter furs of a strill
- Suede leggings waxed with fireproof resin

NAU'UR KAD BESKAR'GAM

The Mandalorian art of forging—*nau'ur kad beskar'gam* (literally the "lighting of iron skin")—is a time-honored process that refuses to be industrialized. The skill and equipment required are tightly guarded secrets within Mandalorian space to prevent the smithing techniques from spreading to the galaxy at large. Even after the Empire annexed Mandalore, Imperial scientists were unable to replicate the craft, despite intense efforts. The forge is the beating heart of a Mandalorian covert, a way to keep a piece of their home planet and heritage alive.

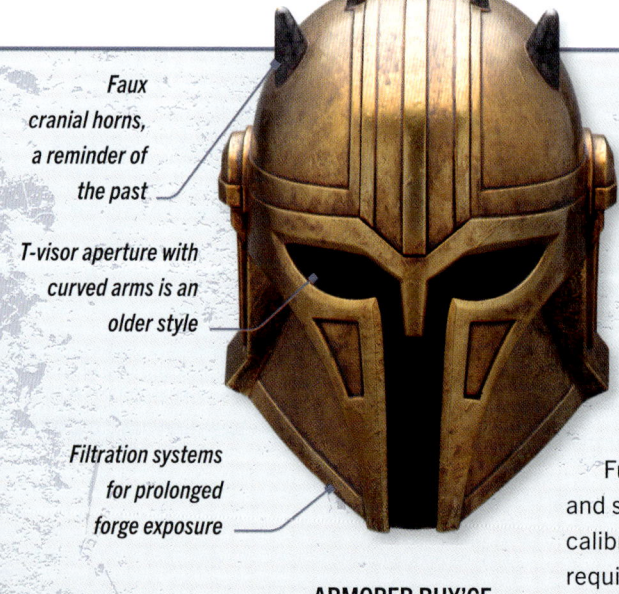

- Faux cranial horns, a reminder of the past
- T-visor aperture with curved arms is an older style
- Filtration systems for prolonged forge exposure

ARMORER BUY'CE

HELM OF THE FORGE

While Armorers eschew signets or other clan-based markings, their helms are unique. The ornate, ceremonial T-visor suggests a shamanistic dimension to this profession. Some Armorers are known to have animalistic designs incorporated into their helmets. Functionally, the helm electronics and sensor systems are nano-calibrated for the intricate work required of the craft.

The Armorer is also a skilled electrical and mechanical engineer, capable of crafting and maintaining jetpack designs.

FORGING THE FUTURE

As is demanded by the Way, the Armorer sets aside a portion of the proffered beskar into a trove devoted to the foundlings. It is for the preservation of their heritage that Mandalorians carefully ration their supplies of the cherished steel.

The Armorer places a sheet of annealed beskar into the firing ring of the cryofurnace.

- Beskar cuirass with bronzium finish
- Bronzium-and-durasteel leveling instrument
- Variable mass repulsor core
- Strill-hide suede gloves
- Utility belt holds frequently used tools
- Layered leather tanning apron

> "WHEN ONE CHOOSES TO WALK THE WAY OF THE MANDALORE, YOU ARE BOTH HUNTER AND PREY."
> – THE ARMORER

DATA FILE

SUBJECT	The Armorer
HOMEWORLD	Mandalore
SPECIES	Unknown
AFFILIATION	Nevarro Mandalore covert
HEIGHT	1.7 m (5 ft 7 in)

PART I: A NEW COMPANION

THE ARMORER'S WORKSHOP

The covert's most honored alcove is a place of sacred tradition. Powered by Nevarro's natural geothermal energies, the forge's extremes of temperature—conjured by ancient devices and processes—are harnessed to temper beskar steel into Mandalorian armor and weaponry. The Armorer decides what is suitable to forge, and she alone operates the equipment. She fits the design to her understanding of a Mandalorian's needs and their place on their lifelong journey following the Way.

> "THIS CAN FORM A FULL CUIRASS. THIS WOULD BE IN ORDER FOR YOUR STATION."
> – THE ARMORER TO THE MANDALORIAN

MYTHOSAUR SKULL
The entrance to the heart of the Mandalorian covert is marked by a large, stylized skull of the mythosaur, a Mandalorian creature. The skull is crafted by the Armorer out of pure beskar and is a revered symbol of perseverance.

Sagittal crest sculpted into skull

Gore-horns

Shroud dissipates exhaust through sewer network

Cryojet array

Scale and macroanalysis table

Duranium anvil

The Armorer in preparation

WHAT REMAINS
When the Imperial remnant takes over Nevarro, its forces infiltrate the covert. Many Mandalorians fall, but the Armorer stays behind to guard her station. She battles the stormtroopers with only her tools. No matter what fragments of the forge are left behind, they are useless without a skilled armorer.

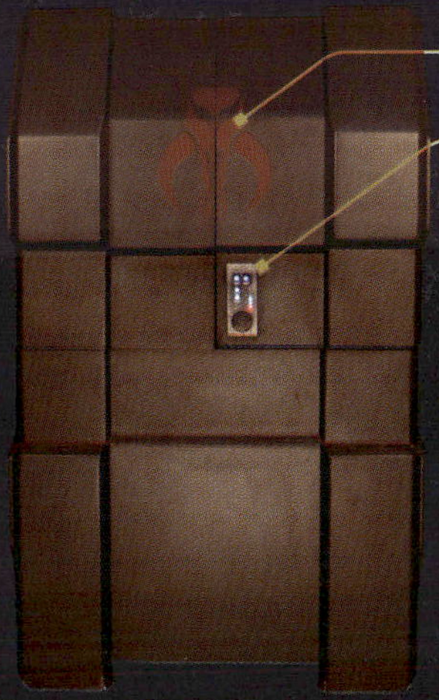

- *Painted mythosaur emblem*
- *Locking system*

THE ARMORER'S CABINET
Most of the Armorer's tools are kept in a massive cabinet, which is portable to meet the needs of a nomadic life traveling from covert to covert. The Armorer alone can unlock the cabinet, revealing a work station of polished veshok wood and an array of tools stowed in specific positions. The layout is determined by tradition, not preference.

CLOSED CABINET

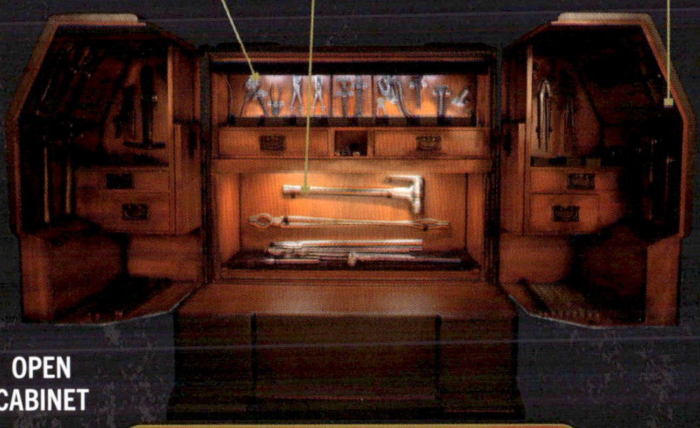

- *Crimping tool*
- *Planishing hammer*
- *Centenarian veshok wood*

OPEN CABINET

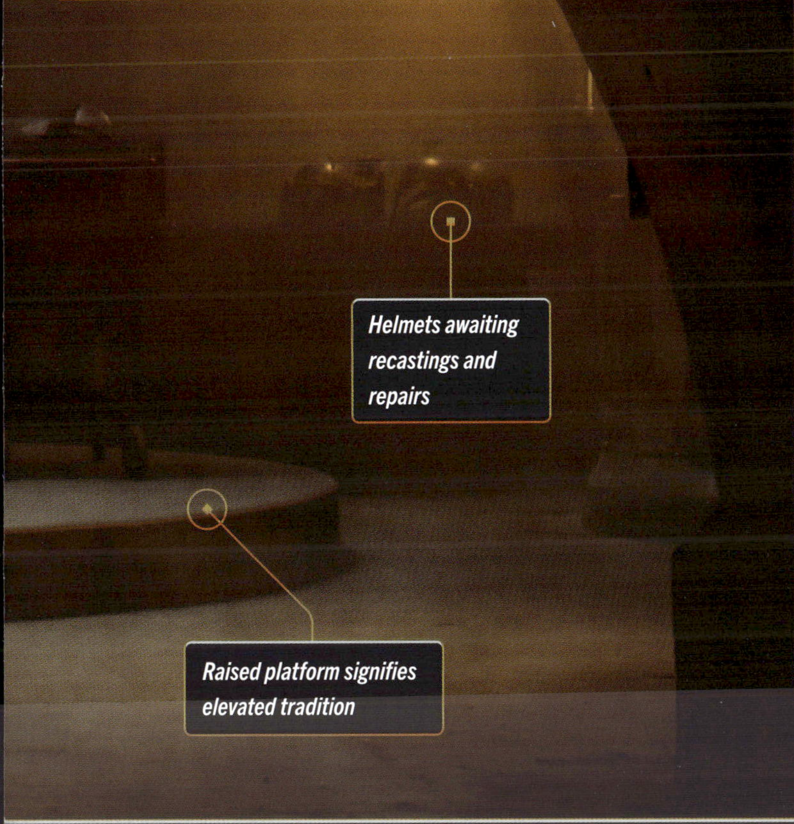

Helmets awaiting recastings and repairs

Raised platform signifies elevated tradition

THE MYSTERIOUS PROCESS

The Mandalorian method for forging beskar is a closely guarded secret, a type of near-mythical alchemy intended to keep ancient armor intact. What follows is an incomplete analysis of some of the steps involved.

THE BATH OF PURITY
The Armorer uses magnetic tongs to place the ingot into a cryoflux bath. The chemical reacts and acts as a purifying agent during the forging process.

SHAPELESSNESS
Coated with cryoflux, the beskar becomes mercurial as it endures syncopated bursts of intense heat and quenching cold.

A BUILDING BLOCK
Localized destabilization fields keep the beskar malleable as it is roll-forged into the billet—an undifferentiated shape—and the molding process begins.

ENDURING BLOWS
The Armorer's gravity hammer uses inverse repulsor fields to increase the kinetic blows of its heavy core as it attenuates the billet.

FINDING FUNCTION
The destabilization field is recalibrated as the billet is hammer-forged around a shaping mandrel that describes its eventual form.

REPETITION AND PATIENCE
The billet is hammered and reshaped as it is drawn into specific shapes, its molecular alignment stabilizing meanwhile into a more hardened form.

FIRE AND ICE
Repeated hot and cold blasts burn off the cryoflux, taking away any deeply rooted impurities. When there is not enough beskar to make a shape, an additive is introduced.

FINAL MEASURE
The Armorer anneals the piece and affixes it to a technological mounting truss. She uses nanocalipers to get a true reading of its form and examine its tolerances.

PART I: A NEW COMPANION

ARVALA-7

One of dozens of moons shaken loose from a gas giant by a cometary calamity, Arvala-7 eventually came into its own stable orbit closer to the system's sun. It is now a small, desert planetoid that soaks up seasonal rainfall, producing hardy life-forms that can survive months without another deluge. Arvala-7 is loosely settled, one of countless Outer Rim worlds that fall off official maps due to lack of significance. In short, it is an ideal hiding place.

DATA FILE
REGION Outer Rim
SECTOR Sevetta
SYSTEM Arvala
DIAMETER 2,375 km (1,475 miles)
TERRAIN Dry, hardened mud
MOONS None
POPULATION Less than 1 million

Nikto camp

> "THOSE THAT LIVE HERE COME TO SEEK PEACE."
> – KUIIL

Scattered lommite deposits

Sinking badlands

Tonzir settlement (abandoned)

Saturated mud sea

GORVIN SNU LIZARD
Inquisitive and speedy gorvin snu emerge from tunnels to devour washed-out worms and insects after a rainfall.

ITEMS OF INTEREST

MUDHORN CAVE
Excavated by a massive animal, the mudhorn cave is built low in the terrain, retaining the moisture of the desert rains.

KUIIL'S VAPOR RANCH
Kuiil the Ugnaught came to Arvala-7 for the solitude and tranquility. The asset that Mando and others seek is a cause of disruption.

DURIPAN PLAINS
The desert soil dries rapidly after rainfall, producing enormous hardpan flats where no grasses grow. The intersecting crevasses teem with tiny creatures.

NIKTO CAMP
Well-armed Nikto thugs have moved into an abandoned estate and are decidedly unneighborly to any who dare approach.

Unlike the Jawas on Tatooine, this clan does not have a central camp and instead stays perpetually mobile in its sandcrawler home.

EVOLVING LANDSCAPE
Evidence of Arvala-7's past geological torment can be seen in the striations that mark the mountains and rounded bluffs. More recent climate conditions have further shaped these structures, smoothing out edges and creating intermittent river beds that become navigable pathways through the badlands. Jawas have mapped these roads, albeit aware of their potential impermanence.

The sandcrawler moves deeper into the canyons

Pronounced geological striations

Shadowed valley leading to the mudhorn cave

Piled scree deposits

PART I: A NEW COMPANION
KUIIL

Having witnessed enough hardship to last several lifetimes, Kuiil seeks tranquil retirement, tending an expansive vapor ranch on Arvala-7, harvesting subterranean crops, and raising blurrgs. The arrival of bounty hunters tracking a quarry brings strife back to his comfortable life, but Kuiil sees promise in the Mandalorian's ability to settle this disruptive matter. Though Kuiil wishes for peace, he is no daydreamer. Taciturn and weathered, he is pragmatic, with a weary wisdom earned through decades of toil.

Kuiil has spent most of his life as an indentured worker, trading his mechanical skills to pay off his clan's debt. The Empire was the final holder of his indenture, and Kuiil's talents kept Imperial war machinery operational. Kuiil earned his freedom and sought the simplicity of a self-sufficient life, yet he still enjoys tinkering away at projects on his workbench, which bears a TIE fighter viewport as a reminder of the past.

Kuiil has a peaceful relationship with the Jawas on Arvala-7, and he brokers a peace between them and the Mandalorian after they strip the *Razor Crest* bare. Viewing Mando as a guest, Kuiil helps reassemble the now-skeletal starship in record time and refuses payment for the feat.

TECHNICAL SKILLS
With quiet focus, Kuiil can work mechanical miracles. He is able to patch together the *Razor Crest* into working condition overnight. Kuiil can even refashion complex droid programming to transform an assassin droid into a helpful ranch hand. Ugnaughts have a reputation for their mechanical skills, and Kuiil far exceeds it.

WORK GOGGLES
- Removable frames hold lenses in threaded retaining socket
- Adjustable head strap
- Leather skullcap with noise-activated ear protection
- Wavelength-attenuating, polycarbonate lenses

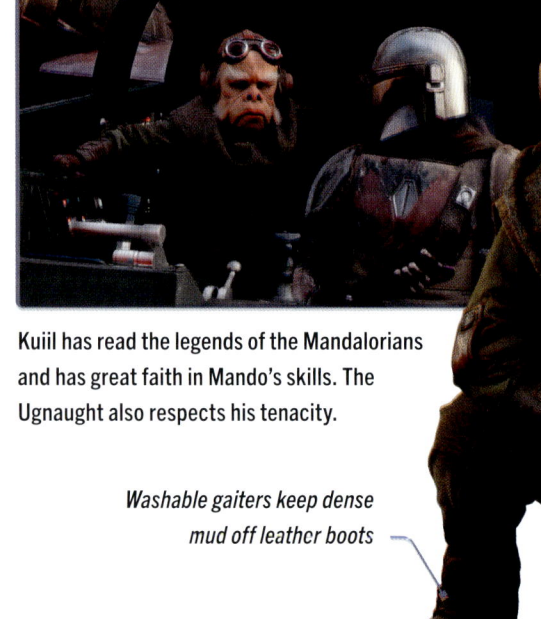

Kuiil has read the legends of the Mandalorians and has great faith in Mando's skills. The Ugnaught also respects his tenacity.

Washable gaiters keep dense mud off leather boots

HARSH HISTORY
Ugnaughts hail from the planet Gentes, and their technical expertise, unflagging endurance, and relatively small size have unfortunately made them the target of enslavers and others that would exploit their labor. During the days of the Old Republic, Zygerrians enslaved entire Ugnaught tribes—from aged elders to helpless Ugletts—and the species was scattered across the galaxy. The Galactic Republic did what it could to free Ugnaughts from bondage, but the majority of this despicable crime took place beyond its borders.

MUZZLELOADER PROJECTILE THROWER

- Targeting sight
- Acceleration chamber
- Gauss-action barrel
- Lockable safety trigger
- Weathered leather strap

STUN DART

- Neuro-electric stun charge conductor
- Stabilizer plume

Kuiil meets Mando when the latter is beset by wild blurrgs and silences the beasts with well-placed stun darts.

- Humorless, age-etched gaze

DATA FILE
SUBJECT	Kuiil
HOMEWORLD	Arvala-7
SPECIES	Ugnaught
AFFILIATION	Independent
HEIGHT	1.45 m (4 ft 9 in)

"I HAVE SPOKEN."
— KUIIL

- Stiffened tovhog-leather gloves help resist blurrg bites
- Desert scarf protects against the Arvalan elements
- Paired tool panniers worn on belt
- Coarse-woven plant-fiber fabric trousers

THE GREATER GOOD
Aged and flinty, with a strong moral compass, Kuiil will risk his life for a greater cause. He has no love for the Empire or any who would threaten peace and freedom. He has a soft spot for Grogu and wishes to shield him from the dangers of the galaxy.

PART I: A NEW COMPANION
BLURRGS

Blurrgs are tough-skinned, dim-witted omnivorous reptiles found on scattered worlds in the Outer Rim, including Arvala-7, Miv'rah, the Forest Moon of Endor, and Ryloth. An adult blurrg has a brain the size of a jubba nut, which makes them relatively easy to train provided one is as obstinate as the beast is. Their high-domed, thick skulls and low centers of gravity make them adept at ramming attacks. Agitated blurrgs will charge and trample indiscriminately.

Well-muscled legs give blurrgs a surprising jumping range, which is a valuable trait on Arvala-7's cracked duripan plains.

> "THE WAY IS IMPOSSIBLE TO PASS WITHOUT A BLURRG MOUNT."
> – KUIIL

A BLURRG IS BORN

Born in clutches of five or six eggs, blurrgets are dependent on their mother for protection and food. Upon hatching, the blurrgets are treated to a feast of partially digested meat regurgitated by the mother. The meal is all that remains of the father, who is devoured after mating. The father's body nourishes the mother up to when she lays eggs and, due to her slowed digestive process at this stage of reproduction, remains of nutritional value through to hatching.

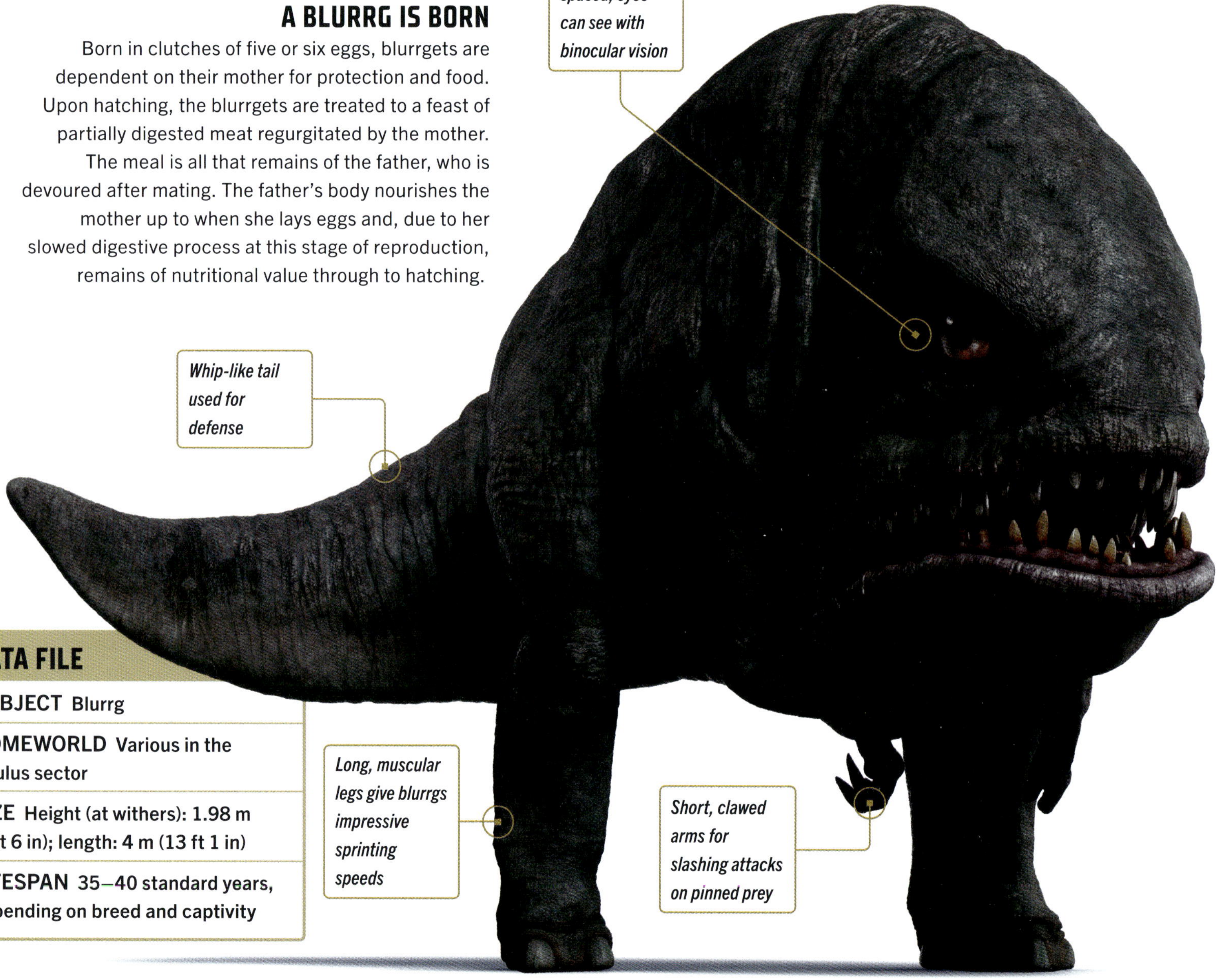

Though widely spaced, eyes can see with binocular vision

Whip-like tail used for defense

Long, muscular legs give blurrgs impressive sprinting speeds

Short, clawed arms for slashing attacks on pinned prey

DATA FILE

SUBJECT Blurrg

HOMEWORLD Various in the Gaulus sector

SIZE Height (at withers): 1.98 m (6 ft 6 in); length: 4 m (13 ft 1 in)

LIFESPAN 35–40 standard years, depending on breed and captivity

Nostrils seal to keep out water or insects

Gaping mouth helps regulate internal body heat

Teeth continue to grow throughout life

BLURRG RUN
Strains of blurrgs raised on scattered worlds evolve or are bred to have different characteristics and advantages. The Rylothian blurrgs are the fastest, while the forest blurrgs of Endor are more plodding—perhaps never accessing the open land that necessitates swift, long-distance runs. The Arvalan blurrg is somewhere in the middle, with a sprinting speed of up to 75 kph (47 mph).

Hefty tail serves as counterbalance as blurrg launches forward

FACT FILE

DIET
Blurrgs are omnivorous, though too much meat makes them logy; Kuiil feeds his blurrgs a mix of pummeled maize-stalk, water, and arges frogs

HABITAT
Blurrgs are most comfortable in semi-arid, temperate settings but are remarkably adaptable; they cannot survive in subzero environments

BLURRGS OF BURDEN

Blurrgs can be trained to pull heavy loads, as they transform their speed into drafting power. Their endurance and obtuse stubbornness are both of benefit, as a trained blurrg can be tempted by the promise of food for hours on end. Kuiil uses blurrgs to haul a repulsorlift sled, which is made considerably lighter to move by its antigravity generators. On primitive Endor, blurrgs receive no such advantage. The Sanyassan Marauders known to inhabit the Dragon's Pelt savannah force their blurrgs to tow wheeled wagons.

Young, wild blurrgs can be territorial toward non-blurrgs, especially when resources are sparse.

TO TAME A BLURRG
To find the asset, the Mandalorian must learn to tame and ride a blurrg foal. Though Mando is a seasoned warrior of impressive repute, blurrg-riding is not among his skills. The recalcitrant beast throws him off repeatedly, until he is able to exert control over her. Despite a few bumps—and a slightly bruised ego, perhaps—Mando breaks the wild beast. He does not name the blurrg as Kuiil thinks such an act is too sentimental.

PART I: A NEW COMPANION

IG-11

One of a series of dangerous assassin droids largely outlawed in the galaxy, IG-11 is a hired gun programmed to follow Bounty Hunters Guild protocols to the glyph. Reliable and durable, IG-11's thin body is built on an armored substrate that can withstand repeated assaults. It is against his manufacturer's protocol to allow himself to be captured, and he has a built-in, self-destructive, baradium charge to prevent that from ever happening.

IG-11 takes on the assignment to track down the Client's asset on Arvala-7, which leads the droid to a Nikto camp in the desert wilderness. The Mandalorian and IG-11—both Guild members—decide to cooperate to blast their way past the Nikto mercenaries protecting the asset.

IG-11 is under the directive to bring the target in dead, something Mando violently disagrees with. Mando blasts a hole in IG-11's cranial processor, leaving the droid as little more than battlefield detritus. The Ugnaught rancher Kuiil discovers the remains of IG-11, and claims him as salvage. He reconstitutes the droid's programming core for a new function: that of protector.

NOTABLE IG UNITS

Funded by the InterGalactic Banking Clan, Holowan Laboratories' controversial Project Phlutdroid resulted in numerous notorious droids in the IG series. A sampling follows:

IG-88: Perhaps the most infamous of the IG assassin droids to become a bounty hunter, Imperial records officially credit IG-88 with more than 150 deaths.

IG-72: An assassin and bounty droid that self-destructs during the hunt for Republic-era fugitive Adar Tallon on Tatooine.

IG-90: A red-hued assassin droid active during the Galactic Civil War and involved in the targeting of Dr. Chelli Aphra.

HELIOS-3D: An IG-86 sentinel droid and a member of Cad Bane's posse that engineers a hostage crisis in the Galactic Republic Senate during the Clone Wars.

ALWAYS COMBAT READY

IG units feature a basic, unembellished mechanical design, free of sleek adornments or manufacturer trademarks. Such a simplified construction reduces the chance of mechanical failure or cascading damage from combat. Thanks to his rotating trunk and head, IG-11 can instantly turn around with a turn of a servomotor tumbler. IG-11 uses this maneuver to his advantage in disorienting its foes.

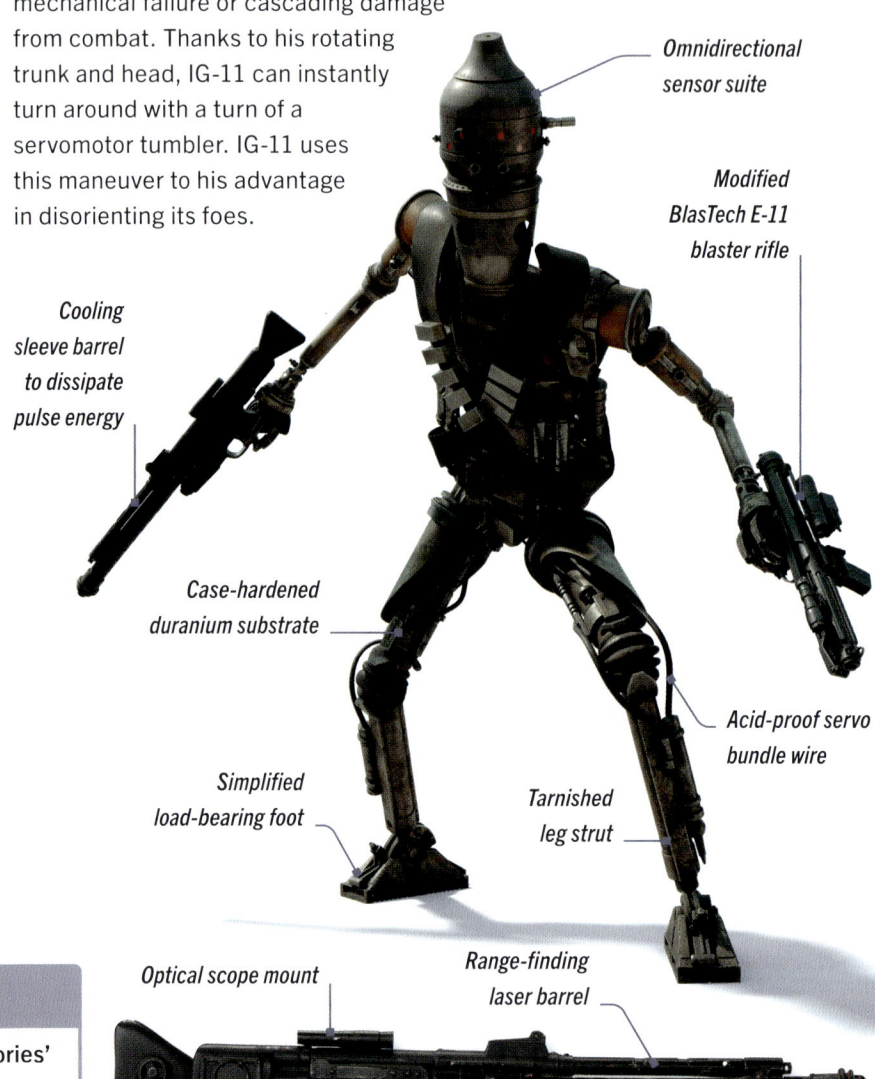

- Omnidirectional sensor suite
- Modified BlasTech E-11 blaster rifle
- Cooling sleeve barrel to dissipate pulse energy
- Case-hardened duranium substrate
- Acid-proof servo bundle wire
- Simplified load-bearing foot
- Tarnished leg strut
- Optical scope mount
- Range-finding laser barrel
- Magnatomic adhesion grip

BLASTECH DLT-20A BLASTER RIFLE

Even in protector mode, IG-11 is still extremely dangerous, delivering a crushing hold to a hapless scout trooper that threatens his charge.

After reawakening, IG-11 is no longer a hunter. He becomes Kuiil's protector and a strong ranch hand.

Heat/motion sensors on rotating band

THE REFORMATTING
IG-11's shallow personality manifests mostly as shouting ultimatums, quoting Guild protocol or uttering calculations of success. Mando's pointblank blast erases his neural harness. With great difficulty, Kuiil rebuilds it. The droid has to learn the basics of interaction. With patience and repetition, Kuiil reinforces his development, resulting in a loyal, even gentle, personality.

> "SUBPARAGRAPH SIXTEEN OF THE BONDSMAN GUILD PROTOCOL WAIVER COMPELS YOU TO IMMEDIATELY PRODUCE SAID ASSET!"
> – IG-11

Ball-joint servomotor

Blaster ammunition cell bandolier

Pincer hand with integral industrial laser cutter

Shielded computer interface ports

Tempered blast armor

Cups crafted from local clay

ARVALAN TEA SET

Tray edge minimizes risk of spillages

Harvested by Kuiil

Pneumatic leg joint in accordioning sleeve

HEATING TRAY

PHEDRA-SHRUB BLOSSOM TEA

DATA FILE
SUBJECT	IG-11
HOMEWORLD	Unknown
SERIES	IG assassin droid
AFFILIATION	Formerly Bounty Hunters Guild; later loyal to Kuiil
HEIGHT	2.19 m (7 ft 2 in)

PART I: A NEW COMPANION
GROGU

Very little is known about Grogu—a mysterious alien known initially only as "the Child" and pursued by bounty hunters on behalf of Imperial interests. When Mando takes the lucrative assignment for an Imperial Client, he cannot predict the true nature of his quarry and is given very little tangible information. Grogu has no chain code—no official identification—save for a record of his age. Incongruously, he is 50 standard years old, indicating a life cycle far different from most humanoid norms.

Though Mando completes the assignment, and is handsomely rewarded for it, he ultimately reneges on the deal. To do so breaks Guild protocol in favor of following his conscience as well as the Way. Grogu is a foundling, left alone by the turmoil of war or by war's aftermath. It is a quality both Mando and Grogu share, a bond stronger than even a Bounty Hunters Guild agreement. The Mandalorian infiltrates the Client's safe house and absconds with Grogu.

While Grogu speaks no words, his eyes and ears clearly express his feelings of joy, uncertainty, or fear. He is intensely curious about his surroundings and the strange, wonderful places Mando's journeys take them.

> "SO, THIS LITTLE BOGWING IS WHAT ALL THE FUSS WAS ABOUT. WHAT A PRECIOUS LITTLE CREATURE."
> – GREEF KARGA

UNUSUALLY GIFTED
Grogu is touched with the power of the Force. In moments of crisis, he exhibits telekinetic ability, and is able to move objects many times his size with just the power of his mind. Completing such a task exhausts Grogu, who then slumbers until refreshed. He also has the rare ability to heal wounds by touch.

CONVEYANCE
Though Grogu is capable of walking, his toddling gait and tiny steps make it impossible for him to keep pace with the adult world. Instead, he usually sits in a hover pram, held aloft on a cushion of repulsorlift energy. A programmable homing sensor on the pram keeps it following the Mandalorian.

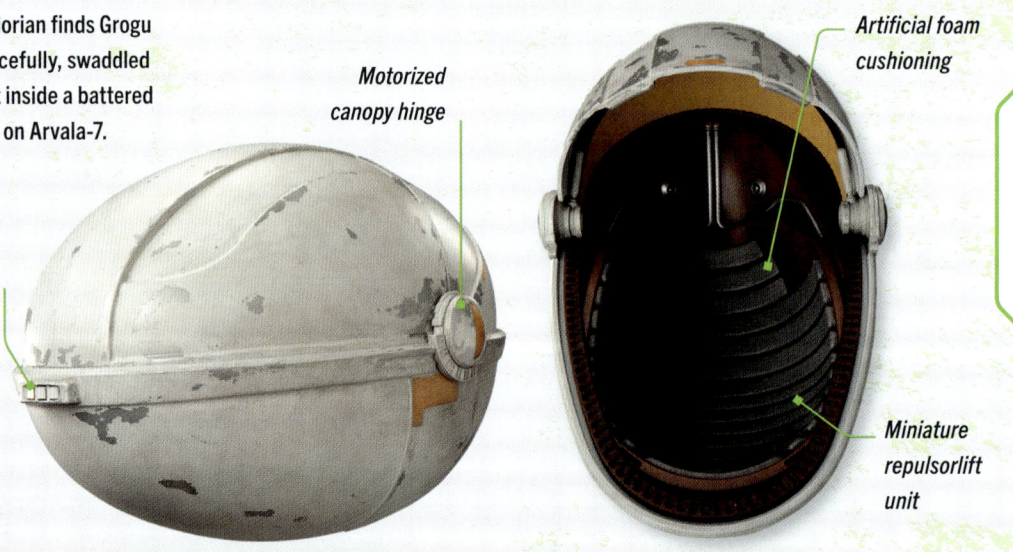

The Mandalorian finds Grogu resting peacefully, swaddled in a blanket inside a battered hover pram on Arvala-7.

- Safety seal switches
- Motorized canopy hinge
- Artificial foam cushioning
- Miniature repulsorlift unit

HOVER PRAM (CLOSED) HOVER PRAM (OPEN)

Mando at first imagines he can find a peaceful world where he can leave Grogu, but he realizes that they are safest together.

FROG FEAST
Grogu exhibits a healthy appetite—and a notable taste for amphibians. The eager child can devour a fat frog in surprisingly few gulps, bones and all.

Strong hind legs for traversing muddy spawning pits

Monocular vision

ARVALAN ARGES FROG

DATA FILE
SUBJECT	Grogu
HOMEWORLD	Unknown
SPECIES	Unknown
AFFILIATION	The Mandalorian
HEIGHT	0.34 m (1 ft 1 in)
AGE	50

Downy vellus hair

Wide, sensitive ears help dissipate heat

1.25 mm threaded channel

BELOVED SHIFTER KNOB

THE ASSET
The Client seeks Grogu—or as he callously calls him, the asset—for scientific research. The Client's henchman Dr. Pershing, an Imperial scientist, immediately begins subjecting Grogu to medical exams to better understand his alien physiology and how it connects to his supernatural talents.

Small keratin nails will harden with age

PART I: A NEW COMPANION
OFFWORLD JAWAS

Jawas are an unusual sight beyond their native Tatooine deserts, but members of this hardy species can be found on Arvala-7 and Nevarro. One offworld tribe on Arvala-7 operates its sandcrawler home in the customary Jawa way: traversing the craggy terrain collecting scrap to refurbish and sell to settlers.

Moisture vaporators for water collection

Droid-holding cage

Stretched tarpaulin shade

Loading dock hatch (sealed)

ADAPTING TO ARVALA-7

The original ore crawler design boasted simplified mechanical engineering that proved adaptable to a wide range of environmental conditions. On Arvala-7, muck clearing becomes of greater importance, and roles devoted to cleaning out the mud built up on the crawler's treads are valued in the tribe. Spotters live in camps atop the upper deck and are able to steer the crawler away from craggy areas or from enormous quagmires.

Fuel-loading door

DATA FILE

MANUFACTURER Corellia Mining Corporation

MODEL Mobile refinery/digger crawler

TYPE Treaded transport

DIMENSIONS Height: 28 m (92 ft); width: 23.2 m (76 ft); length: 49.9 m (164 ft)

SPEED 30 kph (18.6 mph)

WEAPONS None

AFFILIATION Offworld Jawas

Reddened eyes distinguish offworlder from yellow-eyed Tatooine Jawa

Squill-leather bandolier

JAWA ELDER

The elder enforces a strict hierarchy aboard his sandcrawler, but his ways are not just those of hard rule. He knows the value of sharing good fortune across the entire tribe and can even be described as "generous." It is a word with no direct translation in Jawaese, so it must be cobbled together from word fragments.

Precious necklace symbolizes status in tribe

Sensor suite attuned to metallic deposits

Ionization charge (inside belt pouch)

Recurved kukri machete

Control cabin windows

Concealed, well-muscled legs from constant ladder climbing

Sharpshooter's perfect vision

JAWA HUNTER

A Jawa hunter is one of the tribe entrusted with an ionization blaster. His piercing eyes grant him pinpoint accuracy. Since Jawa weapons tend to be short-range affairs, he lends his acuity to spotting dangers from the sandcrawler cockpit. He fires an ionization charge that incapacitates the Mandalorian's armor.

JAWA SCAVENGER

This Jawa has an important role in his tribe as he is a preparer. This job entails taking hunted prey that is not able to be reused whole and dissecting it for valuable parts. He has an impressive inferred and instinctive knowledge of galactic technology. He could make a living apart from the tribe should he decide to do so.

Tools concealed up sleeve

PART I: A NEW COMPANION
MUDHORN

Found on Arvala-7 and a handful of other worlds, the mudhorn is a lumbering ungulate. Its most distinguishing feature, as evidenced by its name, is an immense, thick horn sprouting from its forehead, which it uses for defense and to carve out a home in the wilderness. The mudhorn is omnivorous, grinding down plants, lichen-covered stones, and the bones of trespassers with its flat teeth. Extremely territorial, it is best avoided.

FIERCE DEFENDER
Arvala-7 is an unforgiving desert of a world marked by periods of flash flooding that turn the desert hardpan into muddy trenches. Only the most tenacious plants take root in such an environment, and their rarity leads to territoriality among those higher up the food chain. Mudhorns stake out a gully to call their own, using their horns to dig and widen cave burrows, which they defend.

> "SOOGA! SOOGA! SOOGA!"
> – JAWAS CHANTING FOR A MUDHORN EGG

- Keratinous horn with calcium deposits
- Powerful neck muscle pulls back weighty horn
- Hypsodont teeth with strong enamel for a mudhorn's tough diet
- Broad foot pads distribute weight on muddy surfaces

DATA FILE
SUBJECT	Mudhorn
HOMEWORLD	Arvala-7
SIZE	Height (at withers): 2.57 m (8 ft 5 in); width: 1.82 m (6 ft); length: 5.47 m (17 ft 11 in)
LIFESPAN	Unknown

Upper mud coat has dried to a shell

Big game hunters have made the horn a prized trophy

Eyesight is better suited for caves or night

Mudhorns can run up to 30 kph (19 mph)

Dense fur matted with mud

COAT OF MUD

Mudhorns have endothermic mammalian metabolisms. They avoid the harsh desert heat by sleeping in their caves through the day, emerging at night protected from the cold by their thick, wooly coats. During especially hot days they wallow and coat their bodies in thick, cooling mud—the source of their name. The mud is so effective, it renders a mudhorn invisible to infrared sensors.

FACT FILE

DIET
Omnivorous; mostly roots and lichens found in damp caves; bones of dead intruders for calcium

HABITAT
Mud plains and desert hardpan on Arvala-7; mudhorns carve their own caves for sleeping and rearing of young

During the Mandalorian's tangle with a mudhorn, the Child demonstrates remarkable Force ability, telekinetically lifting the charging beast so that Mando can deliver a killing blow.

THE JAWAS' PRIZE

The mudhorn is an example of an oviparous (egg-laying) mammal. Female mudhorns only produce one egg during mating season and protect it fiercely. The Jawa settlers of Arvala-7 consider a mudhorn egg an extremely rare delicacy, placing great value on it. Mando seeks an egg to exchange for his stolen ship parts.

Obscured T-visor

Amban phase-pulse rifle, inoperative from clog

Cape heavy with mud

Chest plate with compromised integrity

Mudhorn egg, covered in furry shell

Battered pauldron knocked loose

Broken gauntlet in need of repair

PART I: A NEW COMPANION
PAZ VIZSLA

Mandalorian traditions endure, thanks to the fervent loyalty of those keeping the flames alive, even after repeated hardships over the decades. Paz Vizsla is part of the underground Mandalorian enclave on Nevarro. He resents the fate of his proud people and will not forgive the Empire for the Great Purge. He passionately believes the path forward for his people lies in the past—adherence to the Way, a hardline Mandalorian orthodoxy espoused by the Children of the Watch, a particularly strict sect.

While Paz has a simmering temper, he can be defused by words of wisdom from the Armorer, whom he respects for her role within the enclave. Paz does not hold the same regard for the Mandalorian, looking down upon his profession. He also disdains Mando for taking Imperial payment. When Mando returns from a successful hunt with a camtono filled with beskar stamped with the mark of an Imperial smelter, Vizsla's ire boils over, and the pair nearly come to blows. However, Mando also follows the Way, and for this, Vizsla can overlook their differences; loyalty to the few remaining enclaves of their people matters more.

- Lightweight duralumin carbide cross-frame
- Gyroscopic flight control systems (beneath cone shell)
- Heat dissipation grille
- Compact repulsorlift load-balancing generator
- Paired variable thrust nozzle
- Tandem-port high-capacity power cell

MS-EJT4 JETPACK
Vizsla's jetpack is heavier than the model traditionally worn by adherents of the Way. The robust engine keeps his armored frame aloft and feeds power into his devastating repeating blaster.

FAMILY HISTORY
Paz Vizsla bears the family name of House Vizsla, one of the most troubled political factions in recent Mandalorian history. During the Clone Wars House Vizsla, led by Pre Vizsla, engineered a coup against Duchess Satine Kryze and her pacifistic ideals, but collusion with dark conspirators led to Pre's death and the catastrophic Siege of Mandalore.

- Extensible rangefinder
- T-visor macrobinocular viewplate
- Traditional House Vizsla livery

PAZ VIZSLA'S HELMET

- BlasTech M-55 medium repeating blaster
- Jetpack power cell connects to rifle via articulated cable

FIREPOWER UNLEASHED
Paz Vizsla's specialized armor and weaponry fit his battlefield role as a heavy infantry trooper. His medium repeating blaster has three alternating barrels to facilitate cooling during blast syncopation. The cannon draws power through an articulated galven-modulated power cable, whose circuitry pre-cycles the energy before it enters the rifle for added destructive yield.

Vizsla and the other warriors of the hidden enclave spring into action to assist Mando against the Bounty Hunters Guild.

Reinforced helmet with integrated targeting array

DATA FILE

SUBJECT	Paz Vizsla
HOMEWORLD	Concordia, moon of Mandalore
SPECIES	Human
AFFILIATION	Children of the Watch
HEIGHT	1.91 m (6 ft 3 in)

House Vizsla pauldron emblem

Beskar-reinforced breastplate

Pauldron armor

Ultrasonic generator concealed in handle

Flexible fuel pipe connects flame emitter to jetpack

Reinforced durasteel blade

VIBROBAYONET

Utility belt with blaster and jetpack maintenance tools

Programmable activation switches for armor systems

Large-gauge flame emitter on gauntlet

SKILLED WARRIOR

As much as Vizsla relishes the long-range striking power of his jetpack and cannon, he is also eager for melee combat. In such contests, he draws a long vibrobayonet from where it is concealed in his boot. The weapon contains a generator in its base, which sends high-frequency tremors through the blade, increasing its lacerating power.

PART I: A NEW COMPANION
UPGRADED ARMOR

The armor the Mandalorian wears to Arvala-7 receives a beating from a mudhorn. Crumpled, gored, and speared by the raging creature, the suit loses its integrity and dangles limply from Mando's body. He repairs it as best he can, but it requires replacement. With the hefty bounty procured from the Client, Mando can improve his armor, and, under guidance from the Armorer, add a few powerful "extras" to his mobile arsenal.

SIGNETLESS PAULDRON

In the absence of a clan or house marker, Mandalorian followers of the Way adorn their pauldron with a signet denoting a noteworthy and honorable kill. Commemorating the ancient past when Mandalorians had to tame the hostile wilderness of their worlds, this signet is often that of a predator. Though Mando slays the mudhorn, he does not consider it a worthy kill due to the Child's help.

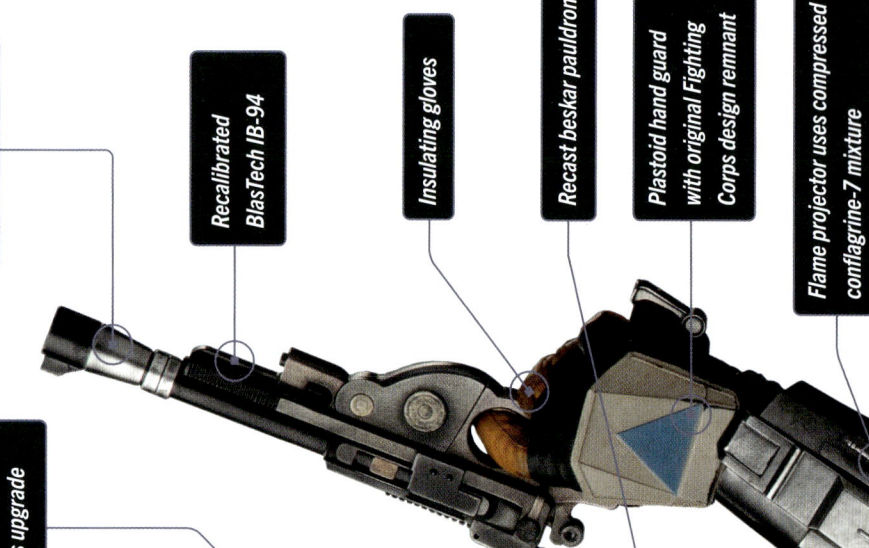

- *Replaceable barrel assembly to ensure accuracy*
- *Recalibrated BlasTech IB-94*
- *Insulating gloves*
- *Recast beskar pauldron*
- *Plastoid hand guard with original Fighting Corps design remnant*
- *Flame projector uses compressed conflagrine-7 mixture*
- *T-visor with "Mandovision" systems upgrade*
- *Repolished helmet dome*

DATA FILE

THIS IS THE WAY

The particular Creed followed by the Mandalorian covert on Nevarro is one orthodoxy. The Mandalorian diaspora after the Great Purge means other coverts have different beliefs.

A MARKET FOR BESKAR

Though Mandalorians revere beskar for its traditional role in their culture, the material is valued for its industrial qualities across the galaxy. However, only Mandalorian metallurgy can unlock beskar's true potential.

Mando's cuirass gleams with the sheen of pure, polished beskar. It draws attention but also warns others of his prowess.

"THEY'RE ALL WEIGHING THE BESKAR IN THEIR MINDS, BUT NOT ME."
– GREEF KARGA, UPON SEEING THE UPGRADES

A NEW CUIRASS

The Armorer decides the Mandalorian warrants a new cuirass. She melts down the delivered ingots to craft a new articulated chest plate, measured and fitted precisely to a holographic proxy of the Mandalorian's torso. When annealed and finally quenched, the armor hardens to a finish capable of withstanding close-range blaster shots. The man beneath is still flesh and blood, and there is a limit to the concussive damage he can take.

- Exactingly dried veshok wood stock
- Magnatomically affixed pauldron
- Beskar tasset
- Impact-deflecting angled plane
- High grade disruptor power charges
- Segmented cuirass permits greater flexibility
- Rifle bandolier
- All-weather survival boots

LEFT VAMBRACE
- Customizable control panel
- Beskar "seedhead" launcher cone
- Service access hatch
- Magnetic acceleration sleeve
- Cooling intake

RIGHT VAMBRACE
- Flame projector nozzle
- Armored fuel line
- Status indicator readout

WHISTLING BIRDS

When Mando declines a signet on the reasoning that an enemy assisted in his kill, the Armorer decides to use the apportioned beskar to create a whistling birds (jair-senaar) launcher instead. Whistling birds are nested durasteel-tipped explosive darts launched from a beskar gauntlet. The darts swarm towards specific heat-sources, which Mando can program parameters to exclude.

PART I: A NEW COMPANION

SORGAN

A sanctuary deep in the Outer Rim, Sorgan is a sparsely settled, verdant world. Copses of conifer trees are threaded by rivers, which spill their banks and deposit krill into catch pools dug out by farmers. Ramshackle villages sprout around the most bountiful rivers. Sorgan has no starport, no industrial centers, and no settlements large enough to be considered cities. The planet is known for its export of spotchka, a luminescent blue beverage brewed by the locals.

> "NO POPULATION DENSITY. REAL BACKWATER SKUG HOLE. WHICH MEANS IT'S PERFECT FOR US."
> – MANDO TO THE CHILD

- Northern archipelago
- Mineral-rich soil deposits at northern delta
- Temperate weather patterns encourage life to flourish
- Grinjer herds roam the inland plains
- River settlement that Mando approaches

DATA FILE

REGION	Outer Rim
SECTOR	Karthakk
SYSTEM	Sorgan
DIAMETER	8,742 km (5,432 miles)
TERRAIN	Rivers; grasslands; coniferous forests
MOONS	2
POPULATION	Under 10,000 estimated; no census data

KRILL
Non-industrialized inland krill farming brings a labor-intensive yet rewarding harvest for the settlers of Sorgan.

A SURVEY OF SORGAN

WETLAND FORESTS
The shifting soils of the wetlands prevent conifers from establishing the necessary roots to grow to towering heights.

FOREST CLEARING
The Mandalorian lands the *Razor Crest* in a dry upland clearing a few kilometers away from a farming village.

SORGAN COMMON HOUSE
A place for travelers to eat, drink, and seek work or refuge, the common house serves spotchka and bone broth.

RAIDER WIKIUP
Klatooinian raiders have constructed a temporary camp of brushwood and grass from which to launch their attacks.

FARMERS' VILLAGE
Several generations old, the krill farmers' village was originally a grinjer-trapper's settlement whose focus changed once krill-farming methods were made more reliable. It is home to about a dozen families. Its residents now take any excess spotchka that they have and sell it to the nearby common house for resale or export.

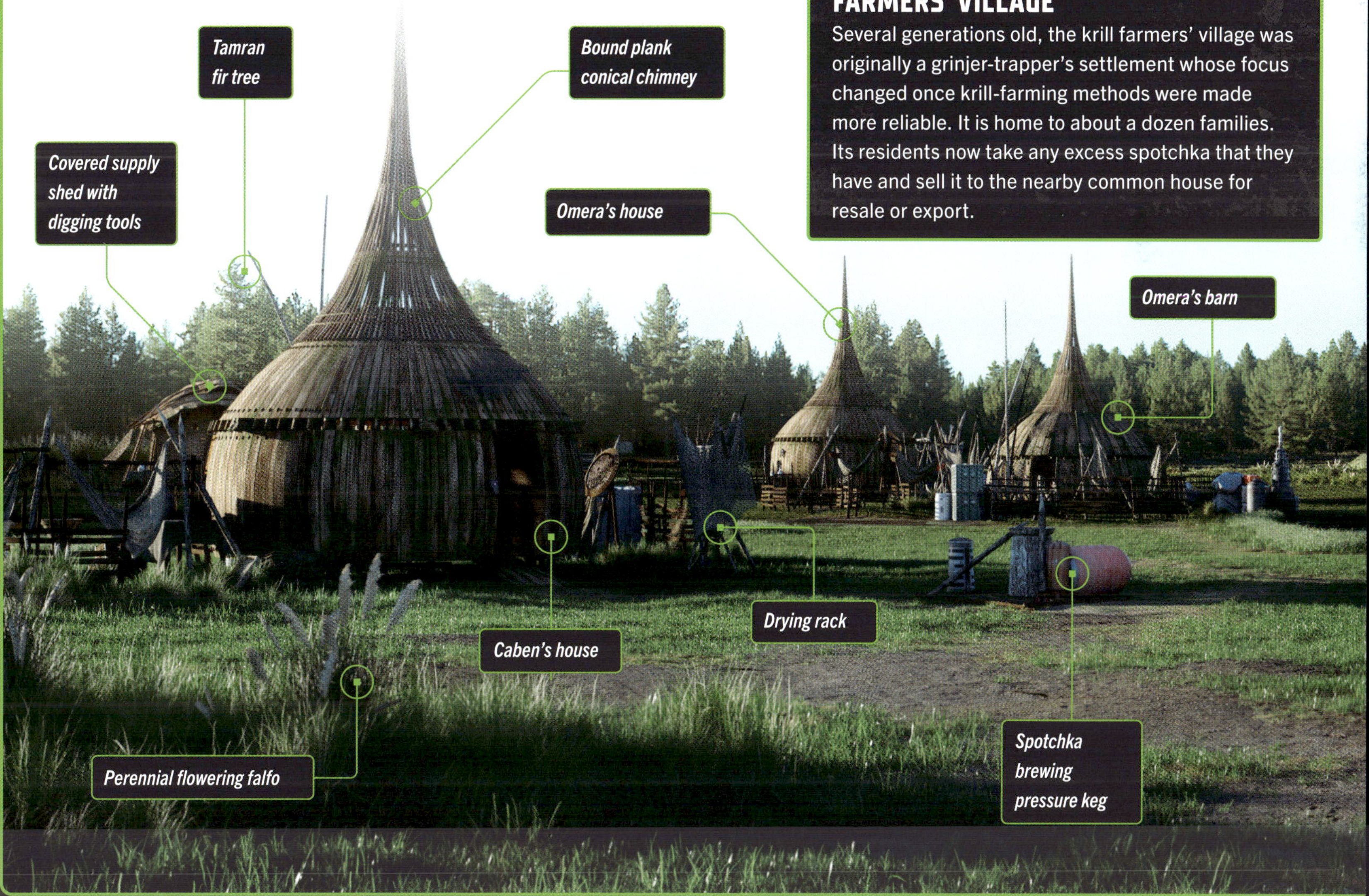

- Tamran fir tree
- Bound plank conical chimney
- Covered supply shed with digging tools
- Omera's house
- Omera's barn
- Caben's house
- Drying rack
- Perennial flowering falfo
- Spotchka brewing pressure keg

PART I: A NEW COMPANION
SORGAN VILLAGE

Self-described as living in "the middle of nowhere," the Sorgan farm villagers enjoy the isolation of rural life and the community that it fosters. For generations, they have drawn krill to their containment pools, luring them with seeded algae that keeps the teal crustaceans from returning to the river. Villagers wade hip-deep into the pools, panning for fully grown krill with baskets made of reeds and baleen. The fleshiest specimens are sifted from the smaller fry and placed into wicker hoppers. Within venerated huts, these krill have their shells harvested to make spotchka brew.

Cubed grinjer cuts and squawkfowl tenders form the building blocks of sizzling, delicious kebabs.

SORGAN SUSTENANCE

Spotchka is made from crushed krill casings and Sorgan river water fermented in casks made from local wood. This brewing process means homegrown spotchka has a distinct flavor and potency that offworld brands cannot match. In fact, connoisseurs are content to pay a premium for the authenticity. Grinjers are local, large game animals that are hunted as they can provide a wide variety of foods, including bone broth, stew, and steaks. Lotus biscuits, fir-cones, float-apples, mosschop, and reedroot are hearty, nutritious alternatives for the strictly herbivorous.

Netting allows bottles to be hung from hooks

SPOTCHKA JUGS

Basket full of lotus biscuits

Polished stone porringer

BONE BROTH BOWL

Upper support timbers

Lined chimney flue

Freshwater fill-up counter

FAVORITE SPOT

Vish's welcoming nature and her establishment's gentle atmosphere make the common house and the nearby lodging a favorite place for regulars. Each one feels that they have made a discovery—the galaxy's best kept secret—in the comforting fare found here. Strangers are welcome provided they don't ruin a good thing.

OMERA

Omera cares deeply for her daughter Winta, wishing the best for her while teaching her the skills to thrive on Sorgan. The community is of great help in this regard. Of all the villagers, Omera seems the most comfortable and competent with blaster weaponry, suggesting some previous training at an earlier age.

Krill-dyed collar with beetle-carapace and mollusk-shell embroidery

Farmer's apron with tool pockets

OMERA AND MANDO
Omera is drawn to Mando because of his devotion to his ward, the Child, recognizing in him the focus and sacrifice that comes with parenting. She is intensely curious about this mysterious man.

Krill-stained waterproof waders

Winta's mother, Omera, has warned her to stay away from the tree line, for raiders lurk there.

WINTA

Winta is a playful, sociable girl who has many friends among the other kids in the village. She plays wickerlimmie with them when not doing her chores. Should Winta find herself alone, she amuses herself by chasing froglings. Winta grows fond of Grogu and is sad to see him leave when he departs with Mando.

Collar made by Omera

Decorative belt

PART I: A NEW COMPANION
CARA DUNE

A veteran of the Galactic Civil War who fought under the banner of the Rebellion and the nascent New Republic, Cara Dune is a seasoned warrior. She speaks little of her past, but her Alderaanian heritage makes it easy to surmise what centers her animus for the Empire. No planet suffered quite like Alderaan did, obliterated as it was by the blast of the Death Star. The teardrop tattoo on her cheek, which upon closer inspection is an Alliance crest, is a tiny indicator of the enormous loss she carries.

Dune is an intimidating brawler as well as a crack shot. As the galaxy transformed with the scattering of Imperial power, Dune found herself losing focus and direction. What once had been clear-cut combat missions turned into peacekeeping assignments, escorting potentates, or quelling riots. It was not what she had signed up for, so she resigned her commission, reinventing herself as a mercenary. This way of life erased much of the valor she earned as a veteran. Questionable jobs have brought a bounty on her head, and she now avoids New Republic space.

Cara arrived on Sorgan about a week before Mando. At first, she assumes he is there to collect a bounty on her.

> "IF ANYBODY RUNS MY CHAIN CODE, I'LL ROT IN A CELL FOR THE REST OF MY LIFE."
> – CARA DUNE

Hair dyed dark, no longer regulation length

SHOCKTROOPER TRAINING
Cara Dune served with the Alliance 6th Spinward Fleet, training under grizzled fighters at the tail end of the Galactic Civil War. She saw most of her action following the Battle of Endor, mopping up bastions held by Imperial warlords. Dune was a Dropper, serving on commando missions where rebel soldiers plummeted from high-altitude ships for fast and quiet insertion. Though she can boast a string of successful missions, they were not without cost. In addition to her agility and aim, Dune is a combat medic skilled in field medicine.

Pressure belt from drop suit

Kinetic-absorbent internal honeycomb structure in stock

Drop suit's magnatomic plate to affix gear

Stowed hunting knife

Carrying and stabilizing handle

Upper barrel

Cyclic power generator drum

M-32 LIGHT REPEATING BLASTER RIFLE
Following her military career, Cara is a stickler for maintaining her weapons. Demanding frequent maintenance, her M-32 rifle cycles powerful blasts at a rapid rate through syncopated barrels.

Self-sharpening sheath

HUNTING KNIFE

Cara finds the Mandalorian intriguing and asks him for details about his mysterious culture. She is bemused by its intractable rules.

Teardrop tattoo is a symbol of lost homeworld

LONE WARRIOR

During her early missions with the Rebel Droppers, Cara became accustomed to being welcomed as a liberator by the beleaguered citizens of one-time Imperial worlds, who would greet the commandos with feasts and flowers. As the promised glory of the New Republic fails to materialize, Dune becomes more of a lone operative.

Broken, blood-stripe Rebel Dropper tattoo

Chest seal switches from her Dropper vac-suit

Belt has mounting loops for utility pouches

Forearm guard is piece of Dropper vac-suit armor

Unpowered optical scope

DDC MT2 blaster pistol has been modified to maximize each blaster bolt's intensity by using up ammo cells faster.

Cara fills time, earns credits, and exercises in crowd-pleasing tether-brawls against overconfident opponents, like ill-fated challenger Taur Deeves.

DATA FILE

SUBJECT Carasynthia Dune

HOMEWORLD Alderaan

SPECIES Human

AFFILIATION Formerly Rebel Alliance; formerly New Republic; now independent

HEIGHT 1.73 m (5 ft 8 in)

PART I: A NEW COMPANION
KLATOOINIAN RAIDERS

These Klatooinian bandits are a ruthless gang of marauders that preys on the krill farmers of Sorgan. The group once worked for Hutt crime lords like their fellow Nikto and Vodran henchmen. The Klatooinians have since gone independent in the wake of the massive upheaval in the criminal underworld following Jabba the Hutt's death. Though this gang has sacrificed its standing in organized crime, its members relish their freedom.

At first, the raiders seemed content to simply extort a cut of the harvest from the villagers, but bloodlust has led their leader, Sastos, to violence. Sastos and his raiders seem unstoppable as they own a powerful weapon—a reclaimed AT-ST walker cast off by the Empire after the end of the Galactic Civil War. They had not counted on their victims showing courage, and the villagers are now armed, trained, and ready to fight back.

- Welded armor plate
- Armored viewport
- Light blaster cannon
- Femoral strut
- Dangling drive engine fluidic lines
- Ankle joint tensioner
- Ankle joint (bound by flexorcord)
- Fence-cutting blade

DATA FILE
MANUFACTURER Kuat Drive Yards
MODEL All Terrain Scout Transport
TYPE Scout walker
DIMENSIONS Height: 9.04 m (29 ft 8 in); width: 4.58 m (15 ft); length: 6.43 m (21 ft)
SPEED 65 kph (40 mph); slowed by damaged leg bearings
WEAPONS 1 twin laser cannon, 1 light blaster cannon, 1 concussion grenade launcher (spent)
AFFILIATION Klatooinian raiders

AT-ST RAIDER

This battered All Terrain Scout Transport was stationed at an Imperial outpost on Dom-Bradden but never saw action. With the collapse of the Empire, the base was abandoned. Sastos and his crew found the outpost during their escape from Hutt Space. The Klatooinian mechanics activated the walker and repainted it in tribal war colors. Over the years, the gang has used the vehicle in a string of raids to deliver devastating firepower.

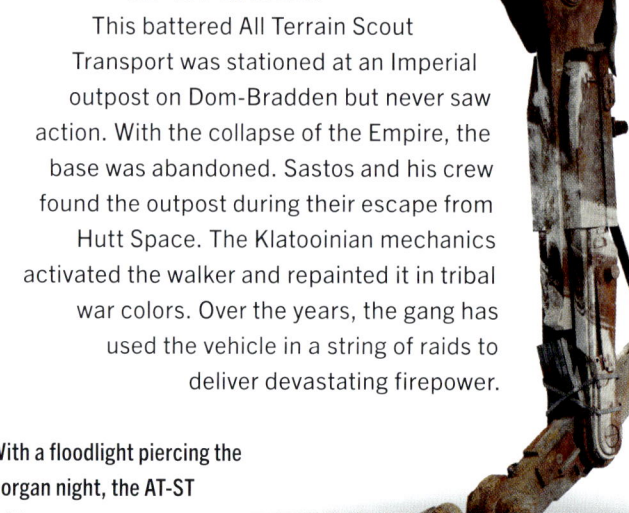

With a floodlight piercing the Sorgan night, the AT-ST raider seems even more frightening. Some see it as more of a supernatural beast than a machine.

Emerging from the tree line in the morning mists with weapons brandished, the terrifying raiders attack the unarmed villagers.

FACT FILE

PATH OF DESTRUCTION
Since acquiring the walker, the raiders have also struck on Andasala, Svivren, Reuss VIII, and Midani.

WALKER UPKEEP
Without Imperial engineers or resources, the AT-ST is worse for wear after five years of use. The Klatooinians make do with improvised repairs and additions to the craft.

> "I'VE SEEN THAT THING TAKE OUT ENTIRE COMPANIES OF SOLDIERS IN A MATTER OF MINUTES."
> – CARA DUNE, REGARDING THE AT-ST

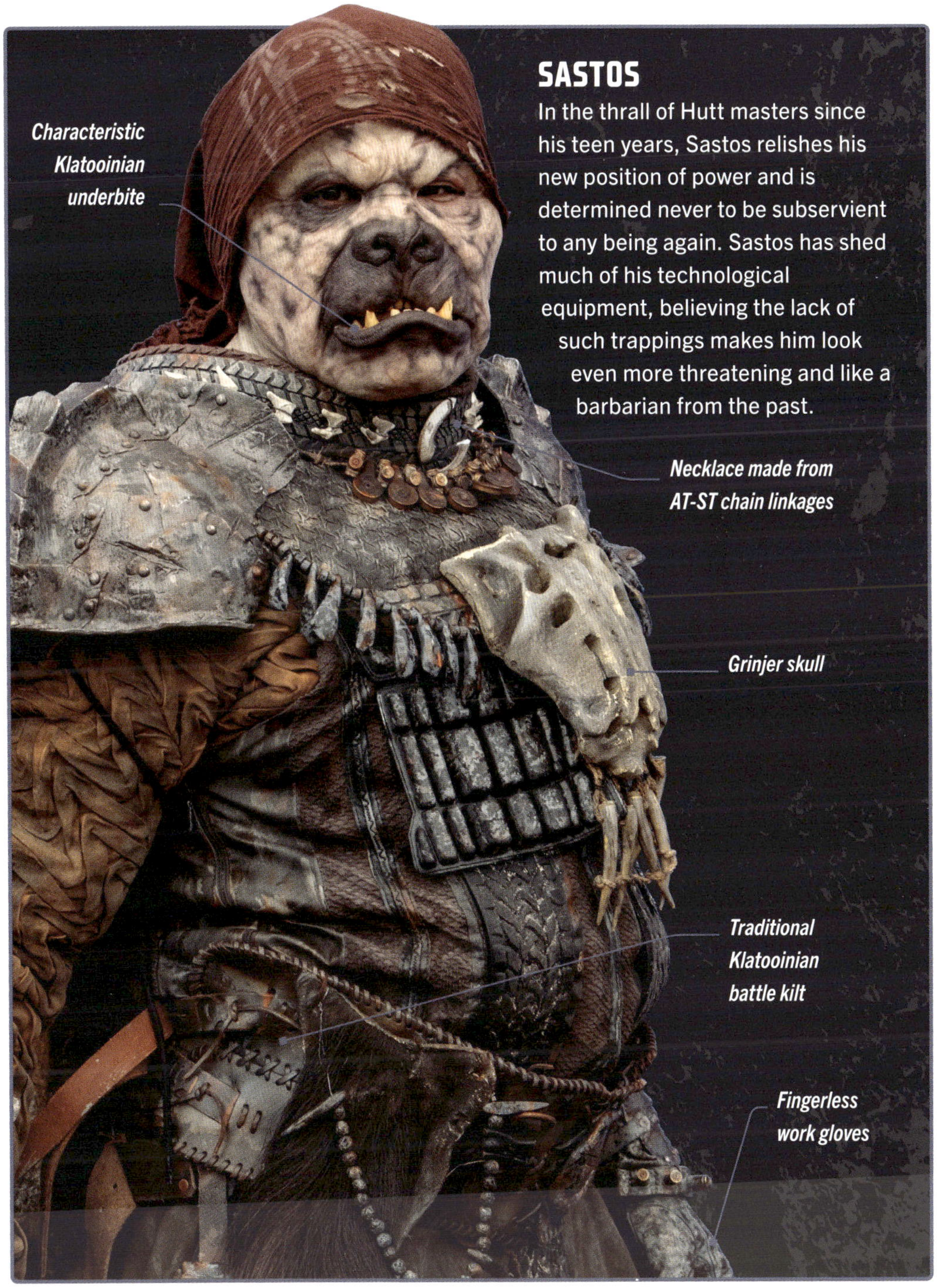

SASTOS

In the thrall of Hutt masters since his teen years, Sastos relishes his new position of power and is determined never to be subservient to any being again. Sastos has shed much of his technological equipment, believing the lack of such trappings makes him look even more threatening and like a barbarian from the past.

- Characteristic Klatooinian underbite
- Necklace made from AT-ST chain linkages
- Grinjer skull
- Traditional Klatooinian battle kilt
- Fingerless work gloves

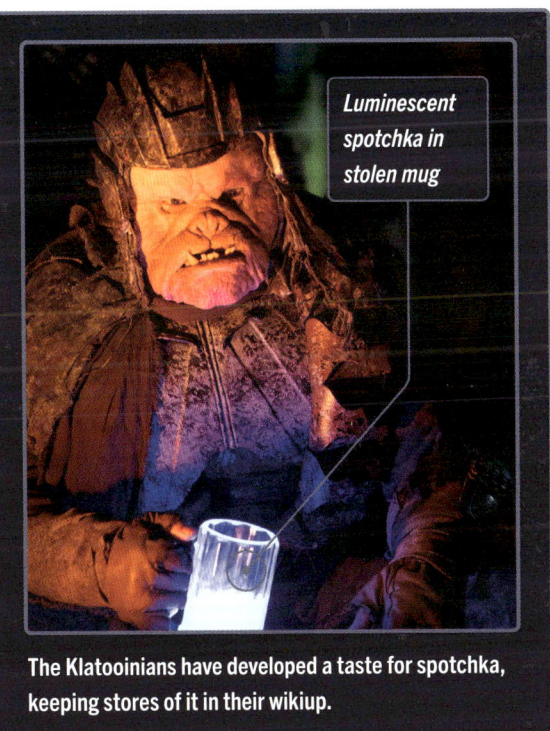

Luminescent spotchka in stolen mug

The Klatooinians have developed a taste for spotchka, keeping stores of it in their wikiup.

EMBEGGU

Embeggu learned the secrets of spotchka through intimidating captive farmers, and he is now an accomplished brewer. Now the raiders don't need to steal casks of finished spotchka and can destroy them. Instead, they steal the raw krill so Embeggu can create brews that appeal more to Klatooinian tastes.

RIOT MAR
Giving chase in his starfighter, bounty hunter Riot Mar lands a serious blow on the *Razor Crest*'s starboard engine pylon.

RIOT MAR'S SHIP

PART I: A NEW COMPANION
PELI MOTTO

Peli Motto is the acerbic and short-tempered attendant of Docking Bay 3-5 at the Mos Eisley Spaceport. She runs the facility with the help of an energetic pit droid trio. Peli tends to the *Razor Crest* when Mando comes to Tatooine attempting to keep a low profile. Though Peli isn't entirely hospitable to the armored hunter, her grouchy exterior melts away to show a tenderness toward the Child. She coddles little "bright eyes" (as she calls him), and sees that he is looked after and fed, for an additional fee, while Mando carries out business in the port city and beyond.

In time, Peli becomes a valued contact for Mando, a friendly face on an otherwise unwelcoming world. No doubt it is her fondness for the Child that enamors Peli to the duo and keeps her from swindling them. On subsequent visits, Peli connects Djarin to a rumored Mandalorian operating out of Mos Pelgo, reunites Mando and Child after their brief separation, and equips the Mandalorian with an N-1 starfighter when he needs a vessel.

DOCKING BAY 3-5
Docking Bay 3-5 is one of a multitude of crater-like launch stations that dot Mos Eisley Spaceport. The landing facility is primarily sunken below ground level, with stairs and a service ramp leading up to street level. The mid-sized hangar has repair and diagnostic equipment as well as fueling supplies. It can be rented for 24 credits a day, not counting repair fees, which is where Peli really makes her money. Peli also maintains a cramped and cluttered office within the bay.

Wide-bore donderbus blaster rifle

Professional survival training, paid for with repair services

TOUGH TIMES
The shifting tides of galactic politics have made the already lawless Mos Eisley even more tumultuous. Following the volatile fallout of the collapse of the Empire and the death of Jabba the Hutt, Tatooine eventually settled, falling even further from prominence without Jabba's presence or an Imperial garrison. Peli earns a meager living off her attendant duties, as her bay often stands vacant. She supplements her pay with high-stakes sabacc games played at the neighborhood cantina. Peli practices her skills playing against her droids, who often cheat.

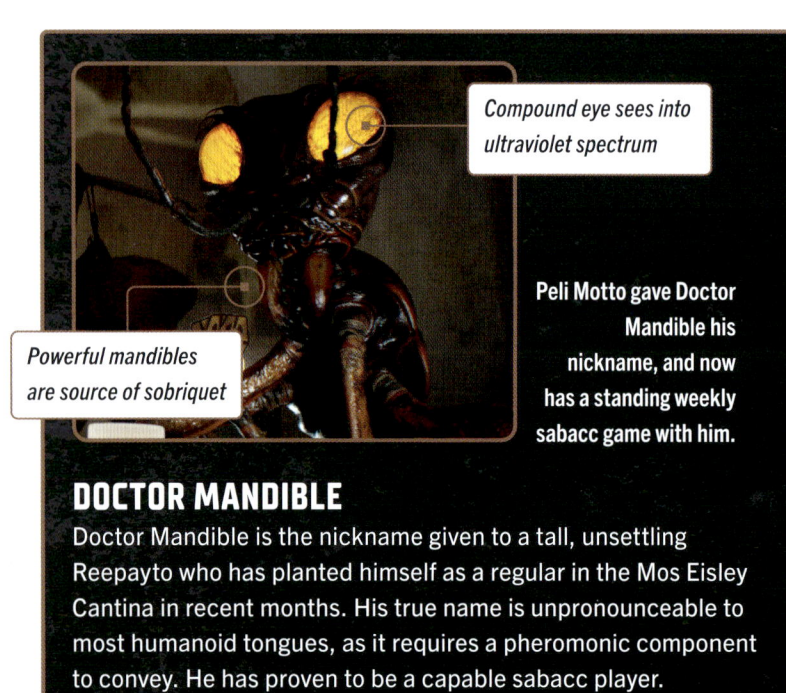

Compound eye sees into ultraviolet spectrum

Powerful mandibles are source of sobriquet

Peli Motto gave Doctor Mandible his nickname, and now has a standing weekly sabacc game with him.

DOCTOR MANDIBLE
Doctor Mandible is the nickname given to a tall, unsettling Reepayto who has planted himself as a regular in the Mos Eisley Cantina in recent months. His true name is unpronounceable to most humanoid tongues, as it requires a pheromonic component to convey. He has proven to be a capable sabacc player.

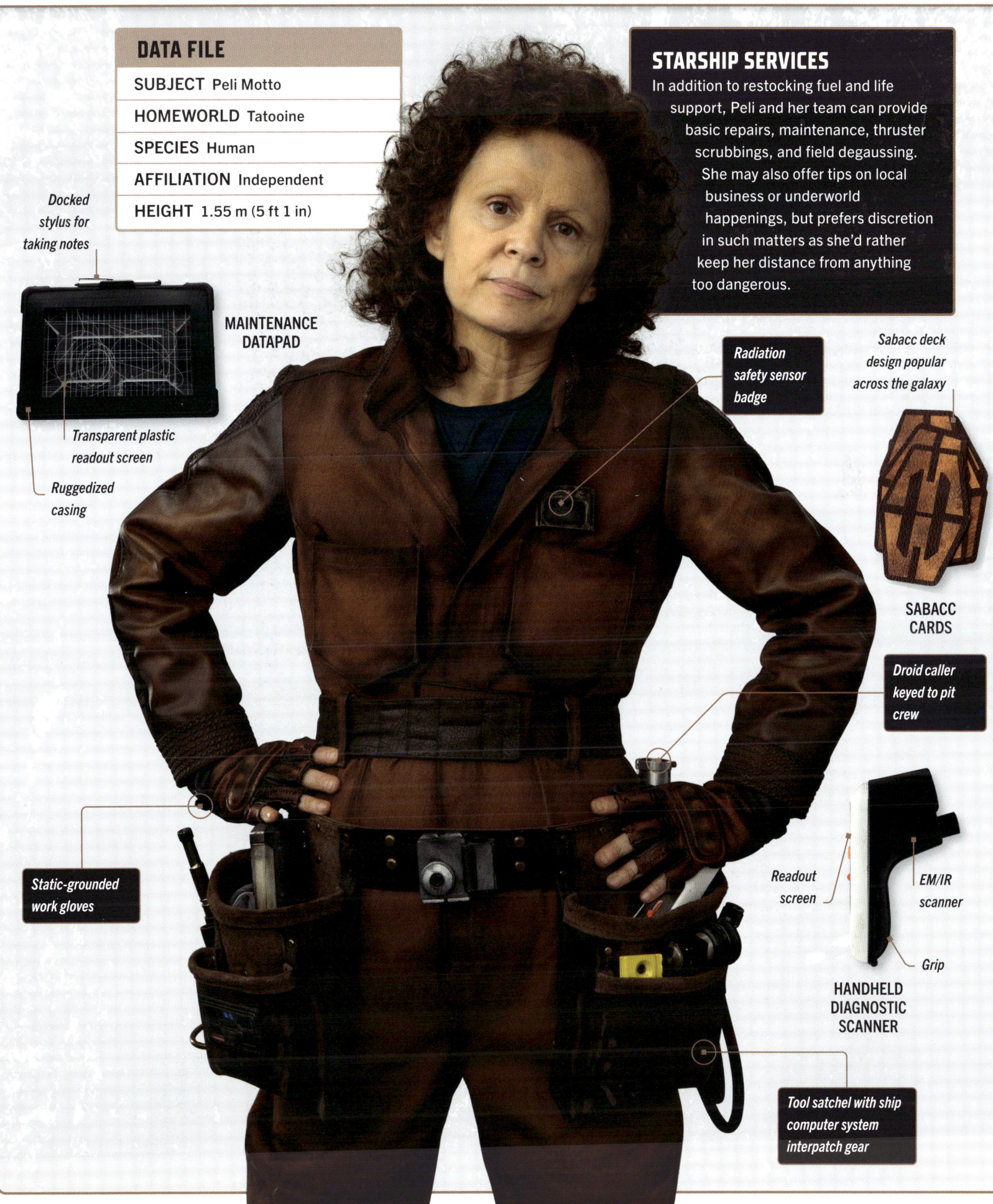

PART I: A NEW COMPANION
PELI'S DROIDS

The turbulence following Jabba the Hutt's death and the eventual rise of Boba Fett's leadership strains Tatooine's chronically rickety economy. To make ends meet beyond the docking fees she can charge during an uncertain era of visitors to Tatooine, Peli Motto also offers mechanical repair services to anyone in the central Mos Eisley Spaceport district who may need it.

Knowing how untrustworthy some of the local repair work can be—especially given her close association with Jawas in the past—Peli promises all-droid services, meaning she can keep her costs affordable. Or, at least, that's her pitch—she is not above overcharging gullible visitors she doesn't expect to see again. For local clientele and trusted regulars—Din Djarin included—Peli drives a fair bargain for her mechanical expertise and her misfit team of droid fixers.

BD-72 shines a spotlight on the work-in-progress N-1 starfighter, and holorecords the construction, keeping a precise inventory of parts and procedure for future examination, analysis, and troubleshooting—helpful for Peli's loosely structured approach.

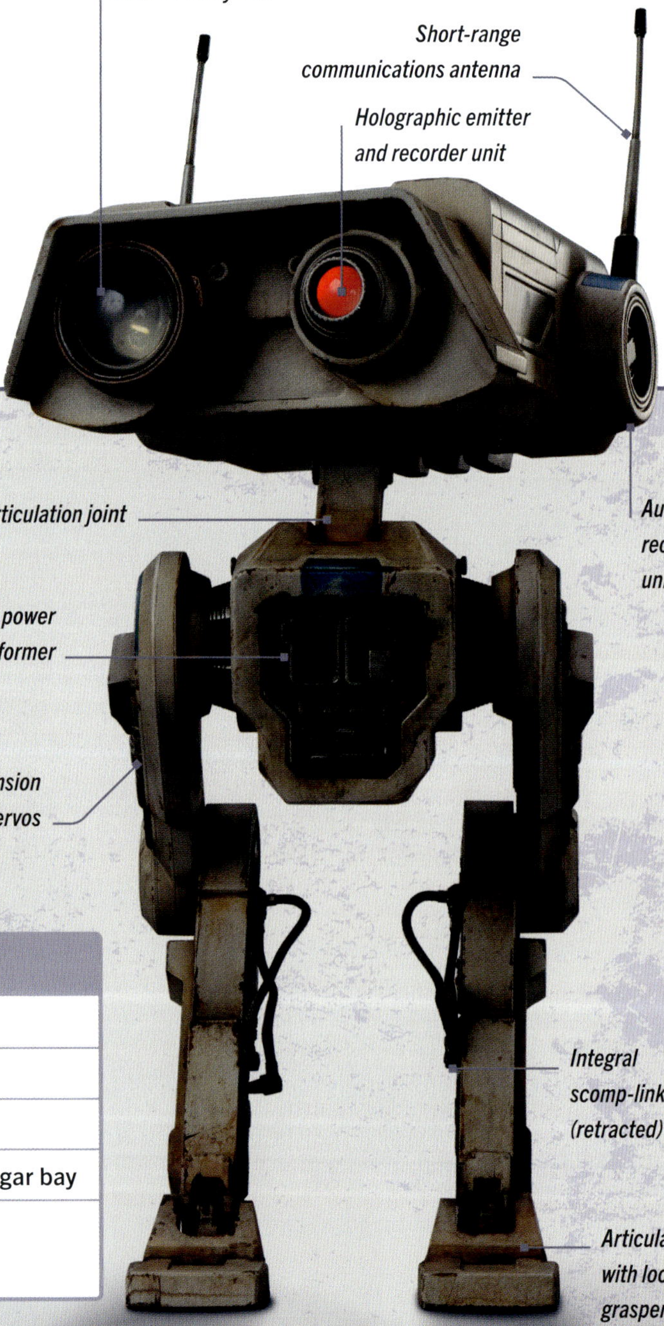

- Spotlight and active scanner array lens
- Short-range communications antenna
- Holographic emitter and recorder unit
- Audio receptor unit
- Neck articulation joint
- Integral power transformer
- High-tension gyro-balance servos
- Activated holorecorder
- Integral scomp-link (retracted)
- Articulated foot with lockable graspers

BD-72
A repurposed vintage Behold-Urwar Droid Concepts explorer unit, BD-72's motivational firmware has a deeply encoded sense of curiosity meant to drive it beyond any fear of the unknown. As a repair assistant, this inquisitiveness is channeled into eagerly finding the best way to apply its integral toolset to help its fellow mechanics.

BD-72, OBSERVER MODE

DATA FILE
SUBJECT	BD-72
HOMEWORLD	Tatooine
SERIES	BD explorer droid
AFFILIATION	Peli Motto's hangar bay
HEIGHT	0.43 m (1 ft 5 in) (not including antenna)

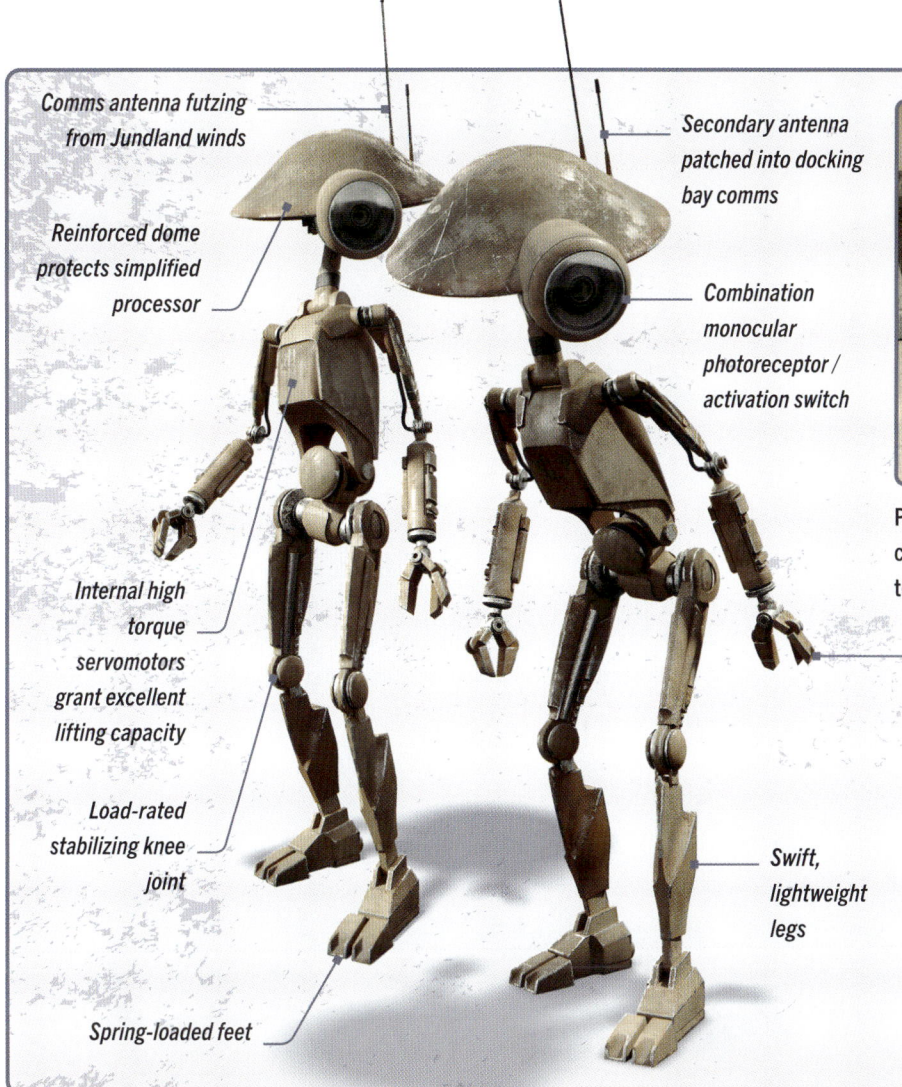

- Comms antenna futzing from Jundland winds
- Reinforced dome protects simplified processor
- Internal high torque servomotors grant excellent lifting capacity
- Load-rated stabilizing knee joint
- Spring-loaded feet
- Secondary antenna patched into docking bay comms
- Combination monocular photoreceptor / activation switch
- Versatile tool-grasping manipulators
- Swift, lightweight legs

Peli programs the pit droids to carry out such scams as the classic "Grand Theft Jawa," wherein they alter a stolen speeder to appear as a different one to sell to the original owner.

PIT DROIDS

Peli's principal repair crew consists of a trio of aged DUM-series pit droids that chirp and scuttle about. They help Peli with a range of repair tasks, join her for sabacc games, and even discreetly cover for less-than-legal transactions. When not needed, the three fold up and recharge in a stowed configuration, springing open as soon as the situation warrants.

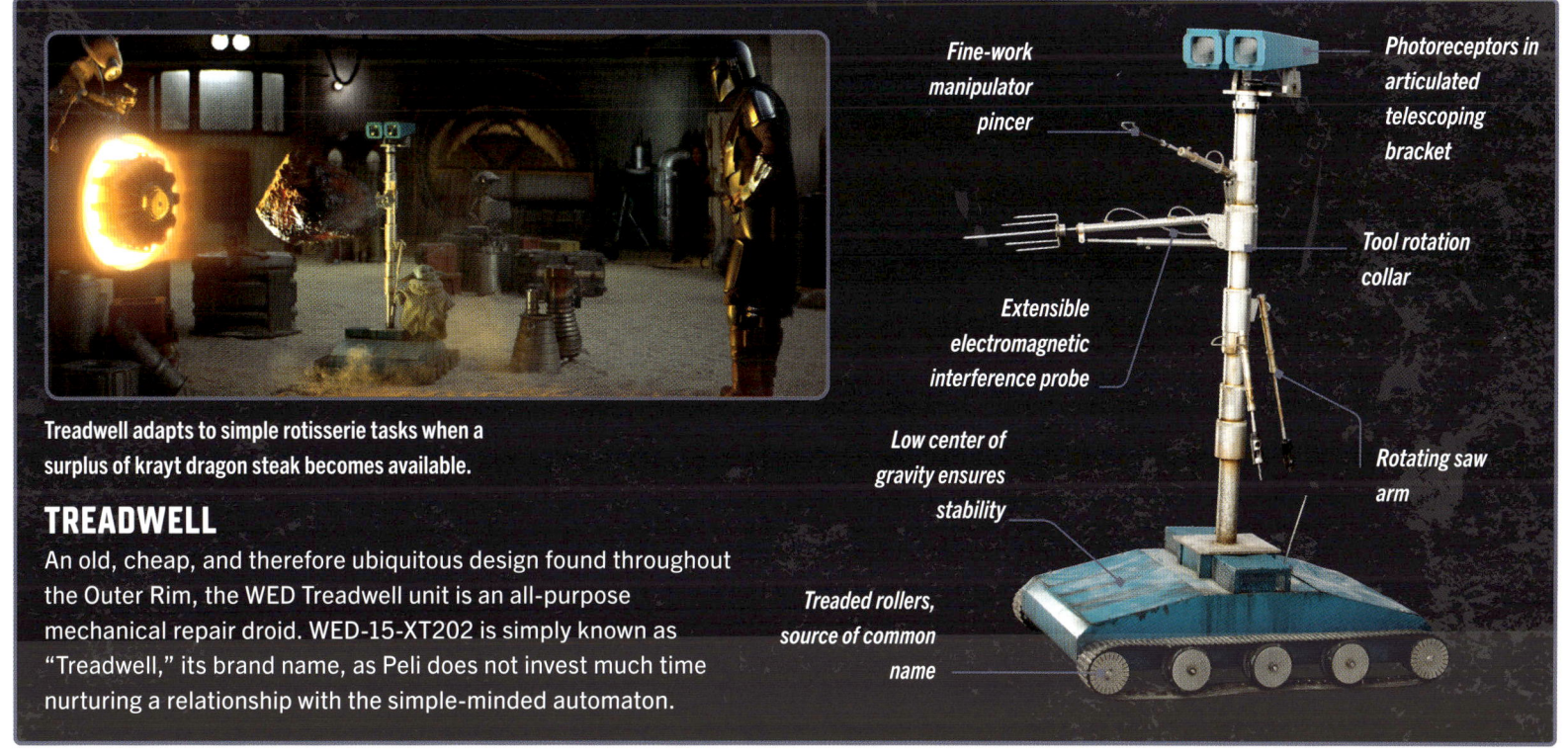

Treadwell adapts to simple rotisserie tasks when a surplus of krayt dragon steak becomes available.

TREADWELL

An old, cheap, and therefore ubiquitous design found throughout the Outer Rim, the WED Treadwell unit is an all-purpose mechanical repair droid. WED-15-XT202 is simply known as "Treadwell," its brand name, as Peli does not invest much time nurturing a relationship with the simple-minded automaton.

- Fine-work manipulator pincer
- Extensible electromagnetic interference probe
- Low center of gravity ensures stability
- Treaded rollers, source of common name
- Photoreceptors in articulated telescoping bracket
- Tool rotation collar
- Rotating saw arm

PART I: A NEW COMPANION
TORO CALICAN

A rookie bounty hunter, Toro Calican hopes to join the Bounty Hunters Guild. An abundance of confidence and ambition exudes from Calican, not quite covering up the telltale signs of youthful inexperience. Toro acquires a bounty puck signaling 10,000 credits for the capture of Fennec Shand, and the corresponding tracking fob points in the direction of the Dune Sea.

What Toro lacks is an appreciation of the danger that Fennec represents, but the Mandalorian supplies it when Toro tries to persuade him into a working partnership. Mando accepts the job and requests the tracking fob, but Toro is wary of being made inconsequential, so smashes it against the wall. Now, Toro's mind alone retains the positional data.

The two head into the dunes on rented speeder bikes, following Toro's memorized coordinates. Shand has hunkered down on a ridge, and has her pursuers in her snipers' sights. The partners hold out until dark before making a coordinated move to outflank Shand. Throughout their trek, Toro questions Mando's wisdom, even though Mando's skill saves the younger man from multiple missteps.

HEAVY BLASTER PISTOL
Toro keeps a well-maintained DL-75 heavy blaster pistol. It is a stripped-down rifle with its barrel and stalk removed—a common underworld modification. The pistol retains a rifle's punch, but at close range and with considerable recoil.

- Model 40 Marksman scope

CAPTURING SHAND
Under cover of darkness, Mando and Toro race toward Shand on their speeder bikes. They take turns launching flash charges—brilliant projectiles that hinder the sniper's night vision—into the sky, and outmaneuver Fennec at the cost of Mando's speeder bike. Mando leaves to fetch a wandering dewback so they can transport their bounty back to port, leaving Toro alone with their acquisition. Fennec successfully ascertains Toro's ambition as the night ends. She points out that Mando is a much more valuable quarry and is also wanted by the Guild.

- DL-75 heavy blaster pistol
- Breathable synth-fabric neck buff protects against sun and sand
- Buckled straps to tighten trouser legs

DATA FILE
MANUFACTURER
Aratech Repulsor Company

MODEL 712 AvA

TYPE Speeder bike

DIMENSIONS Height: 0.82 m (2 ft 8 in); width: 0.72 m (2 ft 4 in); length: 3.45 m (11 ft 4 in)

SPEED
325 kph (202 mph)

WEAPONS None

AFFILIATION
Ridden by Toro Calican

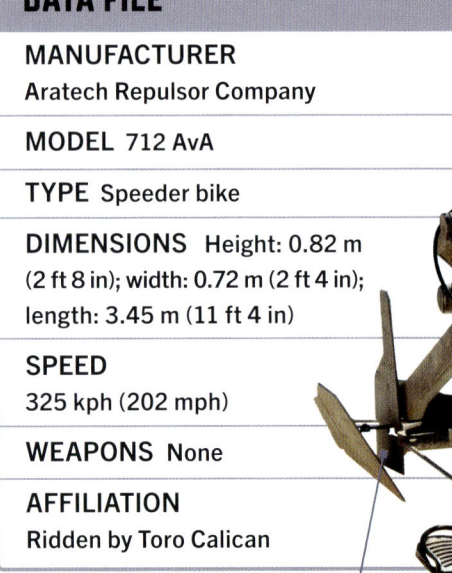

- Tarp for wilderness shelter
- Inner steering vane
- Leather pannier bags

712 AVA SPEEDER BIKE
The 712 AvA speeder bike is an old civilian version of an even older Imperial design. This bike has had much of its communications instrumentation stripped out, forcing the driver to rely on handheld comlinks for contact and navigation. The pivot-mounted outriggers add extra maneuverability provided the driver muscles the steering column.

TORO'S END
To Fennec's surprise, Toro shoots her, leaving her badly wounded in the desert. He speeds ahead to Mando's ship. Using the Child and docking attendant Peli Motto as hostages, he forces Mando to surrender. But Mando blinds the inattentive Calican with a flash charge and then finishes the wannabe legend with a blaster shot.

- Manual adjustment control
- Primary electronic lens
- Image balance lens

NEURO-SAAV MODEL TD2.5 ELECTROBINOCULARS
The fact that Toro's electrobinoculars are newly out-of-the-box indicates how inexperienced Toro is. At 250 New Republic credits they are a pricey piece of optical hardware, featuring advanced magnification and low-light enhanced imaging systems.

- Weather-coated racing goggles
- Perforated emitter nozzle
- Gunslinger-cut leather holster and belt
- Padded nerf-leather vest over upper bodyglove
- Glowrod pouch
- Scandoc pouch
- Medpac items distributed in small stowage pouches

DATA FILE
SUBJECT	Toro Calican
HOMEWORLD	Coruscant
SPECIES	Human
AFFILIATION	Aspiring for Bounty Hunter Guild membership
HEIGHT	1.75 m (5 ft 9 in)
AGE	24 standard years

PART I: A NEW COMPANION
DEWBACKS

Dewbacks are large lizards native to Tatooine. There are two main dewback breeds on the planet: the witla and the pearled. These beasts are well adapted to the desert environment, and are used as riding mounts as well as sources of draft labor, food, and skins. Dewbacks are diurnal, active when the Tatooine suns shine their brightest. At night, dewbacks become sluggish as temperatures dip into the single digits. Tatooine's populace tamed these handy animals long ago, and various breeds are available for sale or rent at the planet's scattered spaceports.

FALLEN RIDER
In the Dune Sea, Mando and Toro Calican discover a domesticated pearled dewback trekking aimlessly while dragging the dead body of a one-time rider. The corpse is that of Jird Loomis, a bounty hunter who fell foul of Fennec Shand and now serves as bait for a trap she has set.

WHAT'S IN A NAME?
In the wild, dewbacks travel in small herds for protection. They cluster together at night, huddling for warmth. During the cooler nighttime temperatures, moisture collects on their thick skin.
In the morning, the dewbacks reinforce their social bonds and acquire vital moisture by licking the collected dew from the backs of their neighbors—the source of the species' name. Their muscular bodies, thick hides, and strong tails mean they have few natural enemies, but their eggs are vulnerable to predators.

FACT FILE
SUBJECT Pearled dewback

HOMEWORLD Tatooine

SIZE Average height (at withers): 1.7 m (5 ft 7 in); average length: 2.5 m (8 ft 2 in)

LIFESPAN Average 30 standard years (domesticated)

- Dew collects on back overnight
- Pebbled skin is tough to pierce
- Fire-roasted dewback tail is a popular port meal at Mos Eisley and Mos Espa
- Skilled riders set a dewback at ease before riding with gentle pressure on its tail
- Smaller footprint than the witla dewback

- Leather pannier bags
- Universal handgrip
- Outer steering vane
- Unspooled fuel lines
- Accelerator pedals

ZEPHYR-J SPEEDER BIKE
While not exactly the finest racing machine to come out of Corellia, the Zephyr-J is nonetheless a reliable bike favored in the Outer Rim for its durability. Its percussive engine purrs like a narglatch rather than whispering like the noise-suppressed models more common in larger settlements.

DATA FILE

MANUFACTURER Mobquet Swoops and Speeders

MODEL Zephyr-J

TYPE Speeder bike

DIMENSIONS Height: 0.96 m (3 ft 2 in); width: 0.7 m (2 ft 4 in); length: 3.29 m (10 ft 10 in)

SPEED 325 kph (202 mph)

WEAPONS None

AFFILIATION Ridden by the Mandalorian

- Patchy, insulating fur for colder nights
- Eyes have a nictitating membrane to protect against blowing sand
- Strong lips can strip the husks off of desert grasses
- Pearled dewbacks have thick claws for scratching at sandstone

DATA FILE

DIET
Dewbacks are omnivores, catching scurriers and similar-sized to smaller prey or feeding off desert grasses, sages, and underground tubers

HABITAT
Depends on breed; witlas prefer the Dune Sea; pearled dewbacks are often found in rockier areas

PART I: A NEW COMPANION
FENNEC SHAND

> Elite mercenary and assassin Fennec Shand has been operating in the criminal underworld since the early days of the Empire, making a name for herself by ruthlessly carrying out difficult assignments. During her decades-long career she's scored hits for all the top criminal syndicates, including the notorious Hutt Clan.

With the coming of the New Republic and its commitment to restoring peaceful order in the galaxy, Fennec faces fresh challenges. Justice agents for the New Republic begin systematically locking down her top employers, and Shand starts a life on the run, as she is now the target of a hefty bounty.

Fennec's fugitive path takes her to the desolate Tatooine. An aspiring young bounty hunter named Toro Calican traces her position to beyond the Dune Sea, and looks to make Shand his first acquisition. But the rookie needs help, and hires the Mandalorian as a mentor. The ambitious Calican gets more than he bargains for when he tracks down Shand, but Fennec too underestimates her mark, and she suffers a near-fatal blaster wound for her efforts.

DEADLY BETRAYAL
In addition to her martial skills and piloting ability, Fennec Shand is adept at reading people, ferreting out their weaknesses and exploiting them. Toro Calican's inexperience radiates from him like a beacon, and Fennec lures him into betraying Mando with word of the armored warrior's falling-out with the Guild and the sizable bounty on his head. While she had hoped to negotiate her freedom, she misjudges just how rash Toro can be. Toro blasts Fennec, leaving her wounded in the sand.

FENNEC'S HELMET
- Plastoid battle helmet
- Adjustment dial loosens faceplate
- Slit visor keeps Shand focused on her target
- Carry slot and blade concealed in shoulder stock
- Sleeveless jacket constructed of rancor leather
- Armorweave skirt
- Orange-accented energy discharge pleats
- All-weather boots
- Silent tread

MERR-SONN MUNITIONS 785MK FIREPUNCHER-X SNIPER RIFLE
Elongated triple-printed galven circuitry lining the barrel length strengthens bolt cohesion for longer, more accurate fire.

- Light-gathering amplification plate
- Replaceable barrel head
- Calibrated-tension trigger

In a profession filled with rookie hot heads, Shand favors the slow methodical approach of lining up the perfect shot.

A CLOSE CALL

Fennec is en route to Mos Espa to secure transit off-world when she encounters several bounty hunters. She kills one dewback-riding bondsman and nearly incapacitates Mando with her sniper rifle. Mando and Calican capture her, though she is confident she can hold out long enough to devise a means of escape.

- Long hair kept in a thick braid
- Scrambled comlink on chest-mount
- Upgraded GA Model 84 night-targeting optical macroscope
- Internal seals keep contaminants like desert sand out of her gloves
- Gun sling has mounted ammunition cells for easy access

Shand briefly overpowers the inexperienced Calican, but his seasoned backup man Din Djarin blocks her attempted flight into the desert.

THROWING BLADE
- Knuckle grip
- Weight-reducing holes

Fennec nearly closes a deal with Calican, but he betrays her. It is not the end for Shand, however.

DATA FILE
- **SUBJECT** Fennec Shand
- **HOMEWORLD** Unknown
- **SPECIES** Human
- **AFFILIATION** Currently independent
- **HEIGHT** 1.63 m (5 ft 4 in)

PART I: A NEW COMPANION

THE ROOST

The Roost is a deep space shadowport operated by Ranzar Malk. The station is an old industrial design, and its habitable interior is devoted to a cluttered chop-shop spread across four hangar bays. Access to the Roost is invitation-only and personally vetted by Malk. He runs a profitable enterprise as an outlaw tech, outfitting starships with all the illegal modifications a captain can afford. Malk's mercenary crew of thieves and pirates also uses the Roost as its base of operations. He has known the Mandalorian for years: they used to run underworld jobs together.

DATA FILE	
MANUFACTURER	Torranix ICC
MODEL	Deep space industrial processing station, *RKDA*-class
TYPE	Repurposed starship repair station
DIMENSIONS	Height: 95 m (312 ft); width: 41.1 m (135 ft)
WEAPONS	None; relies on carried security craft
AFFILIATION	Ranzar Malk

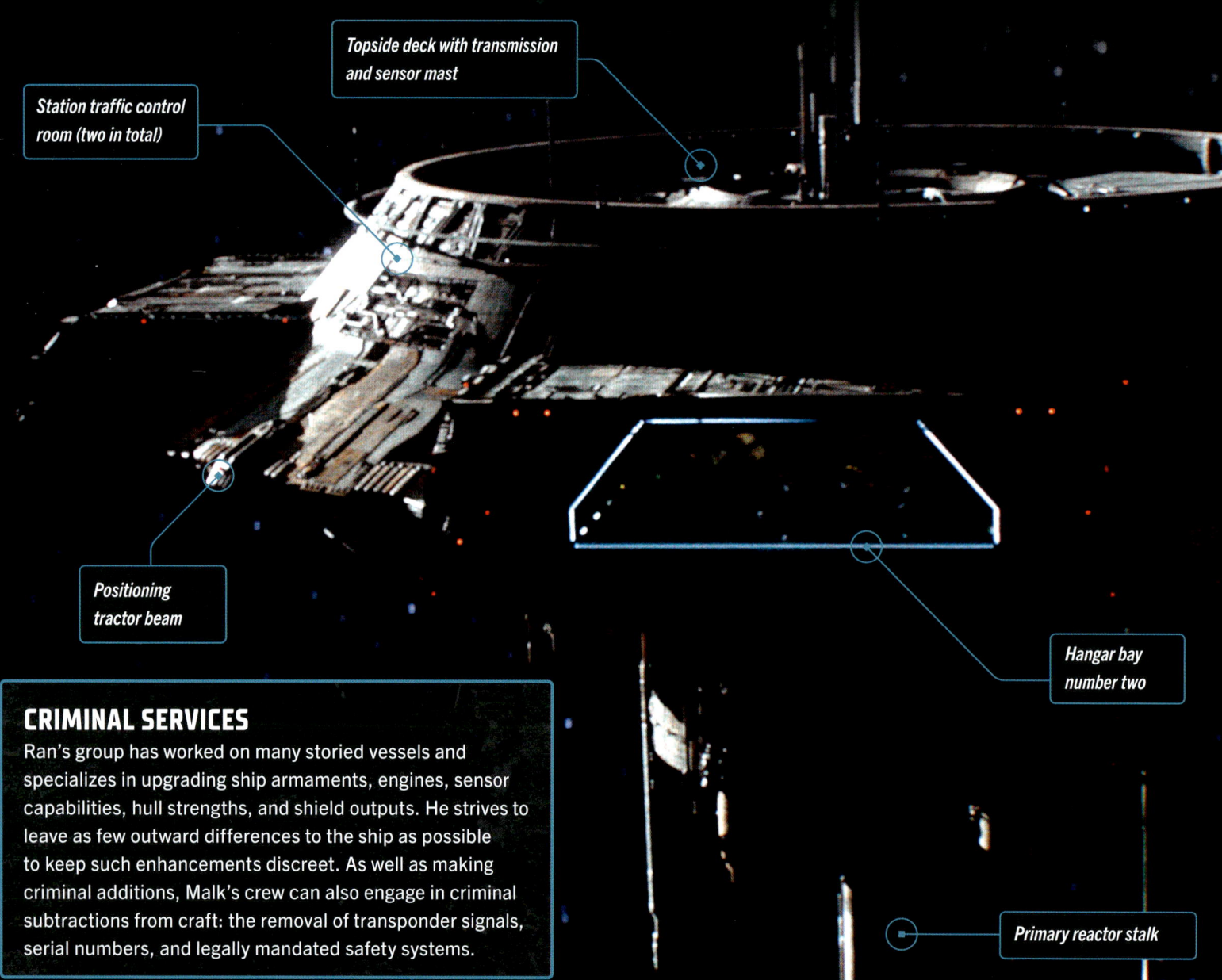

Topside deck with transmission and sensor mast

Station traffic control room (two in total)

Positioning tractor beam

Hangar bay number two

Primary reactor stalk

CRIMINAL SERVICES

Ran's group has worked on many storied vessels and specializes in upgrading ship armaments, engines, sensor capabilities, hull strengths, and shield outputs. He strives to leave as few outward differences to the ship as possible to keep such enhancements discreet. As well as making criminal additions, Malk's crew can also engage in criminal subtractions from craft: the removal of transponder signals, serial numbers, and legally mandated safety systems.

REPURPOSED STATION

Roost station was commissioned as an orbital launch base for local starfighter security forces. Its four hangar bays along cardinal points expedite emergency launches along any approach vector. While the Roost does have a shielding system, the station relies on carried craft for defense as it has no offensive weaponry.

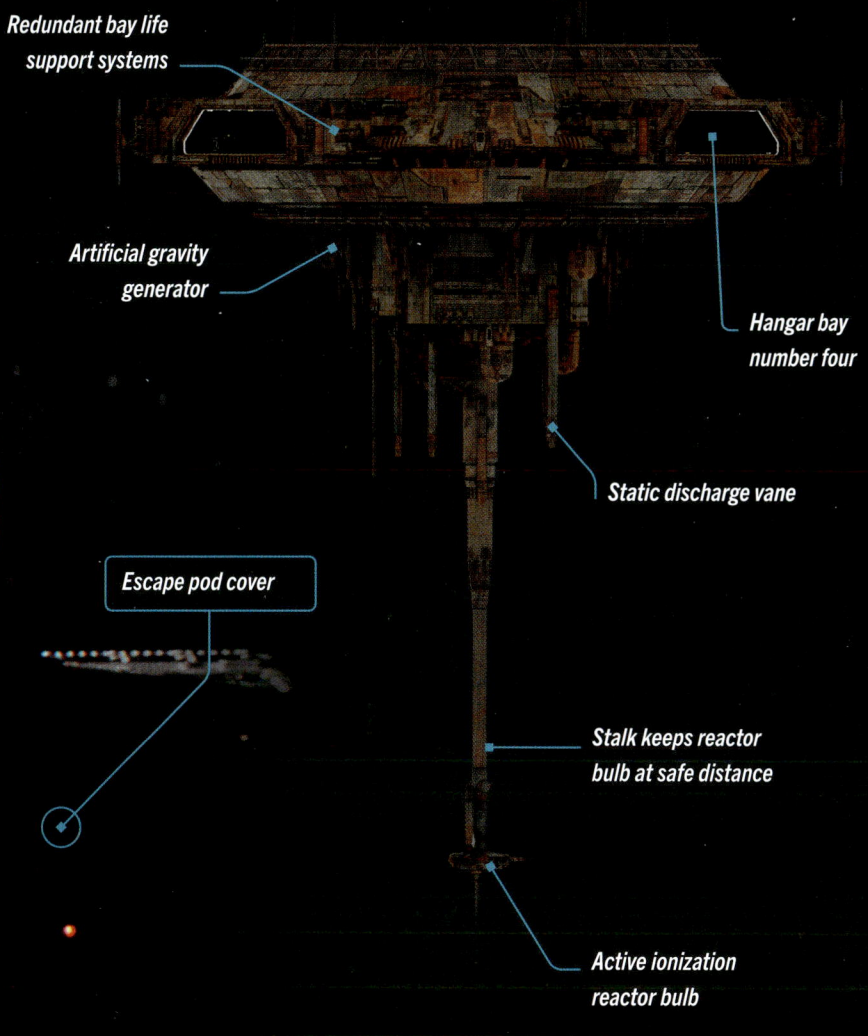

- Subspace transmission relay
- Redundant bay life support systems
- Artificial gravity generator
- Hangar bay number four
- Escape pod cover
- Static discharge vane
- Stalk keeps reactor bulb at safe distance
- Active ionization reactor bulb

RANZAR "RAN" MALK

- Grizzled beard gives him the air of a criminal elder statesman
- Technician's synth-leather vest
- EM-field and radiation detection safety sensor
- Sleeve piping includes heating filaments
- Work gloves with insulated palms
- Reinforced kneepads for low work
- Mechanic's spatter guards

> "YOU KNOW THE POLICY: NO QUESTIONS."
> – RANZAR MALK

ROGUE-CLASS GUNSHIP

Tucked away below deck in a hidden hangar bay of the Roost is a *Rogue*-class Porax-38 starfighter that is heavily armed and modified into a gunship. Ran has augmented the Clone Wars-era craft with new shipboard electronics from the modern era. He intends to tie up any loose ends by launching the fighter to destroy the *Razor Crest*.

PART I: A NEW COMPANION
MIGS MAYFELD

> An ex-Imperial sharpshooter, Migs Mayfeld is the smart-mouthed leader of Malk's infiltration crew. Cocky and argumentative, Mayfeld doesn't seem too impressed with the Mandalorian or the *Razor Crest*. Despite Mayfeld's disagreeable attitude, Ran vouches for him based on past capers. Mayfeld introduces Mando to the rest of his crew, and they depart to intercept the New Republic fortified prison transport.

Leadership tradition states Mayfeld goes in first. With Mando overriding the door controls while the ships dock, Mayfeld leaps from the *Razor Crest* onto the *Bothan-5*, two of his five carried guns at the ready. When the crew runs into New Republic sentry droids, Mayfeld's shooting skills prove to be more than just boastful talk. His mission planning skills, though, aren't as sharp—things go awry as the prison ship that was supposed to be crewed only by droids turns out to have a New Republic officer aboard, who sets off a distress signal calling for reinforcements. With only minutes to spare, it is a scramble to carry out their prison break before a flight of X-wings arrives.

When boasting about his past Imperial marksmanship status, Mayfeld is quick to point out he was no stormtrooper.

HITTING THE MARK
Mayfeld's elite Imperial Army Special Missions service record is marked equally with commendations for combat and demerits for insubordination. Superior officers tolerated his impertinence because of his battlefield results. Mayfeld boasted he could split a credit coin half a kilometer (a third of a mile) away in a rainstorm. His insults were similarly well aimed, but it was his eye that gained him his reputation. As the Galactic Civil War came to a close, Mayfeld reinvented himself as a mercenary, being several guns for hire in one.

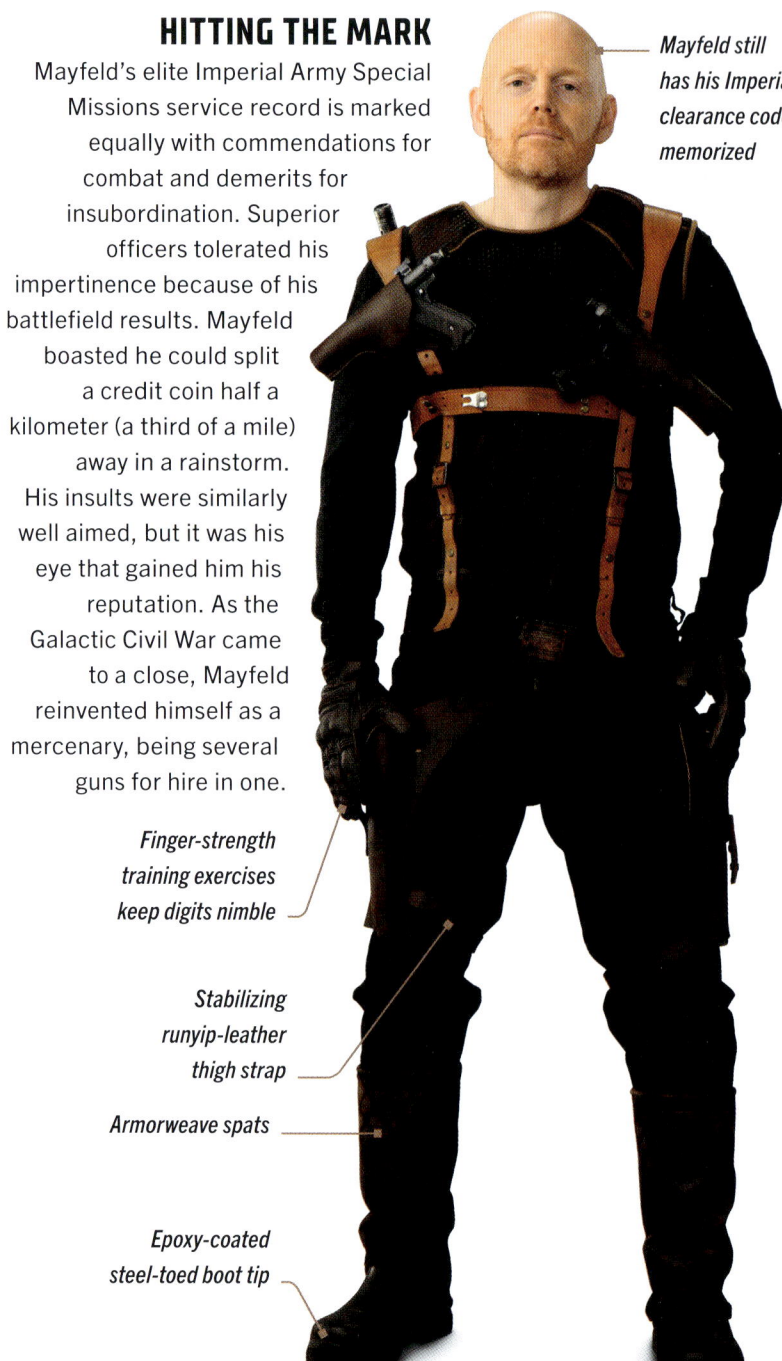

Mayfeld still has his Imperial clearance codes memorized

Finger-strength training exercises keep digits nimble

Stabilizing runyip-leather thigh strap

Armorweave spats

Epoxy-coated steel-toed boot tip

After having been betrayed by Mayfeld's crew, a vengeful Mando wreaks havoc using the *Bothan-5*'s control room.

85

- Mind busy assessing shooting angles and variables
- Shirt piping keeps shoulder holster from slipping

DATA FILE
- **SUBJECT** Migs Mayfeld
- **HOMEWORLD** Woostri
- **SPECIES** Human
- **AFFILIATION** Malk's gang
- **HEIGHT** 1.78 m (5 ft 10 in)

Mayfeld is wary of the new variables the Mandalorian represents.

- Merr-Sonn Munitions W-SP73 pistol
- 3BT Brainthree neuro-link automated weapons solution pack

> "WE GET IN, WE GET OUT, AND YOU DON'T HAVE TO SEE OUR FACES ANYMORE."
> – MIGS MAYFELD

Mayfeld can fire around corners without breaking cover with a mechanical arm affixed with a BlasTech DT-12. An electrode-contact neuro-link allows him to point the arm with his mind.

TURNABOUT
Mayfeld and his crew betray Mando, imprisoning him in the former cell of the prisoner they have just freed. However, Mando escapes his confinement and makes his way past his newfound adversaries, sparing their lives as they did his. He tosses Mayfeld, Burg, and Xi'an into an empty cell aboard the prison ship. The New Republic sentences Mayfeld to 50 years of hard labor in the Karthon Chop Fields as inmate 34667.

- Cromax 2B-MAL comlink pre-scrambled by Q9-0
- Cautionary pulse generator in handle buzzes if ammo is low

PART I: A NEW COMPANION
MALK'S CREW

> Led by sharpshooter Migs Mayfeld, Mando finds himself part of a fractious gang. However, each member brings a key element to the mission. Beyond his own varied skillset, Mando brings the *Razor Crest* with its rare, ghost-like status. Q9-0's response time and piloting skills enable them to sneak up on the prison transport and dock without being detected. Burg and Xi'an are both skilled warriors with completely different fighting styles.

After a bumpy transition from hyperspace to realspace, Q9-0 sidles the *Razor Crest* up to the *Bothan-5* and links the two ships via their airlocks. The infiltration team transfers onto the prison ship, with Q9-0 keeping tabs on their movements, transmitted via their local comlink signals as well as the patched-in *Bothan-5* internal sensors. Q9-0 oversees the mission from this vantage point—including when it goes awry, in no small part due to his teammates.

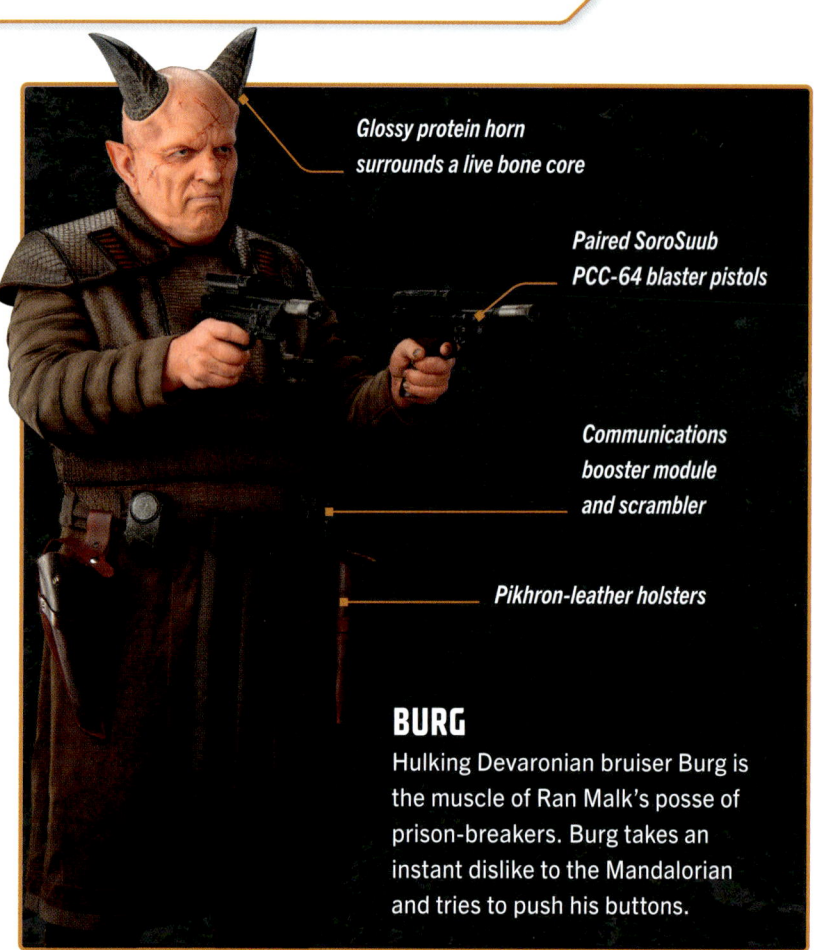

Glossy protein horn surrounds a live bone core

Paired SoroSuub PCC-64 blaster pistols

Communications booster module and scrambler

Pikhron-leather holsters

BURG
Hulking Devaronian bruiser Burg is the muscle of Ran Malk's posse of prison-breakers. Burg takes an instant dislike to the Mandalorian and tries to push his buttons.

SEARCHING FOR THE CHILD
In the *Razor Crest*'s comms logs, Q9-0 finds a transmission from Greef Karga that details Mando's fallout with the Bounty Hunters Guild, and what triggered it. Q9-0 calculates the Child's bounty value, and prioritizes capturing him. He does not predict that Mando would return to the *Crest* in time to stop him.

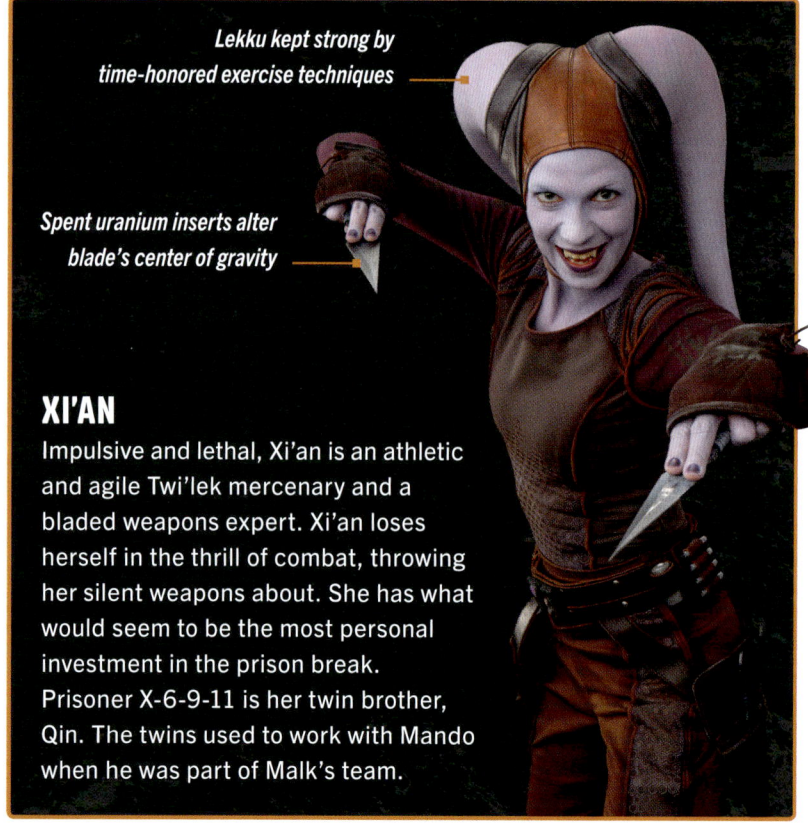

Lekku kept strong by time-honored exercise techniques

Spent uranium inserts alter blade's center of gravity

XI'AN
Impulsive and lethal, Xi'an is an athletic and agile Twi'lek mercenary and a bladed weapons expert. Xi'an loses herself in the thrill of combat, throwing her silent weapons about. She has what would seem to be the most personal investment in the prison break. Prisoner X-6-9-11 is her twin brother, Qin. The twins used to work with Mando when he was part of Malk's team.

DATA FILE

SUBJECT Q9-0 (Zero)
HOMEWORLD Roost Station
MODEL Modified Arakyd RA-90
AFFILIATION Malk's gang
HEIGHT 1.75 m (5 ft 9 in)

Multifaceted photoreceptors behind mirrored domes

Manipulators conceal multiple-gauge scomp link adaptors

Two-axis rotational glenohumeral articulation

Vambraces improve accuracy and reaction time

Recharge coupling port

Boosted cabling drives additional power into added hardware

Tactical stowage holding blaster repair implements

Integral accelerometers in femur

Q9-0

Q9-0 started as an RA-90 protocol droid, a remote, outworld boutique alternative to the classic RA-7 design. Designed for worlds with less refined infrastructure, the droid has an improved pelvic servomotor assembly giving it a more confident gait and surer balance compared to older RA models. Its neural harness can accommodate warranty-voiding combat upgrades. Q9-0 sports the popular LOM-series mercenary overlay developed by black market slicers. To Ran Malk's specifications, Q9-0 became "Zero," no longer just an expert in etiquette and protocol but a criminal strategist as well.

PART I: A NEW COMPANION
BOTHAN-5

The New Republic correctional transport *Bothan-5* is a high-security prison ship meant to move convicted criminals from temporary jails to penal colonies. Intelligence gathered by Ran Malk's operation uncovers that the *Bothan-5* will be dropping to sublight in the Dilestri system, to recalculate the next leg of its hyperspace journey. This leaves the craft exposed for a prison break caper to free prisoner X-6-9-11.

The *Razor Crest* stealthily sidles up to *Bothan-5*, alighting atop its hull and establishing an airlock juncture without detection.

MAX SECURITY

The first line of security for *Bothan-5* is the secret travel routes that avoid busy hyperspace lanes. Prisoners aboard are separated into individual, fortified cells that prevent close collaboration or contact. A security team made up entirely of droids prevents coercion or disloyalty. Finally, an emergency beacon with a direct tie to New Republic X-wing patrols is a last resort.

At first, *Bothan-5* appears to offer little that truly challenges Malk's crew of skilled mercenaries.

DATA FILE

MANUFACTURER
Corellian Engineering Corporation

MODEL CR-225T

TYPE Fortified transport ship

DIMENSIONS Height: 26.85 m (88 ft 1 in); length: 173 m (576 ft 7 in); width: 44 m (144 ft 4 in)

WEAPONS
Three double laser cannon turrets

AFFILIATION
New Republic Correctional Corps

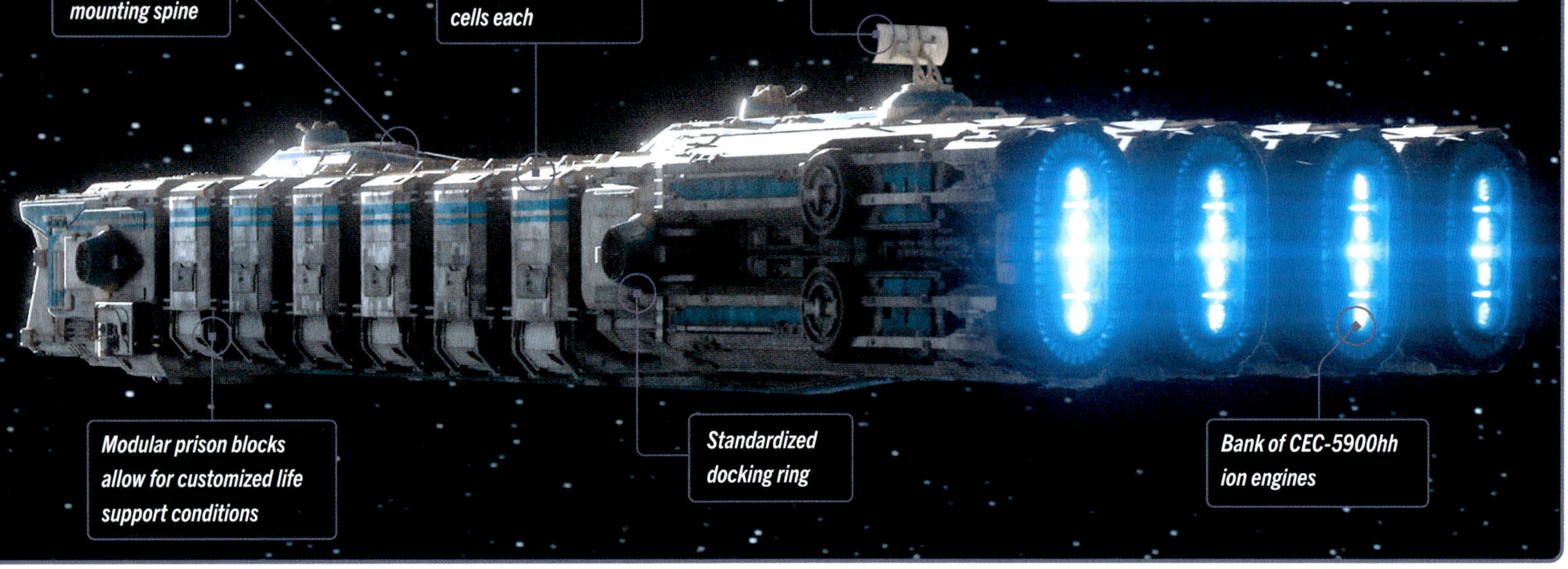

- Central hull mounting spine
- One of 14 modular prison blocks of 80 cells each
- Primary sensor/communications rectenna
- Modular prison blocks allow for customized life support conditions
- Standardized docking ring
- Bank of CEC-5900hh ion engines

Qin and Ran conspire to get the gang back together, minus Mando.

> "THE PACKAGE IS BEING MOVED ON A FORTIFIED TRANSPORT SHIP."
> – MIGS MAYFELD

QIN

The prisoner set for pickup by Malk's crew is the Twi'lek criminal Qin. He is surprised to see the Mandalorian's helmet when cell door 221 opens up and will not forgive Mando for leaving him behind when last they parted. Until his escape, Qin was destined for hard labor at the Karthon Chop Fields.

Karthon work gloves

Quilted leather spats scanned for weaponry

DATA FILE

SUBJECT	Qin
HOMEWORLD	Ryloth
SPECIES	Twi'lek
AFFILIATION	Malk's gang
HEIGHT	1.8 m (5 ft 11 in)

PART I: A NEW COMPANION
BOTHAN-5 CREW

According to Mayfeld's intelligence, the *Bothan-5* is operating with an all-droid crew. The Mandalorian in particular is dismayed to find a human officer aboard, as he has taken care to avoid any major entanglements with the New Republic. Completing the mission while also sparing the life of the officer proves impossible to the impulsive criminals. This deadly complication starts a countdown to a New Republic reprisal. No matter how indifferent he is toward the galactic government, the last thing Mando needs is another enemy.

> **"THERE WERE ONLY SUPPOSED TO BE DROIDS ON THIS SHIP."**
> – THE MANDALORIAN

- Helmet inspired by classic Alderaanian design
- BlasTech A180 blaster pistol
- Official New Republic blue
- Belt buckle with NRCC officer's disc
- Synth-leather holster
- Paneling replaces outmoded flared design of past generation
- Synth-leather boots with positive grip soles

OFFICER DAVAN
New Republic Correctional Corps officer Lant Davan is fatally inexperienced. Though his posting requires combat training and to be in proximity to hardened criminals, heavy bulkheads and squads of security droids separate him from direct contact with such unsavory company. Nervous Davan orders the trespassers to surrender their weapons, but the more seasoned infiltrators are not intimidated by his shaky efforts.

CALLING FOR HELP
Davan carries an emergency tracking beacon, a compact S-thread transmitter that sends a coded signal on a New Republic frequency to a roving X-wing patrol. Reinforcements are a mere 20 minutes away.

- Compressed hyperpole antenna
- Broadcast indicator
- Activator switch

TRACKING BEACON

DATA FILE
SUBJECT	Lant Davan
HOMEWORLD	Chandrila
SPECIES	Human
AFFILIATION	New Republic Correctional Corps
HEIGHT	1.78 m (5 ft 10 in)

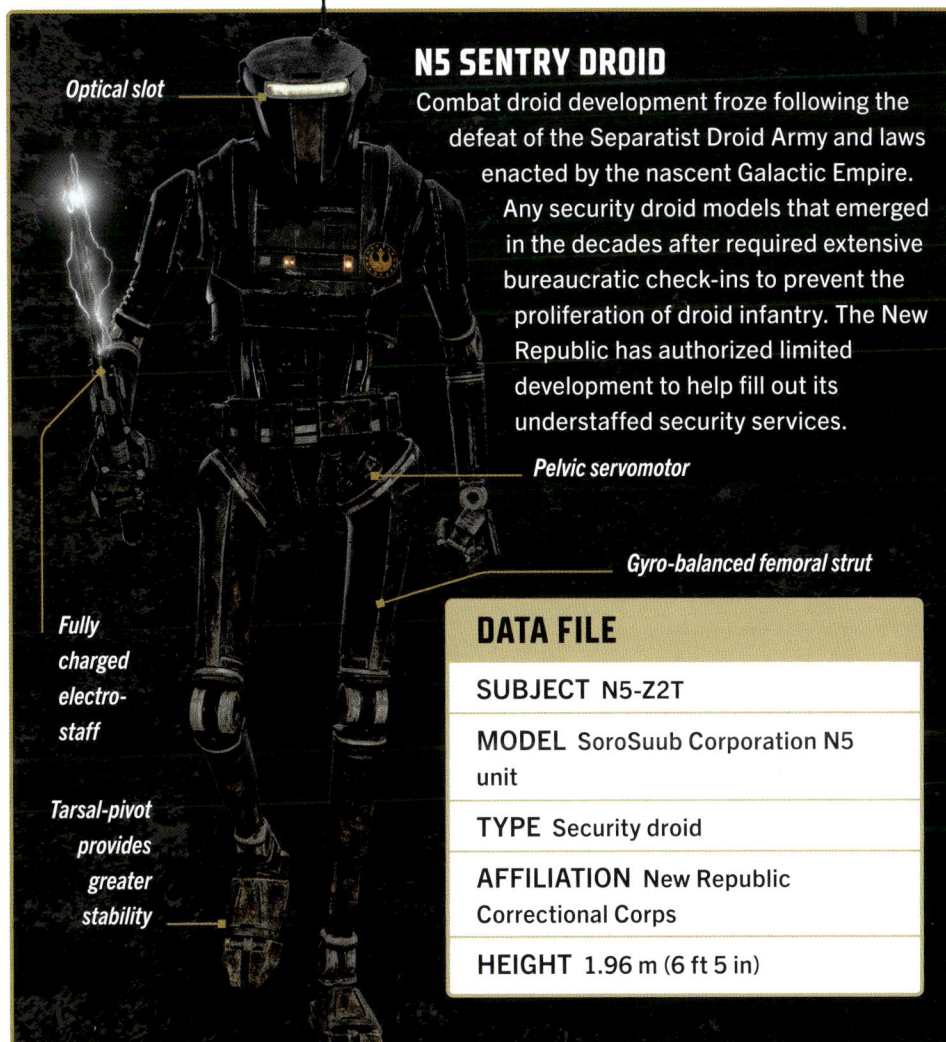

Hardly intimidated by the R1s, Burg charges, tackling one of the units and then tossing its dented body at its squad mates.

- Air-cooled heavy blaster cannon
- Access panel/display indicators
- Power cell mount
- Programming board (behind panel)
- Retractable manipulator arms
- Repulsorlift generator base

R1 SECURITY DROID

Industrial Automaton found new life for antiquated surplus R1 units by repurposing them for sentry duty and selling them at discount to the fledgling New Republic Correctional Corps. The original treaded unipod has been replaced with a more versatile repulsorlift base. The comlink transmitter has been swapped out for a heavy blaster cannon, and the Mark II reactor drone shell serves as security armor.

DATA FILE

SUBJECT R1-G106

MODEL Industrial Automaton R1-NRCC

TYPE Repurposed sentry droid

AFFILIATION New Republic Correctional Corps

HEIGHT 2 m (6 ft 7 in)

N5 SENTRY DROID

- Optical slot
- Pelvic servomotor
- Gyro-balanced femoral strut
- Fully charged electro-staff
- Tarsal-pivot provides greater stability

Combat droid development froze following the defeat of the Separatist Droid Army and laws enacted by the nascent Galactic Empire. Any security droid models that emerged in the decades after required extensive bureaucratic check-ins to prevent the proliferation of droid infantry. The New Republic has authorized limited development to help fill out its understaffed security services.

DATA FILE

SUBJECT N5-Z2T

MODEL SoroSuub Corporation N5 unit

TYPE Security droid

AFFILIATION New Republic Correctional Corps

HEIGHT 1.96 m (6 ft 5 in)

FACT FILE

MONITORED MILITARY
Though the New Republic has made efforts to halt military expansion among member worlds, special dispensation is allowed for security droids provided their entire operational cycles are well documented.

PRISON PLACEMENT
N5 droids also serve as prison guards on New Republic penitentiary outposts, including Delrian, Wobani, Karthon, Sunspot, and Valfin.

Mando proves his mettle to a skeptical Mayfeld by single-handedly taking out a squad of patrol droids in close combat.

PART I: A NEW COMPANION

MOFF GIDEON

A methodical and calculating Imperial stalwart, Moff Gideon is the mastermind behind the machinations that have led to the hunting of the Child. New Republic records show that Gideon was executed for war crimes, but clearly such reports are inaccurate. He not only lives, but he commands a sizable splinter of the Imperial remnant operating near Nevarro.

> "YOUR ASTUTE PANIC SUGGESTS THAT YOU UNDERSTAND YOUR SITUATION."
> – MOFF GIDEON

Gideon brings his authoritative might and armored forces to the Nevarro City square, planning for a final confrontation that will see the Child delivered to him. Gideon's forces assemble an E-Web heavy repeating blaster and stand ready to raze the Crossroads Common House. He gives the occupants trapped inside—Mando, Cara Dune, and Greef Karga—until nightfall to surrender the asset.

The Mandalorian recognizes the name Gideon, and the truth behind the Imperial's identity becomes clear. The well-researched Gideon calls out Mando by his real name—Din Djarin. It is a name that only exists in the archives of Mandalore. During the Purge, an Imperial Security Bureau officer would have had access to this information. That officer was Gideon.

REMNANT REVEALED
Under the Client's command, the Imperial presence on Nevarro seemed weak and furtive. This appearance was a calculated front. Far from the city there is an Imperial outpost, mistakenly believed to be abandoned. It is from here that Gideon musters combat-ready forces that arrive by transport and take up attack positions while he himself arrives in his TIE fighter. The Client has served his purpose and failed Gideon, so the Moff has his troops eliminate that loose end. Gideon has no compunctions about eliminating underlings.

SURROUNDED
A blistering hail of blaster fire tears through the window of the Common House, killing the Client and causing Mando and his compatriots to seek cover. Overwhelming firepower surrounds the riddled refuge.

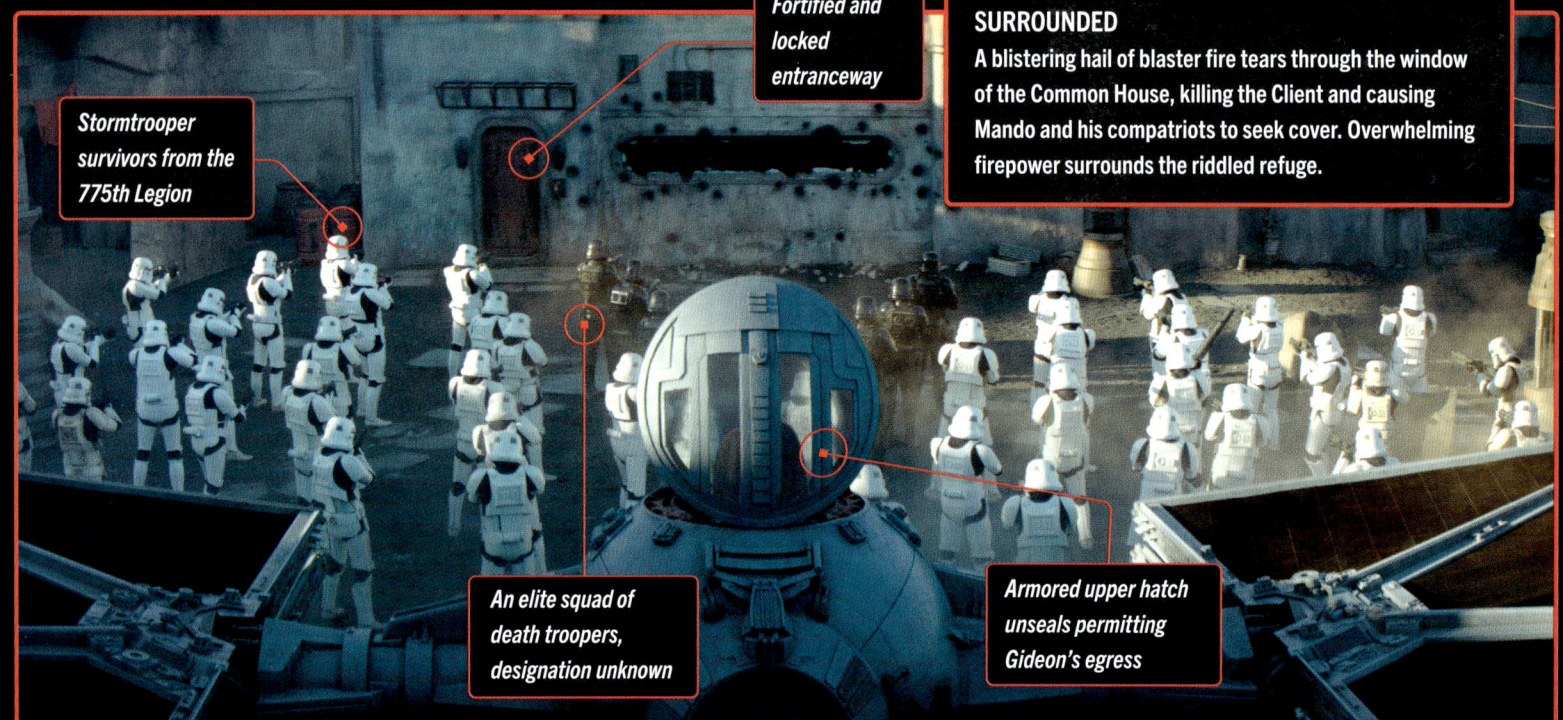

- Stormtrooper survivors from the 775th Legion
- Fortified and locked entranceway
- An elite squad of death troopers, designation unknown
- Armored upper hatch unseals permitting Gideon's egress

EXPANDED FORCES

Beyond Moff Gideon's presence on Nevarro, he has other scattered Imperial remnant troops and assets under his control. Gideon travels to them aboard his command ship, an *Arquitens*-class Imperial light cruiser. With such authority, it seems unusual that Moff Gideon is so singularly drawn to the Child.

DATA FILE

SUBJECT	Moff Gideon
HOMEWORLD	Unknown
SPECIES	Human
AFFILIATION	Imperial remnant
HEIGHT	1.73 m (5 ft 8 in)

DDC D-16 BLASTER PISTOL
This compact blaster pistol can be expanded with optional stalk and range-extending barrel assemblies.

Adjustable optical scope with low-light enhancers

Shoulder strap with rank/unit indicators

Advanced pilot's life support and armor chest plate

Feedback-enabled piloting gloves

Kyber-field generated blade shape

Red lining evokes regal imagery of Imperial past

PART I: A NEW COMPANION

THE DARKSABER

As a relic of the past and an omen of the future, the long lost Mandalorian Darksaber is a burdensome weapon, laden with history and tragedy. It is a unique artifact from a bygone era, a product of an unlikely collaboration when the Mandalorians and the Jedi Order bridged their violent differences. It was crafted by the only known Mandalorian accepted as a Jedi, forged by his hand to create a lightsaber like no other: one with a flattened energy blade that scintillates with an absence of color.

In the centuries after its construction, the Darksaber became an icon of unification among the Mandalorians, especially in the era without a Mand'alor to rule them. As per Mandalorian tradition, the Darksaber can only be earned through conflict—to wield it without right would be to invite calamity that not even the mighty weapon could defend against.

Following his crash on Nevarro, Moff Gideon uses the legendary Darksaber to extricate himself from the wreckage of his TIE fighter.

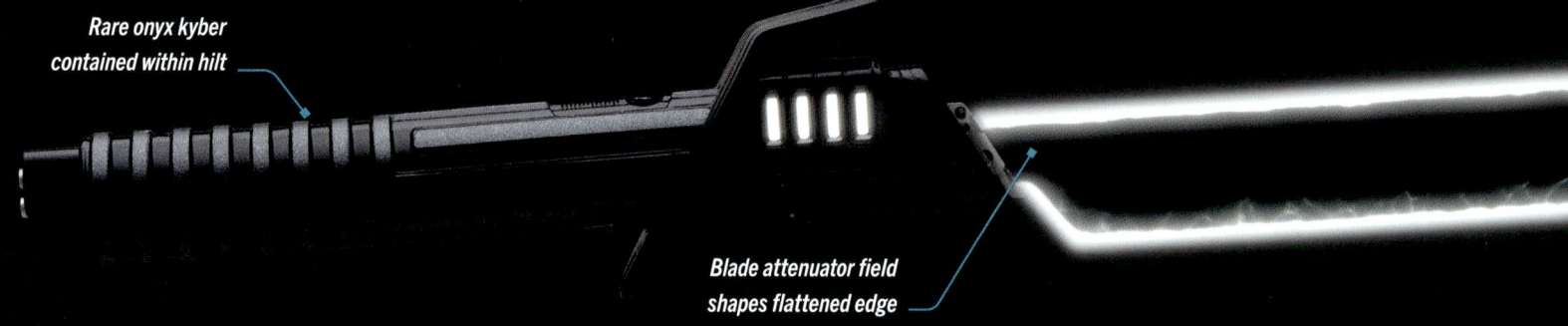

Rare onyx kyber contained within hilt

Blade attenuator field shapes flattened edge

GIDEON'S CUSTODY

Moff Gideon plucked the Darksaber from Bo-Katan Kryze as a spoil of war, cementing his dominance over the capitulated Mandalorians. He won it not in personal combat but through the might of the Empire, satisfying—at least by his own egoist view—the Mandalorian custom and marking himself as the rightful wielder.

CURSED BLADE

Bo-Katan is hardly a superstitious traditionalist. She accepted the Darksaber freely as a gift from Sabine Wren during the Imperial occupation. The disasters that follow drive her to properly reclaim the blade.

Cabur *stance keeps blade at the defensive ready*

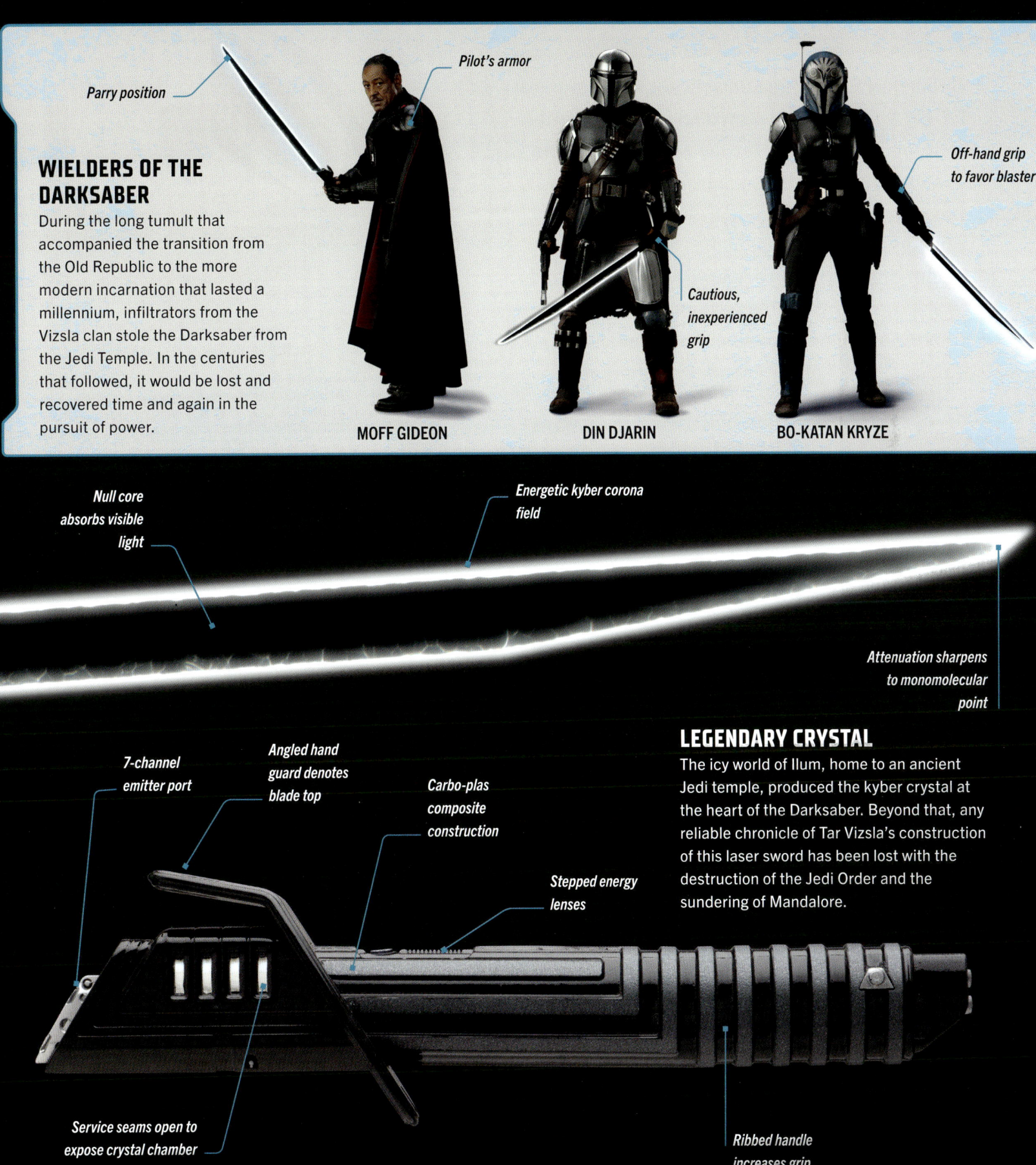

WIELDERS OF THE DARKSABER

During the long tumult that accompanied the transition from the Old Republic to the more modern incarnation that lasted a millennium, infiltrators from the Vizsla clan stole the Darksaber from the Jedi Temple. In the centuries that followed, it would be lost and recovered time and again in the pursuit of power.

- Parry position
- Pilot's armor
- Cautious, inexperienced grip
- Off-hand grip to favor blaster

MOFF GIDEON **DIN DJARIN** **BO-KATAN KRYZE**

- Null core absorbs visible light
- Energetic kyber corona field
- Attenuation sharpens to monomolecular point

LEGENDARY CRYSTAL

The icy world of Ilum, home to an ancient Jedi temple, produced the kyber crystal at the heart of the Darksaber. Beyond that, any reliable chronicle of Tar Vizsla's construction of this laser sword has been lost with the destruction of the Jedi Order and the sundering of Mandalore.

- 7-channel emitter port
- Angled hand guard denotes blade top
- Carbo-plas composite construction
- Stepped energy lenses
- Service seams open to expose crystal chamber
- Ribbed handle increases grip

PART I: A NEW COMPANION

GIDEON'S TIE FIGHTER

Throughout most of the Galactic Civil War, Imperial TIE fighters benefited from docking bays, carrier craft, or base facilities for their launches. It was rare for a TIE fighter to set down in the wilderness. The standard TIE was optimized for supported landings, with final approaches assisted by tractor beams and access to the craft facilitated by walkways or portable ladders. In the wild, amenities like these could not be found. Gideon's model of TIE provides an alternative.

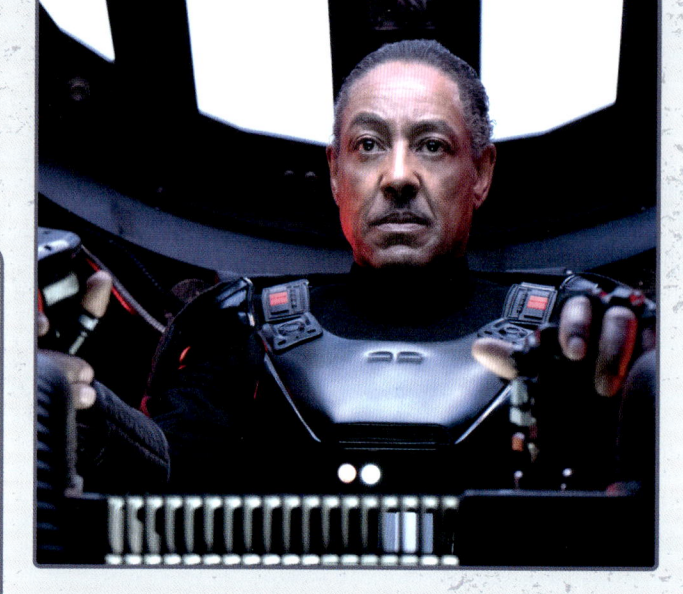

GIDEON IN FLIGHT
Though some Imperial officials are content to let underlings handle their transport and flight missions, Gideon is not only instrument-rated on TIE fighter craft but keeps in active practice in both simulations and actual flight operations. Gideon routinely ferries himself aboard a TIE fighter from his Imperial light cruiser to his destination.

The Mandalorian, having jetpacked up to Moff Gideon's TIE fighter, clings to the outside of the craft's cockpit.

- Densely corrugated solar energy collector
- Articulation servos in wing spar
- Accumulator lines concealed beneath solar cells
- Reinforced support frame

LANDING MECHANISM
Standard TIEs rest on the edges of their hexagonal panels. TIE fuselages are lightweight enough for this not to cause undue strain, though standard Imperial naval procedure was to suspend TIEs on racks to keep the panels unburdened. This TIE has been adjusted with configurable wings and a tripodal landing gear to facilitate touching down in wilderness conditions or on uneven terrain.

DATA FILE

MANUFACTURER Sienar Fleet Systems

MODEL TIE/ln space superiority fighter

TYPE Combat starfighter

DIMENSIONS (FLIGHT MODE) Height: 8.82 m (29 ft); width: 6.68 m (22 ft); length: 7.24 m (23 ft)

WEAPONS 2 SFS L-s7.2 laser cannons

AFFILIATION Galactic Empire, Imperial remnant

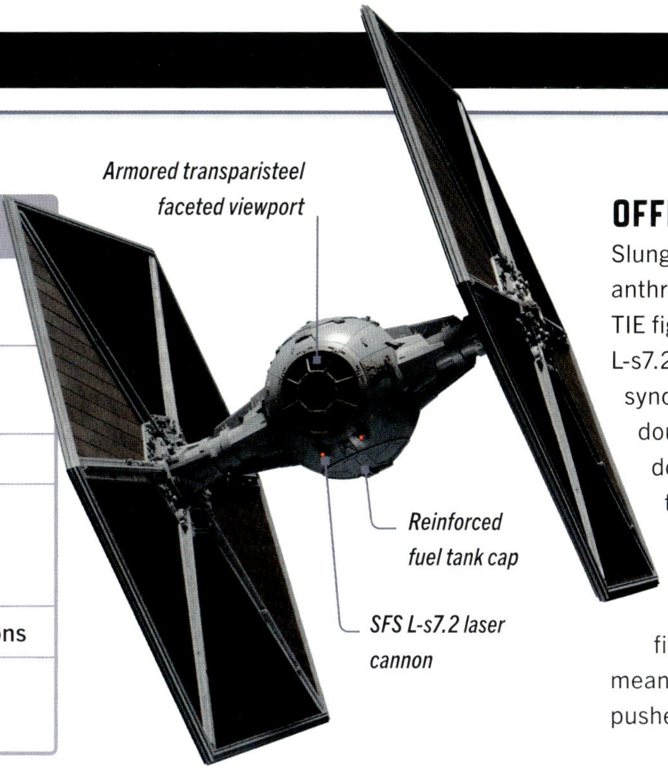

Armored transparisteel faceted viewport

Reinforced fuel tank cap

SFS L-s7.2 laser cannon

OFFENSIVE CAPABILITIES

Slung beneath the cockpit viewport, on what is anthropomorphically called the "chin" of the TIE fighter, are a pair of Sienar Fleet Systems L-s7.2 laser cannons. The linked cannons are synchronized to fire simultaneously, as a double blast is a more efficient way of doubling the TIE's destructive yield without taxing the ship's power distribution and cooling systems. The pilot controls the firing by thumb-activated buttons atop the engine control sticks. The linked-fire nature of the weapons configuration means only one of the two buttons needs to be pushed, but pilots instinctively press both.

> "OUR BLASTERS ARE USELESS AGAINST HIM!"
> – CARA DUNE

TIE fighter hulls are relatively thin compared to those of most other starfighters, making Mando's well-placed grav charges all the more destructive.

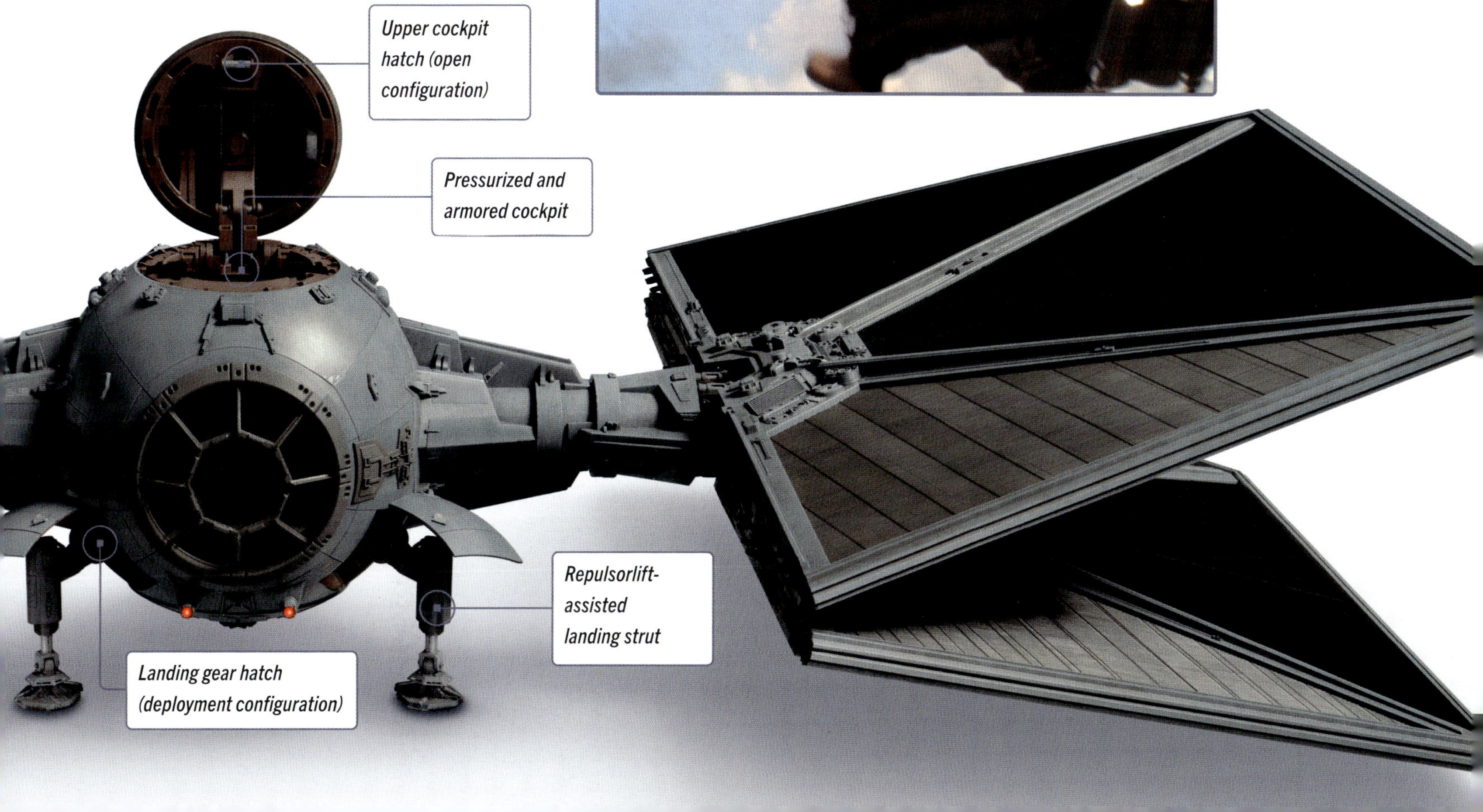

Upper cockpit hatch (open configuration)

Pressurized and armored cockpit

Repulsorlift-assisted landing strut

Landing gear hatch (deployment configuration)

PART I: A NEW COMPANION

GIDEON'S ASSAULT

On orders from Moff Gideon, an unusually large collection of Imperial remnant forces encloses the Crossroads Common House. To an onlooker, dozens and dozens of stormtroopers are a reminder of the time when the Empire ruled unchallenged, and when its militarized might could be brought down upon any transgression. The sight is a clear indicator of how seriously Gideon takes recapturing the asset.

A squad of death troopers conveys Gideon's disappointment with the Imperial Client by riddling him and his guards with blaster bolts.

- Integrated combat sensor systems
- Featureless pauldron denotes status when seen through trooper visors

DEATH TROOPER

Death troopers are elite operatives and were once assigned to special Imperial projects or high-ranking officers. They are an exceedingly rare sight during the New Republic era. These soldiers have classified cybernetic augmentation.

The incinerator trooper fans a gout of flame past the Common House doorway, pushing back any concealed ambushers.

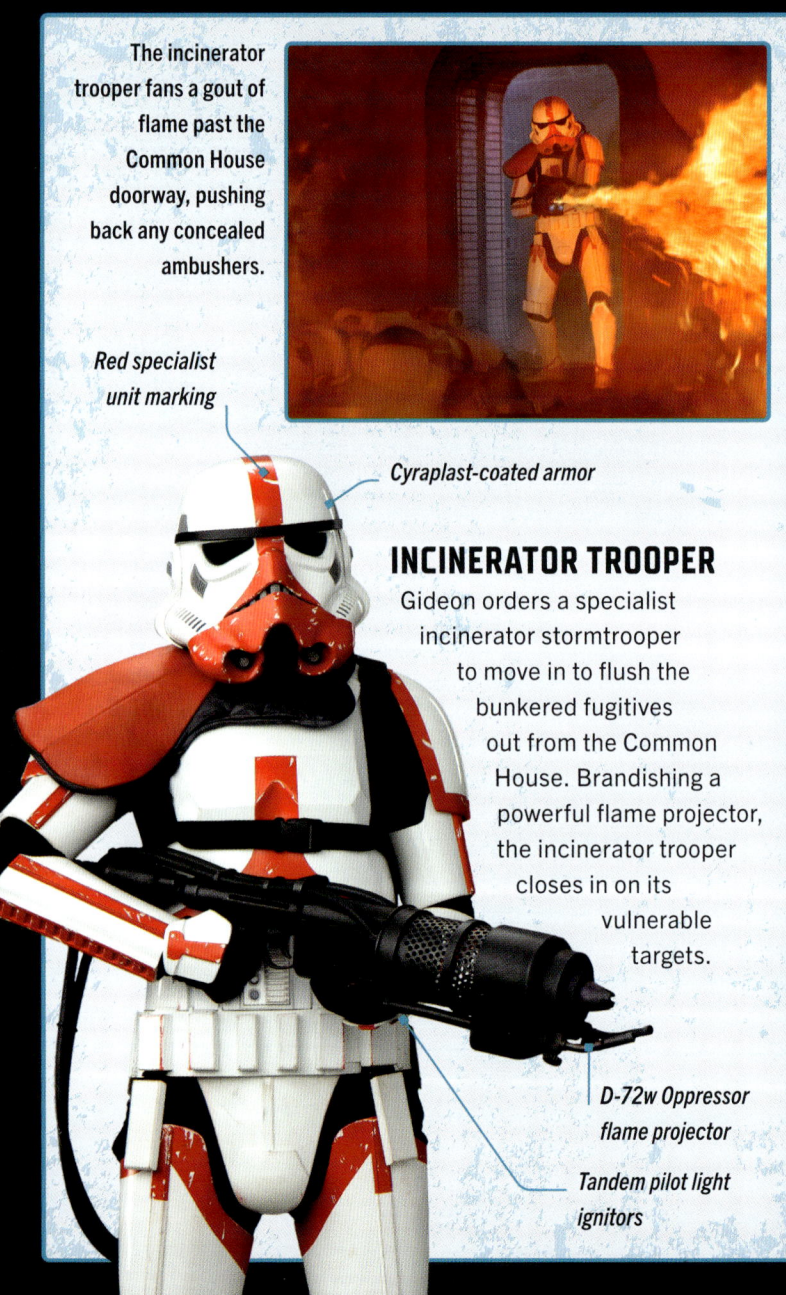

- Red specialist unit marking
- Cyraplast-coated armor

INCINERATOR TROOPER

Gideon orders a specialist incinerator stormtrooper to move in to flush the bunkered fugitives out from the Common House. Brandishing a powerful flame projector, the incinerator trooper closes in on its vulnerable targets.

- D-72w Oppressor flame projector
- Tandem pilot light ignitors

- Sight with infrared adapted viewing scope
- Air-cooled emitter nozzle
- Tripod-tension adjust
- Flashback suppressor
- BlasTech TR-62 auto-cushion tripod

E-WEB 15

An upgrade to the EWHB-10 (emplacement weapon, heavy blaster cannon), the E-Web 15 is a tripod-mounted repeating blaster capable of overwhelming a fire zone with intense bursts of destructive energy. Its attached Gk7 Cryocooler supplies a continuous power flow for up to an hour of sustained operation without risk of overheating.

74-Z SPEEDER BIKE

Patrolling the streets and outskirts of the city are pairs of scout troopers on Aratech 74-Z speeder bikes, a model in military use since the time of the Clone Wars.

- High-speed steering vanes
- Tempered outriggers resist torque
- Streamlined chassis
- Universal handgrips
- Scout trooper hunched to reduce air resistance

DATA FILE

MANUFACTURER	Aratech Repulsor Company
MODEL	74-Z
TYPE	Speeder bike
DIMENSIONS	Length: 0.99 m (3 ft 3 in); width: 0.67 m (2 ft 2 in); height: 3.4 m (11 ft 2 in)
SPEED	500 kph (311 mph)
WEAPONS	1 light blaster cannon
AFFILIATION	Imperial remnant

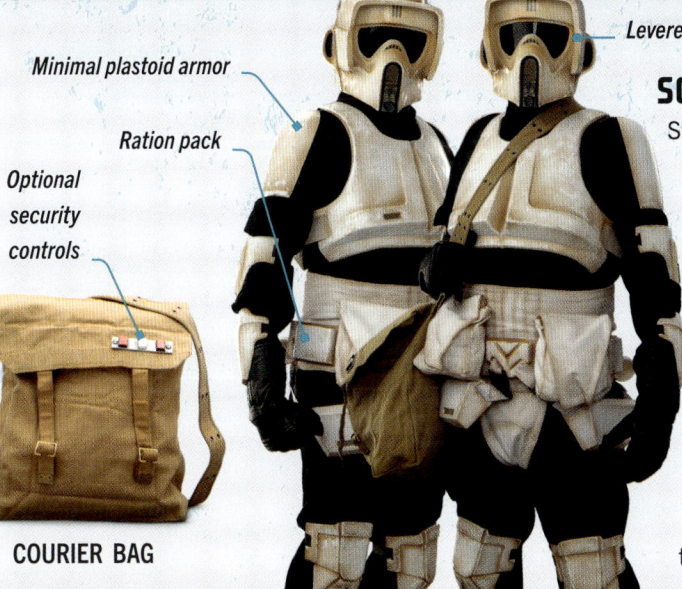

- Minimal plastoid armor
- Ration pack
- Optional security controls
- Levered visor with focusing shroud

COURIER BAG

SCOUT PATROL

Stationed at the Nevarro City gate are two scout troopers assigned to keep watch on newcomers and to scan the horizon for impending trouble. Given the paucity of traffic to Nevarro, it is not a demanding assignment. AP-1982 and JS-1975 nevertheless manage to disappoint.

STORMTROOPERS

The stormtroopers who respond to Moff Gideon's commands are much more precise and disciplined than the Client's limited pool of soldiers. They hearken back to the well-trained legions of the Empire.

IMPERIAL TROOP TRANSPORT

Barreling into the city square with inexorable mass and momentum are the brick-like ITTs, brimming with stormtroopers ready to spill out and take position. An inelegant design, the ITT takes the brutalism of Imperial architecture and mounts it on repulsorlifts. Similar models are designed to hold prisoners and serve as riot control in urban areas.

- Armored transparisteel viewport
- Troop deployment doors
- Dorsal heavy laser cannon turret

DATA FILE

MANUFACTURER	Ubrikkian Industries
MODEL	ITT K79-H20
TYPE	Armored troop transport
DIMENSIONS	Height: 2.45 m (8 ft); width: 3.18 m (10 ft 5 in); length: 8.06 m (26 ft 5 in)
SPEED	120 kph (75 mph)
WEAPONS	2 dorsal laser cannons in turret, 2 forward fixed laser cannons
AFFILIATION	Imperial remnant

PART I: A NEW COMPANION

UNDERGROUND ESCAPE

Gideon's targets barely escape with their lives from the shootout at the Common House. They flee through the sewers, arriving at the Mandalorian Covert. Mando discovers that the covert lies in ruins and most of the hidden Mandalorians have been killed. The Armorer remains, salvaging what armor she can from the fallen. She does not know if any of her people survived, but has hope that some escaped offworld. The Armorer points the group toward a subterranean lava river that will take them back to the surface.

Once more the Mandalorians court extinction. It was a great risk to emerge from the covert to come to Mando's aid, and this is the price. The Empire invades the sewers and destroys the hidden sanctuary.

Thixotropic flow keeps from solidifying

Reinforced magmatic rock hull

STONE KEELBOAT

A decrepit keelboat sits at the end of a passageway, its stony hull gelled to the river bank by time-cooled lava. Cara Dune blasts it free with her weapon, and the team climbs aboard, letting the lazy flow of the Charon River pull them beyond the city's limits toward the plains.

Pushed along by a reinforced pole operated by a ferry droid, the keelboat is also known as a lava punt.

LAVA MEERKATS

Indigenous to the Nevarro lava banks, these silicate suricates are heat-resistant mammals whose oily coats are fireproof. The glittery-eyed meerkats are regarded as nuisances, little more than sewer vermin, by most Nevarro denizens.

> "IF YOU FOLLOW THE DESCENDING TUNNEL, IT WILL LEAD YOU TO THE UNDERGROUND RIVER. IT FLOWS DOWNSTREAM TOWARD THE LAVA FLATS."
>
> – THE ARMORER

IG-11's actions are far removed from his original programming—he heals Djarin's grievous wounds, then walks through a lava river to sacrifice himself for his allies.

Archway part of original civic planning efforts

Lava meerkat scrounges for fire ticks

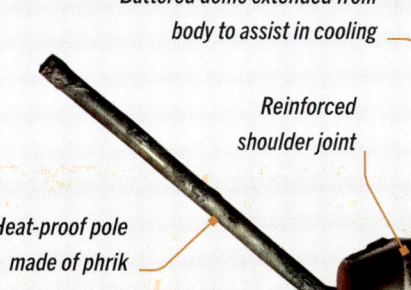

Who built MA-13 is unknown, but the level of soot contamination suggests it has been active for decades.

KEELBOAT ASTROMECH

MA-13 is an antiquated ferry droid built out of a discarded R-series shell. The droid has been in an extended slumber, encrusted with cooled lava and soot deposits, and is awakened by the presence of passengers. It creakily stands to its full height and fulfills its function of pushing the punt downriver with its four arms.

Battered dome extended from body to assist in cooling

Carbon-scoring

Reinforced shoulder joint

Heat-proof pole made of phrik

DATA FILE	
SUBJECT	MA-13
MODEL	Modified Industrial Automaton R-series unit
TYPE	Repurposed astromech droid
AFFILIATION	Independent
HEIGHT	2.46 m (8 ft 1 in)

PART I: A NEW COMPANION
RISING PHOENIX

The discarded armor from the fallen Mandalorian Covert finds new life thanks to the Armorer's salvage efforts. She not only adorns Mando with a long overdue signet, but also bestows upon him the gift of the Rising Phoenix, or *Munad Tracyn-senaar* in Mando'a. This is the traditional name of both the jetpack technology and the skill to operate it. Mando, having been saved by the jetpack-equipped Fighting Corps of the Death Watch, has witnessed the Rising Phoenix. Now, he also has the hardware.

> "THIS WILL MAKE YOU COMPLETE."
> – THE ARMORER

- Helmet transmitter port connects to jetpack
- Central hollow channels air to mini-turbines
- Armored ignition chamber redirects thrust
- Thrust cone from directional nozzle
- Treated cape fabric is flame retardant
- Feedback sensors in shin guard translate to jetpack control
- Shifting balance can change exhaust vector
- Weighted leg cuff adds additional aerial control

With Moff Gideon strafing from his TIE fighter, Mando has no option but to give aerial pursuit with his new jetpack.

FACT FILE

JETPACK HERITAGE
Jango Fett's experience in Rising Phoenix led to some clone troopers learning to use jetpacks, which in turn led to specialized units of Imperial airborne infantry.

FOCUS REQUIRED
Since precise jetpack adjustments derive from body movements, Rising Phoenix demands discipline and no distraction, otherwise a clumsy misstep could lead to a jetpack misfiring.

OPERATING A JETPACK
Jetpack operation, particularly of Mandalorian design, is a learned skill that is an extension of armor usage. The gauntlet and helmet controls can seamlessly connect to jetpack navigation systems so that subtle muscle movement, pupil-tracking, weight distribution, and gestures create a language the jetpack can process and act on. Rising Phoenix is the Mandalorian martial art of physicality behind this language.

CLAN OF TWO

Mando originally sees the Child as an asset for capture, categorizing him as an enemy, but later breaks the Bounty Hunters Guild code to rescue the infant. By Mandalorian Creed, this act made the Child his foundling to care for and nurture, and the two of them a clan. The killing of the mudhorn therefore came from a clan alliance and is worthy of earning the signet.

MANDO'S RIGHT PAULDRON
- Raised and polished beskar signet
- Stylized mudhorn skull and horn

JETPACK RESCUE

Years ago, Mandalorians bearing the Death Watch signet came to Din Djarin's rescue, finding the boy cowering in a cellar. As per the Way, these Mandalorians identified Djarin as a foundling. Young Djarin then devoted himself to the Creed and left his past identity behind.

Callouts
- Jet intake cap (and projectile expansion port)
- Stowed flare launcher
- Cooling vent
- Rigid air-frame
- Beskar-armored fuel tank
- Magnetic attachment points
- Directional exhaust nozzle
- Directional servo

DATA FILE

MANUFACTURER The Armorer, with componentry from Merr-Sonn Munitions and Mitrinomon Transports

MODEL Custom modified JTZ-18

TYPE Personal jetpack

DIMENSIONS Height: 0.56 m (1 ft 10 in); width: 0.32 m (1 ft 1 in)

SPEED 280 kph (174 mph)

WEAPONS None

AFFILIATION The Mandalorian

ARMORER'S DESIGN

The core of Mando's jetpack is a JTZ-18 design modified extensively for Mandalorian usage by the Armorer. Conventional controls are replaced by Rising Phoenix interfaces. A beskar skin, salvaged from the fallen of the covert, gives the jetpack a distinctive patina and a durable shell. Should the need arise, Mando can use the controls on his gauntlet to operate the jetpack at a distance.

PART II:
A NEW QUEST

In their time together, the Mandalorian and the Child form an unmistakable bond and drive to protect one another. The Armorer recognizes in the Child remarkable abilities characteristic of the Jedi Order. By the Creed, it is Djarin's responsibility to protect the Child and reunite him with his people.

Finding a Jedi will not be easy. Djarin seeks out information from the network of Mandalorian coverts, but finding another Mandalorian in this era also proves difficult… and dangerous! Reports of an armored lawman in the outskirt settlements of Tatooine bring Mando back to the desert planet, where he uncovers the lost armor of Boba Fett. On Trask, Mando meets Bo-Katan Kryze, uncovering more history that was lost to him. Kryze and her Nite Owls are of a very different sect of Mandalorians who do not adhere to Djarin's orthodoxy. She shocks Djarin by removing her helmet in front of him. Despite their differences in beliefs, the Mandalorian and Bo-Katan exhibit effective teamwork, as he helps the Nite Owls in their capture of an Imperial freighter.

Information supplied by Bo-Katan brings the Mandalorian closer to finding a proper place for the Child, as the youngster's abilities require study and honing. The discovery that the Imperial remnant has foul designs on the Child adds urgency to Mando's quest. On the planet Corvus, Mando meets the former Jedi Ahsoka Tano, who unlocks many of the Child's secrets, including his name—Grogu—and history, and suggests a path to find the young one training.

PART II: A NEW QUEST
FIGHT NIGHT

Tenuous rumors suggest that the gangster Gor Koresh is interested in Mandalorian culture and therefore might be able to provide Mando with a location for a covert. The Mandalorian travels to RTK111, a spent mining world of so little interest it doesn't even warrant a name, in pursuit of Koresh. The planet is the ideal place for unscrupulous individuals like Koresh, who has turned a crumbling company town into his power base. Beyond the graffiti-covered structures and slums overrun by feral hounds, there is a fortified honky-tonk where Koresh holds court.

Inside is an improvised arena, with a raised hexagonal ring where combatants spar. Gor profits from the drinks served and from a cut of wagers made. Koresh is delighted to see the Mandalorian in his venue, because he's fond of beskar armor. A collector of rarities, and a shrewd judge of valuable items in a turbulent economy, Koresh hopes to peel the armor off of Mando and sell it piece by piece.

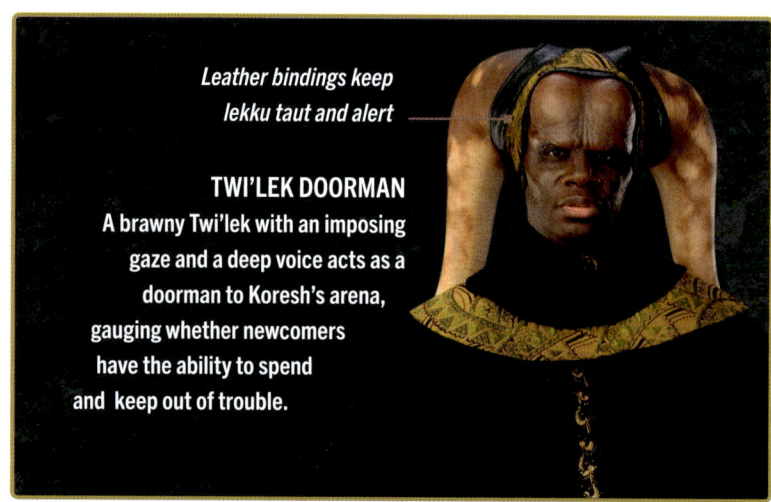

Leather bindings keep lekku taut and alert

TWI'LEK DOORMAN
A brawny Twi'lek with an imposing gaze and a deep voice acts as a doorman to Koresh's arena, gauging whether newcomers have the ability to spend and keep out of trouble.

GAMORREAN FIGHTER
This dim-witted warrior is one of a pair of prize Gamorrean cruiserweight champs that Koresh has brawl for sport. He and his opponent are kept apart between brawls to let animosity grow. He is driven to succeed, but has been disappointing Koresh recently so the gangster is looking to unload him.

Scar from dirty move

Sensitive snout

Canine tusk

Traditional leather and fur trunks

Mando walks through the dilapidated slums enlivened by colorful graffiti and the glowing eyes of light-avoiding night hounds.

GAMORREAN SPARRING AX
- Repulsorfield conducting cables
- Vibro-setting touch plate

GAMORREAN CHAMP

After Koresh eliminates his opponent with a well-aimed blaster shot, this fighter finds himself victorious in his longstanding rivalry, albeit only by default. He has little time to sift through his confusion and savor victory, because a different type of combat erupts in the arena. He attempts a flying tackle of the Mandalorian, but falls short—and unconscious.

- Raised ax signals victory
- Broken horn
- Arm binding assists with identification
- Belt of reigning champion for his class
- Dwoob-fur lining
- Gladiator sandals

Abyssin sportsman Koresh proposes a wager to the Mandalorian for his armor.

GOR KORESH

Gor Koresh started in the criminal underworld through an alliance with the Droid Gotra. As part of this agreement, he shifted from droid gladiatorial combat to strictly organic pit fighting. Though Koresh fancies himself a gentleman of sophisticated tastes, the bar for such a claim is appallingly low on RTK111.

KESSLER DB-41 SPORTING BLASTER PISTOL
- Barrel physically braced to scope for accuracy
- Monocular vision with doubled retinal focusing planes
- Scope aligned for his Abyssin sight
- Hexagonal sigil denotes his trademark arena

PART II: A NEW QUEST

MOS PELGO

About 300 kilometers (186 miles) northwest of Mos Eisley is the hamlet of Mos Pelgo. The tiny settlement has been known at times as Freetown, at first for its promise of freedom from the crime, pollution, and crowds of the larger port cities, and later for surviving Tatooine's turbulent liberation from Imperial occupation. Mos Pelgo began as a small mining venture that succeeded in finding enough silicax oxalate to ensure its independence, but this untapped wealth has attracted trouble.

Articulated facemask prevents this Manjtoo from being mistaken for a Jawa

A greedy Manjtoo sees more value in Mando's jetpack than in the Child as a hostage, an ultimately fatal choice.

DESERT BANDITS
The Mandalorian and the Child are still targets, despite the settling of old Guild scores and the apparent disappearance of Moff Gideon. Mando's armor will forever make him prey as long as beskar remains valuable. Bandits jump him in the desert wilderness, hoping to score a fortune.

Saloon's upper deck (closed during the day)

Pretormin Environmental GX-6c moisture vaporator

Raised platforms reduce predator-attracting vibrations

Marshal Cobb Vanth's custom swoop

OLD MINING SETTLEMENT
The complex cross-polytopic internal structure of the mineral silicax oxalate grants it valuable properties in data storage and navcomputing, making even a small amount worth a fortune. As a small venture, Mos Pelgo only extracted small nuggets. The rapacious Mining Collective forced the townsfolk to dig deeper for even greater lodes.

The Weequay bartender keeps a wary eye on a confrontation between the marshal and a Mandalorian stranger.

DATA FILE

SUBJECT Taanti
HOMEWORLD Sriluur
SPECIES Weequay
AFFILIATION Loyal to Marshal Vanth
HEIGHT 1.83 m (6 ft)

Wrinkled skin common among Weequays

TAANTI

Mos Pelgo became a haven for those who had crossed the wrong people or incurred debilitating debts in the larger cities. Those down on their luck could start a new life here.

The Child seeks cover in a (fortunately) dry spittoon before a gunfight breaks out in Mos Pelgo's sleepy saloon.

Culzer's General Store

Jundland Wastes on the horizon

Vane-style anemometer

Torsuch's boarding house offers affordable accommodations for travelers

712-AvA speeder bike once used by Toro Calican

Subterranean ventilation stack

Mining hopper turned into animal water trough

PART II: A NEW QUEST

COBB VANTH

The Marshal of Mos Pelgo stands between the cruelest elements of desert life and the townsfolk of Freetown. A self-appointed lawman, de facto mayor, and trusted veteran of Tatooinian survival, Vanth recognized the danger of the power vacuum left by the toppling of both Jabba the Hutt's criminal enterprise and the Galactic Empire. While some celebrated newfound freedom, Cobb worried.

Power players such as the Red Key Raiders and their backing agents, the Mining Collective, could make life miserable for the people of Mos Pelgo. Vanth's fears proved well founded when goons from the Mining Collective rounded up the Mos Pelgo villagers and forced them to work the very mines that were supposed to set the town free. With Mining Collective equipment and local toil, the bounty of silicax oxalate could be extracted from the ground at a far more profitable rate than ever before. Vanth escaped capture with a camtono of silicax, and was able to trade the precious mineral to Jawas in exchange for a peculiar prize aboard their sandcrawler: the salvaged armor of Boba Fett.

Targeting rangefinder (retracted)

Single missile can destroy an armored landspeeder

HOMING MISSILE

STORIED SALVAGE
The corrosive gut fluids of the sarlacc scarred the armor's durasteel coating, but the beskar's integrity and many of the subsystems are intact.

Blast dissipation cuirass

Quickdraw woodoo-leather holster

Fuel tank

Kneepad rocket dart launchers

REPAIRED MITRINOMON Z-6 JETPACK

Directional exhaust nozzle

DATA FILE

MANUFACTURER	Custom special made from salvage
MODEL	Radon-Ulzer 620C podracer engine
TYPE	Modified speeder
DIMENSIONS	Height: 0.98 m (3 ft 3 in); width: 1.65 m (5 ft 5 in); length: 5.18 m (17 ft)
SPEED	480 kph (298 mph)
WEAPONS	None

Repurposed speeder bike handlebar rig

SCAVENGED SWOOP

A common mechanic's saying is that a swoop is little more than an engine with a seat. Cobb Vanth's swoop is a literal realization of what was always supposed to be an exaggeration. Cobb needs swift conveyance to deal with the many dangers that threaten Mos Pelgo. His vehicle more than suffices.

Debris-deflecting cowling

Turbine drive motor

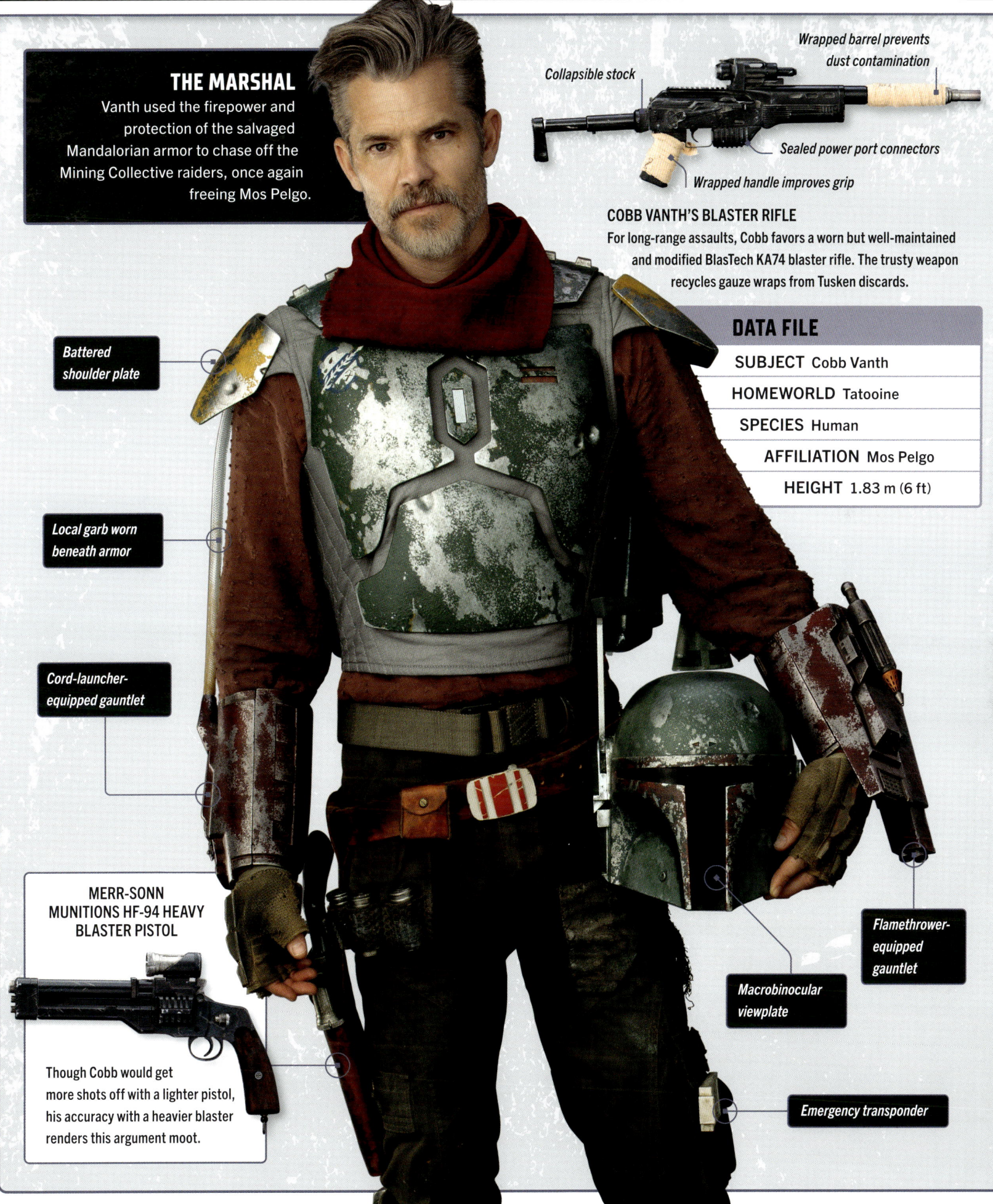

THE MARSHAL

Vanth used the firepower and protection of the salvaged Mandalorian armor to chase off the Mining Collective raiders, once again freeing Mos Pelgo.

COBB VANTH'S BLASTER RIFLE

For long-range assaults, Cobb favors a worn but well-maintained and modified BlasTech KA74 blaster rifle. The trusty weapon recycles gauze wraps from Tusken discards.

- Collapsible stock
- Wrapped barrel prevents dust contamination
- Sealed power port connectors
- Wrapped handle improves grip

DATA FILE

SUBJECT	Cobb Vanth
HOMEWORLD	Tatooine
SPECIES	Human
AFFILIATION	Mos Pelgo
HEIGHT	1.83 m (6 ft)

- Battered shoulder plate
- Local garb worn beneath armor
- Cord-launcher-equipped gauntlet
- Flamethrower-equipped gauntlet
- Macrobinocular viewplate
- Emergency transponder

MERR-SONN MUNITIONS HF-94 HEAVY BLASTER PISTOL

Though Cobb would get more shots off with a lighter pistol, his accuracy with a heavier blaster renders this argument moot.

PART II: A NEW QUEST
TUSKENS

Tuskens, or "sand people," are desert nomads, who are fiercely territorial of the craggy lands that line the Dune Sea. Tatooine's moisture farmers and colonists falsely view them as "savages." In truth, Tuskens have a complex culture and are extremely guarded against outsiders. The Mandalorian is one of the few outlanders to have taken the time to understand their customs, for he recognizes the value of their survival skills and knowledge of the desert.

Tusken scouts spot the approach of the outlanders from kilometers away. The Tuskens cautiously see an opportunity to negotiate for goods.

Tuskens share their succulent black melons in discussion with Marshal Vanth and the Mandalorian, as they parley peacefully.

TUSKEN SPOTTER
An elder spotter is one of a quartet of scouts who travel single file atop their bantha mounts along the Dune Sea fringes. He is more patient than the impulsive youths under his command, and when Mando stops a respectful distance from their banthas, he recognizes an opportunity for peaceful transaction.

- Sand-filtering breathmask
- Ammunition packet attached to bandolier
- Woodoo-leather strap
- Long-barreled cycler rifle

TUSKEN SCOUT
This scout from a Tusken tribe that roams the edges of the Dune Sea is a lesser to the elder spotter. He is eager for bloodshed but knows to keep his temper in check and wait for his leader's command to attack.

- Warrior spikes
- Ammunition pouches
- Weighted club end of gaffi stick
- Thick desert cloak
- Clan-crafted leatherwork

Stabilizing stock, sometimes personalized with carvings

Rifled barrel for long-range accuracy

Trigger

CYCLER RIFLE

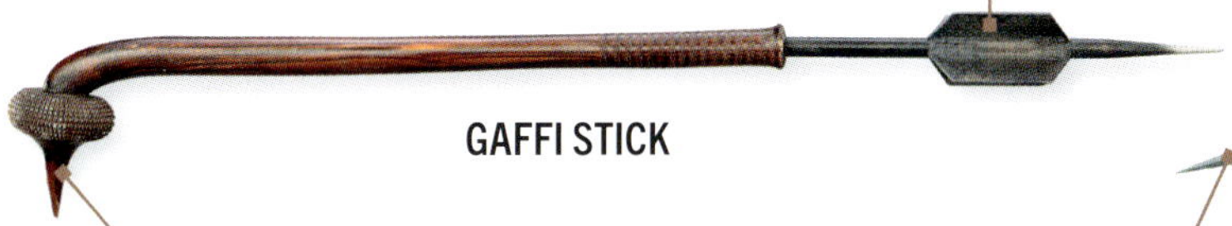

Skein spring tension rollers

Finned end, often coated with sandbat venom

GAFFI STICK

Club end doubles as bantha dental tool

Gaffi bolt resting in slider

Winch levers

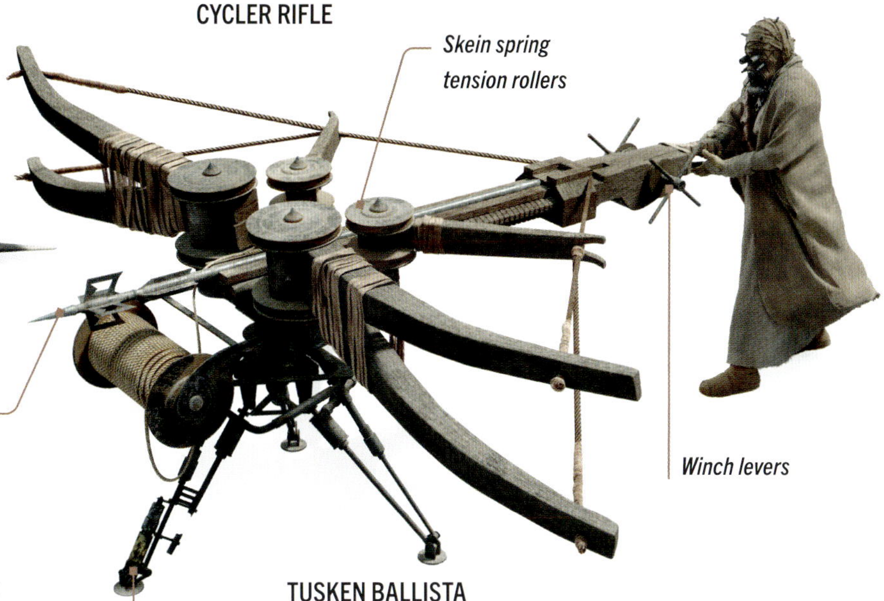

TUSKEN WEAPONRY

The paucity of raw materials means Tusken weapons are made of salvage and colonist discards. Their most distinctive weapon is the gaderffii (or gaffi stick)—a heavy club that Tuskens brandish while howling in fierce displays of dominance. For long-range attacks, they fire projectile-launching cycler rifles that possess simple, weatherproof mechanical functions.

Recycled tripod mount

TUSKEN BALLISTA

The Tusken ballista was made famous by the chroniclers of the assault on Fort Tusken that gave the natives their name and fierce reputation. This weapon is a rare sight as it is made of precious desert wood.

> "TUSKENS THINK THEY'RE THE LOCALS. EVERYONE ELSE IS TRESPASSING."
> – THE MANDALORIAN TO TORO CALICAN

MASSIFFS

Pack animals, massiffs are loyal, protective quadrupeds with bony plate armor. They have extremely precise olfactory senses and can be tamed as trackers— the Tuskens also domesticate them for hunting and to detect intruders to their grounds.

Spiraling horn

Hubba gourd and rockmelon skins collect in teeth, which require cleaning

Thick fur

DATA FILE

SUBJECT	Bantha
HOMEWORLD	Tatooine
SIZE	Height (at top of horn crest): 2.79 m (9 ft 2 in); width: 2.24 m (7 ft 4 in); length (to end of tail): 6.39 m (21 ft)
LIFESPAN	80 standard years

BANTHA BAIT

Banthas are an important staple to the nomadic life of a Tusken. Aside from transportation, a bantha provides valuable raw materials for survival through its horns, fur, milk, and dung. Banthas are afforded status within the tribes, and the sacrifice of one—as was done to an aged beast to lure a krayt dragon to the surface—is not done lightly by the Tuskens.

PART II: A NEW QUEST
KRAYT DRAGON

The greater krayt dragon is the ultimate predator of the Tatooine deserts. A rare few achieve truly prodigious proportions and become leviathan krayt dragons. The massive reptile uses subsonic harmonics generated deep in its throat to fluidize a path of sand before it, essentially swimming through the shifting silica like an oceanic predator. So dire a threat is this behemoth to the settlement of Mos Pelgo that the normally adversarial townsfolk and Tuskens unite to stop it.

DEN OF THE DRAGON
The leviathan krayt has roosted in an abandoned sarlacc pit, presumably after having devoured the host within. Krayt dragons are the only natural predator of sarlaccs.

Anchoring tail

Thick skin lined with osteoderm spikes

The leviathan krayt has 16 limbs in total: 6 hindlimbs, 4 midlimbs, and 6 forelimbs

Four-clawed hind foot with elongated talons

The enormous beast erupts from its lair, striking at the Mos Pelgo townsfolk and Tuskens who scramble to stop it.

FACT FILE

DIET
Leviathans hunt huge prey like sarlaccs and tibidons and can make short meals of whole banthas and dewbacks.

HABITAT
The leviathans spend most of their time asleep, preserving energy within caves or canyons, or beneath the sand.

DATA FILE
SUBJECT Leviathan krayt dragon
HOMEWORLD Tatooine
SIZE Height: 28.68 m (94 ft); width: 45.60 m (149 ft 7 in); length: 184.51 m (605 ft)
LIFESPAN Unknown

Rock- and bone-crunching teeth

Armored cranial dome and horns

Diaphragm emits multilayered subsonic howl

Grasping five-clawed forearm

APEX PREDATOR
The exact number of leviathan krayt dragons is unknown; despite their enormous size, they are rarely spotted above ground. They are one of the few known creatures able to migrate into the searing badlands beyond Tatooine's habitable zones, so their population may never be accounted for. The canyon krayts are far more common.

The leviathan krayt dragon can expel a caustic fluid from its gizzard which can cause severe chemical burns to its prey.

An unlikely sight in the desert wastes: settlers and Tuskens working side by side for the common goal of survival.

TO KILL THE KRAYT DRAGON
A tentative alliance is struck between the Mos Pelgo denizens and the Tuskens, brokered by the Mandalorian and Cobb Vanth. The Tuskens lure the beast out, attempting to drive it across a series of buried explosives from the mining town. This act is not enough to stop the krayt, and Mando must improvise an explosive end to the monster.

PEARL
A krayt's gizzard can hold treasure: precious stones rounded to perfection by its digestive process. The rarity of krayt carcasses only enhances the value of these pearls.

PART II: A NEW QUEST
FROG LADY

The next step in Mando's quest to find his brethren depends on his safe transport of a being known only as Frog Lady in Mos Eisley. By the next equinox, Frog Lady needs her clutch of eggs fertilized by her husband, who resides on the oceanic moon Trask. Ordinarily, it would be a short hyperspace jump to the next system, but the delicate structure of the Querm eggs cannot withstand lightspeed travel. The journey is a slow crawl at sublight, with the *Razor Crest* exposed to potential dangers.

The technologically savvy Frog Lady repurposes the vocabulator of the scrapped Q9-0 to serve as a translator for her.

Frog Lady and her husband's period of producing offspring is coming to a close as they advance in age. The Querm subspecies of Rybet can only fertilize eggs on worlds of exacting conditions, and Trask, which orbits the nearby gas giant of Kol Iben, is one such example.

The trek is fraught with danger, as an attempt to evade a New Republic patrol downs the *Razor Crest* on the frigid outer world of Maldo Kreis. There, Frog Lady will fight not only for her life but for the survival of her spawn.

FROG MAN
Frog Lady's husband, Frog Man, has scouted ahead and settled at an estuary on Trask, finding employment as a dockhand. He had insisted his wife remain on Tatooine until he was established on Trask and knew it was safe, which took longer than expected. Frog Man sees Mandalorians on Trask and informs his wife. This intel is the key that unlocks Frog Lady's passage.

- Protective nictitating inner eyelid
- Worker's oiled coveralls

EGG CARRIER TANK
- Nutrient bath filter
- Gelatinous coat
- Temperature-monitoring gauge
- Reinforced shockproof frame
- Adjustable shoulder strap

CONTINUING THE LINE
Adult female Querm Rybets produce clutches of unfertilized eggs in annual cycles until they reach middle age. If not fertilized, the eggs eventually decay into component proteins. If fertilized by a male, one egg in a clutch is likely to develop into a tadpole, which hatches and can draw nutrition from the other eggs.

The newborn tadpole makes a friend in the inquisitive Child.

QUERM EGGS
- Membranous chalaza

SURVIVAL INSTINCT
On frigid Maldo Kreis, Frog Lady is drawn to geothermal baths to warm her cold-blooded body and keep her eggs viable. When a swarm of ice spiders descends, she uses her whip-like tongue and her prodigious leaping ability to flee to relative safety aboard the crashed *Crest*.

- Motion-sensitive night vision
- Outer tympanic membrane
- Lid designed for ease of access
- Protective extracellular jelly
- Heat-retaining scarf
- Webbed hands with suction cup fingertips

Frog Lady expertly wields a Shard-3A holdout cluster blaster, protecting the Child from ravenous ice spiders.

DATA FILE
SUBJECT "Frog Lady" (alias—real name unknown)
HOMEWORLD Trask
SPECIES Querm Rybet
AFFILIATION Independent
HEIGHT 1.45 m (4 ft 9 in)

FACT FILE

THE RYBETS
The ancient Rybet people have many subspecies scattered across the galaxy, including some who have settled on Quermia.

LANGUAGE
Her croaking language derives meaning mostly from intonation and is very hard for non-amphibious species to speak.

PART II: A NEW QUEST

MALDO KREIS

In the outer Tatoo system is Maldo Kreis, a one-time rogue ice world caught in an irregular orbit. The small planet spends most of its long year in a deep freeze, save for when it passes along a sliver of its revolution around its twin stars. At this stage, the two suns are in conjunction and the resulting intensified stellar radiation is enough for some of Maldo Kreis to thaw. During those times, the few native organisms that dot the glaciated world spring to ravenous life.

The battered *Razor Crest* comes to a disheveled stop within an ice cave as it evades a New Republic patrol.

Maldo Kreis' upper atmosphere fills with suspended ice crystals which help spread the distant starlight into a bright sky.

X-WING CHASE

For its accessory role in the prison break aboard the *Bothan-5*, the *Razor Crest* is deemed a target of interest by a New Republic X-wing patrol. Captain Carson Teva and his wingmate Trapper Wolf give pursuit, and Mando breaks for cover in the atmosphere of Maldo Kreis.

Intense albedo from ice crystals

Carson Teva's X-wing starfighter

Terminator line from rapidly advancing night

DATA FILE

REGION	Outer Rim
SECTOR	Arkanis
SYSTEM	Tatoo
DIAMETER	2,445 km (1,519 miles)
TERRAIN	Frozen
MOONS	0
POPULATION	0

Fully grown apex spider

Chitinous tibia

Compound radial mound and web spinneret

ICE SPIDER

No formal study of Maldo Kreis has ever been commissioned, leaving reports of its life-forms spotty and inconsistent. The arachnids that dwell near the hot springs in the ice caves are similar to other species encountered in the galaxy, such as the kryknas of Atollon and the knobby whites of the Sluis sector, suggesting a common ancient progenitor.

A swarm of ice spiders at various life stages emerges from a deep hibernation with a deadly hunger.

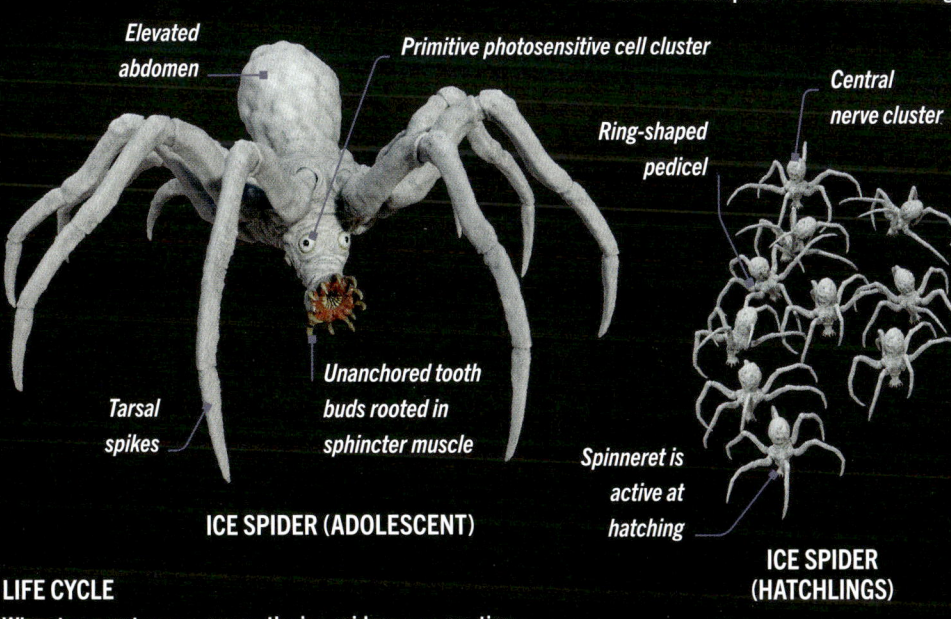

Elevated abdomen

Primitive photosensitive cell cluster

Ring-shaped pedicel

Central nerve cluster

Tarsal spikes

Unanchored tooth buds rooted in sphincter muscle

Spinneret is active at hatching

ICE SPIDER (ADOLESCENT)

ICE SPIDER (HATCHLINGS)

FACT FILE

SUBJECT	Ice spider
HOMEWORLD	Maldo Kreis
SIZE	Up to 9.2 m (30 ft) tall for fully grown apex spider
LIFESPAN	Unknown

The curious and ever-hungry Child pops a newly hatched ice spider into his mouth for a crunchy meal.

LIFE CYCLE

When temperatures warm up, the ice spiders emerge, tiny and vulnerable, from egg cases that dot the ice cavern floors. They instinctively target sources of heat to devour, using their web strands to snare prey and their radial mouths to feed.

PART II: A NEW QUEST
ALLIANCE VETERANS

The New Republic built up its defenses with many eager cadets arriving at newly constructed and restored academies. Shifting political tides would limit the size of the galactic military to prevent another full-scale war. The New Republic Defense Force would be modest in comparison to the overgrown war machines of the past, and the nimble starfighter would continue to see storied service. Active veteran pilots of the Rebel Alliance serve as inspiration for the new generation.

Captain Carson Teva bears witness to a cautious bureaucratic government replacing the maverick impulses of Rebel Alliance operations.

CARSON TEVA

Based out of an outpost on Adelphi, Carson Teva leads New Republic policing efforts in stretches of the Outer Rim that include the Arkanis sector. He is one of the few who does not underestimate the lingering Imperial presence in the galactic hinterlands, theorizing that disparate remnants may in fact be coordinated by an unknown command. Teva recognizes that it's only through the vigilance of Outer Rim denizens that the New Republic can keep order.

Teva crosses paths with the Mandalorian during his patrols, growing to respect Din Djarin's resilience. Teva comes to Djarin's aid when his ship is stranded on Maldo Kreis.

- New Republic blue
- Polarized plastex visor
- New Republic provisional-era crest
- Plastoid chin guard and strap cinch
- Koensayr K-22995-nre flight helmet
- Novaldex Diagnostech life support unit
- Pocket contains datapad with bureaucratic forms for his convenience
- BlasTech A280 blaster rifle
- Guidenhauser flight harness connects to ejection seat
- Signal flares

SUBJECT	Carson Teva
HOMEWORLD	Torolis
SPECIES	Human
AFFILIATION	New Republic Starfighter Corps
HEIGHT	1.75 m (5 ft 9 in)

T-65 X-WING

The undisputed symbol of Rebel Alliance starfighter superiority, the T-65 X-wing continues service in the New Republic. It is slowly being replaced by the modern E-wing, which draws favor from fresh Academy graduates. The veteran X-wing pilots make their preference for their beloved battle-proven craft widely known, a stance met with friction in some circles. As the New Republic solidifies, newer craft dominate Coreward deployments, while the elder X-wings and their proponents carry out their assignments in the more distant and dangerous sectors.

DATA FILE

MANUFACTURER Incom Corporation

MODEL T-65C-A2

TYPE Space superiority starfighter

DIMENSIONS Length: 13.40 m (44 ft); width: 11.76 m (38 ft 7 in); height (attack configuration): 4.66 m (15 ft 3 in)

SPEED 1,050 kph (652 mph) (atmosphere)

WEAPONS 4 laser cannons; 2 proton torpedo launchers

AFFILIATION New Republic Defense Force

R2 unit in astromech socket
Variable geometry exhaust nacelle
Deflector shield generator
Microporous cooling blades
Torplex flight computer
Phototropic armored transparisteel canopy
S-foil extends weapons and shields coverage
Sensor array behind scanner-translucent nosecone window
Polarized alloy replaceable laser tip

CARSON TEVA'S X-WING

A routine transponder ping on an unmarked Razor Crest is the start of Carson Teva's relationship with Din Djarin.

TRAPPER WOLF

Trapper Wolf remained a starfighter pilot when many of his contemporaries sought out civilian life at the war's end. Wolf often flies as Captain Teva's wingmate, serving as second-in-command on patrol. Quite often, he and his fellow pilots are the only New Republic presence to be found in outlands.

Raised ridge conceals comlink antenna
Faded lupine unit symbol
Retractable plastex visor
Chin guard and helmet strap

TRAPPER WOLF'S HELMET

PART II: A NEW QUEST

TRASK

Trask is an oceanic moon that orbits the gas giant Kol Iben and is home to colonies of settlers from Mon Cala, with aquatic townships of Quarren and Mon Calamari abounding. Other amphibious species have also found homes here, working away in the dangerous, but profitable, maritime commercial ventures that dominate activity on the moon. Far from the New Republic, the lack of the galactic government's presence has encouraged Imperial remnant holdouts to run cargo from Trask, which in turn has attracted the Mandalorians that Mando seeks.

The ailing *Razor Crest* limps past the roiling gas giant Kol Iben on its way to Trask.

Mando lands at one of the modular docking platforms of a Mon Calamari port frequented by Quarren.

> "A MANDALORIAN COVERT IS CLOSE. IT'S IN THIS SECTOR, ONE SYSTEM TRAILING."
> – PELI MOTTO TO THE MANDALORIAN

Mon Calamari settlement

Quarren town

Nautolan outpost

DATA FILE

REGION	Outer Rim
SECTOR	Arkanis Borderlands
SYSTEM	Kol Iben
DIAMETER	9,720 km (6,040 miles)
TERRAIN	Oceanic
MOONS	1
POPULATION	35.8 million

Mando ensures the hungry Child is served chunky squid chowder while he does business.

TRASK HARBOR INN
Not far from the landing port is a cozy inn that caters mostly to Mon Calamari locals. Though work is discussed here, the management insists everyone orders a meal first.

Chromatophoric skin

Scarf denotes status as staff

Well-worn apron

MON CALAMARI SERVER

MON CALA SETTLERS
The Mon Calamari people were embroiled in the Galactic Civil War due to their overt support of the Rebel Alliance. Those on Trask preferred to remain uninvolved. Lately, many that have retired from galactic conflict have voyaged to the moon to get away from the tangle of politics on their homeworlds.

The salty dockworker is unimpressed with Mando's unassisted landing of the *Razor Crest*.

Pakoukou gelatin has monetary value

CALAMARI FLAN

Swiveling eye with wide peripheral scope

DOCKWORKER

Okrelp-strand sweater

Synth-leather waders

Calloused, six-fingered webbed hand

THE DOCKS
A series of hexagonal docking bays line the wharf area of Mon Ville, with raised walkways connecting to loading areas and commercial fairways. The outermost—and cheapest—port facilities are simple landing platforms that extend off the docks. Landing is usually facilitated by following a carrier signal from Trask Port Control.

Heavy Industrial Crane Transport (HI-CT walker)

Neritic Gulper container barge

Modular shipping containers

Saltwater-logged Razor Crest trailing okrelp

PART II: A NEW QUEST
HIGH SEAS TREACHERY

Mando's search for his people leads him toward a Quarren fishing vessel whose captain promises to bring him to other Mandalorians. The captain's lie is quickly exposed: he has no intention of honoring his deal, wishing only to capture Mando's valuable beskar armor for himself. What the Quarren has not counted on is that Mando's presence would draw more beskar his way—in the form of a trio of Mandalorian warriors who rocket to Djarin's defense.

Despite their captain's deceitful nature, the crew of the vessel do make an honest living, fishing these waters for tongthunn.

QUARREN CREW

The shoal of Quarren workers aboard the fishing vessel are extended family, originating from a Dac colony. They are loyal only to each other and are humble in the presence of their bullying captain, who proved his dominance at an early age. The captain's word is law both on and off the fishing vessel.

The treacherous captain bats the Child's hover pram into the mamacore hold, forcing Mando to leap into the tank.

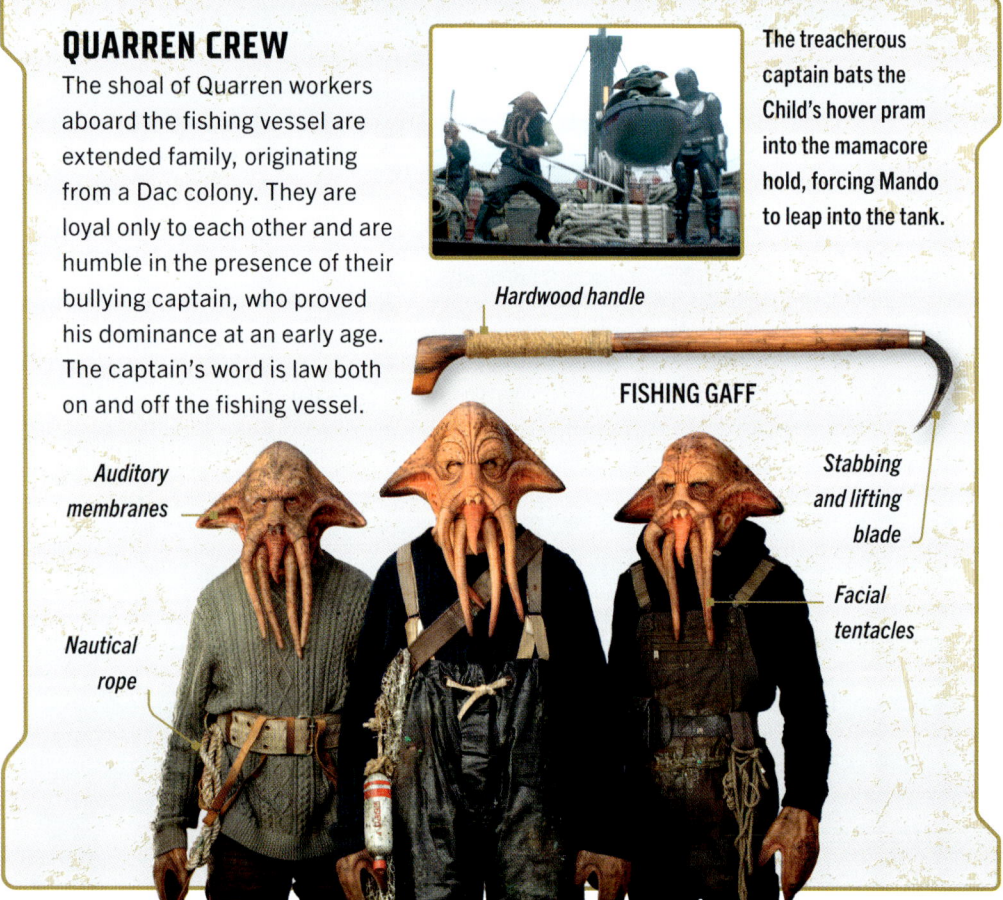

FISHING GAFF
- Hardwood handle
- Stabbing and lifting blade

- Auditory membranes
- Nautical rope
- Facial tentacles

- Long-range communications rig
- Directional mast adorned with fleet logo
- Forward repulsorlift ballast generator
- Bow steering foil

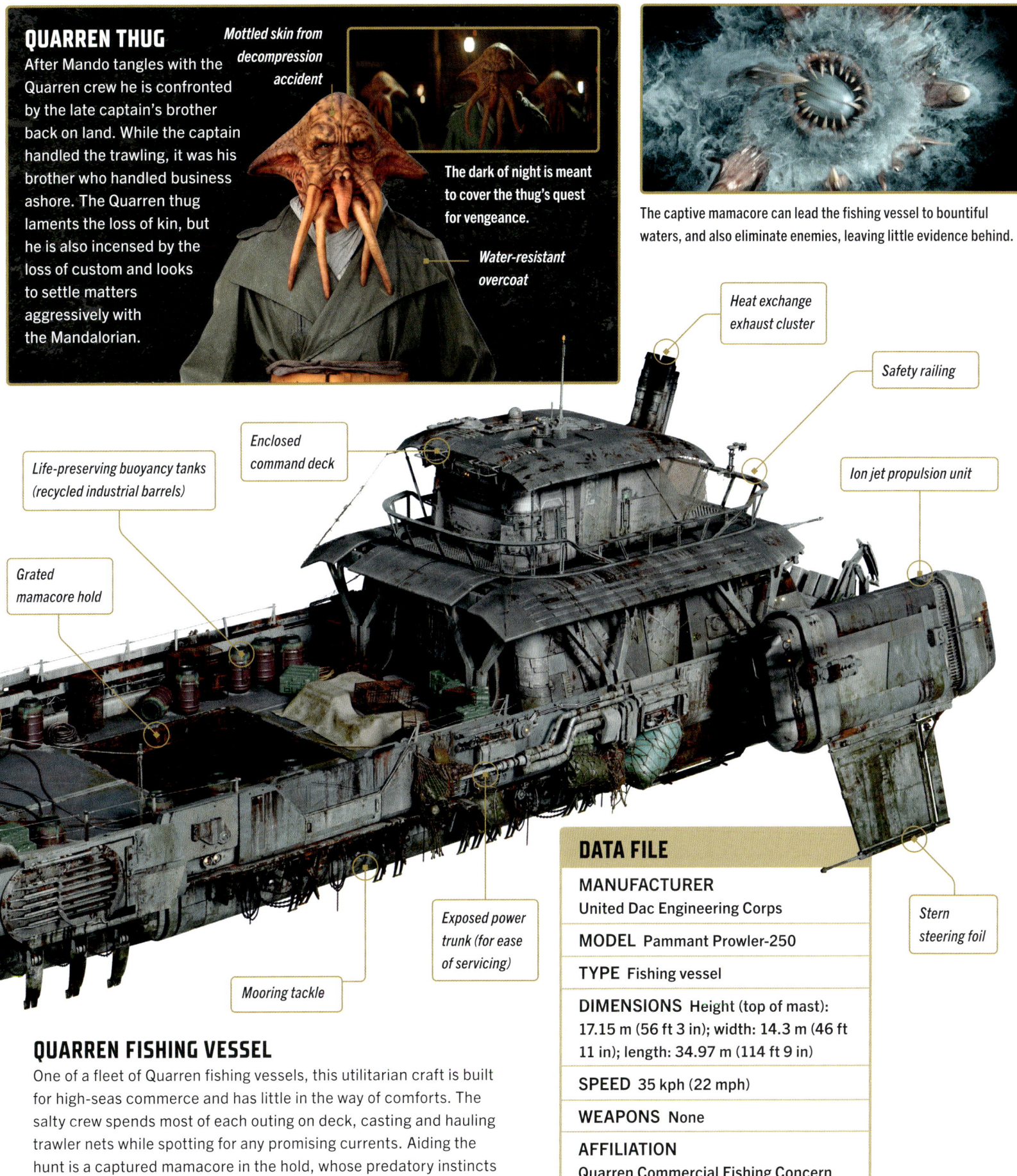

QUARREN THUG

After Mando tangles with the Quarren crew he is confronted by the late captain's brother back on land. While the captain handled the trawling, it was his brother who handled business ashore. The Quarren thug laments the loss of kin, but he is also incensed by the loss of custom and looks to settle matters aggressively with the Mandalorian.

Mottled skin from decompression accident

The dark of night is meant to cover the thug's quest for vengeance.

Water-resistant overcoat

The captive mamacore can lead the fishing vessel to bountiful waters, and also eliminate enemies, leaving little evidence behind.

Heat exchange exhaust cluster

Safety railing

Enclosed command deck

Ion jet propulsion unit

Life-preserving buoyancy tanks (recycled industrial barrels)

Grated mamacore hold

Exposed power trunk (for ease of servicing)

Stern steering foil

Mooring tackle

QUARREN FISHING VESSEL

One of a fleet of Quarren fishing vessels, this utilitarian craft is built for high-seas commerce and has little in the way of comforts. The salty crew spends most of each outing on deck, casting and hauling trawler nets while spotting for any promising currents. Aiding the hunt is a captured mamacore in the hold, whose predatory instincts often point to troups of tongthunn.

DATA FILE

MANUFACTURER United Dac Engineering Corps

MODEL Pammant Prowler-250

TYPE Fishing vessel

DIMENSIONS Height (top of mast): 17.15 m (56 ft 3 in); width: 14.3 m (46 ft 11 in); length: 34.97 m (114 ft 9 in)

SPEED 35 kph (22 mph)

WEAPONS None

AFFILIATION Quarren Commercial Fishing Concern

PART II: A NEW QUEST
BO-KATAN KRYZE

A veteran of the strife that has shaped modern Mandalore, Bo-Katan Kryze is the heiress to the planet's rule, having once wielded the unifying Darksaber as a champion of her people against external occupation. Bo-Katan shares the twisting fortunes of Mandalore, as she now lives in exile far from her home and throne. She has not given up dreams of returning Mandalore to its remembered glory, but the stark reality of harsh circumstance has made her more pragmatic and measured than she was before.

In her youth she was overshadowed by her stately sister, Duchess Satine Kryze, who brought a largely welcomed pacifism to Mandalore that Bo-Katan rejected. Impulsively, Bo-Katan allied herself with zealots who longed for the more martial ways of the past. This radical group, named Death Watch, struck a devilish pact with former Sith Lord Maul, who later betrayed its members, killing Satine and usurping power for himself. Bo-Katan fled the Watch, leading a loyalist force determined to reclaim her world. Though they succeeded with the help of the Republic—and the former Jedi Ahsoka Tano—the coming of the Empire would undo their progress.

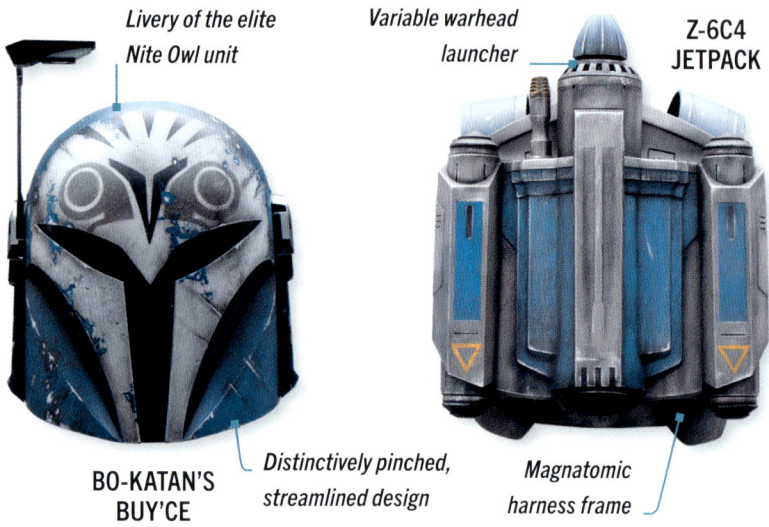

- Livery of the elite Nite Owl unit
- Variable warhead launcher
- **Z-6C4 JETPACK**
- **BO-KATAN'S BUY'CE** — Distinctively pinched, streamlined design
- Magnatomic harness frame

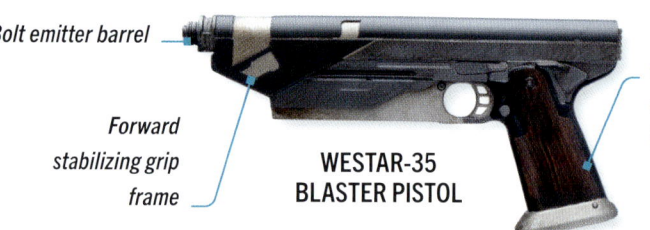

- Bolt emitter barrel
- Forward stabilizing grip frame
- **WESTAR-35 BLASTER PISTOL**
- Power cell encased in handle

VETERAN WARRIOR
Bo-Katan's exposure to conflict since her teenage years has honed her warrior instincts and skills. In addition to her sharpshooter talents, she is skilled in the Rising Phoenix art of acrobatic jetpack combat. She is excellent in unarmed fighting, with a pronounced specialization in bladed weaponry.

- Armor has been in family for three generations
- Paired WESTAR-35s for double-gunslinging
- Beskar patella cover
- Weighted greaves assist in aerial maneuvers

FACE TO FACE
Mando is shocked to witness Bo-Katan casually doff her helmet, as that is a violation of the commandments contained in the Way. Bo-Katan and her compatriots follow a different path, identifying Mando's belief set as that of the Children of the Watch—a zealous, stricter orthodoxy.

Bo-Katan, once a follower, has grown into a capable leader, stirring fierce loyalty in followers who believe in her.

DATA FILE

SUBJECT Bo-Katan Kryze
HOMEWORLD Kalevala
SPECIES Human
AFFILIATION Formerly Death Watch; Mandalorian resistance
HEIGHT 1.67 m (5 ft 6 in)

Articulated targeting rangefinder

Retractable vibroblade

Activation plate

Bo-Katan's right vambrace can deploy an 18-centimeter (7-inch) tempered beskar blade with an optional vibrational setting that increases its cutting effect.

Interface tiara which connects with internal helmet systems

FOR MANDALORE

Mandalore was briefly poised to shake off Imperial rule with the overthrow of Imperial governor and Mandalorian turncoat Gar Saxon. However, this streak of independence precipitated the Great Purge, which led to a mass exodus that scattered what few Mandalorians remain. Bo-Katan was the last to wield the Darksaber during these times.

Shoulder armor with Nite Owl symbol

Tactical pouches containing compact explosives

Gauntlet-mounted Whistling Bird launcher

Synth-leather gloves

PART II: A NEW QUEST
BO-KATAN'S UNIT

There was a time when Bo-Katan Kryze could have commanded legions of Mandalorians. Now, with her people scattered and their world lost, she can only muster a small team of trusted allies. They believe in her and her cause, joining Kryze in her quest to reclaim the Darksaber from Moff Gideon and to acquire the firepower necessary to retake Mandalore. Axe Woves and Koska Reeves may only be two individuals, but each has the firepower and skill to wreak havoc.

NEW ALLY
Word of a new Mandalorian arrival on Trask draws the attention of Bo-Katan Kryze and her unit. They recruit him to their cause in exchange for the promise of information he seeks: a lead to a Jedi Knight. The Mandalorian joins this elite trio in an attack on an Imperial freighter laden with weaponry that Bo-Katan plans to use in an eventual strike against the larger Imperial remnant.

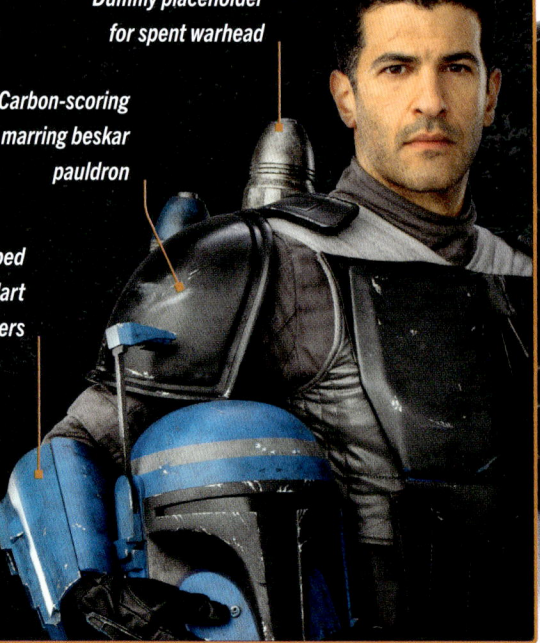

Firing position also communicates tactical moves to partners

Rangefinder in stowed position

AXE WOVES

Kneepad includes dart launchers

Atop the *Razor Crest*, the assembled Mandalorians look out to their prize target, an Imperial Gozanti freighter.

Integral altimeter for high altitude operations
KOSKA REEVES' HELMET

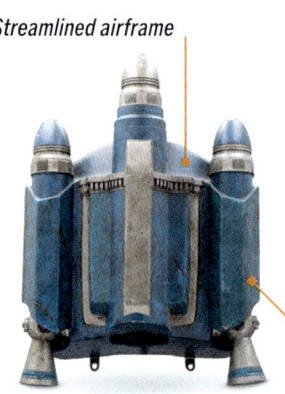
Streamlined airframe
Armored fuel tankage
AXE WOVES' Z-6C2 JETPACK

AXE WOVES
A self-assured warrior who borders on cocky, Axe Woves' confidence is fueled by his marksmanship and his withering opinion of said skill among stormtroopers. Woves is adept at security countermeasures and able to crack Imperial codes with self-made data spikes. Should such technical skullduggery fail, he can blast his way through locked doors.

Dummy placeholder for spent warhead
Carbon-scoring marring beskar pauldron
Vambrace equipped with rocket dart launchers

With a data spike plugged into the external scomp link, Woves opens the emergency airlock seal into the Imperial Gozanti freighter.

TACTICAL TAKEOVER
The Mandalorian infiltrators methodically work their way through the Gozanti freighter, chamber by chamber, clearing each room of Imperial defenders.

A master of hand-to-hand combat, Koska slams multiple Quarren about and flips one over the rail into the deep.

KOSKA REEVES
Koska Reeves is an energetic and agile master of hand-to-hand combat, who has perfected jetpack-assisted dropkicks that send her opponents sprawling. She is not one to look before she leaps, as demonstrated when she dives into a mamacore pen to save the Mandalorian and the Child. She escapes unscathed.

Built-in comlink

Shoulder armor bears Nite Owl sigils

Belt pouches with monomolecular razorwire, garotte, and other silent weapons

Koska inherited her armor from her mother

Synth-leather utility belt with holster

BO-KATAN KRYZE

KOSKA REEVES

Balanced kneeling position for stable fire

PART II: A NEW QUEST

IMPERIAL TARGET

Trask is a black-market port, where the Imperial remnant discreetly transports weaponry and equipment far from the prying eyes of New Republic patrols. Bo-Katan and her unit target an Imperial freighter hauling military-grade small arms and explosives, looking to hijack the shipment for use against the Imperials. It's a four-person job, and the Mandalorian becomes the fourth "pirate" to ambush the ship. Despite being guarded by more than a squad of stormtroopers, the Imperial crew is overwhelmed.

FREIGHTER PILOT
A one-time pit crew member aboard an Imperial Star Destroyer, this lieutenant pines for the glory days of the Empire rather than being stuck behind the controls of a simple freighter.

- Imperial Naval field grays
- Rank code cylinder

DECK OFFICER
The freighter's deck officer watches over the cargo holds of the Gozanti freighter. He commands a squad of stormtroopers to repel any pirates. He makes the fatal error of trapping the Mandalorians in the cargo control area and thus is jettisoned from the cargo bay.

- Officer's cap

FREIGHTER CAPTAIN
Having grown weary of his posting on Trask, this captain longs to return to the Imperial remnant fleet. He longs to prove his worth to Moff Gideon, even if it means sacrificing his life.

- Captain's rank badge
- Holstered SE-14r blaster pistol

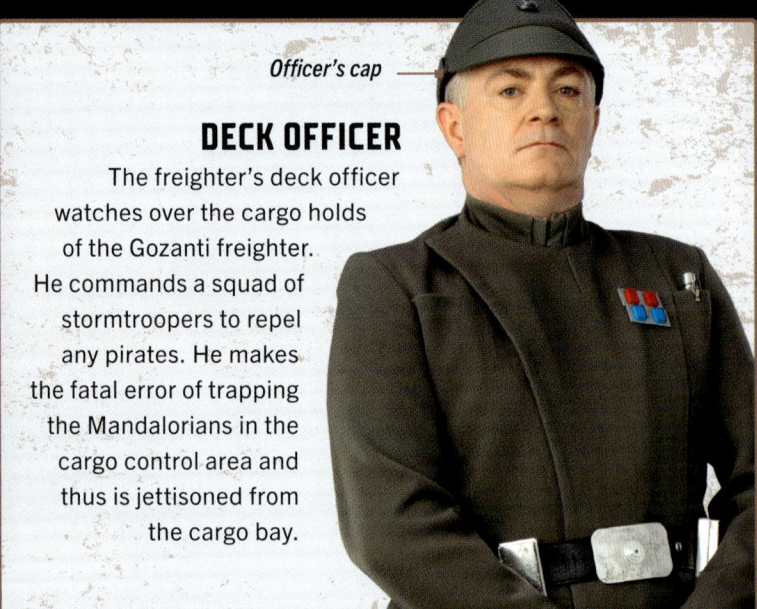

MANDALORIAN PIRATES
As the Gozanti maneuvers out of the shipping zone, it is vulnerable to incursion. The four Mandalorians rocket to its hull with their jetpacks and fight their way past stormtroopers stationed at one of the outer airlock decks. Once aboard, the "pirates" blast onboard security and take over the cargo control area. Captain Tribus, realizing the ship is lost, attempts to scuttle it but is stopped by the Mandalorians. Rather than just steal the Imperial cargo, Bo-Katan absconds with the entire vessel.

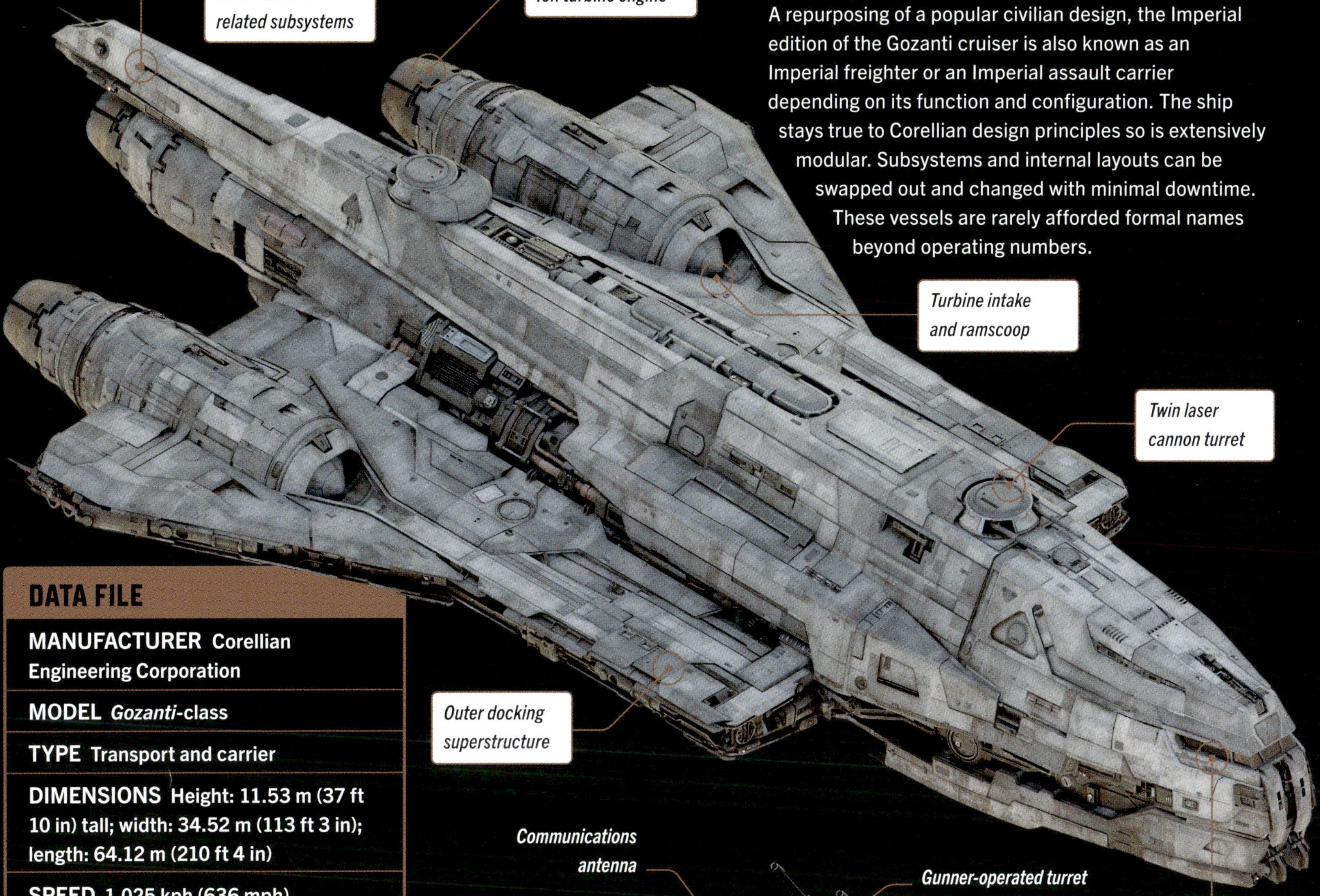

GOZANTI-CLASS CRUISER

A repurposing of a popular civilian design, the Imperial edition of the Gozanti cruiser is also known as an Imperial freighter or an Imperial assault carrier depending on its function and configuration. The ship stays true to Corellian design principles so is extensively modular. Subsystems and internal layouts can be swapped out and changed with minimal downtime. These vessels are rarely afforded formal names beyond operating numbers.

Labels (top view):
- Hyperdrive motivator and related subsystems
- Ion turbine engine
- Turbine intake and ramscoop
- Twin laser cannon turret
- Outer docking superstructure

Labels (front view):
- Communications antenna
- Gunner-operated turret can fire in fixed position from the bridge
- Bridge viewport
- Port stabilizer fin
- Starboard deflector shield emitter
- Articulated docking claw (retracted)
- Medium range active sensor array

FRONT VIEW

DATA FILE

MANUFACTURER Corellian Engineering Corporation

MODEL *Gozanti*-class

TYPE Transport and carrier

DIMENSIONS Height: 11.53 m (37 ft 10 in) tall; width: 34.52 m (113 ft 3 in); length: 64.12 m (210 ft 4 in)

SPEED 1,025 kph (636 mph)

WEAPONS (THIS CONFIGURATION) Three twin laser cannon turrets

AFFILIATION Imperial remnant

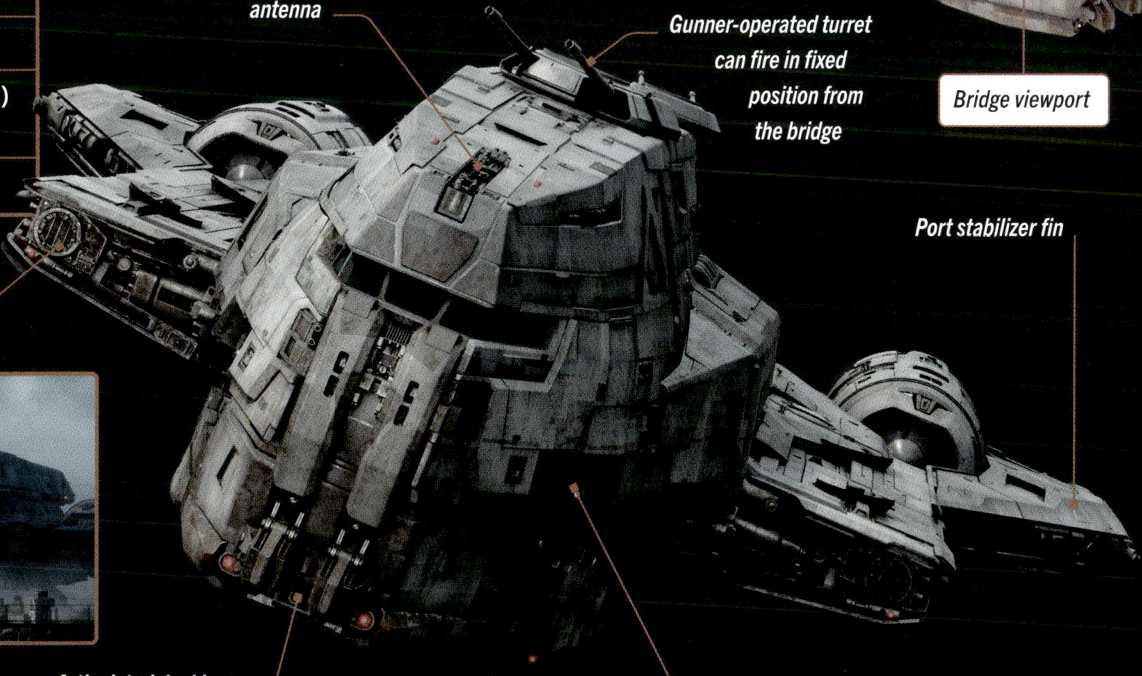

The Trask Gozanti must fly low over the shipping zone to clear the crowded port before gaining altitude to leave the atmosphere.

PART II: A NEW QUEST

NEVARRO REVITALIZED

In Mando's absence from Nevarro, familiar faces have adopted new roles. Greef Karga has regained his title and reputation as magistrate, and his troublesome Mythrol clerk has been reinstated after promising to make restitution. With Mando stuck on Nevarro while the *Razor Crest* is refurbished, he too now gets an opportunity to help clean up the planet.

Karga sees Nevarro and its people as his responsibility. He will not be intimidated by Imperial holdouts or New Republic envoys.

MAGISTRATE KARGA

Greef Karga sees Nevarro's potential to be a trade anchor in the sector if it can be rid of the Imperial outpost and its weaponry. Whereas such goods would undoubtedly bring in a handsome profit on the black market, Greef's primary focus is getting any Imperial traces offworld.

- Ornamental floret over cloak clasp
- Gun belt still necessary
- Magistrate's mantle
- BlasTech PL-42 blaster pistol

The Nevarro landing fields now boast a wider variety of amenities for refueling and restocking visiting ships.

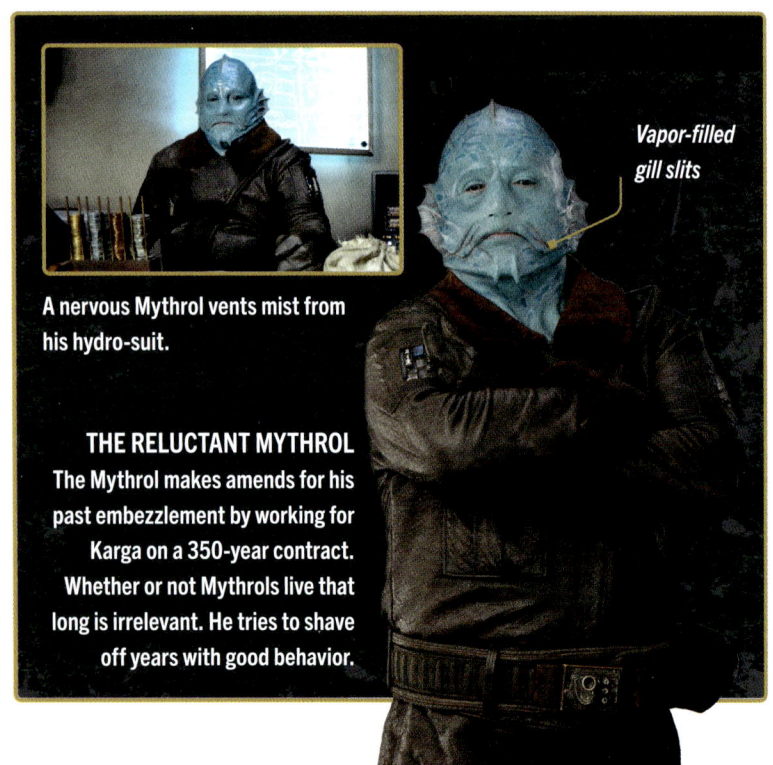

A nervous Mythrol vents mist from his hydro-suit.

- Vapor-filled gill slits

THE RELUCTANT MYTHROL

The Mythrol makes amends for his past embezzlement by working for Karga on a 350-year contract. Whether or not Mythrols live that long is irrelevant. He tries to shave off years with good behavior.

THE SCHOOL

The Crossroads Common House was nearly obliterated during Mando's standoff against Moff Gideon, but the structure was refurbished and has found new life as a schoolhouse. The normally transient visitors to Nevarro now find reasons to stay, as the children in their care can spend worthwhile time learning the basics of a good galactic education. Protocol droid CB-3DU teaches a lesson about the major hyperspace lanes of the galaxy to a classful of subadults, including the Child—who is more interested in a packet of Nevarro nummies.

- Refurbished dropper pauldrons
- Distinctive pentagonal shape
- Raised starbird crest
- M-32 light repeating blaster
- Hunting knife within reach

NEW REPUBLIC MARSHAL BADGE

MARSHAL DUNE

Cara Dune has cleaned up Nevarro's criminal underbelly, deputizing assistants when required but preferring to operate alone. Captain Carson Teva extends an invitation for Cara to join the fledgling New Republic law enforcement efforts in this area of the Outer Rim, which she considers.

- Noise-canceling headset
- Insulated worker's uniform

PORT MECHANIC

This Mimbanese dock worker is in secret contact with the Imperial remnant. In exchange for the promise of credits, he plants a tracking device on the *Razor Crest*.

PART II: A NEW QUEST

IMPERIAL BASE

Located far beyond the canyon capital city of Nevarro is an outpost that dates back to the original Imperial expansion into the sector. Initially thought to be a forward operating base, Greef Karga's fragmented intelligence reveals that it is not quite abandoned and is in fact maintained by a skeleton crew. It was from this outpost that Moff Gideon's reinforcements arrived during the standoff at the Crossroads Common House. Karga recruits Mando to help investigate and destroy the base.

> "IT'S GOT A SKELETON CREW, BUT FOR SOME REASON, IT HASN'T BEEN ABANDONED."
> – MARSHAL CARA DUNE

The rooftop launching pad services a flight of four TIE fighters, which scramble to pursue trespassers.

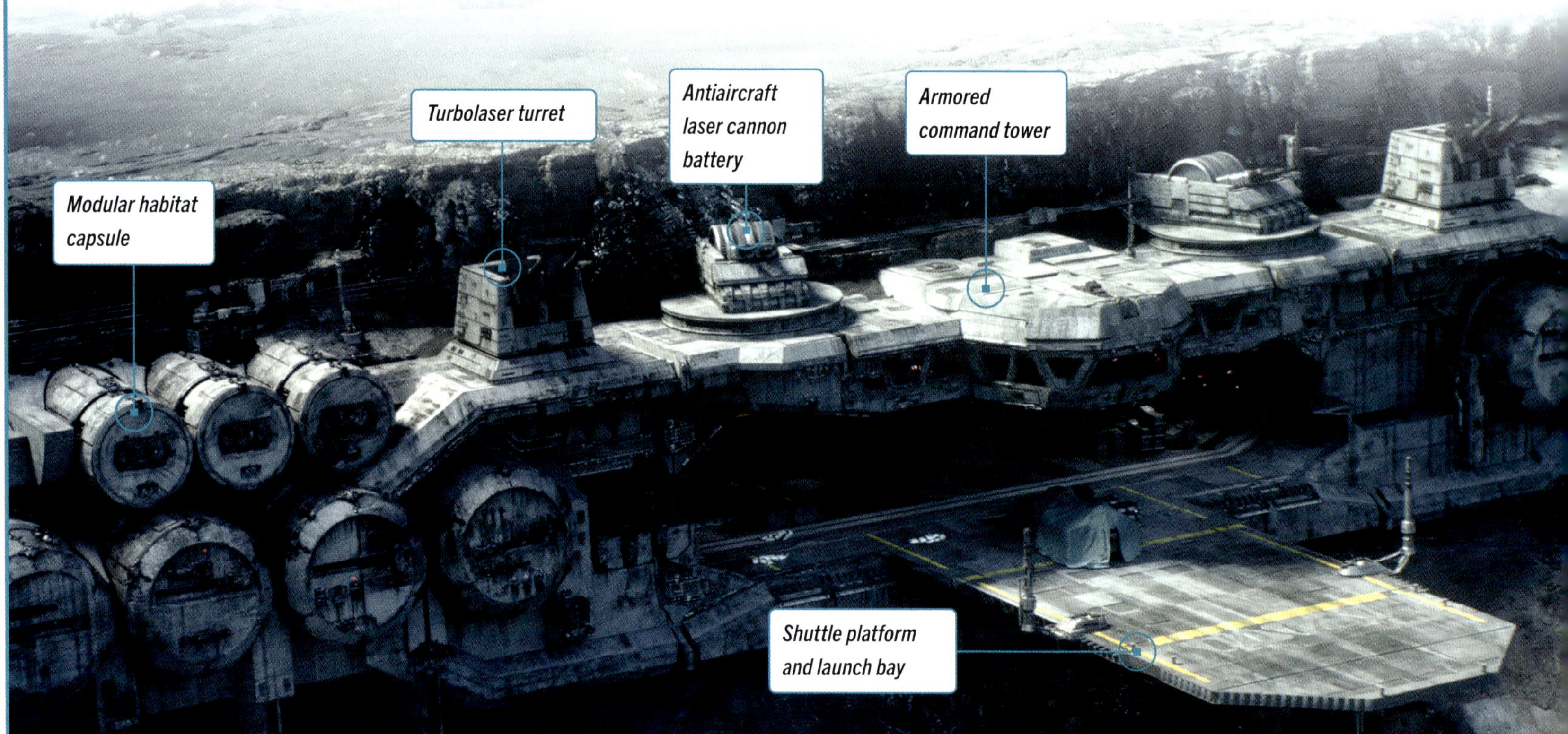

- Modular habitat capsule
- Turbolaser turret
- Antiaircraft laser cannon battery
- Armored command tower
- Shuttle platform and launch bay

LOCAL GARRISON

The Imperial emphasis on standardized, modular design has caused the Nevarro base to face local environmental challenges. Some of the outer doors are not rated to withstand the planet's recurring lava tides. For other threats, an abbreviated contingent of personnel secure the base's perimeter with speeder bike and TIE fighter patrols.

CRITICAL REACTOR

Powering the base is a fusion reactor set into a natural heat shaft. Shielded coolant lines keep the reactor at its optimal operational temperature. Once the Mythrol slices into the controls and shuts off the lines, the reactor goes critical in about 10 minutes.

SECRET PURPOSE

The deeper Karga, Dune, Mando, and the Mythrol penetrate into the outpost, the more its malevolent purpose is revealed. It is not a forward military base, but rather a laboratory staffed by Imperial science officers. A pair of harried scientists desperately purge the data drives to keep the top-secret project classified, but they do not finish. It becomes clear that a cloning operation is underway, and a recording by Doctor Pershing intended for Moff Gideon reveals the Child's blood is rich in midi-chlorians. These discoveries are essential ingredients in this Imperial plot. Ghastly bodies suspended in nutrient baths reveal that this Imperial remnant is implementing outlawed cloning processes to unknown ends.

OVERLOAD
The Mythrol's tampering detonates the base's reactor, which erupts in a fiery blast that ravages the canyon. Several TIE fighters manage to take to the air in time to continue pursuit of the Trexler Marauder.

The TIE fighter flight continues its pursuit even as the escaping Trexler Marauder weaves its way through a narrow canyon.

TREXLER MARAUDER

A short-lived offshoot of the ITT Imperial personnel carrier, the Trexler Marauder is a vehicle-to-vehicle combat-oriented armored speeder. It is considered a collector's item on the black market due to its relative rarity. The passenger section of the standard ITT has been replaced with an enlarged power plant that feeds the expanded weapons loadout.

The turret's sophisticated sensor array visualizes incoming targets.

DATA FILE

MANUFACTURER Ubrikkian Industries

MODEL Trexler Marauder 906

TYPE Armored combat vehicle

DIMENSIONS Height: 2.47 m (8 ft 1 in); width: 3.85 m (12 ft 8 in); length: 8.69 m (28 ft 6 in)

SPEED 150 kph (93 mph)

WEAPONS 2 dorsal laser cannons in turret, 2 forward fixed laser cannons, 2 drum-mounted forward twin laser cannons

AFFILIATION Imperial remnant

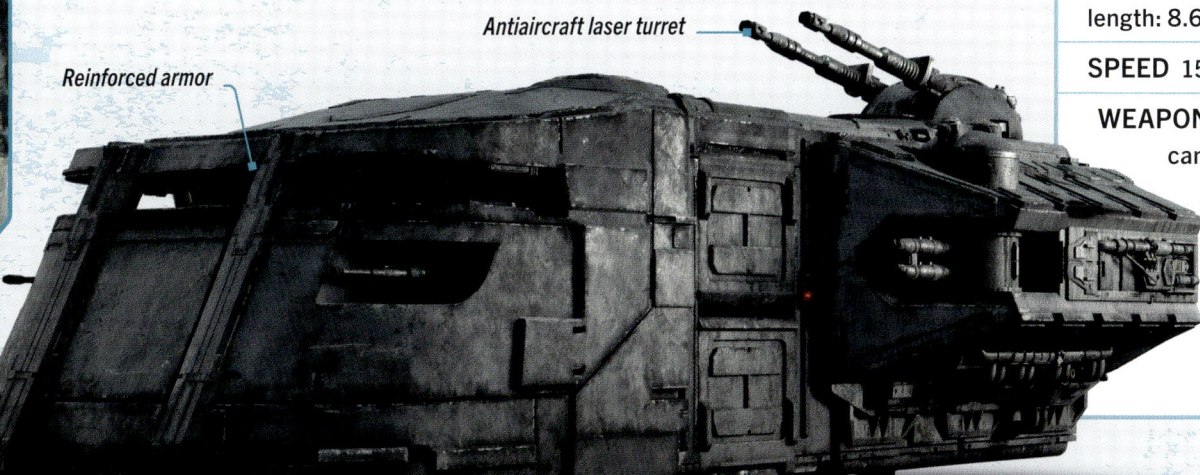

Antiaircraft laser turret

Reinforced armor

PART II: A NEW QUEST

CORVUS

Corvus was at one time a verdant forest world, but conflict and hunger for power has burned much of its vegetation. Scorched forests stand as stark skeletal remains emanating from blackened soil, and rampant mining operations have choked the planet's air with an ever-present fog. The New Republic has no presence on Corvus, which allows the wicked Magistrate Morgan Elsbeth to expand her Imperial-era military manufacturing program. She cruelly subjugates Corvus' citizens in her thirst for power and control. The Mandalorian arrives on Corvus, seeking out a Jedi to train the Child.

Lowing forest-walkers strip what nutrition they can from the charred trunks, which once were bountiful trees covered with fruits and flowers.

WING

A one-time respected community leader in Calodan, Wing is a shadow of his former self, forced to cower in his dwelling to avoid the attention of the magistrate's forces. He surreptitiously helps what citizens he can, avoiding the ire of the guards. At the behest of the townsfolk, Wing takes the magistrate's mantle upon Elsbeth's defeat.

- Magistrate's mantle clasps
- Worker's belt

DATA FILE

REGION	Outer Rim
SECTOR	Cronese Mandate
SYSTEM	Corvus
DIAMETER	6,821 km (4,238 miles)
TERRAIN	Burned forest; low foothills; cracked crust
MOONS	1
POPULATION	3.7 million

- Refurbished Razor Crest makes planetfall
- Port city of Calodan
- Low cloud cover
- Geothermal vents ruptured by unrestrained mining operations

> "NOT MUCH TO SEE OUT HERE… LET'S HEAD INTO TOWN. SEE IF WE CAN PICK UP A LEAD."
> – THE MANDALORIAN TO THE CHILD

Knowing well the Child's appetite, Mando approaches a skittish gorg vendor on Calodan's main street.

CITIZENS OF CALODAN
Calodanians live in fear of the magistrate and her cruel enforcers. What visible faces appear are grim and weary, but most are hidden behind rebreather masks and goggles to survive in the poisoned air.

- *Rebreather mask*
- *Calloused hands in worn work gloves*
- *Baggy clothing hides emaciated build*

CALODAN
The walled city of Calodan stinks of industry and despair. The smokestacks of the mining operation dust all of Calodan with layers of soot that drain the city's vibrancy. Exhausted Calodanians toil in mines or in metalsmithing operations. The path to the magistrate's residence is lined by townsfolk bound to electro-poles in a cruel display of their ruler's capriciousness.

The main gate cupola contains a massive iron bell that chimes at the magistrate's order.

- *Central starport signal beacon*
- *Magistrate's residence*
- *Parapet guard on alert for intruders*
- *Struggling localized air purifier*

PART II: A NEW QUEST
RULE OF THE MAGISTRATE

> From behind her guards, Morgan Elsbeth rules Corvus, stripping the world of its valuable resources. She relies on the compassion of the Calodanians to work against them. They do not wish to see their fellow townsfolk suffer, so she keeps captives on public display to warn all about the price of disloyalty.

Magistrate Elsbeth is bedeviled by a Jedi—or at least, what appears to be a Jedi. The lightsaber-wielding warrior has been stalking her, for Elsbeth is rumored to have information on the whereabouts of the legendary Imperial warlord Grand Admiral Thrawn. The former Jedi Ahsoka Tano seeks Thrawn, the result of some unfinished business from years earlier.

Though a capable warrior herself, Elsbeth knows not to underestimate a Jedi. When the Mandalorian arrives at Calodan, also seeking the Jedi, Elsbeth offers a bounty on Ahsoka's capture: a prize sure to draw a Mandalorian's attention.

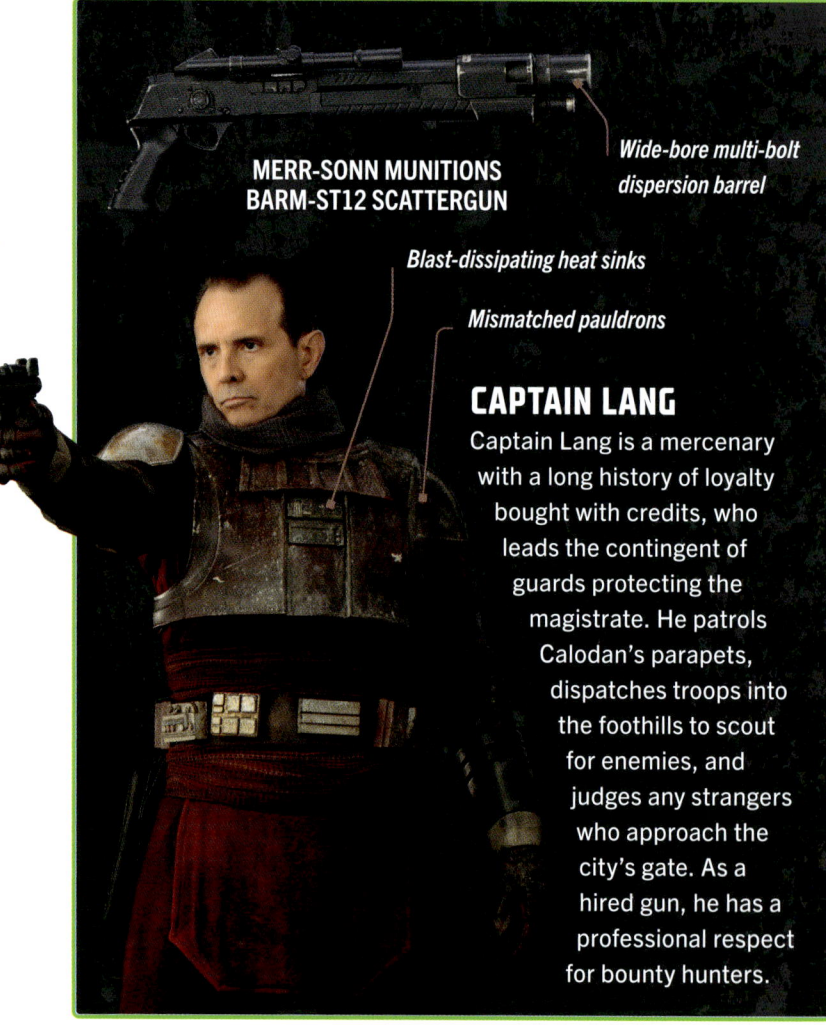

MERR-SONN MUNITIONS BARM-ST12 SCATTERGUN
- Wide-bore multi-bolt dispersion barrel
- Blast-dissipating heat sinks
- Mismatched pauldrons

CAPTAIN LANG
Captain Lang is a mercenary with a long history of loyalty bought with credits, who leads the contingent of guards protecting the magistrate. He patrols Calodan's parapets, dispatches troops into the foothills to scout for enemies, and judges any strangers who approach the city's gate. As a hired gun, he has a professional respect for bounty hunters.

- Armored sensor unit
- Power cell belt
- Highly dexterous digits
- Weighted tibia for stability

HK-87 ASSASSIN DROIDS
A pair of HK assassin droids decorated with half-cloaks serve as bodyguards to the magistrate. Their limbs provide spring-loaded agility, and their antiquated vocoders squawk in guttural Huttese.

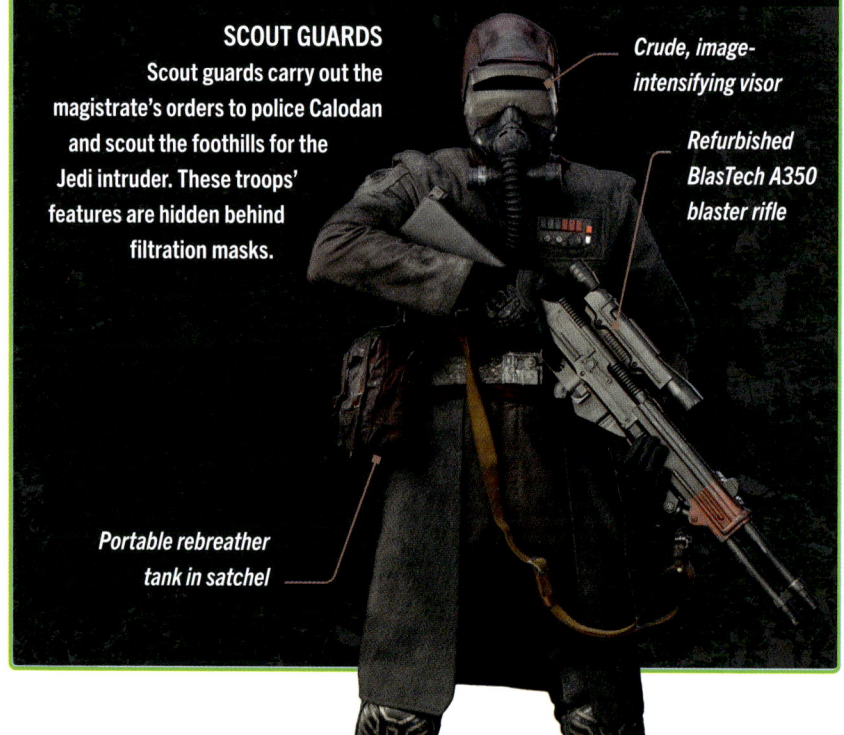

SCOUT GUARDS
Scout guards carry out the magistrate's orders to police Calodan and scout the foothills for the Jedi intruder. These troops' features are hidden behind filtration masks.

- Crude, image-intensifying visor
- Refurbished BlasTech A350 blaster rifle
- Portable rebreather tank in satchel

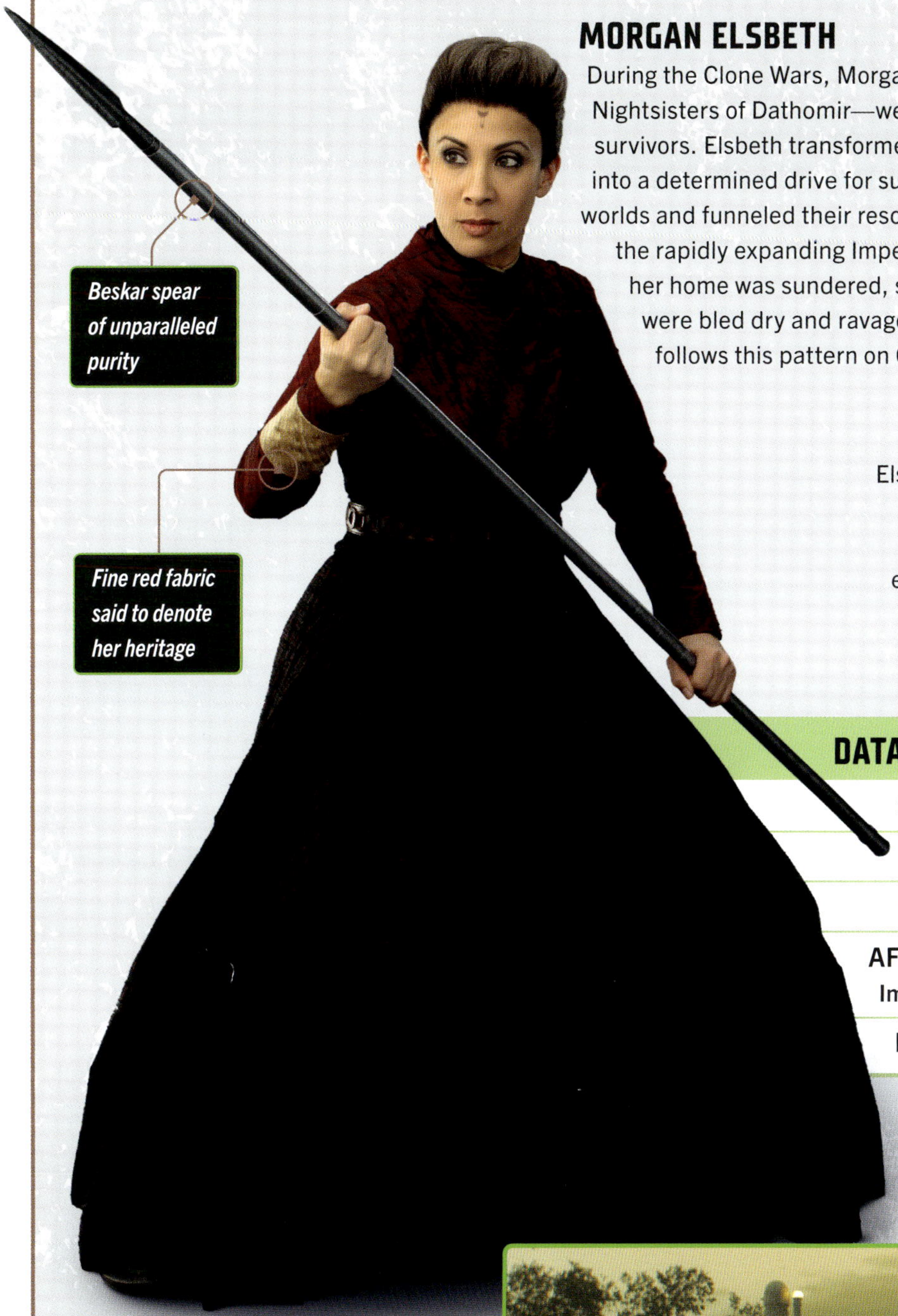

MORGAN ELSBETH

During the Clone Wars, Morgan Elsbeth's people—the Nightsisters of Dathomir—were massacred, leaving few survivors. Elsbeth transformed her sense of loss and outrage into a determined drive for survival. She led the subjugation of worlds and funneled their resources in a manner that benefited the rapidly expanding Imperial fleet. In much the same way her home was sundered, she left entire worlds behind that were bled dry and ravaged for their resources. Elsbeth follows this pattern on Corvus.

Angular blade

Beskar spear of unparalleled purity

Fine red fabric said to denote her heritage

BESKAR SPEAR

Elsbeth wields a spear of beskar which rings with distilled purity when the Mandalorian taps it against his armor. Elsbeth's energetic fighting style combines a variety of exotic forms—Echani firefist, Dathomiri mistdance, and Coruscanti hijkata—making her a truly challenging opponent for Ahsoka Tano.

DATA FILE

SUBJECT	Morgan Elsbeth
HOMEWORLD	Corvus; Dathomir
SPECIES	Human
AFFILIATION	Former Nightsister; former Imperial; loyal to Grand Admiral Thrawn
HEIGHT	1.63 m (5 ft 4 in)

Beskar shaft

The magistrate's opulent residence abuts a serene courtyard lush with greenery that has not been poisoned by the choking elements. A long, low stone bridge splits a tranquil reflecting pool filled with exotic fish.

PART II: A NEW QUEST
AHSOKA TANO

A survivor of much galactic and personal upheaval, Ahsoka Tano walks her own path as the Force directs her. Over the decades, this meandering trek has woven in and out of major events in the galaxy and also kept her hidden. Though she abandoned her standing as a Jedi, freedom from the old orthodoxies has caused Ahsoka to more fully embody what it is to serve the Force and to be a guardian of peace and justice.

As a child, Ahsoka was part of the last generation of the original Jedi Order. During the Clone Wars, she was apprenticed to the Knight Anakin Skywalker, learning much at his side. The travails of the conflict caused her to depart from the Jedi, as she grew disillusioned with an Order so steeped in the machinations of galactic politics.

She narrowly avoided the devastating fallout of Order 66, keeping a low profile while aiding the burgeoning rebellion. Ahsoka worked as an agent code-named Fulcrum, uniting disparate rebel cells before the formation of the Rebel Alliance. She was of great assistance to the early efforts of Phoenix Squadron and the Spectres.

SHADOWS OF THE PAST
A shadow haunts Ahsoka: the knowledge of the fate of her former master. For much of her youth she admired and emulated Anakin Skywalker, impressed by his prowess and spirit. It was heartbreaking for her to discover that so seasoned a Jedi could succumb to the dark side of the Force, driven over the precipice by selfish attachment. She recognizes the danger of such temptations.

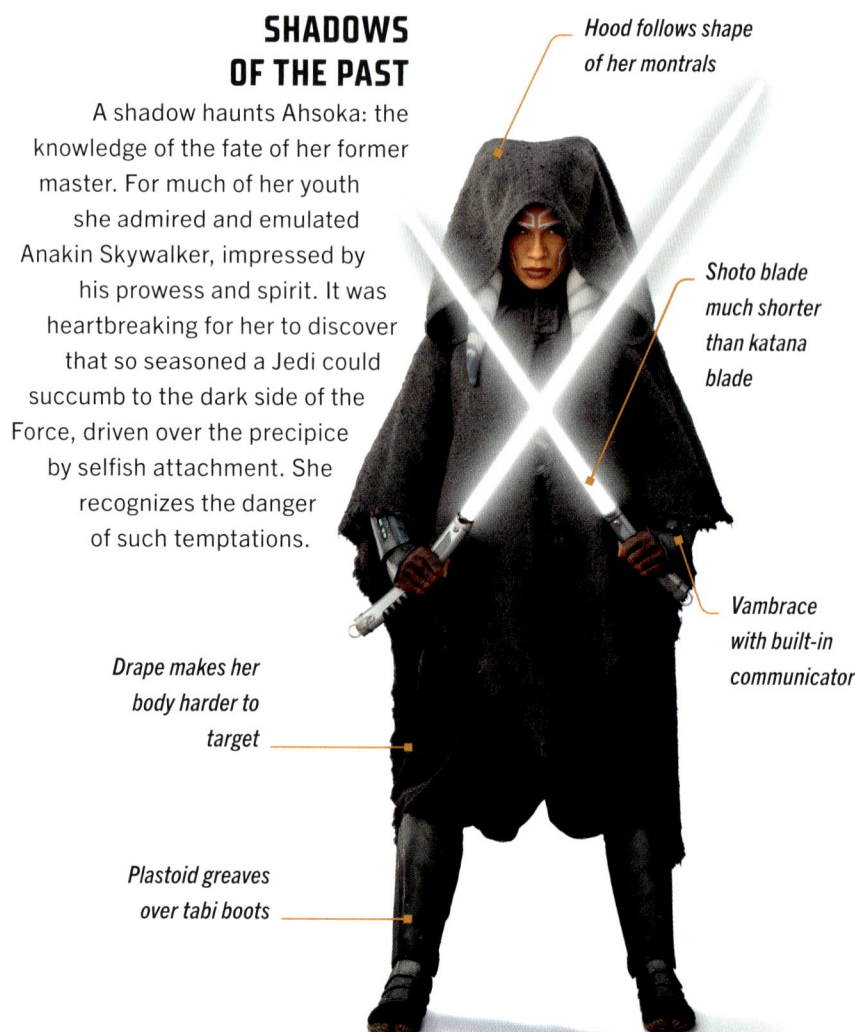

- Hood follows shape of her montrals
- Shoto blade much shorter than katana blade
- Vambrace with built-in communicator
- Drape makes her body harder to target
- Plastoid greaves over tabi boots

AHSOKA'S LIGHTSABERS
During Ahsoka's apprenticeship, Anakin Skywalker crafted for her paired lightsabers meant to extend her reach and maximize her defense against larger foes. She has continued with this form, though her old Jedi blades are long gone. Ahsoka's current lightsabers have pure white blades, the result of specially bonded kyber crystals attuned to her nature.

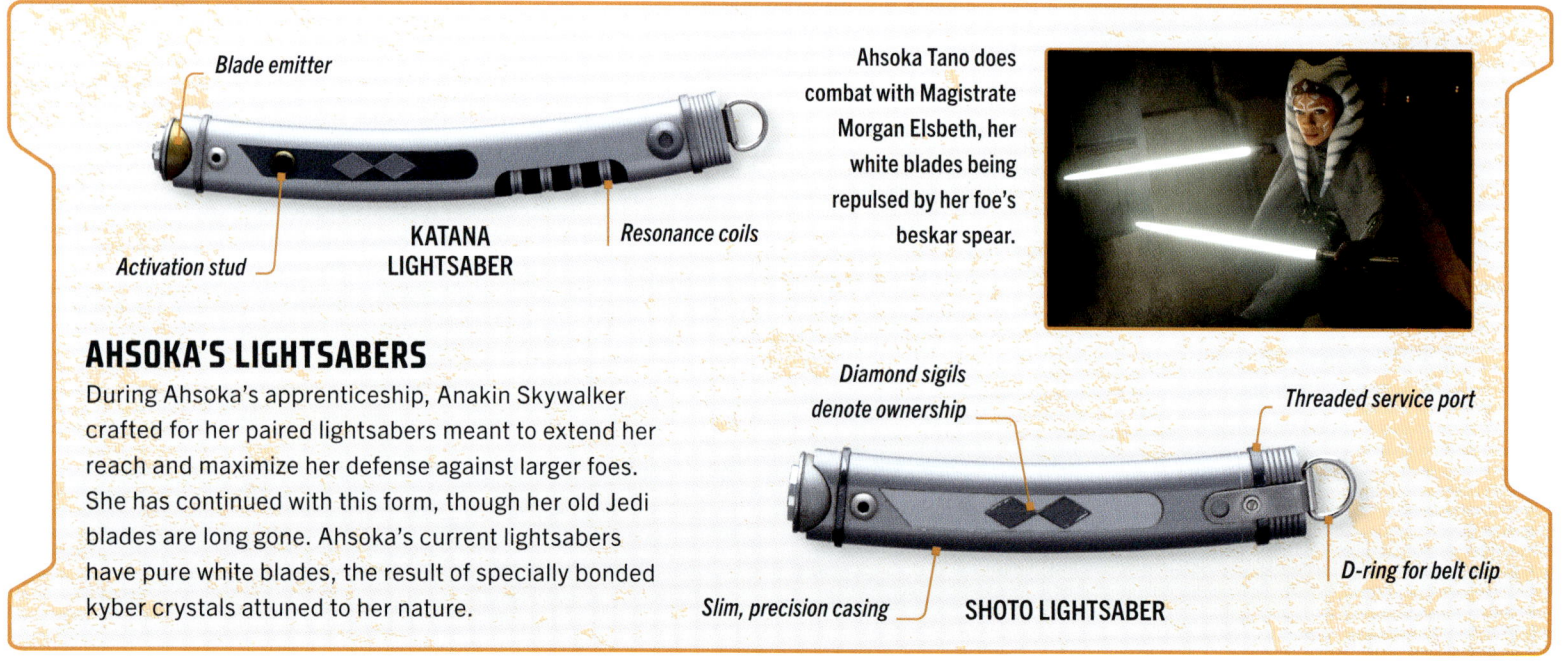

KATANA LIGHTSABER — Blade emitter, Activation stud, Resonance coils

Ahsoka Tano does combat with Magistrate Morgan Elsbeth, her white blades being repulsed by her foe's beskar spear.

SHOTO LIGHTSABER — Diamond sigils denote ownership, Threaded service port, D-ring for belt clip, Slim, precision casing

141

DATA FILE
- **SUBJECT** Ahsoka Tano
- **HOMEWORLD** Raised on Coruscant
- **SPECIES** Togruta
- **AFFILIATION** Former Jedi
- **HEIGHT** 1.76 m (5 ft 9 in)

Headdress

Natural Togruta markings

Togruta lekku

Reverse grip favored since Padawan days

Longer blade held in dominant hand

Katana lightsaber hilt

Belt buckle with arcane carvings

Fabric marked with ancient Jedi glyphs

CONNECTION WITH GROGU
After connecting through the Force, Ahsoka learns more about the Child. His name is Grogu, and he once trained at the Jedi Temple on Coruscant as a Jedi youngling. He has spent decades in hiding, concealing his abilities for survival. Grogu has a strong attachment to the Mandalorian, so Ahsoka refuses to train him.

Ahsoka has only met one other being of Grogu's species—the wise Jedi Master Yoda.

> "I LIKE FIRSTS. GOOD OR BAD, THEY'RE ALWAYS MEMORABLE."
> – AHSOKA TANO

PART II: A NEW QUEST
TYTHON

Tython is an ancient world kept relatively inaccessible by decrepit navigational data, dense stellar clusters, and a lack of commercial interest. The planet is shrouded in mystery and steeped in history. Some scholars contend that the Jedi Order was founded there, but the immense gulf of time between that era and the modern age makes it impossible to prove. For those sensitive to its presence, Tython is said to be strong in the Force. Ahsoka Tano advises Mando to bring Grogu here.

RETURN FROM THE DUNES
Tython proves to be a place where both the ancient and recent past come to life for Mando. Fennec Shand, believed killed by Toro Calican and left to rot in the Dune Sea, proves to be very much alive and paired with another legend who cheated death: Boba Fett. The two are in partnership as Fett seeks to restore his position in the galactic underworld. Fett recovered Shand's wounded body and ensured that she was given life-saving cybernetic implants to put her back into action.

Decades-old battle helmet

Shand's gear does not overly restrict her agility

A concealed homing beacon on the *Razor Crest* draws Imperial troops to Tython, their presence a violation of a sacred site.

A leather wrap conceals Fennec's restorative implants.

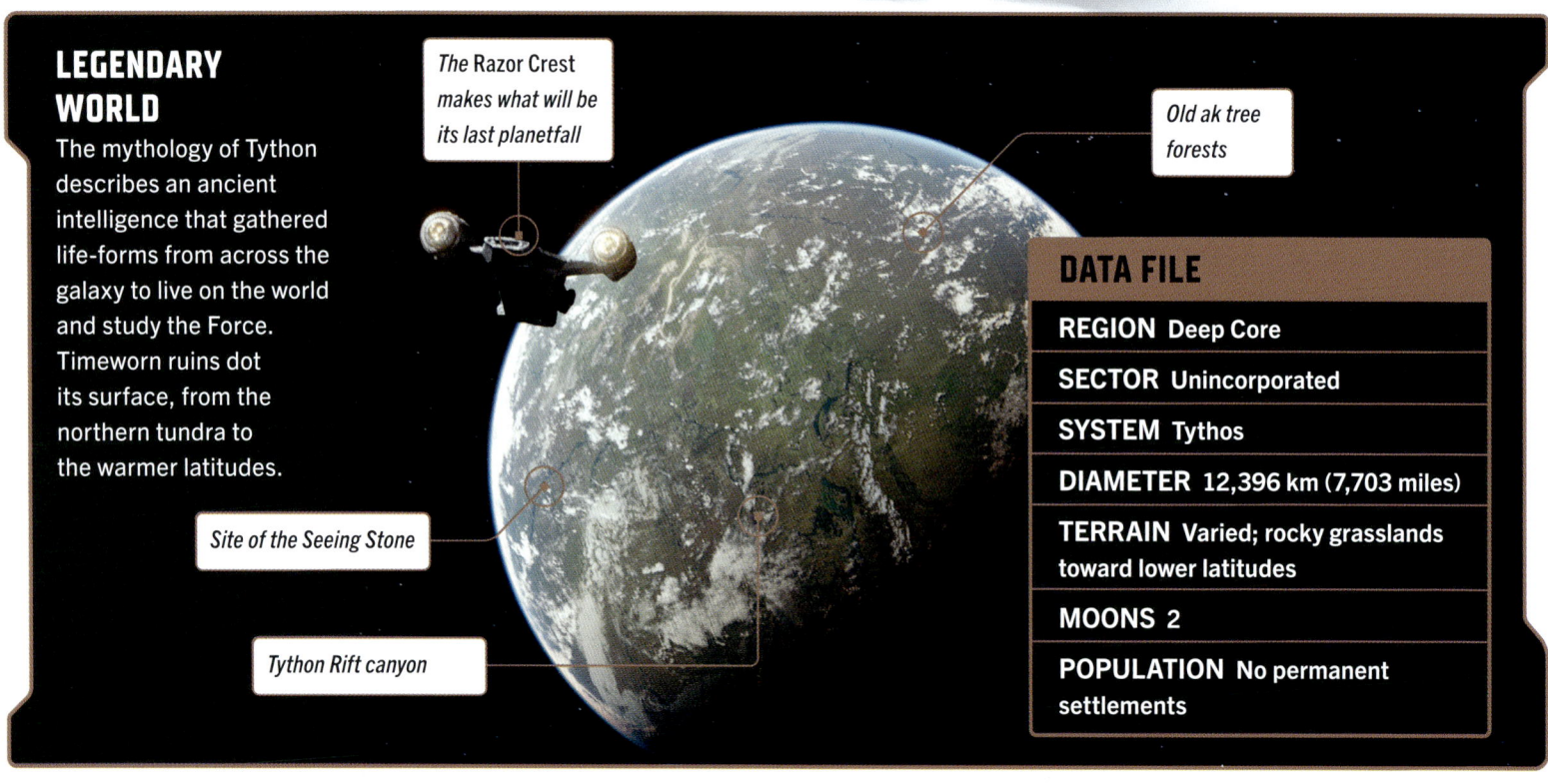

LEGENDARY WORLD
The mythology of Tython describes an ancient intelligence that gathered life-forms from across the galaxy to live on the world and study the Force. Timeworn ruins dot its surface, from the northern tundra to the warmer latitudes.

The Razor Crest makes what will be its last planetfall

Old ak tree forests

Site of the Seeing Stone

Tython Rift canyon

DATA FILE
REGION	Deep Core
SECTOR	Unincorporated
SYSTEM	Tythos
DIAMETER	12,396 km (7,703 miles)
TERRAIN	Varied; rocky grasslands toward lower latitudes
MOONS	2
POPULATION	No permanent settlements

THE CALL

Ancient temples that predate even the Jedi Order dot many worlds across the galaxy and were at one time the subject of detailed study by Jedi archaeologists. The Seeing Stone of Tython is tens of millennia old, but the unusual properties of the stone and surrounding area confound attempts at accurate scientific dating.

A column of focused, visible Force energy

Eroded Loop of the Sages path to the Seeing Stone

Sedimentary rock outcropping

THE SEEING STONE

The stelae of the Seeing Stone temple concentrate the Force, enhancing and magnifying the living energy of Tython.

Stela known as Sixth Brother according to some translations

Inner circle, said to describe the Galactic Core

Mathematically aligned angle maintained by support megalith

Dome believed to represent Tython

Mando brings Grogu to the ancient site

PART II: A NEW QUEST
BOBA FETT

Boba Fett inherited much from his father, Jango—the reputation as the best bounty hunter in the galaxy and the Mandalorian armor that helped cement such esteem. The younger Fett seemingly lost it all when fortune turned against him, and he plummeted into a Sarlacc's gullet during an attempt to execute Luke Skywalker and his companions. The Sarlacc found Fett somewhat indigestible—the nigh indestructible armor helped Fett escape the beast but at great cost. By the time he had healed, Fett found his armor gone and his reputation vanished, washed away by the upheaval sweeping the galaxy.

Most assumed that Boba had died, and in a manner, he did. The old Boba, who chased after bounties for the highest bidder and let the armored mask be his face, had to adapt. Such endurance was in his genes, as he was a perfect duplicate of Jango Fett created by the best cloners on Kamino. In a galaxy where the original age-accelerated soldiers of the Clone Wars were dwindling in number, Boba became the last vestige of Jango Fett's legacy.

Twin suns set over the land that Boba has called home for years, but it is a new dawn for the next phase of his life.

- Bacta therapy cannot erase acid burns
- Bantha-fiber wool coverings
- Gaderffii i-ravu head
- Tusken cycler rifle
- Leather belt with stowed slugthrower ammunition
- Protective gloves

AFTER THE PIT
"New pain and suffering" is a memorable description of the ordeal of being fed to the Sarlacc at the Pit of Carkoon, and Boba Fett is a rare example of a survivor who could testify to its accuracy. Not that the laconic Fett gives much word to this life-altering moment of torment and vulnerability, but that he has emerged speaks volumes. His body and mind bear the scars of the Sarlacc's digestive process.

FAMILY HISTORY
Boba activates a hologram displaying the provenance of his armor, his chain code perfectly matched to its previous owner, Jango Fett. Jango fought in the Mandalorian Civil War, giving Boba—in accordance to certain Mandalorian orthodoxies—status as a foundling.

Reunited with his armor, Boba Fett unleashes wrath against Imperial remnant stormtroopers on Tython.

Variable payload rocket launcher

Power and control linkages sheathed in flexible cable

Refurbished jetpack with reinforced ignition system

Kessler DB-41 blaster pistol sidearm

Binary encoder activation node

Rangefinder power conduit

T-visor with macroscopic viewplate

DATA FILE
SUBJECT	Boba Fett
HOMEWORLD	Kamino
SPECIES	Human (clone)
AFFILIATION	Independent
HEIGHT	1.75 m (5 ft 9 in)

> "I'M A SIMPLE MAN MAKING MY WAY THROUGH THE GALAXY, LIKE MY FATHER BEFORE ME."
> – BOBA FETT

Utility belt with ammunition and armor tools

Right vambrace with cable launcher

WSM1N1 macroscope

NEW BEGINNINGS
Ever the hunter, Fett is tracking down pieces of his legacy—including his armor. It is the last set of armor worn by Jango Fett and has decades of battle scarring as testament to its storied past. After Cobb Vanth gave the armor to the Mandalorian, Fett shadowed Djarin to reclaim it.

PART II: A NEW QUEST
BOBA FETT'S EQUIPMENT

Returning from the Sarlacc pit with nothing to his name, Boba Fett has proved his mettle. His legend may be inextricably tied to armor and equipment, but Fett's effectiveness is not dependent on these tools and is now further tempered by hardship. Having recovered his father's armor from the *Razor Crest*, Fett is terrifyingly lethal against stormtrooper reinforcements rushing Tython, deploying his arsenal of weaponry against them.

Roaming Jawas scavenged Fett's armor, unaware of its importance. Later, Cobb Vanth negotiated its purchase for silicax crystals.

"FATE SOMETIMES STEPS IN TO RESCUE THE WRETCHED."
– BOBA FETT

- Paint from starship hold supplies
- Jerba-leather cummerbund
- Tatooine garb now resembles a traditional kama

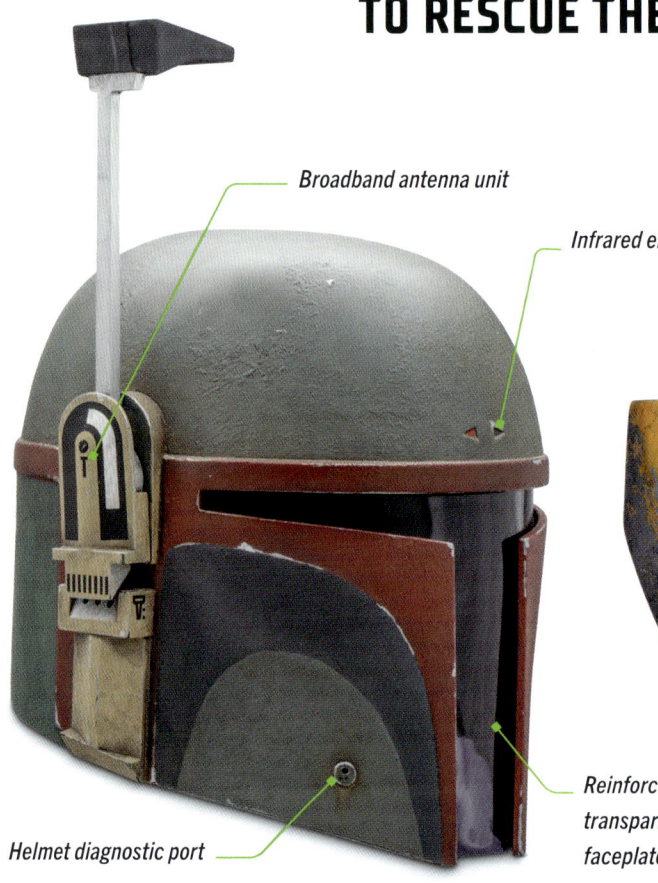

- Broadband antenna unit
- Infrared emitter nodes
- Helmet diagnostic port
- Reinforced transparisteel faceplate

REFURBISHED AND READY
As Fett never walked the traditional Mandalorian path, he relied on his inherited tools and handiwork to keep his armor in shape rather than the tools and wisdom of an Armorer. His armor has durasteel composite pieces and a mix of finishes, so is not as pure as Djarin's predominantly beskar set. Boba has recoated the battered suit, as well as resetting and fortifying its electronic and computerized systems.

- Faded sigil of the fabled mythosaur

LEFT PAULDRON

- Armor control systems line glove

PROTECTIVE GLOVES

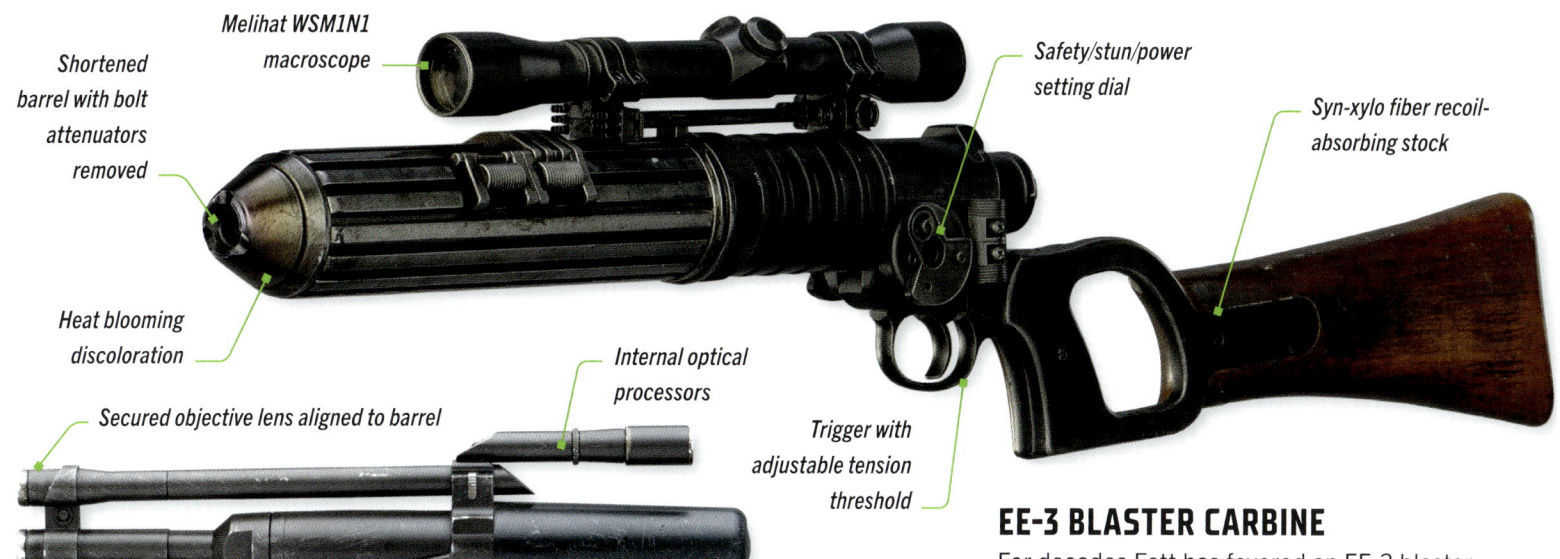

- Shortened barrel with bolt attenuators removed
- Melihat WSM1N1 macroscope
- Safety/stun/power setting dial
- Syn-xylo fiber recoil-absorbing stock
- Heat blooming discoloration
- Internal optical processors
- Trigger with adjustable tension threshold
- Secured objective lens aligned to barrel
- Lasing chamber
- Gas intermix chamber
- Compact power cell in handle
- Low ammunition warning indicator

KESSLER DB-41 BLASTER PISTOL

Once a consumer-grade sporting pistol, this DB-41 has had its power caps clipped and its barrel circuitry resynchronized to increase its lethality. It is rugged, cheap, and lightweight—making for fast draws.

EE-3 BLASTER CARBINE

For decades Fett has favored an EE-3 blaster carbine, having witnessed Zabrak bounty hunter Sugi effectively use one during a shootout at Serolonis. A common modification to the blaster involves shortening the barrel, which cuts its range but increases its firepower. Fett's previous EE-3 was sheared in two during a battle with Luke Skywalker. He finds a replacement among Mando's arsenal aboard the *Razor Crest*.

No longer reliant on advanced technology, Boba has become accustomed to the simple Tusken cycler rifle and its basic optical scope.

LEFT VAMBRACE
- Rocket launcher
- Built-in blaster

WARHEAD
- Guidance fins

ROCKET ATTACKS

Boba's armor includes projectile launchers capable of bypassing defenses designed for energy weapons. His jetpack has a variable payload rocket launcher, while his gauntlet and kneepads are capable of firing simple ballistic flechettes.

GADERFFII ATTACK

In the hands of a Tusken, a gaderffii is a fearsome weapon, able to dispense crushing damage against foes. Settlers on Tatooine commonly call it a gaffi stick, unaware of the cultural details of those they dismissively call "Sand People." Boba respects the nomadic group and has come to appreciate their ways.

Boba Fett hand-crafted his gaderffii using sacred Tusken techniques after embarking on a vision quest while recuperating within a tribe.

BOBA FETT'S GADERFFII
- Ax blade of tempered steel
- Wrapped shaft ensures secure grip
- Weighted club head with stabbing blade

Following an already lethal assault, the darts fired from Boba's kneepads cause the stormtroopers that survive to flee in terror.

PART II: A NEW QUEST
BOBA FETT'S STARSHIP

Boba Fett's modified *Firespray*-class pursuit ship has a distinctive ovoid silhouette, which is a fearsome sight on any fugitive's sensor screens. It has, like its pilot, been given a new lease on life. Recovered from the palace of Jabba the Hutt on Tatooine, the craft is back under Fett's control and is instrumental in his return to the galactic underworld. It has a long history, starting from its days as Jango Fett's ship.

FETT IN CONTROL
Fett learned the basics of starship operation sitting next to his father as Jango piloted the Firespray craft. After Jango's death, bounty hunter Aurra Sing took to piloting the craft before losing the ship to pirate Hondo Ohnaka. Boba Fett would reclaim it once he started his own bounty-hunting career.

The Firespray vessel has an impressive operational range and navicomputer, its hyperdrive swiftly delivering it from Tatooine to the ancient world of Tython.

"LOWER YOUR SHIELDS, DISENGAGE ALL TRANSPONDERS, PREPARE FOR BOARDING."
– BOBA FETT TO AN IMPERIAL SHUTTLE CREW

LANDING CONFIGURATION
The Firespray design is instantly recognizable for its contrasting orientations in landing and flight operations. The ship rests on its engines when grounded and then tilts 90 degrees when flying. The cockpit defaults to match the flight profile (meaning the pilot lies on his back when landed), but the interior passenger cabin rotates to always keep its inhabitants "upright."

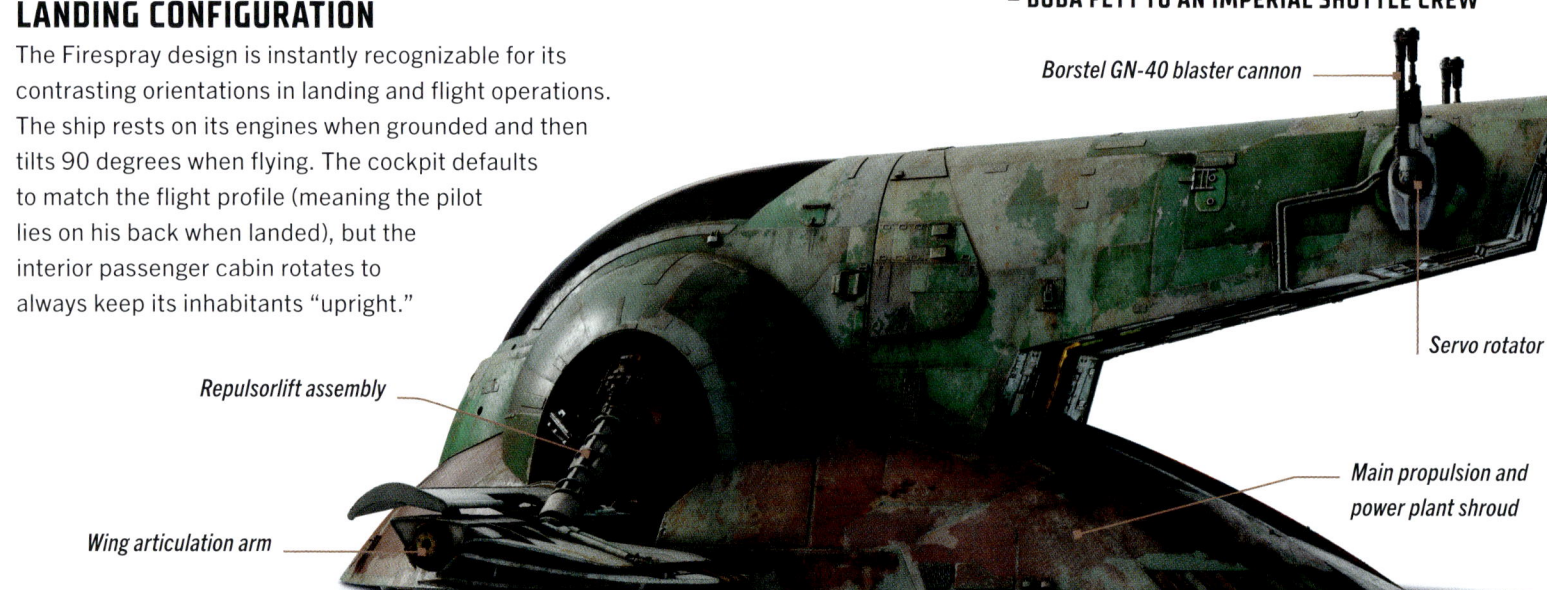

Borstel GN-40 blaster cannon

Servo rotator

Main propulsion and power plant shroud

Repulsorlift assembly

Wing articulation arm

Cockpit and passenger deck canopy

Finned repulsor units for landing maneuvers

Boom arms lock into flight position

Concealed weapons systems

Blasters can switch from ion to laser cannon mode

DATA FILE

MANUFACTURER Kuat Systems Engineering

MODEL Modified *Firespray*-class patrol craft

TYPE Gunship/pursuit ship

DIMENSIONS (IN FLIGHT) Height: 22.62 m (74 ft 3 in); width: 20.23 m (66 ft 4 in); length: 9.82 m (32 ft 3 in)

WEAPONS 2 twin rotating blaster cannons/ion cannons, 2 fixed rapid-fire laser cannons, 2 concealed warhead launchers, 1 tractor beam projector, 1 aft seismic charge layer

AFFILIATION Independent

DEADLY AND DECEPTIVE

Much of the weaponry aboard the ship is tucked away behind armor plates and sliding doors, coaxing foes to overestimate their chances of escape. Rapid-fire cannons are concealed in the ship's spine; a seismic charge layer is at its aft; and its tail-mounted swivel cannons boast a variable configuration system that lets them fire destructive laser and debilitating ion blasts.

A direct hit from the Firespray's ion cannons can easily overload a *Lambda*-class shuttle's onboard electronics.

PART II: A NEW QUEST

TYTHON ASSAULT

Moff Gideon tracks the *Razor Crest*'s location to Tython and dispatches forces to abscond with Grogu. However, a platoon of stormtroopers proves insufficient to get past the combined defenses of the Mandalorian, Fennec Shand, and Boba Fett, so Gideon unleashes his heaviest weapon: experimental droid soldiers called dark troopers.

ARTILLERY STORMTROOPER

Artillery stormtroopers (or informally "shelltroopers") specialize in indirect fire munitions. They carry thermal detonators that can be lobbed from a collapsible mortar launcher. The multifrequency targeting and acquisition system in their helmets is customized to calculate firing solutions.

Artillery stormtroopers wear shock-resistant backpacks filled with canister-shaped thermal detonators.

Axidite-shelled thermal detonator

Merr-Sonn Munitions Model 201 mortar

STORMTROOPER CAPTAIN

Colored pauldrons worn by some Imperial stormtroopers designate rank and/or specialist status, differentiating the soldiers from the standard infantry. A captain with an orange pauldron leads the initial assault on the Seeing Stone and meets a withering defense.

V-82 DROPSHIP

A compact conveyance to ferry soldiers from an orbital transport to a planetary surface, the V-82 is assigned to light capital ships with limited hangar space. Though it carries formidable defense cannons, it is not meant to engage in combat.

DATA FILE

MANUFACTURER	Sienar Fleet Systems
MODEL	V-82 dropship
TYPE	Troop transport
WEAPONS	2 rotating twin heavy laser cannons
AFFILIATION	Imperial remnant

DATA FILE

MANUFACTURER Imperial Department of Military Research

MODEL 3rd-generation combat automata

TYPE Experimental battle droid

HEIGHT 1.9 m (6 ft 3 in)

AFFILIATION Imperial remnant

DARK TROOPER

Any New Republic intelligence on the dark trooper program is fragmentary at best. It is a long-gestating weapons program that took the lessons learned from the Droid Army of the Separatist Alliance and accelerated combat automata to the next level.

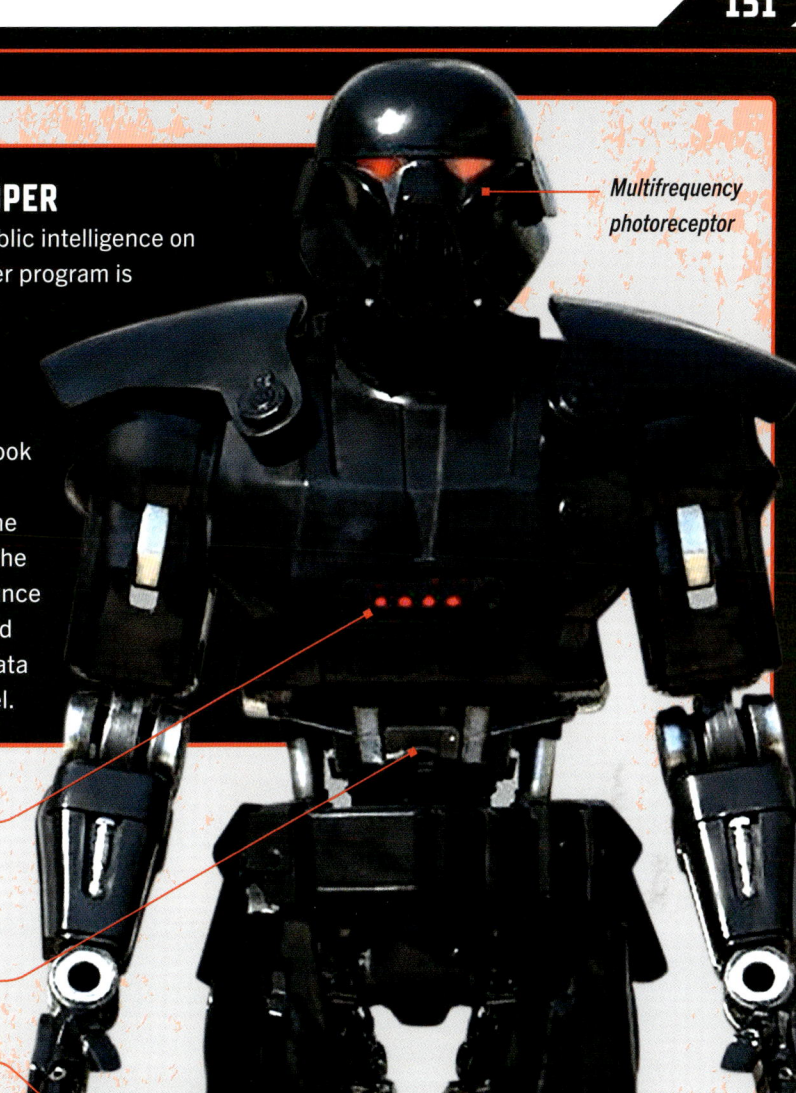

Multifrequency photoreceptor

Power plant status indicators

Cryo-cooled overclocked Stinnet-11 fusion generator

Crushing servo-grip

Directional repulsorfield waveguides

Integral repulsorlift generators, gyroscopic navigation systems, and directional thrusters give dark troopers aerial capabilities.

Wireless synchronized targeting sensor

Reinforced barrel assembly

Short-range ion-charge prod

E-450 "ARC HAMMER" HEAVY BLASTER RIFLE

The third-generation dark troopers are extremely strong but also power-intensive and cannot be used for prolonged engagements without technical and recharge support. These units kidnap an exhausted Grogu.

PART II: A NEW QUEST

MORAK

To track down Moff Gideon's Imperial cruiser and rescue Grogu, Mando recruits inmate 34667 from the Karthon Chop Fields. The prisoner is in fact Migs Mayfeld, who can use his former Imperial connections to secure a solid lead. At Mayfeld's recommendation, Mando and his allies travel to Morak, a site of a secret Imperial mining hub. Cut off from its Coreward and Expansion Region industrial centers, the Imperial remnant maximizes the mineral output of what once would be regarded as a world with minor resources.

Displaced Moraki settlers bitterly glower at the Juggernaut convoy as it rolls through their makeshift village.

- Imperial mining operation
- Freshwater archipelago
- Deep-sea rhydonium deposits too costly to mine

DATA FILE

REGION	Wild Space
SECTOR	Unincorporated
SYSTEM	Morak
DIAMETER	11,421 km (7,097 miles)
TERRAIN	Rainforest; low mountains; riverways; oceans
MOONS	0
POPULATION	Less than 5 million (no official census data)

MORAK

Settlers on Morak have been pushed into squalid conditions by the Imperial mining operation, their vital waterways diverted to serve the refinery. The dynamics of galactic politics are an abstract, academic affair to the average Moraki, who centers their concern on basic survival. Some locals have taken a more aggressive stance.

- Purplish skin of Dopp-muli islanders
- Heat-sensitive ear flaps
- Gear-laden tactical vest
- Detonite charges in storage pouch
- Beaded pouch
- Sash with united clans ribbons

MORAK PIRATES

A clan of crusading raiders, who at one time may have targeted peaceful fishing villages for ransacking, has turned its attention to the Imperial mining convoys. Though the Imperial remnant refers to these raiders as "pirates," these warriors are not interested in theft. They want to rid their world of the Empire's presence by making it too costly—in lives, material, and credits—to stay.

MORAK DRIVER

This driver steers the pirate skiff close enough to the Juggernauts for his compatriots to leap aboard.

- Flaps can clench comlink in place
- Pheoss-fiber tree-leather tunic
- Dopp-fuil clan sash

- Pheoss-tree branch
- Heat-tempered chine
- Top-grip metal band
- Snagging barbs

SCYTHE

- Chiseltooth end
- Elder Pheoss wood

PRYBAR

- Sliding thumb trigger
- Activation indicator light
- Fragmentation shell
- Countdown indicator lights

CLASS-A THERMAL DETONATOR

IMPROVISED WEAPONS

The pirates use hand-crafted tools to pry open the protective seals of a Juggernaut cargo module, allowing them to affix timed thermal detonators to the volatile materials inside.

THE HORDE

The Morak pirates are unaccustomed to the level of determined defense that the Mandalorian delivers. Undeterred, they continue to pile resources into stopping this one stalwart Juggernaut from arriving at its base.

PART II: A NEW QUEST
MORAK IMPERIAL BASE

An Imperial base protects a refinery that processes raw, volatile rhydonium for use as military-grade fuel. Antiaircraft cannons dot the upper structure, while a platoon of security forces patrols the grounds. The outpost is run according to Imperial Security Bureau protocols. Chain-code sniffing sensors, facial trackers, and bio-readers line the installation, making entry very dangerous to anyone on the Empire's wanted list. Mando uncharacteristically volunteers to leave his armor behind, donning captured Imperial armor instead for infiltration.

IMPOSSIBLE SHOT
From the tilting deck of Boba Fett's ship, Mayfeld fires a Tusken cycler rifle with a simple optical scope, hitting a rhydonium canister from hundreds of meters away. His reputation as a sharpshooter is well earned.

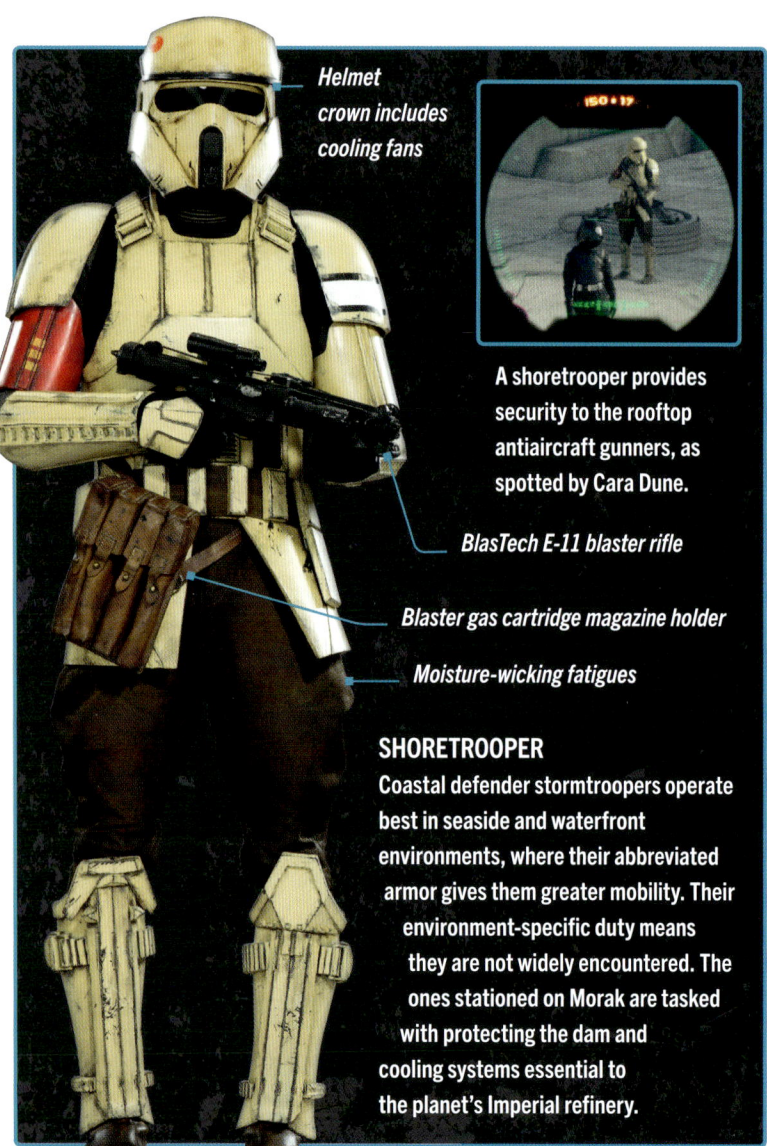

- Helmet crown includes cooling fans

A shoretrooper provides security to the rooftop antiaircraft gunners, as spotted by Cara Dune.

- BlasTech E-11 blaster rifle
- Blaster gas cartridge magazine holder
- Moisture-wicking fatigues

SHORETROOPER
Coastal defender stormtroopers operate best in seaside and waterfront environments, where their abbreviated armor gives them greater mobility. Their environment-specific duty means they are not widely encountered. The ones stationed on Morak are tasked with protecting the dam and cooling systems essential to the planet's Imperial refinery.

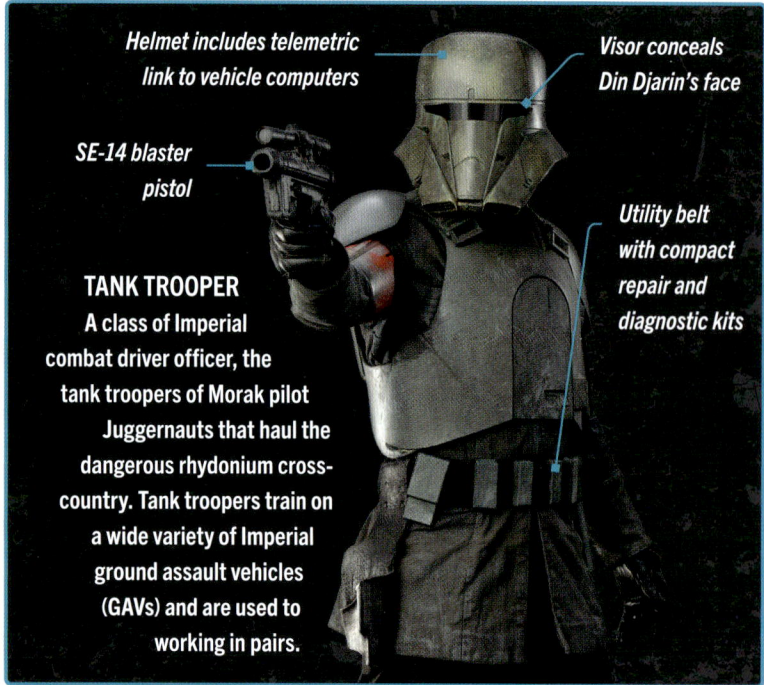

- Helmet includes telemetric link to vehicle computers
- Visor conceals Din Djarin's face
- SE-14 blaster pistol
- Utility belt with compact repair and diagnostic kits

TANK TROOPER
A class of Imperial combat driver officer, the tank troopers of Morak pilot Juggernauts that haul the dangerous rhydonium cross-country. Tank troopers train on a wide variety of Imperial ground assault vehicles (GAVs) and are used to working in pairs.

Combined Imperial stormtrooper forces rush to cover Juggernaut J-5's approach to the refinery, chasing off Shydopp raiders.

VALIN HESS

Valin Hess was once a top general in the Imperial army, having led campaigns on Vestar, Gorbah, and Burnin Konn. He is a true believer in the Imperial cause, and is convinced that the galaxy yearns for order, not freedom. He values his own survival and sees the troops he has sent to their deaths as a means to that end.

- Command disc atop hat
- Private datacards in shockproof case
- Post-Yavin schema rank plaque

The data terminals at the installation scan for known enemies on the Empire's watch list. Din Djarin's unmasked face, not being on any register, allows him access—but at great personal risk.

- Adjustable shoulder strap
- Plastoid pauldron
- Plastoid composite chest plate

RELEASE AND REDEMPTION

At Marshal Dune's request, Migs Mayfeld is released from prison labor to accompany her and Mando on the mission to Morak. Migs' inside knowledge of Imperial operations gives Mando the edge he needs to infiltrate the refinery. Though Migs professes to place pragmatic survival above personal ethics and politics, he risks everything by confronting his former commanding officer Valin Hess. Coming to terms with the death and destruction caused by callous Imperial orders, Mayfeld shoots Hess dead, taking a stance against his past.

- Transparisteel viewport
- Rear module and passenger cabin
- Reinforced carbon rims

JUGGERNAUT

The Juggernaut convoy truck is a relative of the HAVw A6 turbo tank, a wheeled Clone Wars combat vehicle that first earned the Juggernaut nickname. The HCVw A9.2 is a modular design that can be extended in length by adding wheeled segments.

PART II: A NEW QUEST
PREPARING THE ATTACK

The assault on Moff Gideon's cruiser is a mission that requires a hard-to-obtain asset, an Imperial shuttle. With Boba Fett at the helm of his pursuit craft, Mando's crew tracks and targets a shuttle carrying Doctor Pershing, capturing the vessel for their use in infiltrating Gideon's well-armed flagship. With their team assembled, the infiltrators stage a sham of a pursuit from Fett's Firespray, forcing the commandeered shuttle to seek shelter in the cruiser's launch bay.

CAPTURED CLONER
Doctor Pershing is a valued Imperial asset, but this time it's not his specific cloning knowledge that determines his worth. Captured by Mando's crew, Pershing has firsthand intel on the layout of Gideon's vessel, including the location of the brig holding Grogu and where the powered-down dark troopers are bivouacked.

DATA FILE
MANUFACTURER Sienar Fleet Systems
MODEL *Lambda*-class T-4a
TYPE Transport
DIMENSIONS (FLIGHT CONFIGURATION) Height 36.21 m (118 ft 10 in); width 32.72 m (107 ft 4 in); length 23.7 m (77 ft 9 in)
WEAPONS 2 forward-facing double laser cannons, 2 twin wing-mounted laser cannons, 1 retractable rear-mounted double laser cannon
AFFILIATION Imperial remnant

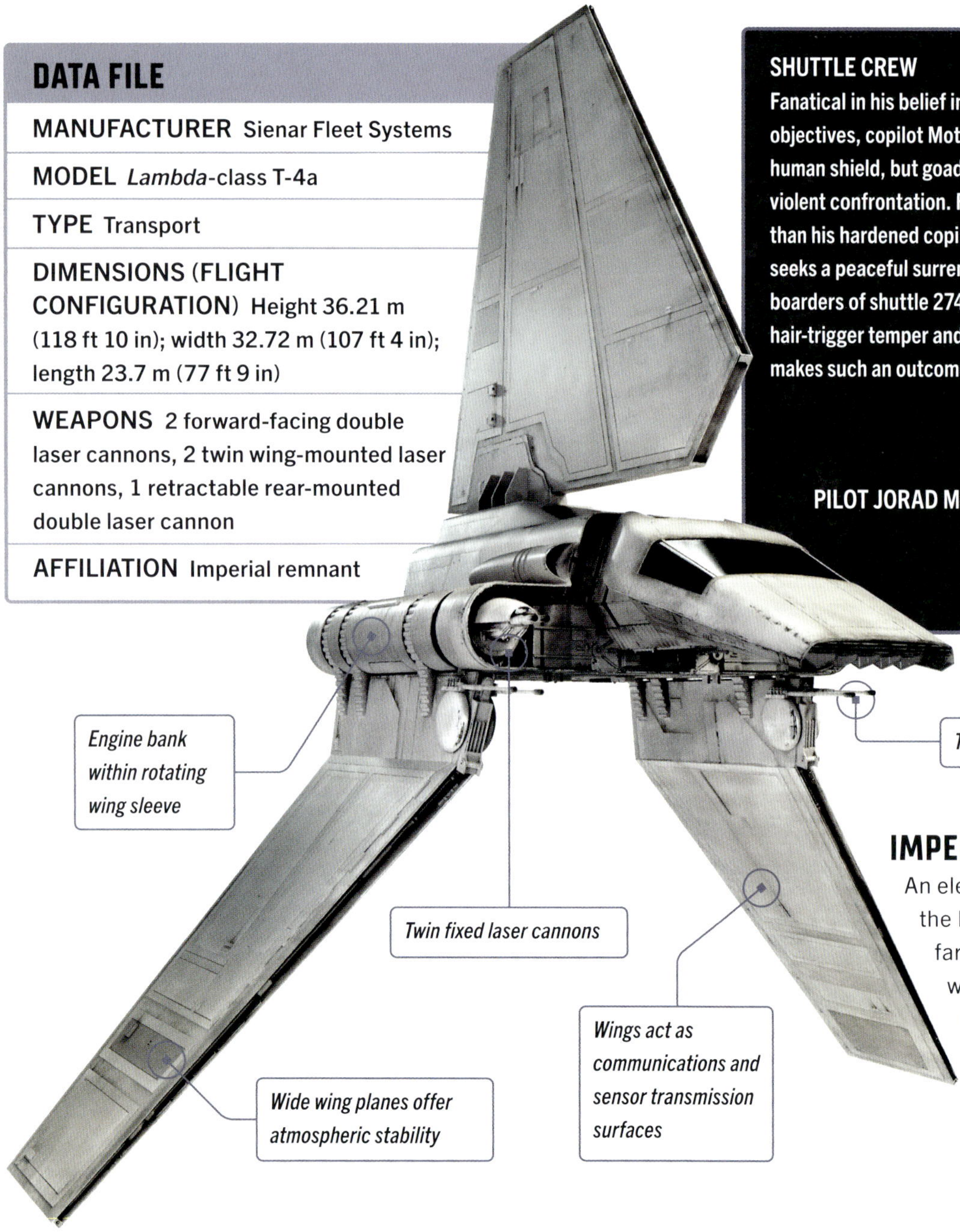

SHUTTLE CREW
Fanatical in his belief in the Empire and its objectives, copilot Mott uses Dr. Pershing as a human shield, but goads Cara Dune into a violent confrontation. Far more nervous than his hardened copilot, pilot Mainos seeks a peaceful surrender to the hostile boarders of shuttle 2743. Mott's hair-trigger temper and dislike of Mainos makes such an outcome impossible.

Sound-suppressing pilot headpiece

PILOT JORAD MAINOS

- Engine bank within rotating wing sleeve
- Twin fixed laser cannons
- Wide wing planes offer atmospheric stability
- Wings act as communications and sensor transmission surfaces
- Twin tilting wing-mounted laser cannons

IMPERIAL *LAMBDA*-CLASS SHUTTLE
An elegant design compared to most transport ships, the Imperial *Lambda*-class shuttle is typically kept far away from combat arenas and usually flies with an escort. The shorthanded nature of the Imperial remnant leaves an unguarded Lambda to be preyed upon by Boba Fett's ship, which neutralizes the shuttle with an ion blast. Mando's crew commandeers the ship for phase one of its mission.

DATA FILE

MANUFACTURER MandalMotors

MODEL *Kom'rk*-class V3.2ma fighter

TYPE Fighter/transport

DIMENSIONS (LANDED) Height: 29.27 m (96 ft); width: 29.1 m (95 ft 6 in); length: 26.46 m (86 ft 10 in)

WEAPONS 2 wingtip laser cannons, 2 fuselage laser cannons

AFFILIATION Bo-Katan Kryze

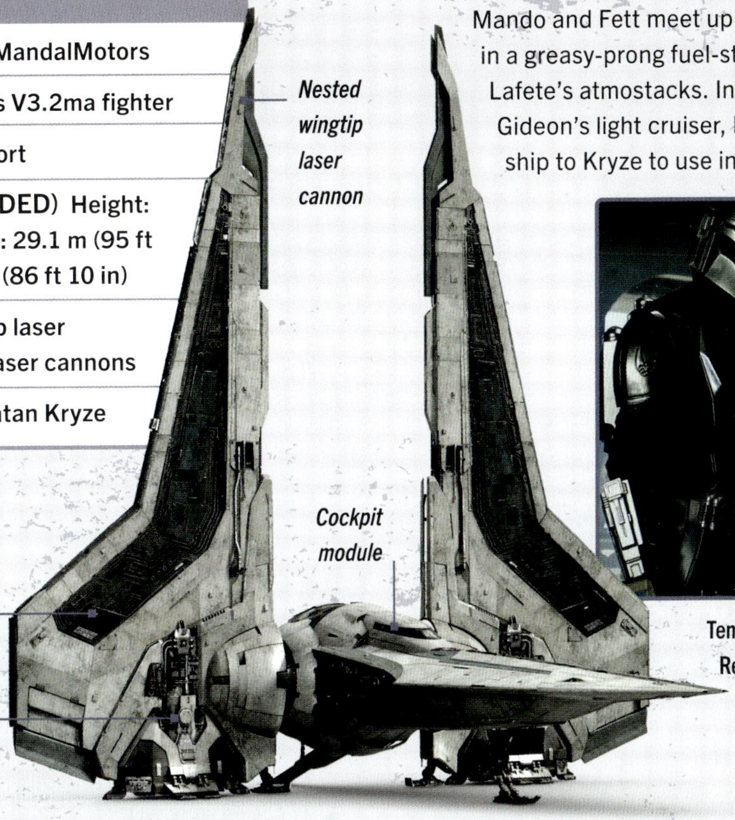

MANDALORIAN BACKUP

Mando and Fett meet up with Bo-Katan Kryze and Koska Reeves in a greasy-prong fuel-stop diner in the shadows of the planet Lafete's atmostacks. In exchange for helping him board Moff Gideon's light cruiser, Mando is willing to pass control of the ship to Kryze to use in retaking Mandalore.

Nested wingtip laser cannon

Cockpit module

Deflector shield projection plane

Reinforced turbojet housing

Tempers flare when Fett meets Mandalorians Kryze and Reeves, who question his right to their proud heritage.

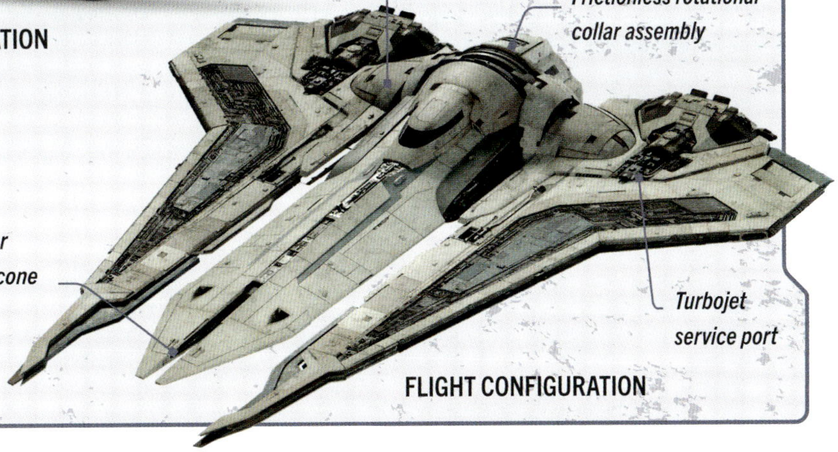

Wing pivot servomotor cradle

Frictionless rotational collar assembly

LANDING CONFIGURATION

GAUNTLET FIGHTER

A classic design unmistakably Mandalorian in origin, this swift and agile Kom'rk Gauntlet fighter is Bo-Katan Kryze's ship. Precision engineering pivots the engine and weapons planes for complex combat maneuvers, and the entire wing assembly can rotate around a central collar with a mechanical grace that would make Verpine shipwrights reek of envy pheromones.

Pursuit sensor suite in nose cone

Turbojet service port

FLIGHT CONFIGURATION

MANDO'S INFILTRATORS

Djarin's team consists of a handful of skilled warriors. Mandalorians Bo-Katan Kryze and Koska Reeves have cultural reasons to wrest control of the Darksaber from Gideon and want to claim the cruiser for their cause. Fennec Shand joins the fray to work off her shared debt with Boba Fett to Mando. Cara Dune is invested in Grogu's return and in dealing out fiery retribution against Imperial targets.

PART II: A NEW QUEST

IMPERIAL LIGHT CRUISER

In an era where the New Republic is vigilant for overt signs of the Imperial remnant, a vessel as enormous as an Imperial Star Destroyer would present an unwelcome target. The ever-pragmatic Moff Gideon leads his mobile operations from the bridge of a light cruiser, a versatile design derived from the venerated Republic *Arquitens*-class warship deployed in the Clone Wars. Automation and modifications have cut down the ship's crew requirements to a fraction of its original needs.

Central sublight engine with primary hyperdrive motivator

Starboard sublight engine service access

Cargo modules

Primary docking port

> "THIS IS MOFF GIDEON'S IMPERIAL LIGHT CRUISER. IN THE OLD DAYS, IT WOULD CARRY A CREW OF SEVERAL HUNDRED. NOW IT OPERATES WITH A TINY FRACTION OF THAT."
> – BO-KATAN KRYZE, PLANNING THE ASSAULT

TIE LAUNCH
Nestled between the light cruiser's forward spars is its launch tube, from which its abbreviated squadron of TIE fighters can be deployed into combat. Tractor beam accelerators, nicknamed "tractorpults" by the pilots, add a boost of velocity as the TIE powers up. The same systems help guide damaged craft in for safe landings. Bo-Katan flies her captured *Lambda*-class shuttle directly into the tube.

Secreted in a cold storage bay is a garrison of dark troopers. They draw too much power to be kept active at all times.

DARK DUEL

Moff Gideon defends himself with the Darksaber and attempts to stop the Mandalorian from absconding with his quarry. Mando's armor and the spear he acquired on Corvus are of a beskar purity sufficient to deflect the blade. Though determined, Gideon is no Jedi. Mando defeats Gideon in combat, taking the Darksaber from him, and in doing so, complicates the return of Bo-Katan Kryze to the title of Mandalore and the throne.

DATA FILE

MANUFACTURER Kuat Drive Yards

MODEL *Arquitens*-class

TYPE Light cruiser

DIMENSIONS Height: 66.72 m (218 ft 11 in); width: 162.99 m (534 ft 9 in); length: 380.34 m (1,248 ft)

WEAPONS 2 dorsal and ventral twin light turbolaser batteries, 4 port and 4 starboard quad laser cannons, 4 forward-mounted concussion missile launchers, 1 forward-mounted medium tractor beam emitter

AFFILIATION Imperial remnant

Command bridge atop shielded conning tower

Portside dorsal twin light turbolaser battery

SERVICE EXTENSION

When the Galactic Republic transitioned to the Galactic Empire with Emperor Palpatine's sweeping proclamations that marked the end of an era, the nascent Imperial Navy had to make do with the warships at hand. Republic light cruisers underwent extensive overhauls, upgrading their engine and combat systems to new, imposing Imperial standards. Gone was the red Republic livery, stripped away so each ship gleamed with a uniform white hull.

Starfighter launch tube

VENTRAL ACCESS

In addition to the forward launch tube, the Imperial light cruiser has a ventral docking area accessible via port and starboard bays. It is from this area that the cruiser launches transport craft and receives replenishment vessels and visitors. When an X-wing fighter suddenly appears on the scopes in the midst of Mando's infiltration mission, its pilot

Starboard sensor arrays

PART II: A NEW QUEST
LUKE SKYWALKER

> A galaxy of conflict has turned foundlings into legends, and Jedi Knight Luke Skywalker is preeminent among the storied heroes who have indelibly shaped history. Luke was raised an orphan of the Clone Wars on a remote moisture farm of Tatooine and had little inkling that he was destined for greatness, or that the blood of one of the Jedi Order's most venerated heroes—and greatest tragedies—coursed through his veins.

Watched over from afar by Obi-Wan Kenobi, a Jedi survivor, Luke was kept safe so he could experience a normal childhood in which he learned responsibility, humility, and compassion from his adoptive parents—Owen and Beru Lars. As Luke came of age, he would embrace his destiny and follow his father's path to become a Jedi.

Learning the truth of his father's fall to the dark side was one of the many burdens Luke would have to bear on his lonely path to Knighthood. Luke's compassion for his father, his refusal to strike him down in anger, and his dousing of his lightsaber blade after a moment of rage were the crucibles of Luke's trials. He emerged as a Jedi.

JEDI IN ACTION
Grogu's call through the Force at the Seeing Stone on Tython has been heard. Luke Skywalker, the first of a new Jedi Order, is once again the person most capable of mounting an impossible rescue. Instinctively guided by Grogu's presence, Skywalker lands his X-wing fighter in the light cruiser's docking bay and effortlessly cuts through the impeding dark troopers holding off Mando's team. As they did before the Jedi of old, mindless battle droids collapse in fragments before his lightsaber.

Defying the Creed, Din Djarin unmasks himself before Grogu, sharing a heartfelt goodbye.

Domed head containing recessed fire suppression gear

Doors on barrel body open to deploy a wide array of tools

R2-D2
Never far from Luke Skywalker's side is his loyal astromech, R2-D2. The droid has witnessed momentous events in the galaxy, though his own peculiar perspective prioritizes his friends' safety rather than the tabulation of history. Aboard Skywalker's X-wing, he provides vital navigational and repair assistance as Luke travels to some of the galaxy's most obscure locales.

Luke can sense the raw talent possessed by Grogu, but recognizes that the child needs training if he is to effectively and reliably wield the Force without being tempted to its dark side. Skywalker offers his guidance.

Hood conceals face

"I WILL GIVE MY LIFE TO PROTECT THE CHILD, BUT HE WILL NOT BE SAFE UNTIL HE MASTERS HIS ABILITIES."
– LUKE SKYWALKER TO THE MANDALORIAN

Luke's mechanical hand serves as a complex reminder of his past missteps

Shimmering green blade of Luke Skywalker's lightsaber

SKYWALKER'S TRAVELS

Luke has vowed to pass on what he has learned. His first student, his sister Leia, has prioritized another path in her life, leaving Luke to traverse the galaxy in his exploration of the Force. Luke is looking to piece together lost knowledge and other scraps of history erased by the Galactic Empire.

Dark cloak evokes a forgotten era

Functional, unadorned black Jedi clothing

DATA FILE

SUBJECT	Luke Skywalker
HOMEWORLD	Polis Massa (born); Tatooine (raised)
SPECIES	Human
AFFILIATION	Jedi Order
HEIGHT	1.72 m (5 ft 8 in)

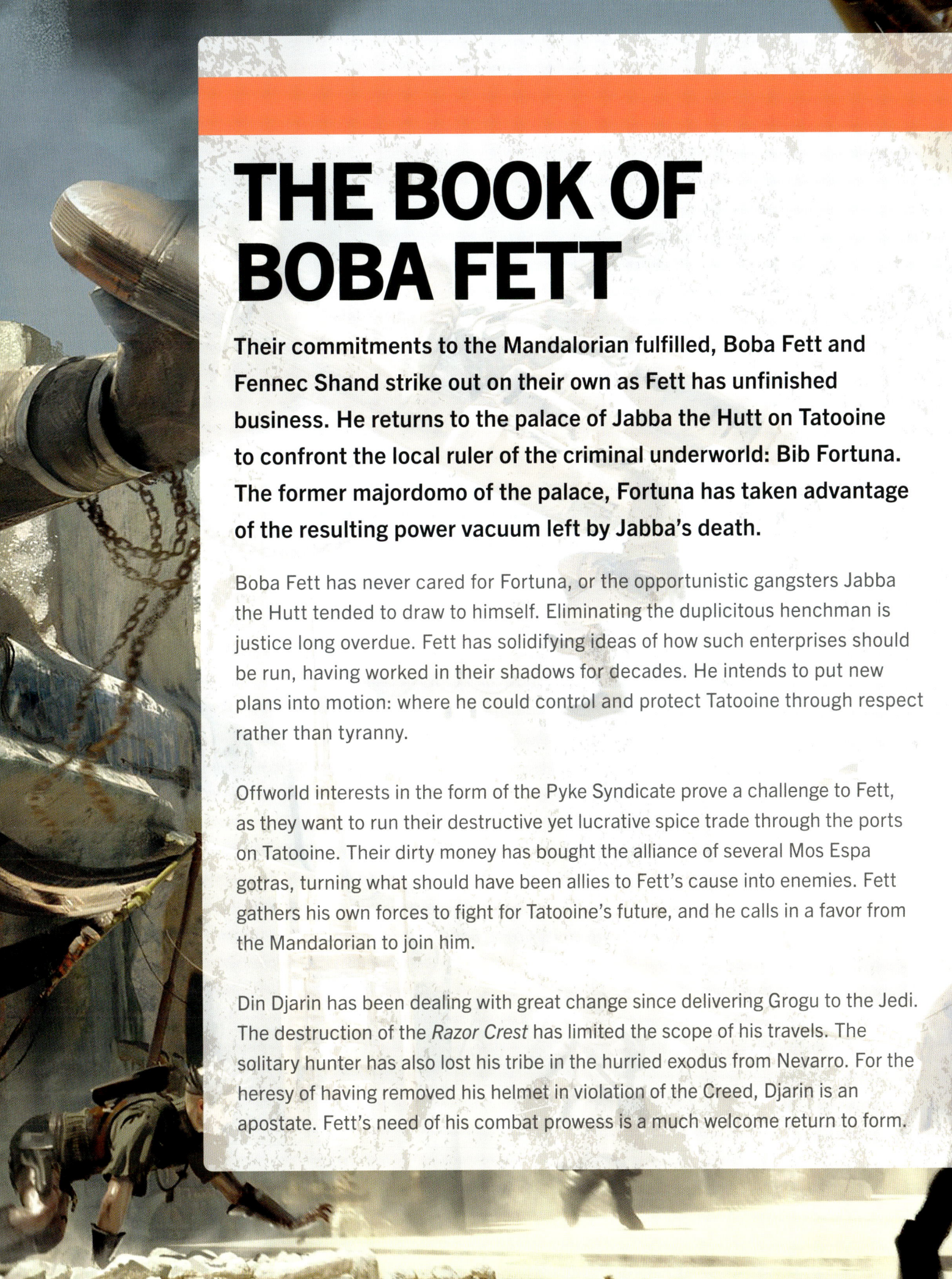

THE BOOK OF BOBA FETT

Their commitments to the Mandalorian fulfilled, Boba Fett and Fennec Shand strike out on their own as Fett has unfinished business. He returns to the palace of Jabba the Hutt on Tatooine to confront the local ruler of the criminal underworld: Bib Fortuna. The former majordomo of the palace, Fortuna has taken advantage of the resulting power vacuum left by Jabba's death.

Boba Fett has never cared for Fortuna, or the opportunistic gangsters Jabba the Hutt tended to draw to himself. Eliminating the duplicitous henchman is justice long overdue. Fett has solidifying ideas of how such enterprises should be run, having worked in their shadows for decades. He intends to put new plans into motion: where he could control and protect Tatooine through respect rather than tyranny.

Offworld interests in the form of the Pyke Syndicate prove a challenge to Fett, as they want to run their destructive yet lucrative spice trade through the ports on Tatooine. Their dirty money has bought the alliance of several Mos Espa gotras, turning what should have been allies to Fett's cause into enemies. Fett gathers his own forces to fight for Tatooine's future, and he calls in a favor from the Mandalorian to join him.

Din Djarin has been dealing with great change since delivering Grogu to the Jedi. The destruction of the *Razor Crest* has limited the scope of his travels. The solitary hunter has also lost his tribe in the hurried exodus from Nevarro. For the heresy of having removed his helmet in violation of the Creed, Djarin is an apostate. Fett's need of his combat prowess is a much welcome return to form.

GLAVIS RINGWORLD

The galaxy is filled with ancient, arcane wonders often ignored by the busy modern traveler. Over the millennia, the stability of Glavis Ringworld invited settlement and expansion, such that it is now an independent toroidal port city. The station's eccentric design makes it an ideal hiding place.

Environmental sensor module

Head with 9,850-credit price on it

KABA BAIZ
A Klatooinian butcher and meat mogul, Kaba Baiz operates out of the Lenapi Meatpacking Degree, until the Mandalorian collects the bounty on his head... and his head.

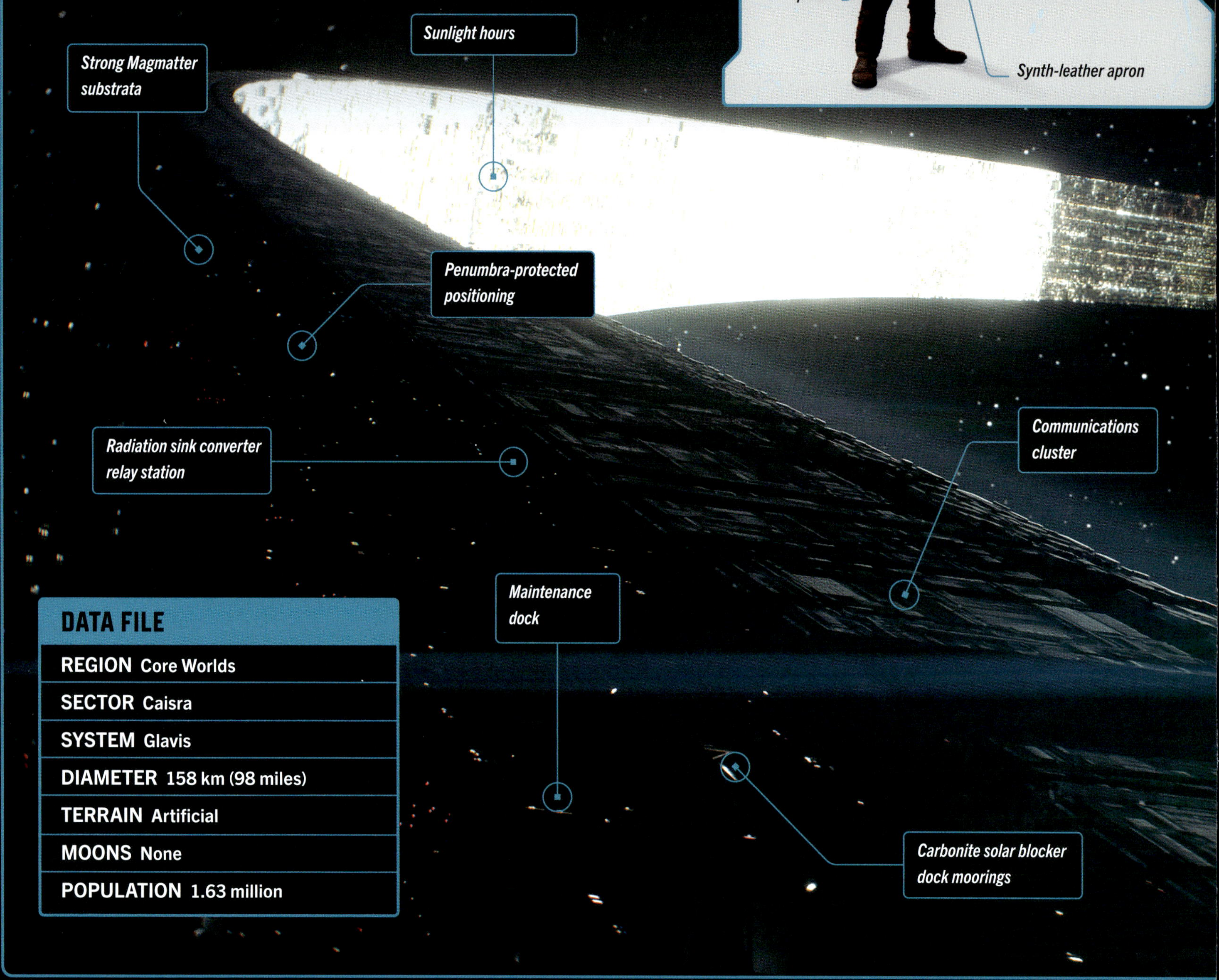

Repaired PRP-152 blaster pistol

Synth-leather apron

Strong Magmatter substrata

Sunlight hours

Penumbra-protected positioning

Radiation sink converter relay station

Communications cluster

Maintenance dock

Carbonite solar blocker dock moorings

DATA FILE	
REGION	Core Worlds
SECTOR	Caisra
SYSTEM	Glavis
DIAMETER	158 km (98 miles)
TERRAIN	Artificial
MOONS	None
POPULATION	1.63 million

INNER CIRCLE

This spacer's neighborhood has the ring's most well-tended docking facilities, refueling ports, and relaxation and recreation amenities for visiting travelers. A wounded and weary Mando seeks out the local Bounty Hunters Guild chapterhouse located atop an observation tower.

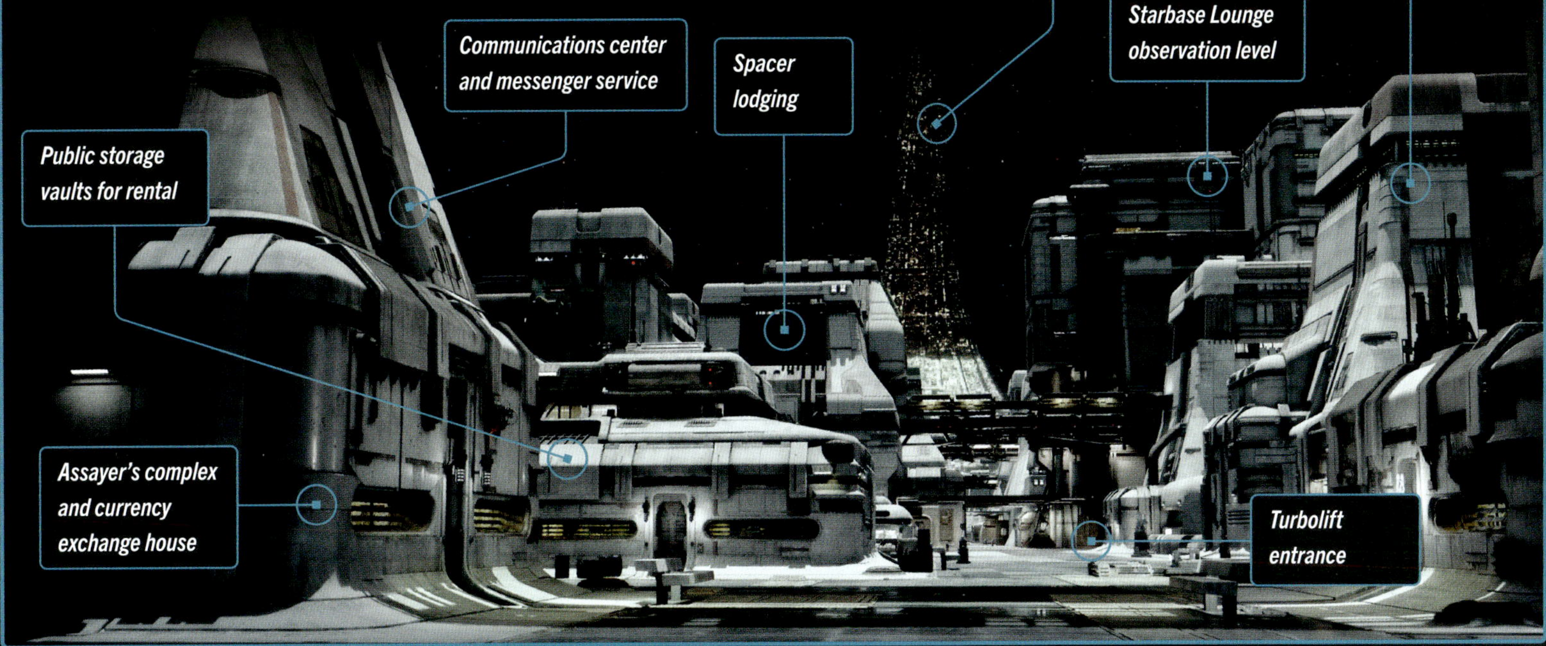

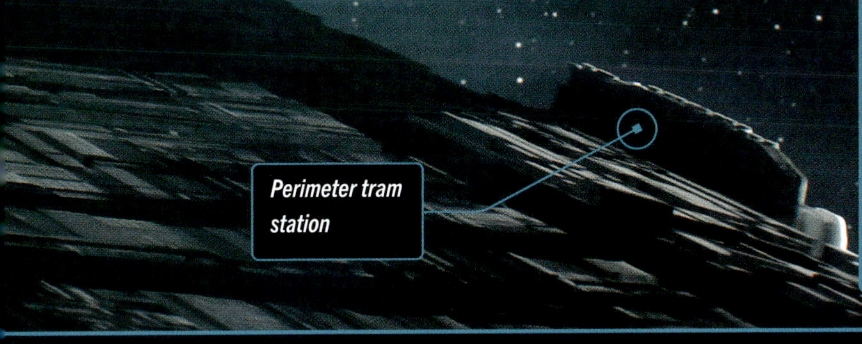

- Solar blocker-provided night cycle
- Consumables processing complex
- Communications center and messenger service
- Spacer lodging
- Starbase Lounge observation level
- Public storage vaults for rental
- Assayer's complex and currency exchange house
- Turbolift entrance
- Starbase Hollow
- Perimeter tram station

The Guildmaster sits in a chic lounge and nightclub complex known as the Starbase. The Ishi Tib invites Djarin to dine, but he has other matters to attend to.

MANDALORIAN COVERT

In the substrata depths below Kalzoc Alley is what little remains of the Nevarro Mandalorian Covert. Scattered since the Imperial assault on their lair, the Children of the Watch await word of a more secure home. On Glavis stands the Forge, tended to by the Armorer and guarded by Paz Vizsla.

The Armorer, skilled at interpreting omens, beholds the recovered Darksaber.

Vizsla challenges Djarin with a rightful ancestral claim to the Darksaber, but he cannot best him in combat.

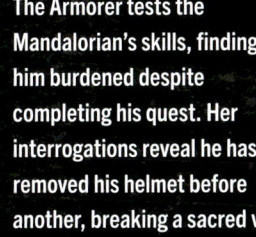

The Armorer tests the Mandalorian's skills, finding him burdened despite completing his quest. Her interrogations reveal he has removed his helmet before another, breaking a sacred vow.

THE BOOK OF BOBA FETT

MANDO'S N-1 STARFIGHTER

Since the sudden destruction of the *Razor Crest*, Din Djarin has had few options when it comes to interstellar travel, even relying on passage booked on commercial liners to get from Glavis Ringworld to Tatooine. But a message from Peli Motto has made the journey worthwhile, for she promises him a replacement for his vessel that meets his exacting criteria: fast, well-armed, and pre-Imperial (and thus off the New Republic registries).

Ionization chamber cleared of scurrier nest

Brushed chromium finish

SOME ASSEMBLY REQUIRED

Mando's arrival is more prompt than expected, so Peli's craft is not ready to fly. The well-connected mechanic has found a vintage hand-crafted Naboo N-1 starfighter. Though the vessel is largely skeletal, Peli has all the parts she needs and then some. With Mando's help, they work together to bring the ship into shape.

Communications array within fore plane

TEAMWORK: MANDO & MOTTO

Mando overcomes his skepticism towards Peli's promises the more he gets his hands on the precision-engineered componentry. With the help of Peli's droids and Jawa neighbors, the N-1 soon boasts modern add-ons and performance boosters that break all baseline records for the craft, creating a ship Peli and Mando take pride in.

Dealmaking stance adopted from Jawa trade language

Peli is pleased once Mando gets young Grogu back in his life, as the youngling delights her.

Microfiber mechanic's shop rag with scratch-free seamless edges

PELI MOTTO

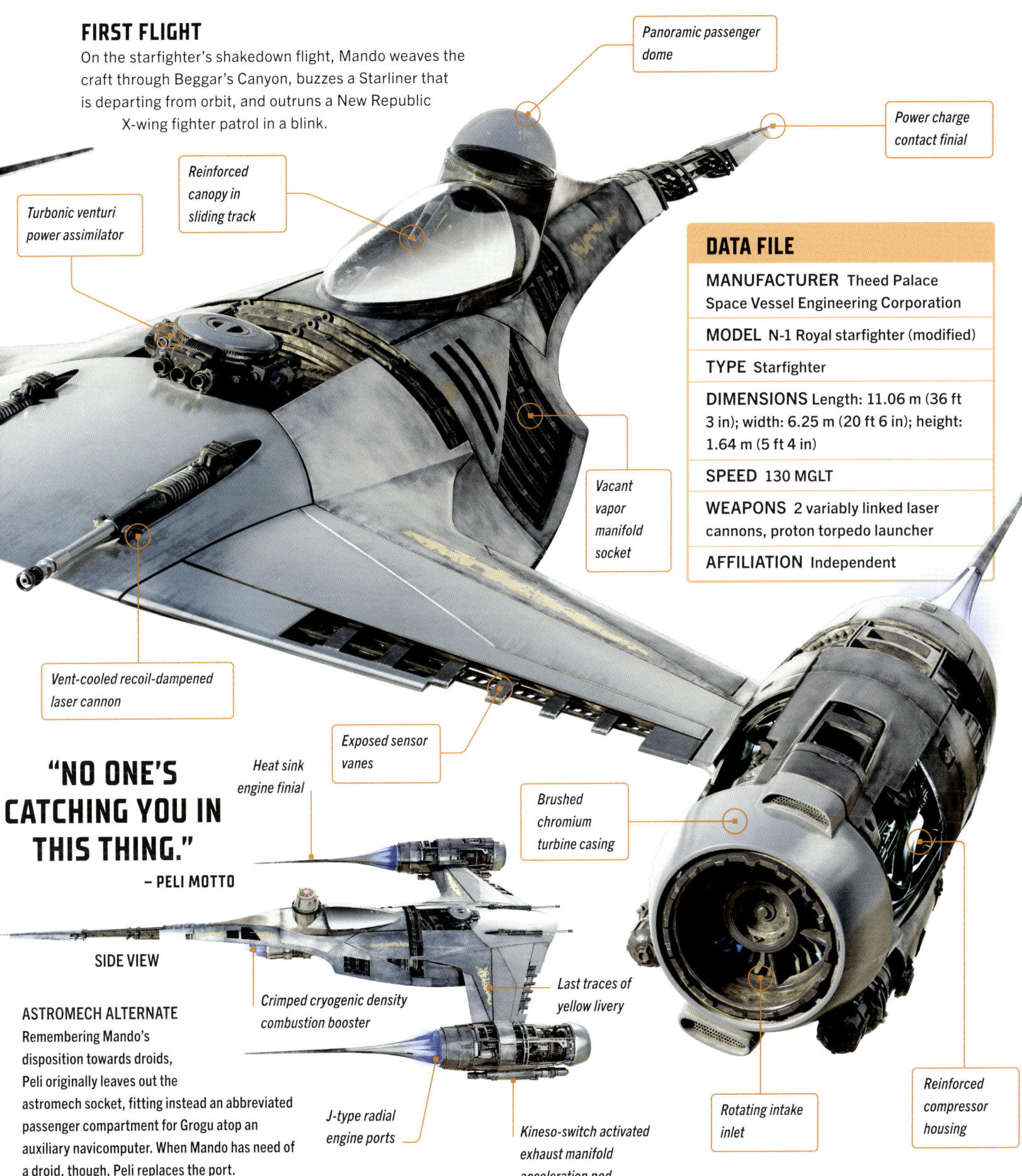

FIRST FLIGHT

On the starfighter's shakedown flight, Mando weaves the craft through Beggar's Canyon, buzzes a Starliner that is departing from orbit, and outruns a New Republic X-wing fighter patrol in a blink.

- Panoramic passenger dome
- Power charge contact finial
- Reinforced canopy in sliding track
- Turbonic venturi power assimilator
- Vacant vapor manifold socket
- Vent-cooled recoil-dampened laser cannon
- Exposed sensor vanes
- Heat sink engine finial
- Brushed chromium turbine casing
- Last traces of yellow livery
- Crimped cryogenic density combustion booster
- J-type radial engine ports
- Kineso-switch activated exhaust manifold acceleration pod
- Rotating intake inlet
- Reinforced compressor housing

DATA FILE

MANUFACTURER Theed Palace Space Vessel Engineering Corporation

MODEL N-1 Royal starfighter (modified)

TYPE Starfighter

DIMENSIONS Length: 11.06 m (36 ft 3 in); width: 6.25 m (20 ft 6 in); height: 1.64 m (5 ft 4 in)

SPEED 130 MGLT

WEAPONS 2 variably linked laser cannons, proton torpedo launcher

AFFILIATION Independent

> "NO ONE'S CATCHING YOU IN THIS THING."
> – PELI MOTTO

SIDE VIEW

ASTROMECH ALTERNATE

Remembering Mando's disposition towards droids, Peli originally leaves out the astromech socket, fitting instead an abbreviated passenger compartment for Grogu atop an auxiliary navicomputer. When Mando has need of a droid, though, Peli replaces the port.

THE BOOK OF BOBA FETT

INSIDE MANDO'S N-1

The handcrafted spaceframe of the N-1 starfighter accommodates all the upgrades Peli Motto can stuff into it. The lack of external cladding means she can adjust the exposed systems as the modifications progress, fine-tuning the vessel to exacting—if occasionally improvised—specification.

Callouts:
- Power charge contact finial
- Exposed power-shedding discharge vane
- Electromagnetic signal receiver
- Astromech-accessible navicomputer
- R5-D4 in swappable astromech socket
- Localized acceleration compensator
- Environmental control systems
- Heat sink finial
- Booster module retracts to allow astromech ingress
- Reinforced ventral booster mount
- Life support access cover (and step)
- Power cell covering
- Cramped cockpit fits armored Mando
- Heat radiating filaments
- Post-reactor radiator ducting
- Late-stage fuel manifold
- Electromagnetic thrust vectoring vanes
- Exhaust manifold acceleration pod
- Compressor bypass ducting

SEATS TWO COMFORTABLY

Starfighters are snug affairs, especially the compact N-1. Peli's modified passenger pod lets Grogu toddle into the cockpit through a small crawlspace. When Mando opts to restore the swappable astromech socket, Grogu rides up front, in his protector's lap, where he can feel safe and also learn the basics of starfighter piloting.

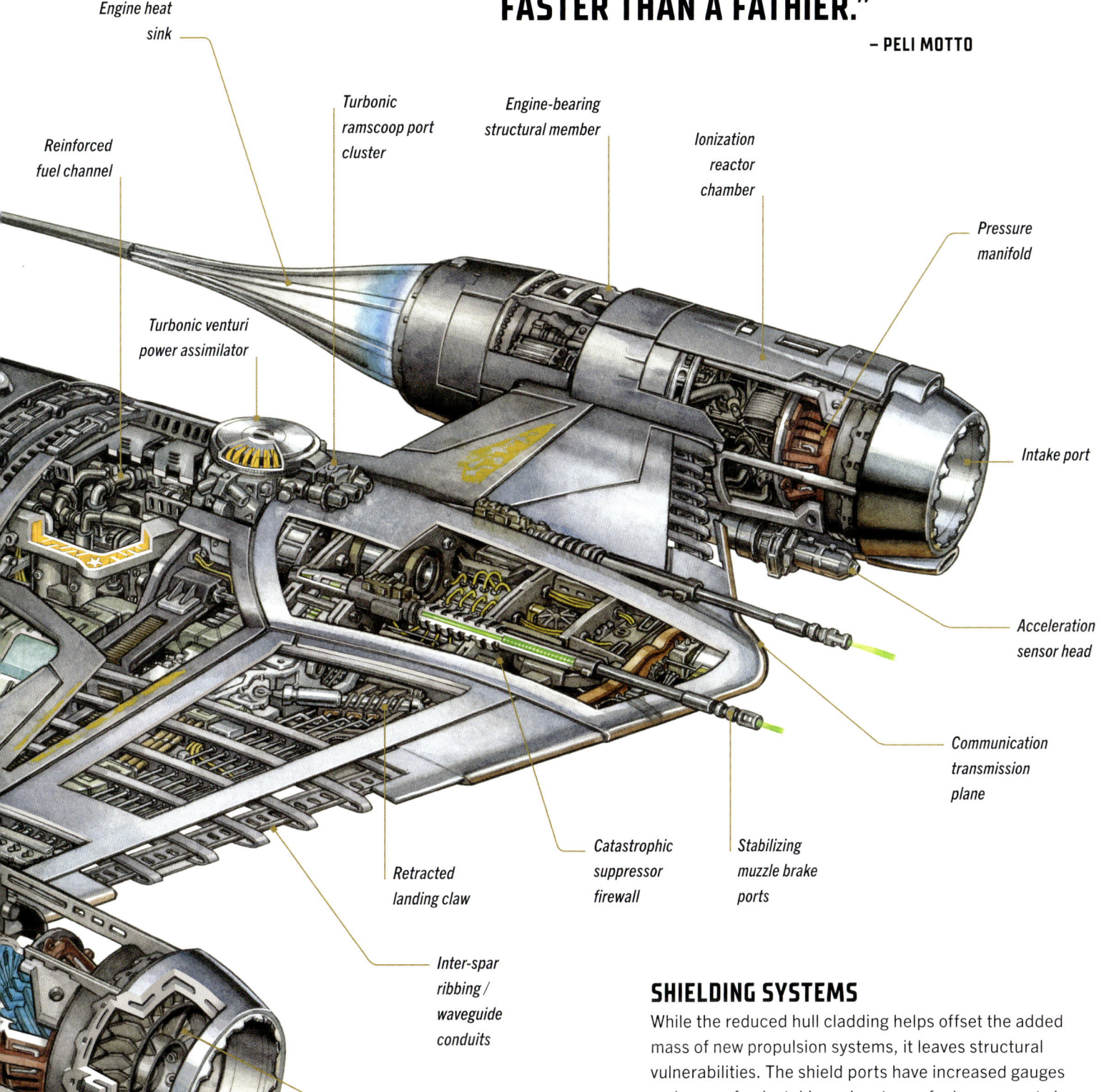

169

> "I'M GONNA ADD ON SOME CUSTOM MODIFICATIONS THAT'LL MAKE HER FASTER THAN A FATHIER."
> – PELI MOTTO

- Engine heat sink
- Reinforced fuel channel
- Turbonic ramscoop port cluster
- Engine-bearing structural member
- Ionization reactor chamber
- Pressure manifold
- Turbonic venturi power assimilator
- Intake port
- Acceleration sensor head
- Communication transmission plane
- Retracted landing claw
- Catastrophic suppressor firewall
- Stabilizing muzzle brake ports
- Inter-spar ribbing / waveguide conduits
- Rotating intake inlet
- Debris extractor port

SHIELDING SYSTEMS

While the reduced hull cladding helps offset the added mass of new propulsion systems, it leaves structural vulnerabilities. The shield ports have increased gauges and power feeds, taking advantage of advancements in deflector manifolds in the decades since the N-1's prime. The swift and nimble craft is hard to hit, but should it take a blast from an enemy, it can quickly dissipate the blow.

THE BOOK OF BOBA FETT

OSSUS

In the years since the defeat of the Sith, Luke Skywalker has been researching the lost history of the Jedi. He has recently uncovered the location of Ossus, a world that was one of several purported to be the homeworld of the Jedi Order. Upon his arrival, Luke discovers a lush world teeming with life. Its true role in the Jedi past remains a mystery, but its promised role in the Order's future has become clear to him.

LIVING LANDSCAPE
Ossus teems with life, a verdant agglomeration of biomes that amplifies the Force with every plant and animal native to the world. Neither technology nor civilization mar its fecund surface.

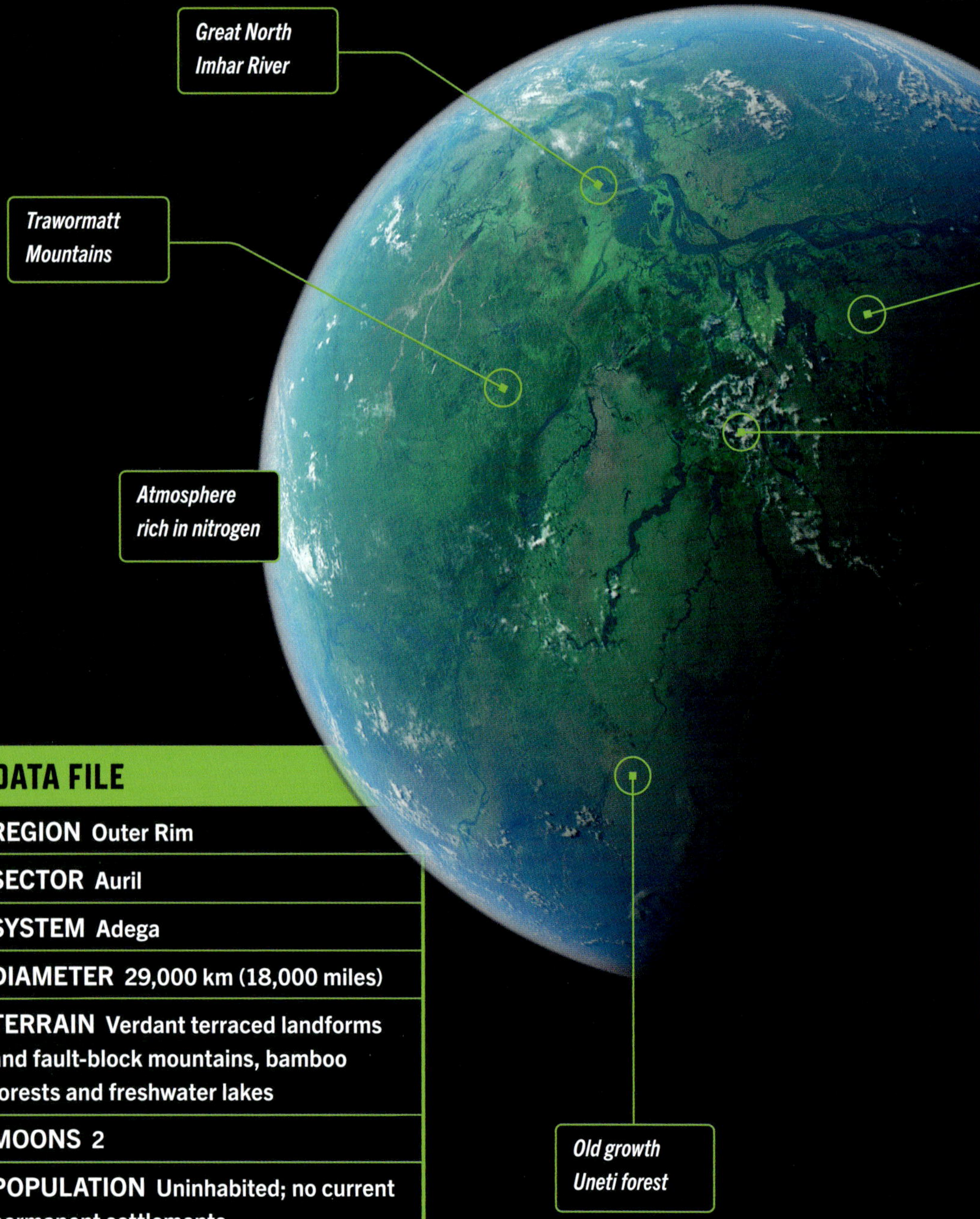

- Great North Imhar River
- Knossos Plateau
- Trawormatt Mountains
- Eocho Mountain Valley
- Atmosphere rich in nitrogen
- Old growth Uneti forest

DATA FILE

REGION Outer Rim
SECTOR Auril
SYSTEM Adega
DIAMETER 29,000 km (18,000 miles)
TERRAIN Verdant terraced landforms and fault-block mountains, bamboo forests and freshwater lakes
MOONS 2
POPULATION Uninhabited; no current permanent settlements

WALLOWING WILDLIFE
Few records properly catalog the abundant Ossus wildlife. This river-dwelling horned ruminant is known simply as a mud yak, as it eats river roots dug up by its prodigious horns.

RONIN JEDI

Ahsoka Tano euphemistically refers to herself as "a friend of the family," and takes great interest in Luke Skywalker's efforts to rebuild the Jedi. Though she opted not to train Grogu, Luke has.

Ahsoka questions whether Mando's desire to deliver a gift to Grogu is as selfless as it seems.

Guarded stance

Shoto lightsaber

Lined tabi boots

AHSOKA TANO

JEDI TRAINING

Luke recognizes that Grogu already has some fundamental training, and at the least offers to hone skills that will allow the youngling to defend himself. A deeper commitment to Jedi study depends on a choice—one that only Grogu can make.

Master Skywalker drills through a variety of lightsaber katas as Grogu watches, rekindling memories of decades earlier in the Child.

Skywalker presents Grogu with a difficult choice of paths ahead.

TEMPLE FOUNDATIONS

Swarms of ant droids gather stones and tirelessly stack them in a beehive configuration, slowly but steadily building what will become Skywalker's Jedi temple on Ossus. Skywalker's own inclinations and upbringing cause him to favor the term "academy" for his future school.

Linked beskar rings

GROGU'S MAIL HAUBERK

A FOUNDLING'S RIGHT

As per the Creed, the Mandalorian wants Grogu to have his first *beskar'gam*, a tunic of beskar mail crafted from Morgan Elsbeth's captured spear. Djarin wants the foundling protected in the Mandalorian way, not just through Jedi abilities.

Industrial Automaton ANT-621 droid

Dry stacked design inspired by ancient Jedi manuscripts

Interior cleared of vegetation

THE BOOK OF BOBA FETT
BATTLE OF MOS ESPA

Upon his return to Tatooine, Boba Fett seeks to upgrade his reputation, moving beyond his previous definition as a bounty hunter. He has his visor set on Jabba the Hutt's (more or less) vacant throne, claiming it so that he can steer the Tatooine underworld in a new direction driven by respect rather than Jabba's excess of wrath and indulgence.

After fending off an attack by the avaricious Hutt Twins who feel entitled to their cousin Jabba's trappings, Fett finds himself mired in criminal intrigue. The opportunistic Pyke Syndicate sows discord among the various gangs in the port city of Mos Espa, abetted by the corrupt mayor Mok Shaiz. The powerful factions include the Klatooinians of the starport and upper sprawl, the Aqualish of the Worker's District, and the Trandoshans of the city center, all arrayed to topple Fett from his assumed position as daimyo.

ASSEMBLED ALLIES

Fett turns to his trusted allies, including the Mandalorian, Fennec Shand, Krrsantan, the townsfolk of Freetown, and local cyborg youth known as the Mods to defend Mos Espa. Fett rides into battle atop his tamed rancor, a beastly mount worthy of Mandalorian heritage.

The furious rancor uses its massive strength to shred an armored scorponek droid.

- Daimyo Boba Fett atop saddle
- EE-3 blaster carbine rifle
- Dense dermal armor of latticed collagen
- Eye drawn to movement
- Fully extended bite radius
- Dense keratin nodule
- Armor-plated tail
- Short, muscular legs
- Stubby hooves

DATA FILE
SUBJECT	Boba Fett's rancor
HOMEWORLD	Tatooine (adopted)
SIZE	Height: 4.9 m (16 ft)
LIFESPAN	Up to 80 standard years in captivity

Grogu uses the Force to calm the enraged rancor, bringing the exhausted beast safely under control.

Hard protein claws

Wide grasp when fingers splayed

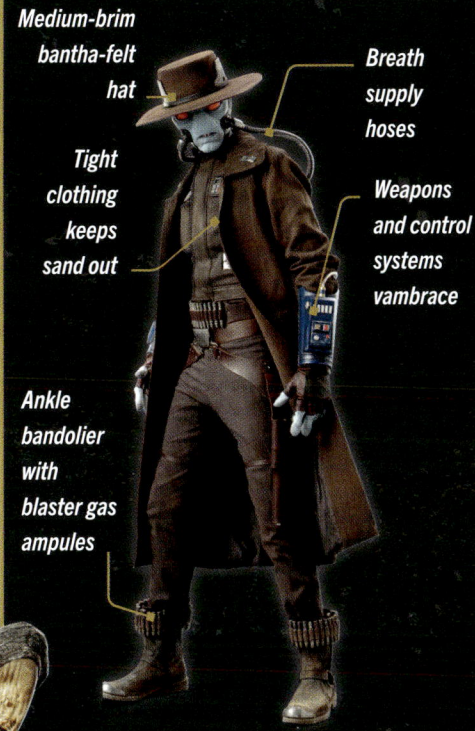

Medium-brim bantha-felt hat

Tight clothing keeps sand out

Ankle bandolier with blaster gas ampules

Breath supply hoses

Weapons and control systems vambrace

CAD BANE

The infamous Duros gun-for-hire has long cast a shadow over Fett's life, having taught him the basics of survival and duplicity in Boba's adolescence during the Clone Wars. Now in the service of the Pykes, Bane is primed for a fateful confrontation with his former protégé.

WW-044 heavy blaster rifle

KRRSANTAN

Former gladiator and current hired muscle, the mighty Wookiee Krrsantan was paid to intimidate Fett out of the Hutt palace. That contract canceled, the two work together.

Spiked tournament armor

Dense duranium plating

Xonti championship belt

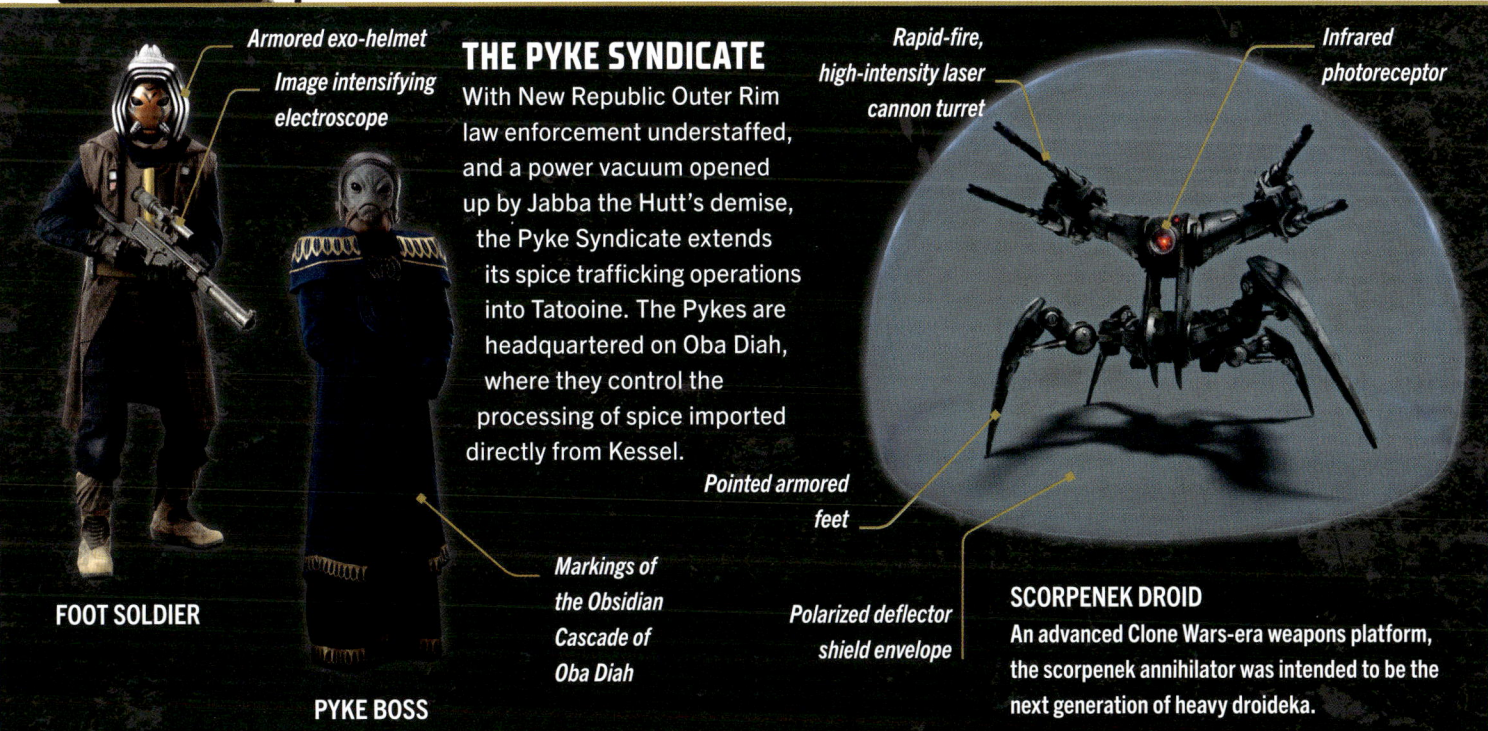

Armored exo-helmet

Image intensifying electroscope

THE PYKE SYNDICATE

With New Republic Outer Rim law enforcement understaffed, and a power vacuum opened up by Jabba the Hutt's demise, the Pyke Syndicate extends its spice trafficking operations into Tatooine. The Pykes are headquartered on Oba Diah, where they control the processing of spice imported directly from Kessel.

Rapid-fire, high-intensity laser cannon turret

Infrared photoreceptor

FOOT SOLDIER

PYKE BOSS

Markings of the Obsidian Cascade of Oba Diah

Pointed armored feet

Polarized deflector shield envelope

SCORPENEK DROID

An advanced Clone Wars-era weapons platform, the scorpenek annihilator was intended to be the next generation of heavy droideka.

PART III:

A NEW HOME

Reunited with Grogu, Din Djarin still feels incomplete as his Mandalorian heritage has been stripped from him. By the tenets of the Creed, the only way Djarin can remove his status as an apostate and return to the Way is by bathing in the Living Waters of Mandalore, a planet believed to be inaccessible.

This rootless existence is one felt by all Mandalorians since the Night of a Thousand Tears. The relentless bombardment of their homeworld by Imperial forces scattered the people across the stars, and many turned their back on a shattered cultural heritage. Those who continue to wear the armor mourn in hiding. Beskar provides little protection against such deep wounds.

Din is driven to prove that Mandalore is not a lost cause. Whispers traveling across the network of coverts have repeated the tales of the planet being not only cursed, but toxic. The irradiated fallout from the Imperial Purge has scoured the planet of life, and there will be no returning to the surface.

The planet has survived such declarations of death before—the Mandalorian civil wars were what scorched the planet of its once lush foliage, forcing its people to live in hermetic domes on the surface. Time and again, Mandalore has risen from the ashes.

The ghostly tales of a world forever lost is an illusion, crafted in part by Moff Gideon. The Imperial warlord has once again eluded capture, somehow escaping from the shuttle transporting him to a New Republic tribunal. His home base of operations and his dark plans deeply involve Mandalore, as the world's tenacious survivors will soon come to know.

PART III: A NEW HOME

THE COVERT RELOCATED

In time, a scout from the Nevarro Mandalorian diaspora discovers a suitable world to be their next covert, and the Armorer brings the Forge with her to rekindle a home fire for the regathered Children of the Watch. It is an uncharted planet that exists solely as a catalog number in the old Imperial registry, a world unlikely to be prioritized in the New Republic's slow inventory of unclaimed territory.

CAVERNS OF REFUGE
The paths of ancient rivers carved a network of caves in the canyon walls of the lakeside covert where the Mandalorians find shelter and privacy. The largest cave closest to the beach is reserved for the Armorer and her forge.

THE LAKESIDE COVERT
The planet has no name, though those in the covert refer to it as the latest *Vheh'yaim*, a Mando'a word denoting a temporary hut. The covert situates itself along the caverns that line the beaches of an enormous freshwater lake. The lake is young, having formed from a river naturally dammed by a rockslide within the last decade. The ecology of the lake is still balancing, and massive predators from the river chains explore the area.

The *susulur*, or witnesses of the helming ritual

Ragnar, Ritual Candidate

Ritual Third

Ritual First

Interbedded shale and sandstone walls

GIANT TURTLE GATOR

The lake draws hungry and curious predators downriver, exploring the dammed depths for prey. A ravenous reptilian titan finds shelled morsels unlike any it has encountered before — dozens of Mandalorians who aggressively defend their covert. The creature's thick hide sloughs off many blows, while its massive bulk threatens to crush the Mandalorians in its mindless thrashings.

Ultimately it takes a blast from a starfighter-scale proton torpedo to kill the menacing beast.

- Laterally compressed armored tail
- Sclerotinized osteoderm plates
- Triple pair of sealable nostrils
- Clawed digits
- Bone-crushing jaws

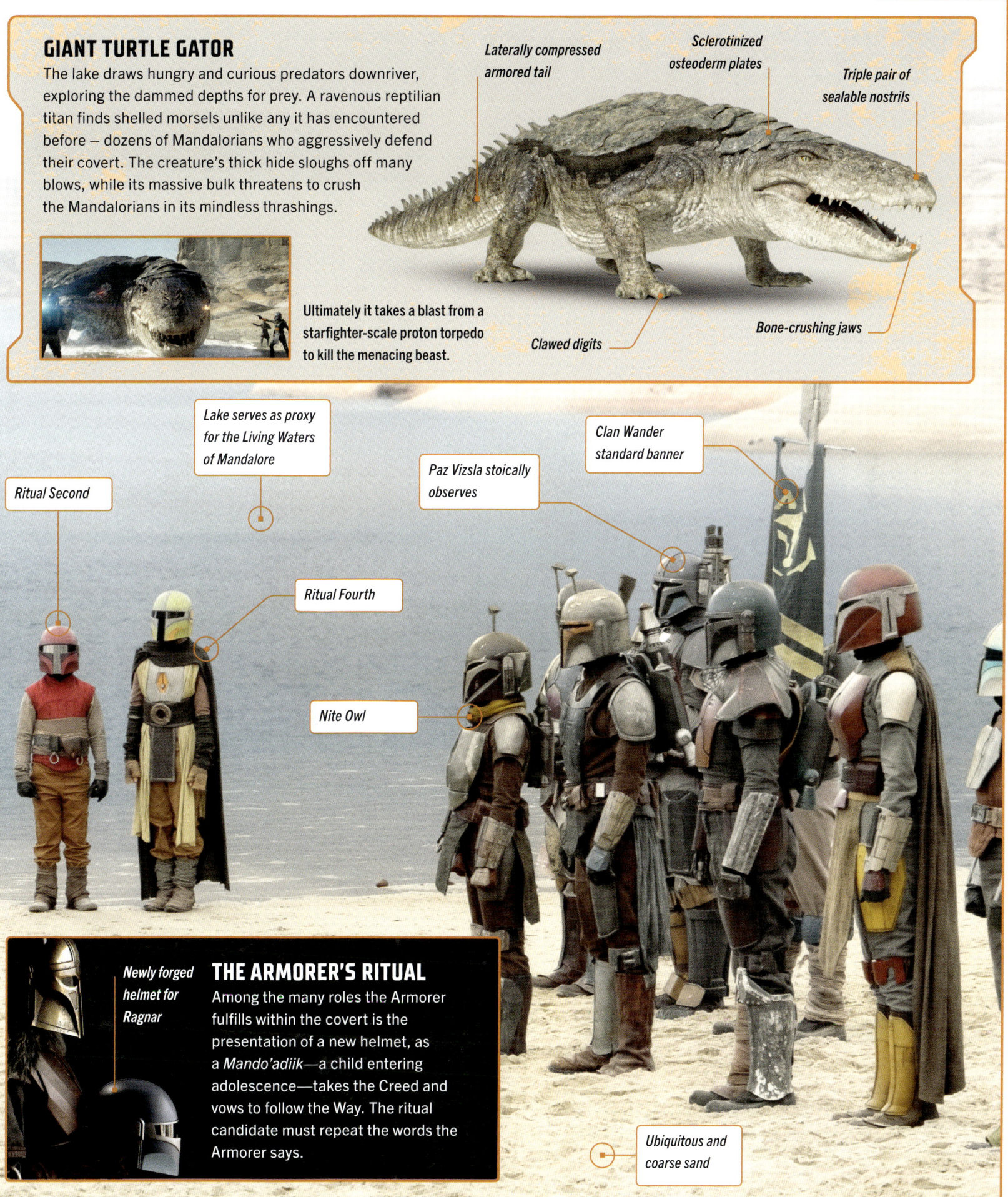

- Ritual Second
- Lake serves as proxy for the Living Waters of Mandalore
- Ritual Fourth
- Paz Vizsla stoically observes
- Clan Wander standard banner
- Nite Owl
- Ubiquitous and coarse sand

THE ARMORER'S RITUAL

Among the many roles the Armorer fulfills within the covert is the presentation of a new helmet, as a *Mando'adiik*—a child entering adolescence—takes the Creed and vows to follow the Way. The ritual candidate must repeat the words the Armorer says.

- Newly forged helmet for Ragnar

PART III: A NEW HOME

RETURN TO NEVARRO

Under the stewardship of Greef Karga, and with the elimination of Imperial holdouts on the planet, Nevarro has prospered. He proclaims it the gem of the Outer Rim, with its port city boasting revitalized shops and markets, and the outlying landscape no longer seen as bleak and inhospitable, but exotically rugged. Karga's boisterous encouragement and ambitious vision for the future resonates with the people of Nevarro, who have long felt neglected by the central systems.

Original upper torso, head and left arm

FALLEN HERO
Afforded a commanding presence in the town square of Nevarro City is a monument to IG-11, the reprogrammed assassin droid that played an instrumental role in ending the Imperial occupation. Metalworking artisans supplemented salvaged components of the exploded droid with bronzium appendages, completing the droid's anatomy in a heroic pose.

"In honor of IG-11 / Here stands a loyal friend and protector / Gone but never forgotten."

CONSTRUCTION BOOM
Karga and his design committee plan out Nevarro's rapid expansion, anticipating the city's growth by holographically plotting out new areas. Now an official trade spur off the Hydian Way, Nevarro sees increased traffic due to lucrative asteroid prospecting in the outer system.

Speeder bike rental shop

Mineral bathhouse and healing spa

Guild Lily AA-C39 freighter

Reconstructed and augmented gateway

Repulsorlift-assisted strongbox

CU-28
Attending to High Magistrate Karga in his administrative affairs is a fastidious protocol droid named CU-28. Karga and his staff usually refer to the droid as Copper for his brilliant finish.

HIGH MAGISTRATE KARGA

The lofty mantle of high magistrate fits well on Greef Karga's broad shoulders. His past among the underworld scoundrels has given him ample experience with what is required to survive in the lawless Outer Rim. When his planet is threatened by pirates, Karga refuses to capitulate or show weakness, despite being heavily outgunned.

From his office view, Karga can see all that Nevarro City is and imagines what it can be.

FOOT DROIDS
To keep his full Mantle of Office free of Nevarro dust, Karga is closely shadowed by a pair of wheeled foot droids.

- Collar of Office set with precious asteroid belt stones
- Fine textured doublet
- Aurodium buckle with sunrise emblem
- Quilted gloves with tightening bands
- Exterior hue evoking Nevarro volcanism
- Interior of magistrate mantle
- First Foot Droid 1BAR-0
- Second Foot Droid 2MAS-N
- Unitread disc
- Padded boots
- Heartfelt Apogee *Taylander-XCE* shuttle
- Under construction transmitter relay tower
- Dorion Discus refitted *Lancer*-class pursuer
- Rental crates ready to return

PART III: A NEW HOME
ANZELLAN DROIDSMITHS

> When Din Djarin requires the complex reactivation of a specialist droid for his return to Mandalore, High Magistrate Greef Karga knows just who to contact. Nevarro is home to a group of Anzellan tinkerers whom Greef tasks to keep his administrative droids—as well as his loyal cape-handling foot droids—operational.

The diminutive trio has found great commercial success amid the economic boom uplifting Nevarro. The belt-mining operations in the outer system rely heavily on automated excavation equipment, and the Anzellans have precise and affordable expertise to keep such crucial machines running under extreme conditions. Their services are in high demand, to the point that the Anzellans have a backlog of work, but they'll pull a favor for a friend of the high magistrate.

Djarin's order is tall—the safe reformatting of a battered IG-unit in an attempt to salvage the work of the late Kuiil, who turned IG-11 from a killer to an ally. A previous attempt to reactivate the scrapped droid resulted in the awakening of a relentless killing machine. But the spokesbeing for the Anzellans has a grim diagnosis: IG-11 is irreparably broken.

POWER DYNAMICS
The hierarchy of the Anzellan droidsmiths—if any—is not known. The smith with blue compression gloves often takes the lead when dealing with clients, though the one with the longest beard, who appears the eldest, may in fact be silently calling the shots (or at least is prone to fits of bossiness). The other member of the group seems to be the silently agreeable one who concentrates on work rather than workplace disagreements.

"NO SQUEEZIE!"
Enamored meeting a being closer to his own scale, the neighborly Grogu enwraps an Anzellan in a big (for those involved) hug, an act of aggressive affection the droidsmith vociferously rejects. Though Djarin tries to smooth matters over by explaining that Grogu is young, the Anzellan is in fact younger than the Mandalorian's charge.

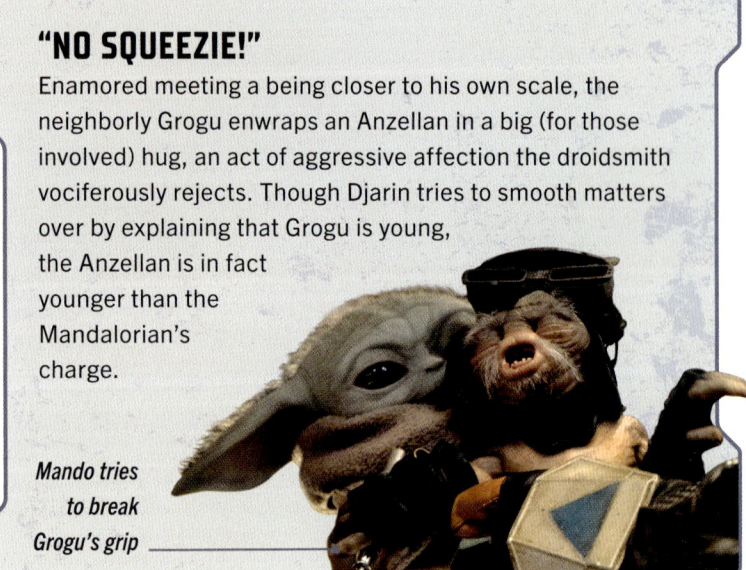

Mando tries to break Grogu's grip

CLOSE QUARTERS
The droidsmith workshop entrance is easy to miss. The whole place fits within the converted crawlspace of a dry goods store above it. A service hatch that can accommodate a crawling humanoid is next to a door scaled for the Anzellans. A cursory examination of the Anzellans' living quarters shows more than three sleeping cubbies, suggesting that their roster grows as work requires it.

With the strongest grasp of Basic, the Anzellans' spokesbeing meets customers at the door.

RESOURCEFUL TRIO

The droidsmiths' skills encompass a wide variety of machinery repair, from droids to speeders to starships. Their tiny proportions allow them to enter the guts of larger devices and operate on their inner workings up-close. Though these Anzellans understand several languages, they speak in a manner that Greef Karga knows well.

FACT FILE

DETAIL ORIENTED
Anzellan eyes naturally have floating corneal lenses that magnify their near vision.

DATA FILE

SUBJECT Anzellan droidsmith
HOMEWORLD Nevarro (current)
SPECIES Anzellan
HEIGHT 0.25 m (10 in)
AGE 34

A heavy equipment certification allows the droidsmith to pilot the experimental IG-12 mech unit, a design project he supervised.

- Loose harness loop
- IR and UV-rated welding specs
- Variable lens magna-goggles
- Insulated fingerless work gloves
- Self-crafted work gloves
- Empty tool pouch often holds snack crickets
- Ascension cable launcher

PART III: A NEW HOME
THE PIRATE KING

> Since the fall of the Empire, the already rambunctious Outer Rim has become even more unruly. For a time, a decrease in Imperial patrols revitalized trade, but it has also brought a corresponding rise in piracy. New Republic patrols cannot keep up, and mercenary protective forces are notoriously unreliable.

The jagged black-and-white livery of the loose-knit Pirate Nation is well known among the interstellar merchants as a sign to power down, drop shields, and deliver the goods in their holds. Piracy has even begun to encroach upon the border worlds of the Mid Rim, an alarming development casting the New Republic as weak and ineffective.

The boisterous leader of the Pirate Nation is its self-crowned monarch, Pirate King Gorian Shard, ruling from a throne within the bridge of his corsair.

DATA FILE
SUBJECT	Pirate King Gorian Shard
HOMEWORLD	Dhania
AFFILIATION	Pirate Nation
HEIGHT	2.01 m (6 ft 7 in)
AGE	Unknown; at least 60 standard years

Shard takes the helm of his corsair, indicating he means business.

TARGET: NEVARRO
Not content to simply pick off ore from the outer belts of the system, Gorian Shard covets Nevarro as a pirate base. He relishes intimidating Greef Karga, a past associate. Shard begins an aerial siege of Nevarro City, raining down devastating cannonades.

- Expressive protoderm brow
- Photosynthesizing tufts
- Fast-growing and aromatic beard
- "Royal" baldric
- Rycrit-hide pauldron
- Corusca gem rings
- Walking stick made from recycled blaster rifle parts
- Tarnoongan frock coat
- Cavalier boots

SHARD'S CREW

The pirate crew's loyalty is maintained by a fair disbursement of captured treasure among the ranks, creating a deeply vested interest in Gorian Shard's continued success. Shard brooks no disloyalty, dispensing fierce punishments for those who would dare hoard loot or not attend to their duties. It's what passes for a code among the amoral lot.

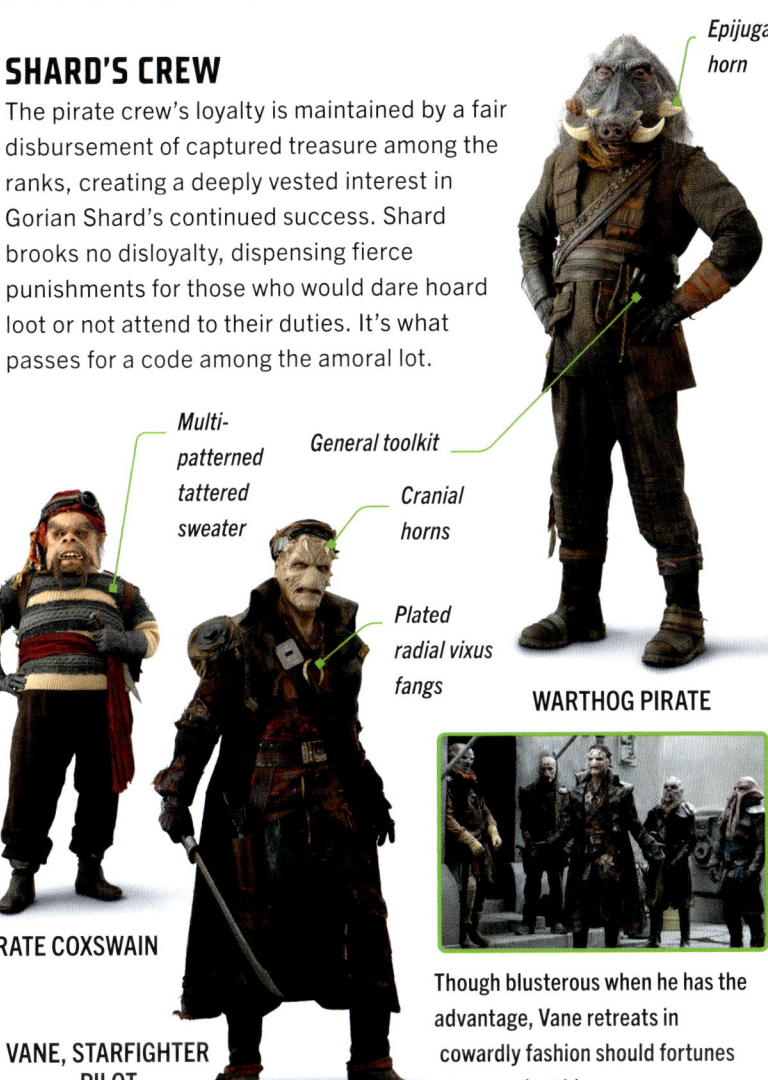

- Multi-patterned tattered sweater
- General toolkit
- Epijugal horn
- Cranial horns
- Plated radial vixus fangs

PIRATE COXSWAIN

VANE, STARFIGHTER PILOT

WARTHOG PIRATE

Though blusterous when he has the advantage, Vane retreats in cowardly fashion should fortunes turn against him.

REPUBLIC INACTION

Nevarro's request for help fails to penetrate the overburdened New Republic bureaucracy. The New Republic Intelligence offices on Coruscant are swamped with weeks of backlog processing, and requisition officers like Colonel Tuttle must prioritize relief efforts favoring member worlds in good standing.

- Regulation uniform officer belt
- Form-fitting tall boots

Though Captain Teva tries to rally help in person, Amnesty Officer G68 reminds Tuttle of Nevarro's independent standing.

COLONEL TUTTLE

PIRATE VESSELS

Pirate King Gorian Shard's flagship is a 125-meter (410-feet) long *Cumulus*-class corsair with 14 retractable multi-ordnance bombardment gunwales on its ventral surface. Its shielded ax-head prow can disrupt enemy shields and penetrate battleship armor. The corsair has rapid launch capabilities to scramble a squadron of outdated but sturdy Rendili StarDrive F3-Vara snubfighters.

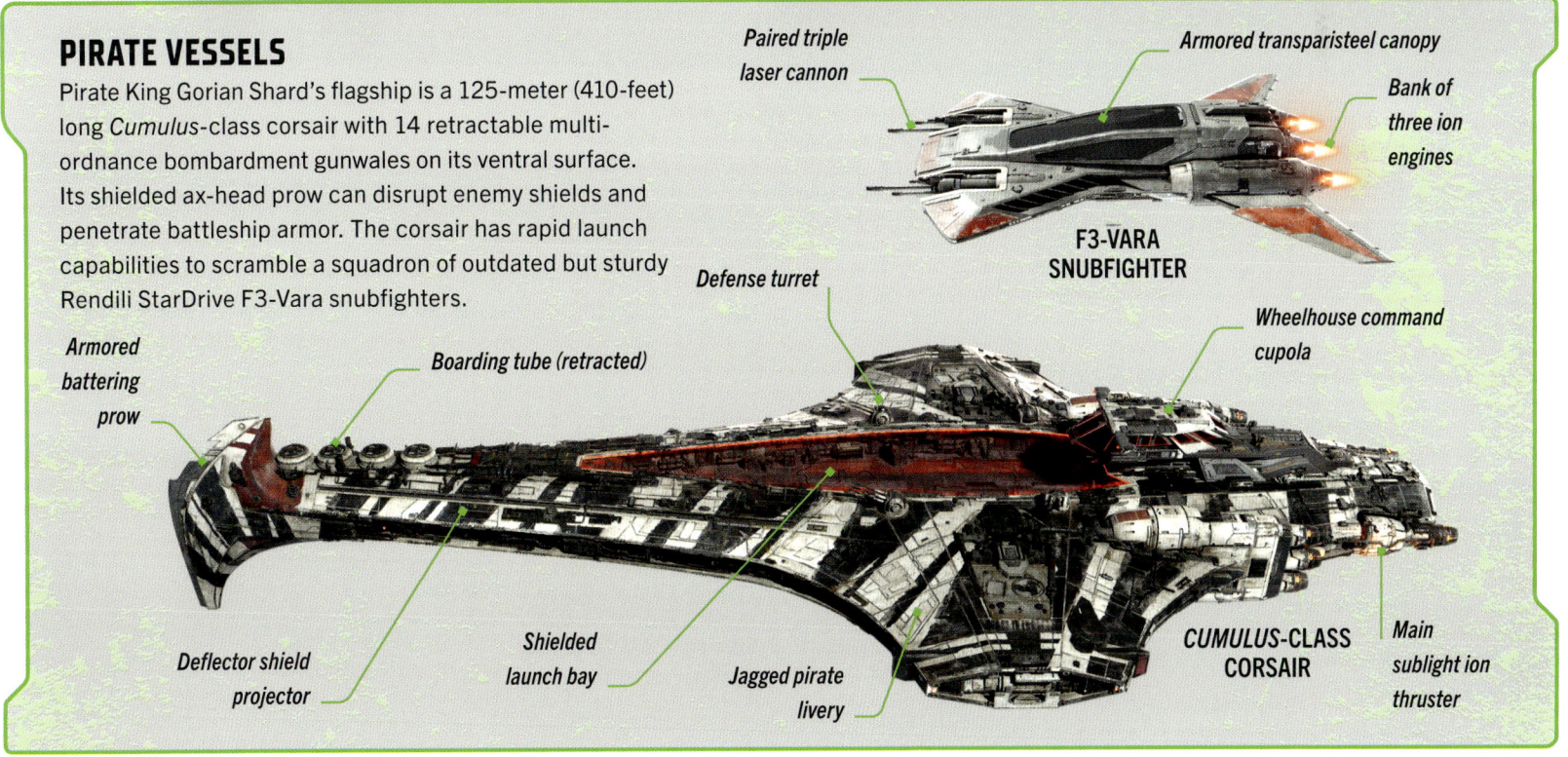

- Paired triple laser cannon
- Armored transparisteel canopy
- Bank of three ion engines

F3-VARA SNUBFIGHTER

- Armored battering prow
- Boarding tube (retracted)
- Defense turret
- Wheelhouse command cupola
- Deflector shield projector
- Shielded launch bay
- Jagged pirate livery
- Main sublight ion thruster

CUMULUS-CLASS CORSAIR

PART III: A NEW HOME

KALEVALA

In the modern era, the Mandalorian throne worlds of the ruling Houses are a shadow of their former selves. Kalevala, which orbits the same principal star as Mandalore, was the domain of one of the most prominent ancient families, House Kryze. It was spared the devastating bombardment that sundered Mandalore, which resulted in a withering blow to Kryze pride: apparently they were not even worth Imperial reprisal. Most of the Kryze lineage has since scattered.

KRYZE FORTRESS
Kryze Fortress holds the marbled throne of the Duchess, which stands at the end of a great hall echoing with a haunting emptiness evoking memories of past glory.

Former site of Kalevala Spaceworks corporate headquarters

Kryze Kot Isle, site of Kryze Fortress

Korkeal Vhettin pasture lands

Site of the ancient Battle of E'tad Alore

Royal Tihaar Vineyards

Mar'eyce Sea

The Mandalorian and Grogu seek alliance with Bo-Katan Kryze, only to discover her own forces have abandoned her.

DATA FILE

REGION	Outer Rim
SECTOR	Mandalore
SYSTEM	Mandalore
DIAMETER	11,450 km (7,115 miles)
TERRAIN	Verdant hills, grasslands, and forested canyons
MOONS	None
POPULATION	425,000 (estimated)

FOOTDROID
A helpful Tac-Spec FIV footman droid attends to Bo-Katan's needs in her spacious palace.

Reinforced chassis

Pelvic servomotor

Precision-articulated limbs

BO-KATAN ABANDONED

Upon her return to the Mandalore system having captured an Imperial freighter at Trask, as well as a light cruiser once belonging to Moff Gideon, Bo-Katan expected to use these military prizes to stage a greater assault on the Imperial remnant. Without the Darksaber to command the Mandalorians, however, she cannot rally an army. It is a bitter realization of the double-edged nature of Mandalorian fealty to custom.

- Nite Owl sigil
- Inherited warrioress cuirass
- Secured tactical belt
- Greaves conceal knife holster
- Outer solar gather panel
- Reinforced transparisteel viewport
- Elongated panels provide power to weapons
- Armored wing spar
- Fuel tank cap

TIE INTERCEPTOR
Squadrons of swift TIE interceptors from an unknown base ambush Kryze and Djarin upon their return from Mandalore.

- Overloading main power generator
- Erupting donjon tower

UNDER SIEGE

The sudden appearance of TIE interceptors forces Kryze to scramble. Djarin ejects from her Gauntlet fighter to jetpack down to his high-speed N-1. The pursuit of the interceptors through coastal canyons distracts the Mandalorians from the arrival of TIE bombers that lay waste to Kryze Fortress. The attackers are short-ranged craft, and no carrier ship appears on the scopes. The disturbing question lingers: where did they launch from?

Bo-Katan Kryze has been threading the coastal gorges in high-speed aircraft since her childhood, a near-reflexive skill now.

Proton bombs dropped from TIE bombers devastate the unshielded fortress, its defenses long stripped away during Duchess Satine Kryze's reign.

- The undercroft survives deep reverberations

PART III: A NEW HOME
R5-D4

The astromechs from Industrial Automaton proved time and again their versatility and resourcefulness in the cause of the Rebellion, with examples that continue into the era of the New Republic. The Rebellion's reliance on snub fighters meant it went through many astromechs during the war, pressing them into frontline service with an intensity unseen since the Clone Wars.

Having been salvaged from a burning sandcrawler on Tatooine by Jawa traders, R5-D4 was encountered by Alliance historian Voren Na'al, who was piecing together Luke Skywalker's remarkable journey from Tatooine farm boy to rebel hero. Na'al purchased R5 at a "fire sale" discount, repaired his motivator, and downloaded an account of the pivotal Jawa droid auction that catapulted Skywalker into history. Rather than let the droid be just a historic footnote, Na'al returned with him to the Rebellion, and R5-D4 was pressed into service as part of Carson Teva's X-wing squadron, participating in several highly classified missions against the Empire.

Following the Alliance victories at Endor and Jakku, R5-D4 was mustered out of starfighter service and given a security-mandated data wipe. Na'al then returned the droid to Tatooine.

HUMBLE ORIGINS
Originally an agromech design, R5-D4 was nicknamed "Red" and put up for sale at the fateful Jawa auction that brought R2-D2 and C-3PO to Luke Skywalker's moisture farm on Tatooine. R5's origins before that are lost to a memory wipe. Red's faulty motivator caused Owen Lars to pass on buying the droid, taking R2-D2 instead.

SPELUNKING DROID
Unable to acquire a working restoration of IG-11 to serve as a spelunking droid to inspect conditions on Mandalore, the Mandalorian instead takes R5-D4 as a loaner from Peli Motto, with the promise that the skittish droid is built for adventure. R5's atmospheric scanners confirm that the planet is not irradiated or poisoned from fallout.

R5-D4 debunks the myth that Mandalore is uninhabitable, prompting Mando and Grogu to continue their exploration of the Sundari ruins.

R5-D4 RESTORED

Although R5-D4's war records have been expunged from his memories, he still has the contact protocols keyed to now-defunct Rebel Alliance signal frequencies. In this way, Carson Teva is able to find his old astromech and reconnect with the droid, now in Mando's service at an uncharted covert. That events should conspire to reunite these people this way gives a skeptical Teva a brief appreciation of destiny.

- High-frequency receiver antenna
- Retractable holographic projector
- Articulated shoulder lifts to reveal booster turbine
- Door conceals universal computer interface arm
- Interference pulse stabilizer
- System lubricant filter/reservoir
- All-terrain drive tread in foot
- Retractable leg stowage compartment
- Spacecraft linkage and control arms (retracted)
- Burtt acoustic signaler
- High-power recharge coupling

DATA FILE

SUBJECT	R5-D4
HOMEWORLD	Tatooine
SERIES	R-series astromech droid
AFFILIATION	Independent, formerly Rebel Alliance
HEIGHT	1.15 m (3 ft 9 in) (not including antenna)

FACT FILE

HIGH FLYING
R5-D4's once empty rocket booster brackets have been refurbished by Peli Motto.

FARM DUTY
R5-D4's programming originally had an R2-AG4 agromech overlay to better condition him for work on irrigation maintenance and crop yield calculations.

PART III: A NEW HOME

MANDALORE

The throne-world of the ancient Mand'alor has weathered millennia of strife, emerging after a devastating period of civil wars to embrace pacifism at the start of the Clone Wars. It was a desperate effort to keep the planet from succumbing to irreparable devastation, but it would not last. The coming of the Empire and the capricious cruelty of Moff Gideon razed Mandalore's surface in what was widely believed to be a final deathblow to the planet.

DATA FILE

REGION	Outer Rim
SECTOR	Mandalore
SYSTEM	Mandalore
DIAMETER	9,200 km (5,716 miles)
TERRAIN	Blasted and fused glass surface
MOONS	2 (Concordia, Mesumika)
POPULATION	Unknown; formerly 4 million

- Keldabe, ancestral capital
- Kyrimorut Peak
- Norg Bral
- Evaporated Apiruna River Valley
- Sundari, former capital
- Former site of Great Veshok Conservatory
- Kelita-Ka

ASH AND DUST
The durability of well-forged beskar means that the cratered cities of Mandalore are grim reminders of the lost. Organic tissue caught in the blasts has vaporized, but the bleached helmets and armored plates remain.

Strained and battered beskar matrix

CLAN KRYZE HELMET

In the ruins of Sundari, Din Djarin lifts a bone-white beskar helmet.

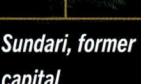

GLASS GRAVES
Imperial bombardment has fused a triple compound of quartz, calcite, and beskar dust into trinitite glass.

Two pairs of eyes with bioluminescent retinas

Powerful mandibles

Primitive tattered rags belted to carry items

Prehensile toes

ALAMITE SCAVENGER

TRIPLE AX

Stone ax heads

TRINITITE CUDGEL

Glass edge split to sharpened point

HAFTED CLUBS

Trinitite head

CYBORG MECH

An unfathomable scavenger lurking in the Sundari wreckage is a being that has been so cybernetically altered out of life-sustaining necessity as to be unrecognizable. The twisted survivor feeds on the blood of his prey—alamites, sewer lizards, and other life-forms it can immobilize with an injection.

SPIDER TANK ARMOR

Armored carapace housing

Articulated limbs

Scissor-claw manipulators

Outside of his armored tank/suit, the spindly mech blasts a debilitating electro-charge.

The cyborg mech prefers live prey, keeping them restrained as it feeds.

Djarin is ambushed by savage alamites in the layered Sundari ruins.

Pale shafts of sunlight from surface

THE MINES OF MANDALORE

Found deep beneath Sundari are the fabled Mines of Mandalore, said to be built atop the original crevasse wherein the very first vein of beskar was harvested by the primordial Mandalorian explorers. Deep waters wind through these stygian caverns.

Cladded air exchange shaft

Remains of modern ore conveyer tubes

Subsidence crevice into lower, older sections

Collapsed ore house

PART III: A NEW HOME
MYTHOSAUR

The earliest accounts of Mandalorian history describe their arrival at a savage world that tested brave settlers with unforgiving wilderness teeming with deadly wildlife. The primordial clans discovered the unique metal—beskar—in the stone that let them tame their world, including the previously indomitable apex beast, the mythosaur. Separating fact from folklore is impossible with the passage of millennia, but the creature is a foundational cultural symbol for the Mandalorians.

MANDALORIAN KYR'BES
The *kyr'bes* is the symbolic depiction of the mythosaur skull as a crown acknowledging the conqueror history of the Mandalorians. Originally the heraldry of the long-extinct Clan Keldau, the symbol now belongs to all Mandalorians, permeating beyond boundaries of clan, bloodline, or status. To be Mandalorian is to have earned the right to wear the symbol.

Caudofemoral musculature aids in swimming

Armored hide has sharp defensive osteoderm spikes

Powerful leg muscles for climbing and swift running speed

Hardened claws with beskar-enriched serrations

FACT FILE
DIET
Amphibious and carnivorous, the mythosaur feasted both on land and in water, able to hunt large prey as well as continually consume small fishes.

HABITAT
The ancient glades and lagoons of Mandalore have vanished along with the mythosaur. The old mines are said to have once been their underground lairs.

DATA FILE	
SUBJECT	Mythosaur
HOMEWORLD	Mandalore
SIZE	Varied by breed; common Mandalore breed averages 30 m (100 ft) in length
LIFESPAN	Unknown

> "THE MYTHOSAUR BELONGS TO ALL MANDALORIANS."
> – THE ARMORER

POWERFUL PORTENT

Generations of conflict—Mandalorians versus Jedi and intense interhouse civil war—scoured Mandalore's surface of vegetation. The devastating Imperial bombardment that followed destroyed any dream that the ancient mythosaur survived into the modern era. The beast was but another fading relic of Mandalorian culture. Bo-Katan Kryze's glimpse of a mythosaur lurking in the Living Waters aligns with prophetic hope that the return of the mythosaur would herald a rejuvenation of Mandalore and its people.

- Trapezial scutes
- Bony supraorbital ridge
- Curved maxillary tusks extending from upper jaw
- Lower jaw often missing from skull samples and artwork
- Ridged sternum; the legendary source of the mask of Mandalore the First

PART III: A NEW HOME

INTRIGUE ON CORUSCANT

Following the end of the Galactic Civil War, the nascent New Republic government operated largely out of Chandrila while the chaos on Coruscant settled down. Still, the New Republic needed the massive apparatus of government on the city planet—the institutions, expertise, personnel, and administrators that had kept galactic society whirring regardless of what regime ruled the capital. It was not without controversy that so much of the New Republic's operational structure came to resemble that of the Empire.

> "AMAZING. ALL THESE PEOPLE WORKING TOGETHER TO MAKE SOMETHING BETTER."
> – PENN PERSHING, AMNESTY SCIENTIST L52

Federal District, old Senate Hall

Holographic Zoo of Extinct Animals

Decommissioning Shipyards

Skydome Botanical Gardens

Water and power distribution node

Industrial District

DATA FILE	
REGION	Core Worlds
SECTOR	Corusca
SYSTEM	Coruscant
DIAMETER	12,240 km (7,605 miles)
TERRAIN	Concentric levels of city sprawl
MOONS	4
POPULATION	Unknown; estimated to be near three trillion, with a third being permanent residents, though a formal census hasn't been performed in decades

PATH TO REDEMPTION

Penn Pershing is a brilliant geneticist and cloning engineer, a top graduate from the Colomus Institute. His focus on cellular repair innovation was sidelined and coopted by Imperial military research, and he spent years on Gideon's secret recombinant projects that were never part of his projected career path. To make amends while in the New Republic Amnesty Program, Pershing wishes to return to science to help others.

Auto-tinting plasspecs lenses

Civilian's tunic

PENN PERSHING

Pershing's doubts about the New Republic bureaucracy are part of official records thanks to his parole droid sessions.

Goaded by Elia Kane to follow his instincts, Pershing breaks amnesty protocols in an attempt to acquire contraband lab equipment.

ELIA KANE

A communications officer aboard Moff Gideon's light cruiser, Elia Kane is now Officer G68 within the New Republic Amnesty Program. She befriends Pershing, coaxing him to take risks and break rules, a ruse to complete her own secret plans.

Amnesty Program uniform and badge

Technical officers, functionaries, and non-military Imperial leadership are given a second chance.

Kane and Pershing never interacted serving Gideon like they do in the Amnesty Housing Complex.

TECHNICAL REHABILITATION

In cases of aggressive transgression, amnesty subjects undergo attunement sessions in a 602 mitigator, a device that uses alpha waves to calm anxious minds.

Pershing is unaware Kane intends to sabotage the process

System control programming interface

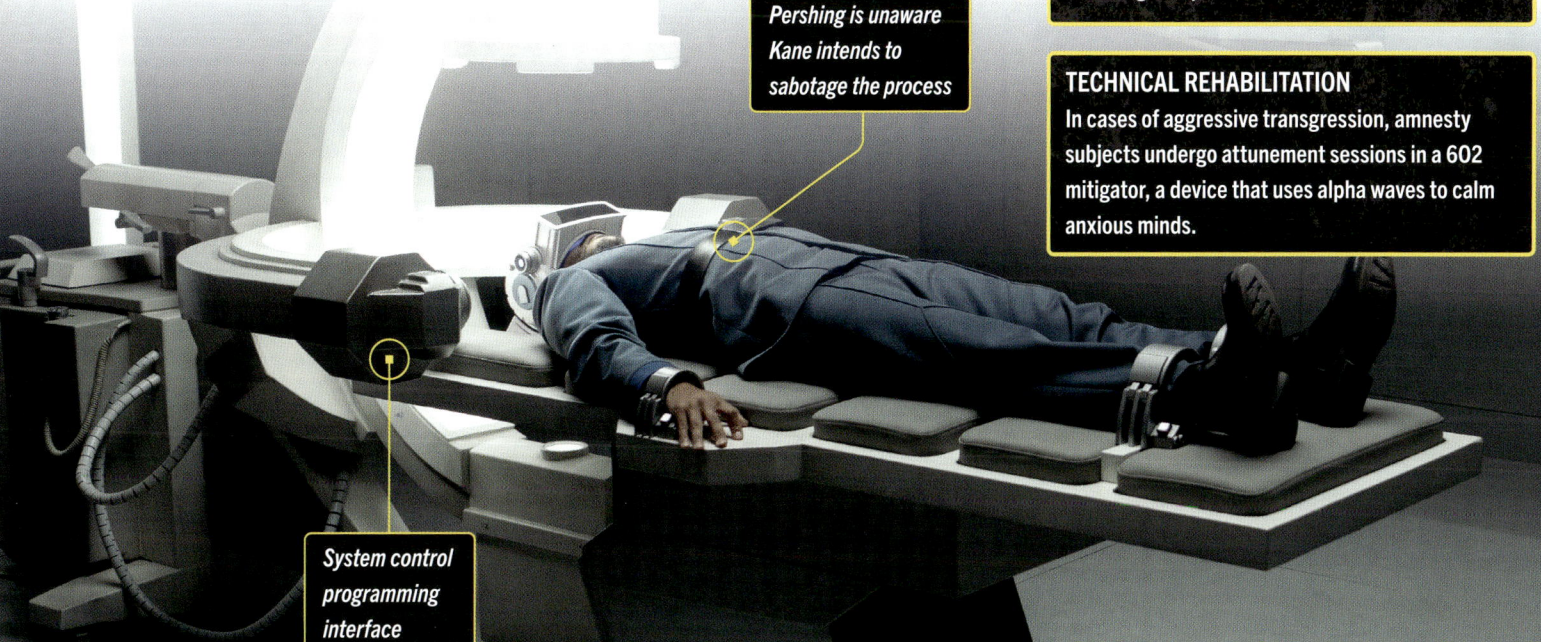

PART III: A NEW HOME

LEARNING THE WAY

> The lakeside beaches form the perfect training grounds for the Children of the Watch, as they undergo their daily drills to keep in peak fighting shape. Target practice, sparring, and Rising Phoenix maneuvers keep the beach abuzz with activities, as Mandalorians of all ages participate. They are monitored by instructors, and their performances judged according to the tenets of the Creed.

The Judge equips both combatants with training dart launchers, capable of firing three darts each. Score R:0, G:0

After witnessing the Child's remarkable abilities, the Mandalorian decides Grogu is ready to begin training in the Way. He leads the Child over to the Judge, who at first decrees Grogu to be too small. But Mando is confident and vouches for him as his ward. Ready to give challenge is Ragnar, who confidently echoes the Judge's dismissal of Grogu.

They engage in a battle of training darts, which proves to be a test of confidence for Grogu, and one of humility for Ragnar.

Instantly, Ragnar fires as the challenge begins. He easily lands a bright green dart splat against his tiny opponent. Score R:1, G:0

SURVIVAL TRADITIONS

Long is the history of parents pushing their hesitant children into daunting challenges. For Mandalorians, a *hibir*, or student, must be forged into a *cuyan*, or survivor. This focus stems from earliest Mandalorian history of survival within their murderous wilderness, a reality that has returned after the purging of their world.

Bo-Katan Kryze shares quiet words of encouragement with an inexperienced Grogu.

For having scored a visible hit, the Judge awards Ragnar a point. The challenge continues. Grogu is promptly hit again. Score R:2, G:0

Grogu acrobatically jumps away from the third dart. Upon landing, Grogu fires three darts against his opponent, winning the challenge. Score R:2, G:3

TRAINING DARTS

Designed for foundlings undergoing training, this wrist-cuff mounted launcher has an adjustable strap that must be tightened to its smallest measure for Grogu. A pneumatic launcher responds to a squeezed fist by firing a dart in sequence. More finessed muscle control can activate each individual barrel, should a Mandalorian opt to vary the dart types.

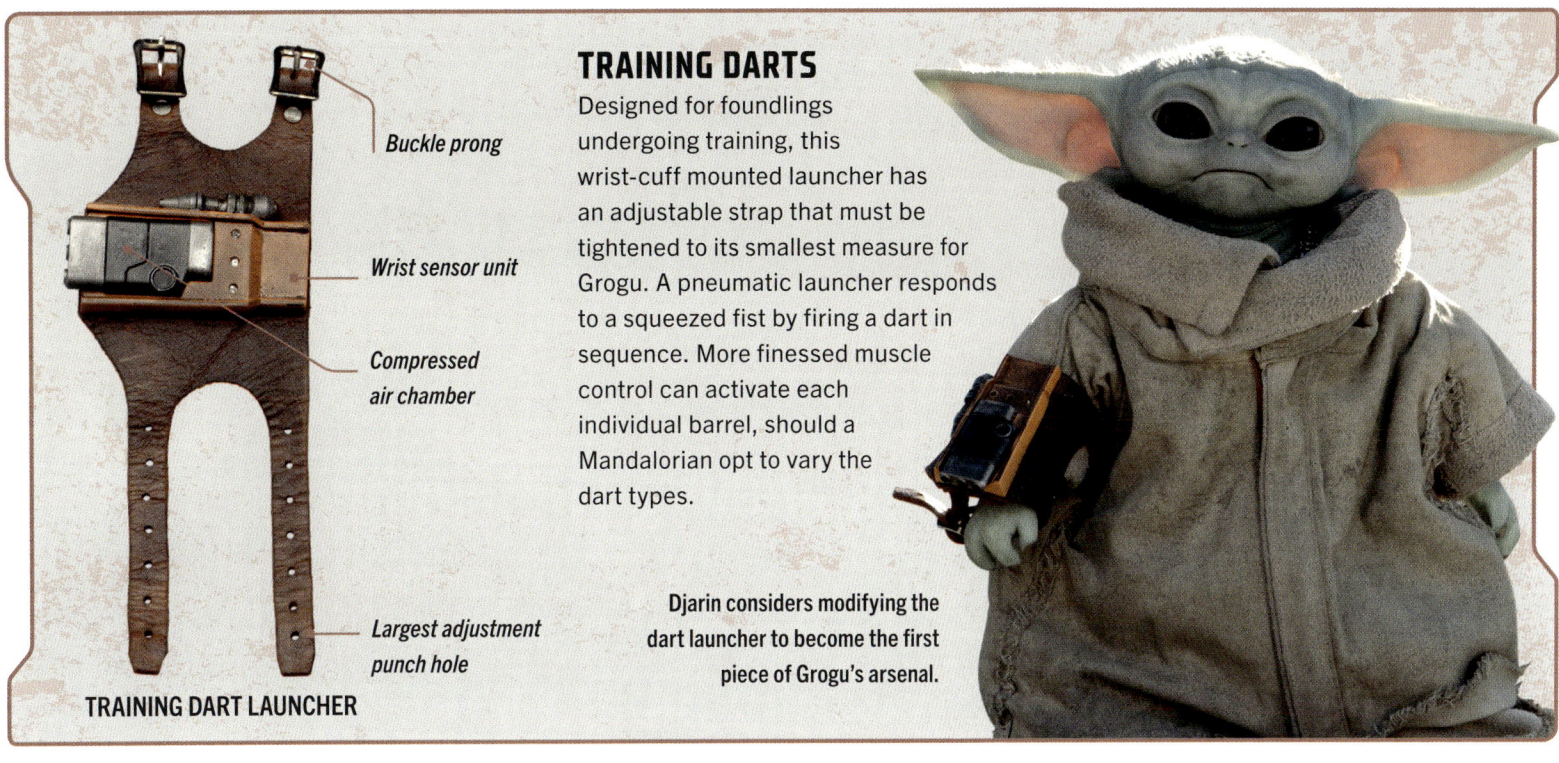

- Buckle prong
- Wrist sensor unit
- Compressed air chamber
- Largest adjustment punch hole

TRAINING DART LAUNCHER

Djarin considers modifying the dart launcher to become the first piece of Grogu's arsenal.

THE JUDGE

Another storied role in Mandalorian culture with a title that supersedes an individual's name and identity is that of Judge. A Judge can weigh personal disputes and has the daily task of adjudicating combat training.

- Z-7D jetpack
- Holstered WESTAR-35 blaster pistol
- Beskar cuisse
- Sniper position schynbald
- Durasteel coated beskar helmet
- Heirloom cuirass
- Adjudicator's cloak
- Weatherproof gaiters

GROGU'S ARMOR

The Armorer crafts for Grogu a protective beskar roundel to affix to his mail shirt, marked with the mudhorn signet he shares with Din Djarin.

The Armorer explains the role of the Forge to Grogu as she works.

The Armorer presents Grogu with the finished roundel, which he will grow into.

- Kinetic capacitor
- Beskar rim
- Inductor unit
- Data storage bead
- Polished surface

BESKAR ROUNDEL (INTERIOR)

BESKAR ROUNDEL (EXTERIOR)

PART III: A NEW HOME
GROGU'S PAST

For Grogu, moments of fear and doubt bring back memories of the tragic night that ended the Clone Wars. A youngling at the Jedi Temple, Grogu was undergoing the rudimentary training among the youngest Jedi hopefuls when darkness infiltrated this most secure of sanctuaries. Clone troopers led by a fallen Jedi marched upon the Temple, filling its polished corridors with deadly blaster fire. With their most capable Knights and masters spread across the galaxy, the valiant Jedi defenders at their Coruscant home were overwhelmed. No one would be spared in the onslaught, not even the younglings.

Jedi Knights, knowing that the future of the very Order was at stake, spirited Grogu to safety. The defenseless Child needed his hover pram for mobility, and like a precious prize, it was carried aloft by a chain of Jedi who fell before the merciless fire of the clone trooper invaders. One determined Jedi, Kelleran Beq, escaped the assault with Grogu accompanying. The Child was saved.

ESCAPE PRAM
Grogu uses a repulsorlift conveyance for transportation. The Jedi Temple had several such prams for species at a similar growth stage. Caretaker programming imprinted on specific Jedi Knights for the pram to follow.

SIDE VIEW

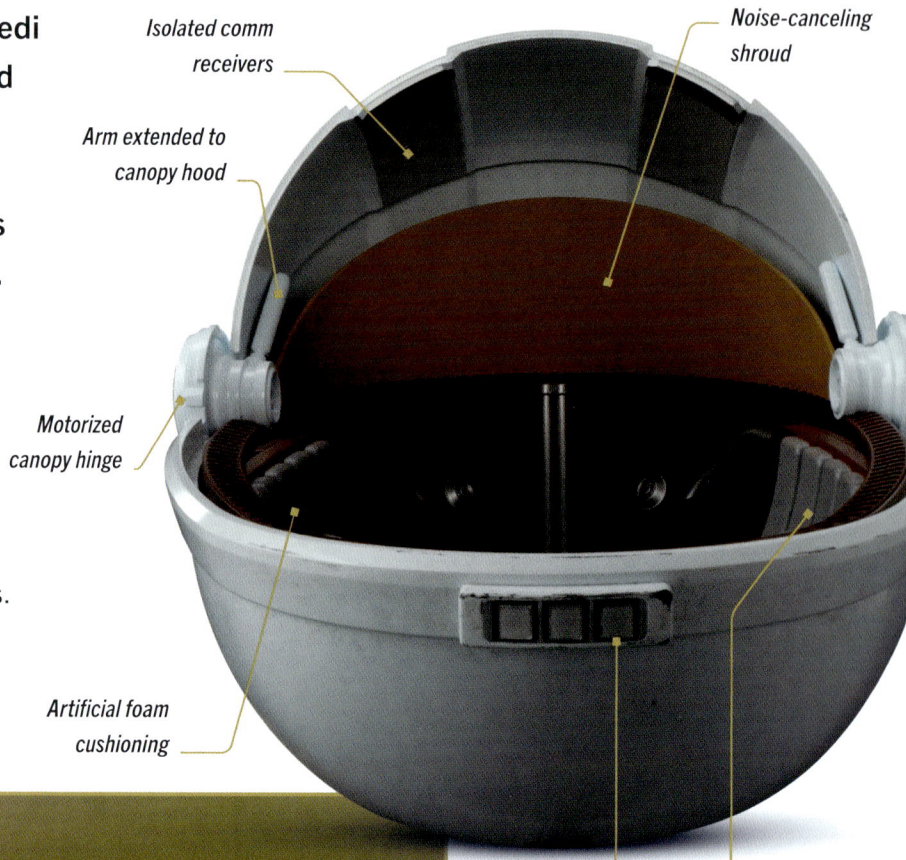

- Isolated comm receivers
- Noise-canceling shroud
- Arm extended to canopy hood
- Motorized canopy hinge
- Artificial foam cushioning
- Air circulation and ventilation channel
- Safety seal switches

Comforting blanket

FEARFUL YOUNGLING
A core Jedi ability is control over the influence of fear. Well trained Jedi Knights can override deeply instinctual fear responses, finding clarity through mental focus. Such instruction starts at a very young age, and little Grogu has much to learn.

501ST LEGION

Fanning out with ordered precision, the elite clone troopers of the 501st Legion were pressed into an emergency assignment to pacify the Jedi Temple. All its inhabitants were decreed by Order 66 as traitors to the Republic.

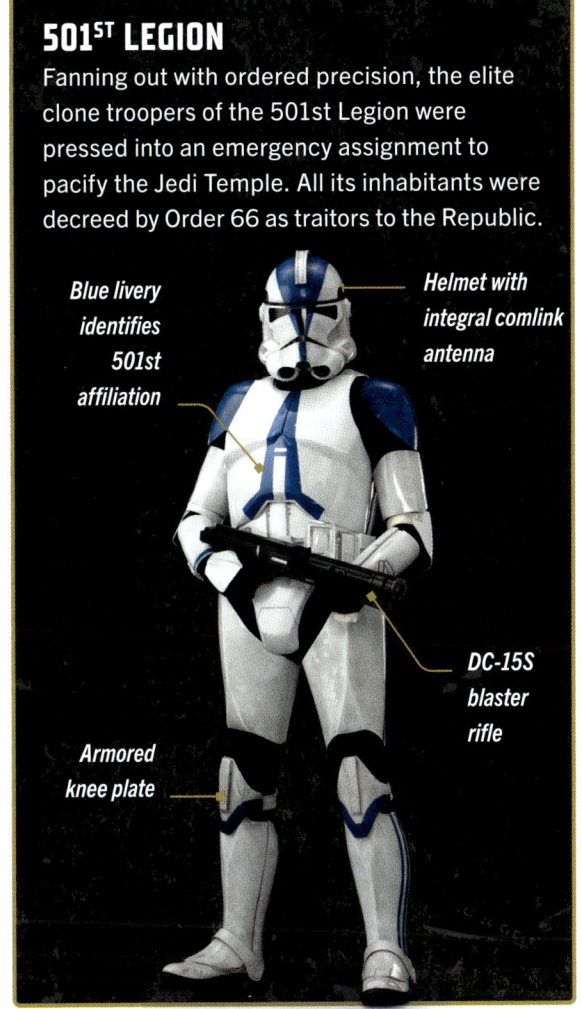

- Blue livery identifies 501st affiliation
- Helmet with integral comlink antenna
- DC-15S blaster rifle
- Armored knee plate

JEDI PROTECTORS

Many Knights and instructors rallied around the most vulnerable of younglings in the Jedi Temple, defending the Order's future against the incoming clone trooper blasterfire with their lightsaber blades.

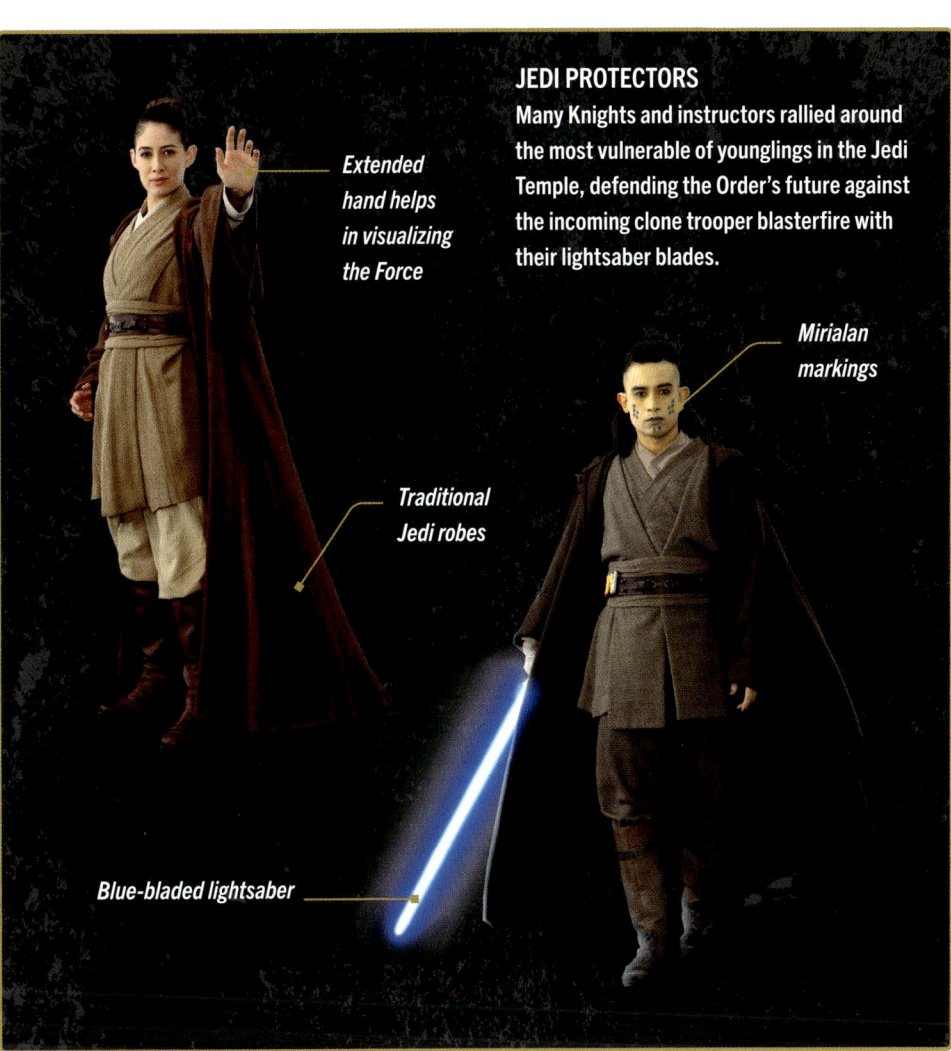

- Extended hand helps in visualizing the Force
- Mirialan markings
- Traditional Jedi robes
- Blue-bladed lightsaber

V-WING

Nimble starfighters from late in the Clone Wars, fielded as improvements over the V-19 Torrent interceptors, the KSE Alpha-3 *Nimbus*-class V-wings are excellent in dogfighting engagements. Their cutting-edge propulsion and maneuverability let clone pilots outfly droid starfighters. As the Empire consolidated its military power, the V-wing was phased out and replaced with TIE-series craft.

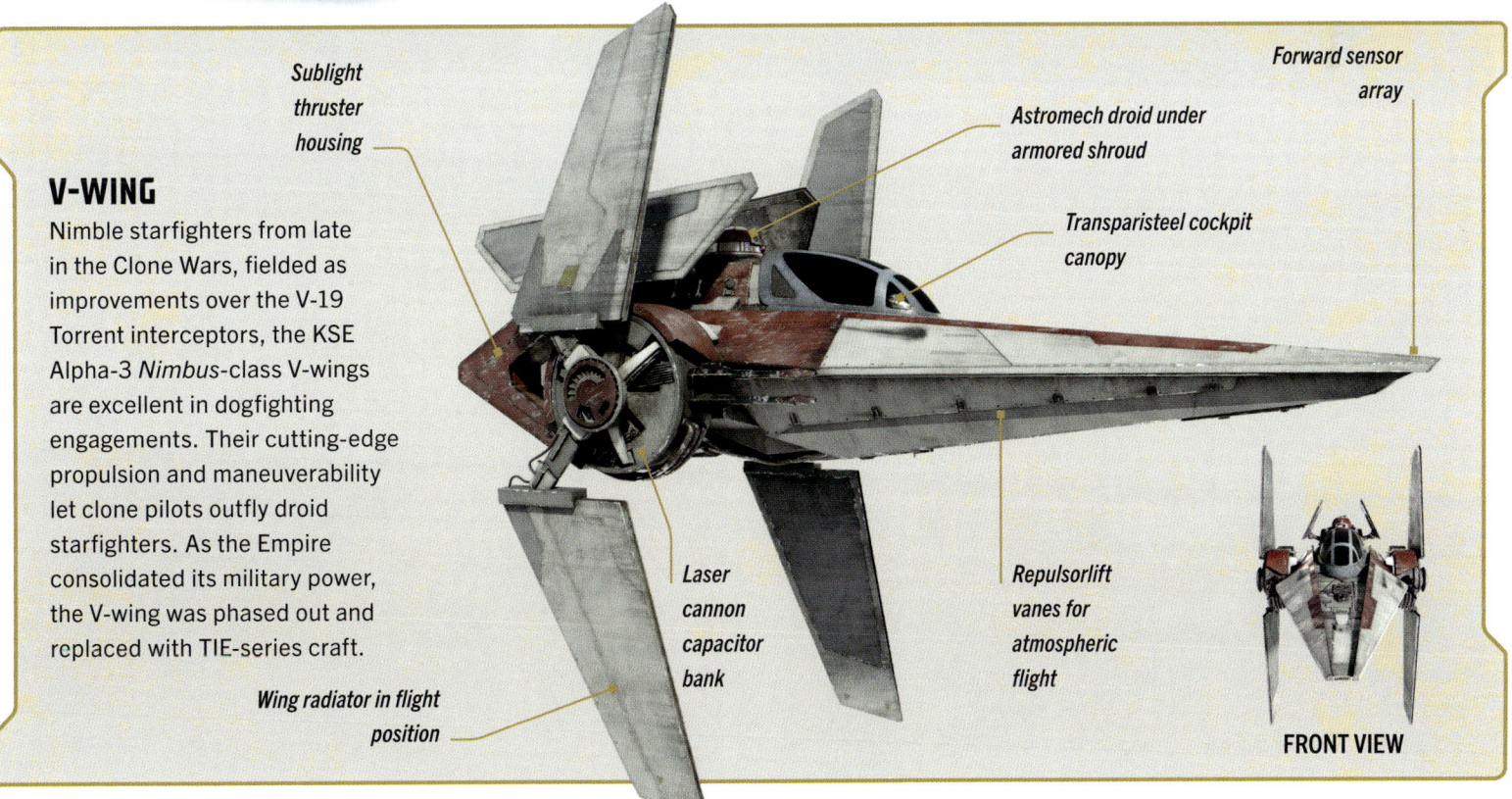

- Sublight thruster housing
- Forward sensor array
- Astromech droid under armored shroud
- Transparisteel cockpit canopy
- Laser cannon capacitor bank
- Repulsorlift vanes for atmospheric flight
- Wing radiator in flight position

FRONT VIEW

PART III: A NEW HOME
KELLERAN BEQ

Green-bladed lightsaber held in high defensive grip

Traditional Jedi tabard

Open hand feeling and focusing the Force

> Chaos engulfed the Jedi Temple on the night of Order 66, as Darth Vader marched a legion of clone troopers into the landmark. Many Jedi were coldly gunned down as they defended their home, scrambling to get the youngest among their ranks to safety. When it came to getting Grogu away, it fell to one of the most trusted guardians among them: Kelleran Beq.

Beq guarded Grogu's hover pram to one of the Temple exits, defending the Child with his paired lightsabers, one of them the blade of a fallen comrade. Beq absconded with a speeder bike that had transported clones to the conflict zone, racing off into the night. Republic gunships gave pursuit, but Beq took the clones on a circuitous chase past Monument Plaza and into the Senate district.

Beq arrived at a Naboo delegation platform where a contingent of Royal Security Guards offered vital covering fire. A chromed yacht was fully fueled and ready to depart. With Grogu secure inside the vessel, Beq outmaneuvered clone V-wing fighters and launched into hyperspace. Grogu was safe… for now.

THE SABERED HAND
A versatile duelist, Beq in particular favored a fighting form that gripped the lightsaber with one hand and freed up the other to help direct the Force with great focus. Beq's perception was greatly attuned to the ebb and flow of the Force surrounding him.

ESCAPE VELOCITY
As one of the few Jedi Knights to escape Coruscant who was witness to the sacking of the Temple, Beq knew that the recall signal that followed was a trap. He fled the capital with Grogu, though where he went next is not known. These dark times are not memories that Grogu revisits often.

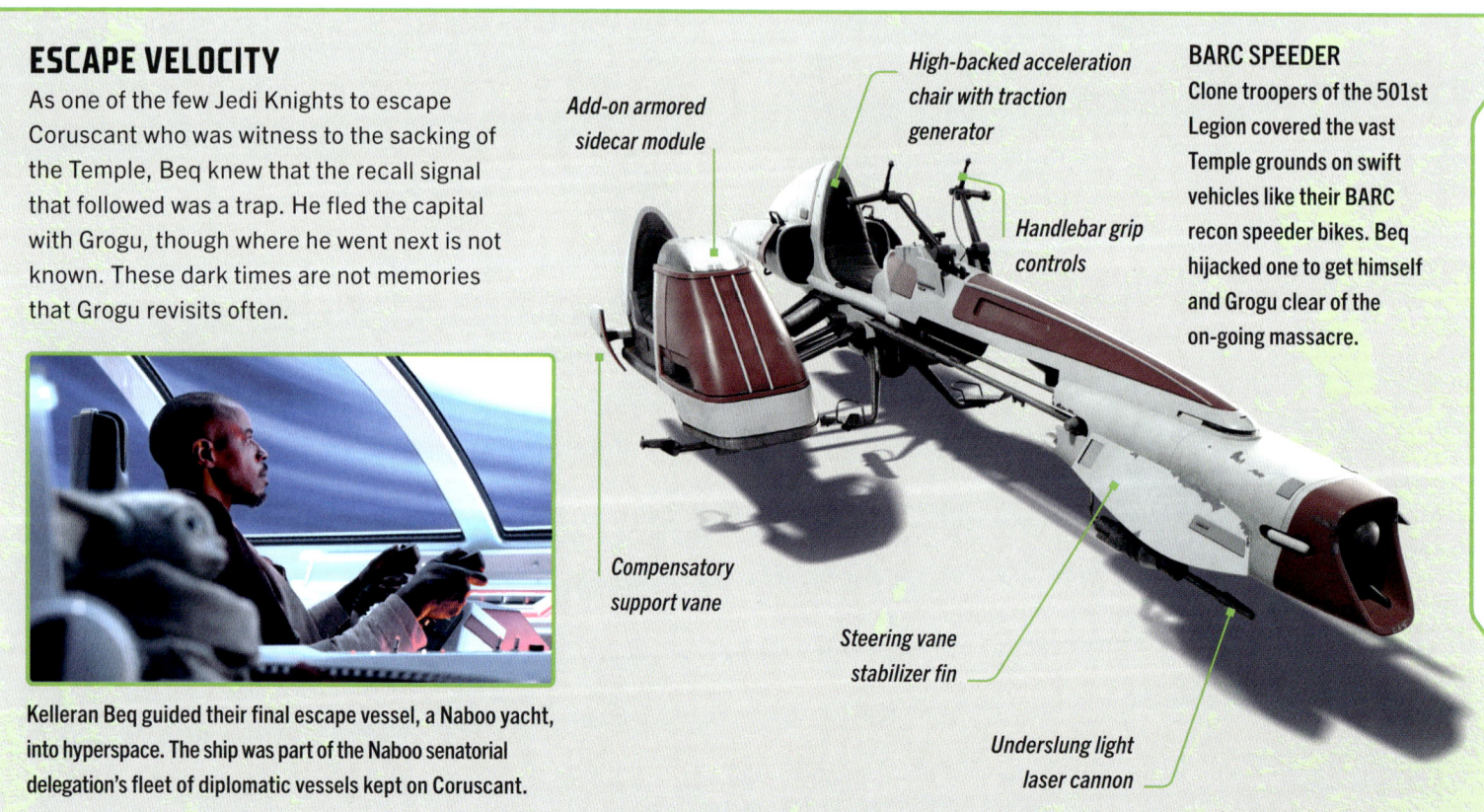

Add-on armored sidecar module

High-backed acceleration chair with traction generator

Handlebar grip controls

Compensatory support vane

Steering vane stabilizer fin

Underslung light laser cannon

BARC SPEEDER
Clone troopers of the 501st Legion covered the vast Temple grounds on swift vehicles like their BARC recon speeder bikes. Beq hijacked one to get himself and Grogu clear of the on-going massacre.

Kelleran Beq guided their final escape vessel, a Naboo yacht, into hyperspace. The ship was part of the Naboo senatorial delegation's fleet of diplomatic vessels kept on Coruscant.

- Embroidery of ancient Jedi symbols
- Upper tabard
- Wrapped sleeves
- Left hand kept empty
- Scintillating green kyber crystal blade
- Dense outer robes

DATA FILE

SUBJECT	Kelleran Beq
HOMEWORLD	Coruscant
SPECIES	Human
AFFILIATION	Jedi Order
HEIGHT	1.88 m (6 ft 2 in)
AGE	48 (as of 19 BBY)

Kelleran Beq secures a BARC speeder for him and Grogu by dispatching a 501st Legion clone trooper.

JEDI TRIAL MASTER

The noble Kelleran Beq personified the strength, knowledge, and bravery required of all Jedi Knights and exemplified these attributes as he oversaw Padawans partaking in their Jedi Trials. Part of his responsibility in the Order was helping masters craft individual Trials that would best test their apprentices. Beq's skill in instruction made him well known and regarded among the younger students at the Jedi Temple. He would hold training sessions aboard the Jedi frigate *Athylia*.

FACT FILE

NEW RECRUITS
Beq served as a Seeker among the Jedi and brought in many promising candidates for testing.

ABLE ASSISTANCE
Helping Beq craft training regimens were the droids AD-3 and LX-R5.

PART III: A NEW HOME
RESCUING RAGNAR

During the early days of settlement in their covert, the Mandalorians had to contend with aerial strikes from native raptors. The armored warriors proved sufficient enough a threat that the direct attacks stopped, though the opportunistic animals would occasionally steal supplies or exposed foodstuffs, leading to lengthy chases down the canyons.

A female raptor with a hungry brood is desperate enough to hunt again. Ignoring the fully grown warriors it instead plucks a foundling from the beach. Young Ragnar, only just having sworn to the Creed, is swept up by the beast, who soars to its distant spire-topping nest.

A Mandalorian hunting team gives pursuit, composed of Din Djarin, Paz Vizsla (the boy's father), Bo-Katan Kryze, and a group of expert jetpack operators known as the Shriek-Hawks. They must take care to employ stealth to avoid alerting the mother raptor, who might kill the boy in its agitation.

AN EVENTFUL YOUTH
Ragnar Vizsla is a born survivor. Only just entering adolescence, young Ragnar has already experienced the danger of Mandalorian life. From the exodus from Nevarro to the resettlement to the lakeside covert, Ragnar witnessed this turbulence with unshielded eyes. Upon donning the helmet, his ritual was interrupted by a monstrous attack, and now the foundling is threatened by the native wildlife anew.

Moments after Ragnar first dons his helmet, before the baptism of Living Waters can conclude, the ceremony is interrupted.

- Freshly forged buy'ce

RAGNAR WITH HELM

- Assured stare meant convey confidence
- Long hair that extends beyond the helmet if untied
- Tailcoat fabric sourced from Nevarro shopkeep
- Ragnar has sewn his clothes
- Equipment loops currently empty
- Tailcoat has hidden pockets
- Scuffed knee from roughhousing
- Weatherproof gaiters
- Reinforced toe

DATA FILE
SUBJECT	Ragnar Vizsla
HOMEWORLD	Nevarro (adopted)
SPECIES	Human
AFFILIATION	Children of the Watch
HEIGHT	1.5 m (4 ft 11 in)
AGE	13 standard years

CANYON RAPTOR

More predacious than the reptavians of Nevarro, the canyon raptors of the new covert world are tenacious hunters. They can fly distances of up to five kilometers (three miles) at a time, beyond the operational range of Mandalorian jetpacks. The solitary beasts protect their young by building inaccessible nests high in the canyon spires.

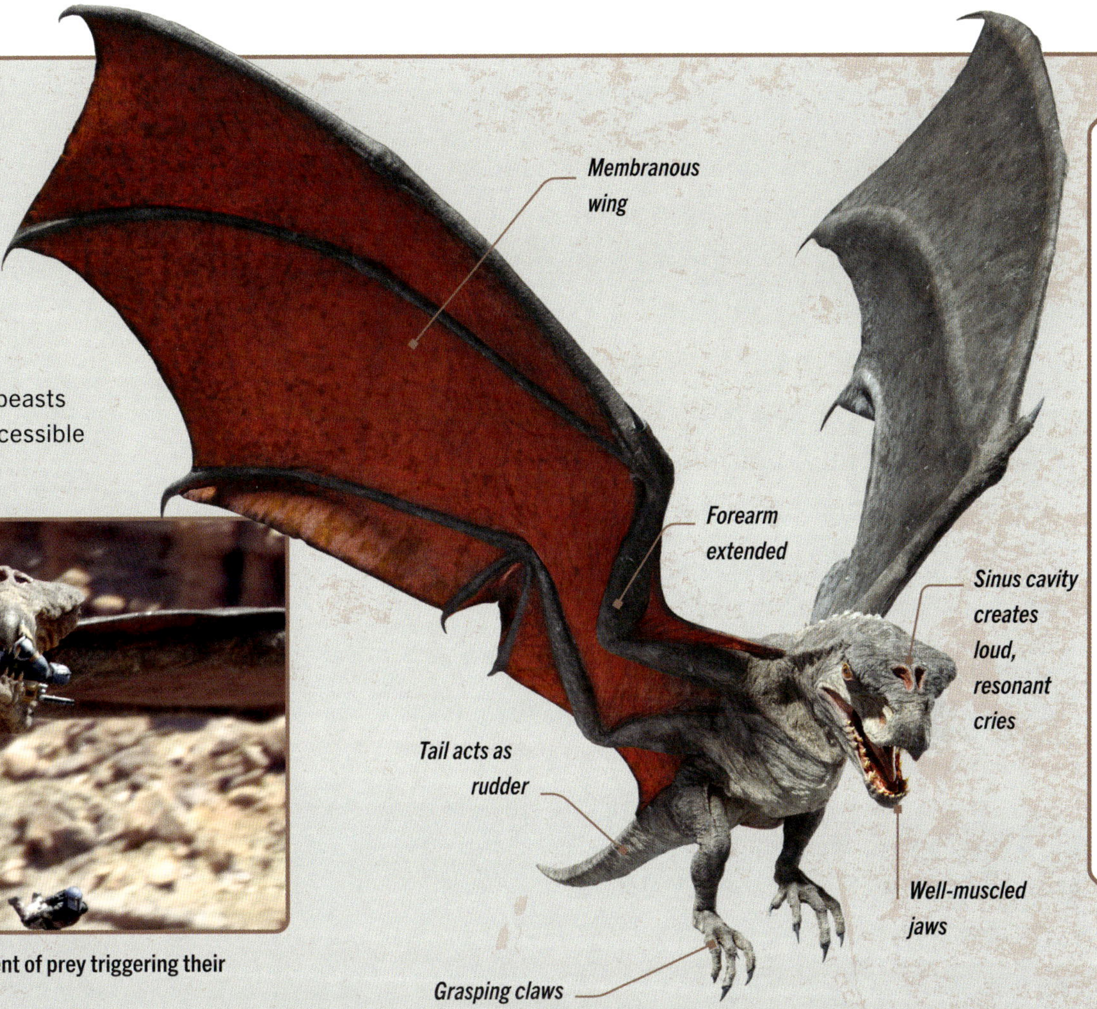

Membranous wing

Forearm extended

Sinus cavity creates loud, resonant cries

Tail acts as rudder

Well-muscled jaws

Grasping claws

Raptor chicks prefer live food, the movement of prey triggering their instincts. This is of faint fortune to Ragnar.

SHRIEK-HAWK TRAINERS

The Shriek-Hawks—or the *Jai'galaar*—of the covert are Mandalorians devoted to the perfection of the Rising Phoenix—the complex defensive and offensive acrobatics of jetpack operation. They join the rescue effort to save Ragnar and kill the hunting raptor. The Shriek-Hawks grant their name to the surviving raptor chicks, retroactively naming the otherwise anonymous creatures as part of their clan.

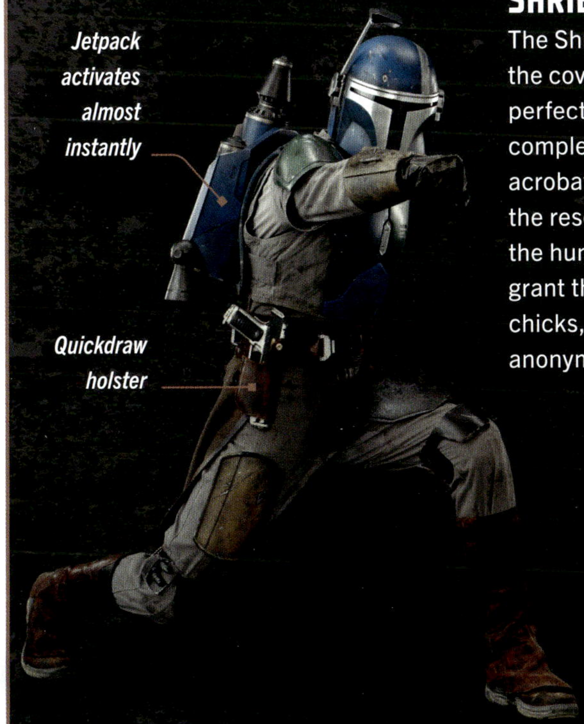

Jetpack activates almost instantly

Quickdraw holster

Optimized viewplate

Relby V-4d blaster rifle

With data gathered from her Gauntlet fighter, Bo-Katan plans a rescue.

PART III: A NEW HOME

IG-12

For the Mandalorian's assistance in ridding Nevarro of pirates, Greef Karga has a gift. Though the Anzellans couldn't restore IG-11 to operational status in time for Din Djarin's return to Mandalore, Karga has them continue their work on the battered droid. They strip IG-11 down to his base motor functions, removing all cognition modules so as not to risk a reboot of any latent assassin droid programming. Then the Anzellans install a pilot's seat within the droid's chest cavity, modifying the design far enough that it warrants a new appellation: IG-12.

This rebuild, in effect, becomes a pilotable mech for young Grogu, a set of battle armor that gives the youngling extra protection in combat. The Mandalorian is initially dismayed at how quickly Grogu takes to the contraption. The loader seat features annunciator buttons that can vocalize Grogu's intentions in a simple binary pairing of "YES" or "NO" statements. The gleeful Child slams the "YES" button repeatedly as he takes to the design.

Refabricated cranial co[ver]

Light detection and ranging emitter surfaces

Telescopic optical sensors

Articulated targeting sight

Audio sensor

Case-hardened broadband antenna surface

Grogu in loader seat

THE NEXT EVOLUTION
The Anzellan Droidsmith pilots the walking droid into Greef Karga's high magistrate office. Grogu is instantly smitten by the machine. He pilots the IG-12 unit into the Nevarro marketplace, getting a feel for the conveyance.

Mando must suddenly reckon with Grogu's newfound independence afforded by the walking droid suit.

FATEFUL ASSISTANCE

As the danger escalates in the pursuit of Moff Gideon and the reclaiming of Mandalore, Grogu is grateful for the IG-12 suit. With it, he keeps pace with the full-sized strides of the Mandalorians. In the heart of Gideon's underground lair, Grogu is essential in distracting a cadre of Praetorian guards away from Djarin.

GUARDIAN GROGU
Thanks to the strength and protection of the IG-12 mech, Grogu gets to switch roles of guardian and protected with Din Djarin, coming to his rescue on Mandalore.

> "THINK OF IT THIS WAY. IT'S MORE OF A VEHICLE. HMM? IT'S SAFER THAT WAY."
> – HIGH MAGISTRATE GREEF KARGA

DATA FILE
SUBJECT	IG-12
HOMEWORLD	Nevarro
SERIES	IG assassin droid
AFFILIATION	Independent
HEIGHT	2.19 m (7 ft 2 in)

- Independently rotating sleeved segments increase sensor coverage

FACT FILE

ORIGINAL VOCABULATOR
The speech synthesizer is still IG-11's original voice saying "YES" and "NO" responses.

MEDICAL ASSISTANCE
The droid still has an integral bacta spray dispenser in his arm.

- Pneumatic arm articulation
- Stabilizers for driver compartment
- Strong pincer manipulators
- Gyroscopic stabilizer rods
- Pneumatic leg articulation
- Weighted foot for stability
- Compressed pneumatic air bottle

PART III: A NEW HOME

ADELPHI

A tropical world of brilliant seas and sunny beaches shaded by palm fronds, Adelphi is mostly unsettled save for a New Republic fighter outpost. The vast expanse of the Outer Rim is too large to effectively police, but the New Republic makes do with scattered outposts from which to launch patrols. Adelphi is one of the most storied, thanks to the veteran pilots who call it a temporary home. Their years of experiences make up for sparse supplies and personnel.

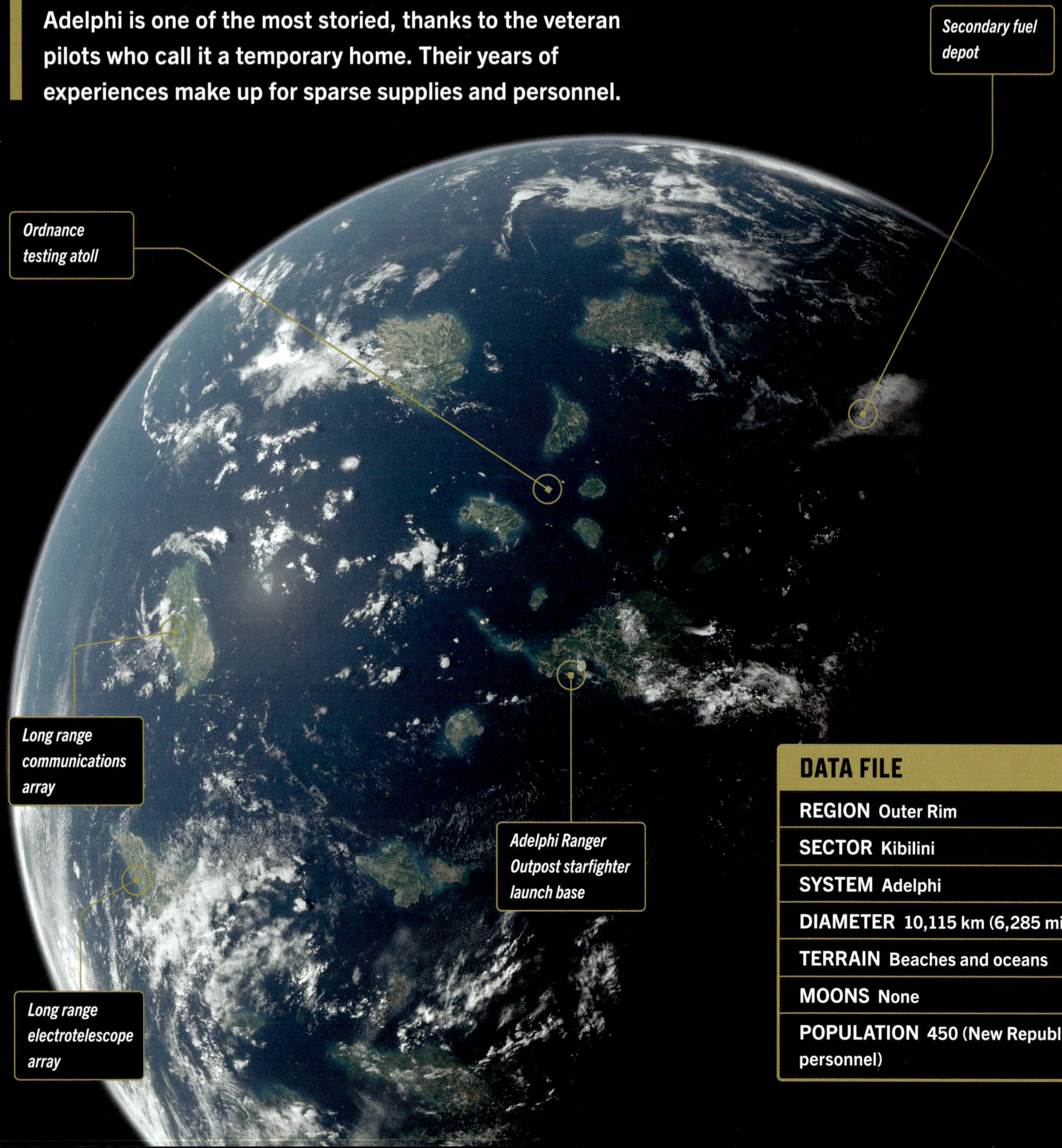

Secondary fuel depot

Ordnance testing atoll

Long range communications array

Adelphi Ranger Outpost starfighter launch base

Long range electrotelescope array

DATA FILE

REGION Outer Rim

SECTOR Kibilini

SYSTEM Adelphi

DIAMETER 10,115 km (6,285 miles)

TERRAIN Beaches and oceans

MOONS None

POPULATION 450 (New Republic personnel)

ALLIANCE VETERANS

While most of the fresh-faced graduates emerging from the New Republic Academies gravitate toward cutting edge designs like the E-wing fighter, Alliance veterans at Adelphi—like Carson Teva and Garazeb Orrelios—far prefer the battle-tested A, X, Y, B, and U-wing fighters of the Galactic Civil War.

- Novaldex Diagnostech life support unit
- Interstellar orange flight suit
- Inflatable FreiTek life vest
- Utility pocket
- Insulated work boots
- Reverse-articulated legs

CARSON TEVA

ZEB ORRELIOS

TIME TO REFUEL

The Pilots' Rest is a place for pilots to unwind, swap stories, play sonic billiards, and get a drink. The fully stocked bar is lined by trophies of captured helmets and Imperial droid fragments, as well as other threats—like an intact assassin droid's head.

Grogu and the Mandalorian enter the Pilots' Rest to propose a new working arrangement to Carson Teva.

A rookie pilot would have a hard time keeping up with the pace of discourse as the veterans hold court.

- Patterned absorbent work smock

SNIVVIAN BARTENDER

ADELPHI RANGER OUTPOST

The tranquil and balmy weather conditions of Adelphi means the ranger outpost itself need not boast too many comforts. The temperature is ideal to most humanoid species, and the bluffs elevate the technology out of reach from any deleterious effects of sea water.

- A Y-wing fighter undergoes avionics systems upgrades
- Quonset hut
- Parked resupply speeder
- Din Djarin's Naboo N-1 starfighter comes in for a landing

PART III: A NEW HOME

FOR LOVE OR MONEY

After breaking ties with Bo-Katan Kryze for her failure to reclaim the Darksaber, her fellow Nite Owls become mercenaries in the Outer Rim. Self-styled as a privateer force, the group is now led by Axe Woves, who offers their services as security forces and even engages in hunting bounties. One such assignment leads them to intercept a Quarren freighter with an outstanding warrant on the head of one of the passengers—a fugitive son of a Mon Calamari noble.

The Quarren vessel stands down, at first assuming the presence of an Imperial light cruiser indicates a remnant force shaking down passing starships for protection money. Woves dispatches an envoy to claim their prize, with Koska Reeves apprehending the target. Such mercenary duty is a far cry from the intended purpose of the newly assembled Mandalorian fleet—to reclaim their homeworld.

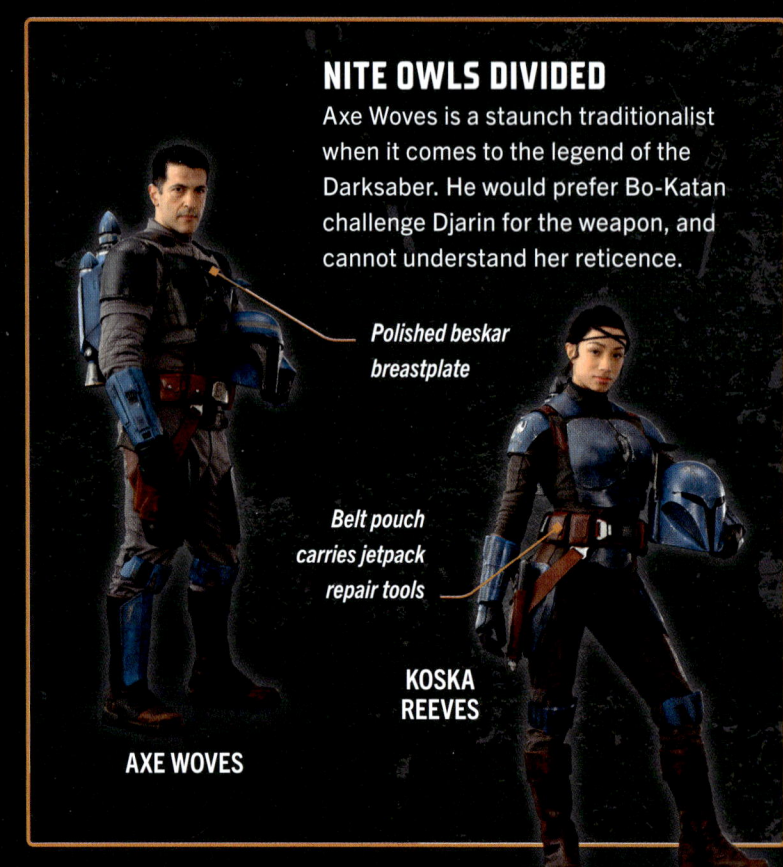

NITE OWLS DIVIDED

Axe Woves is a staunch traditionalist when it comes to the legend of the Darksaber. He would prefer Bo-Katan challenge Djarin for the weapon, and cannot understand her reticence.

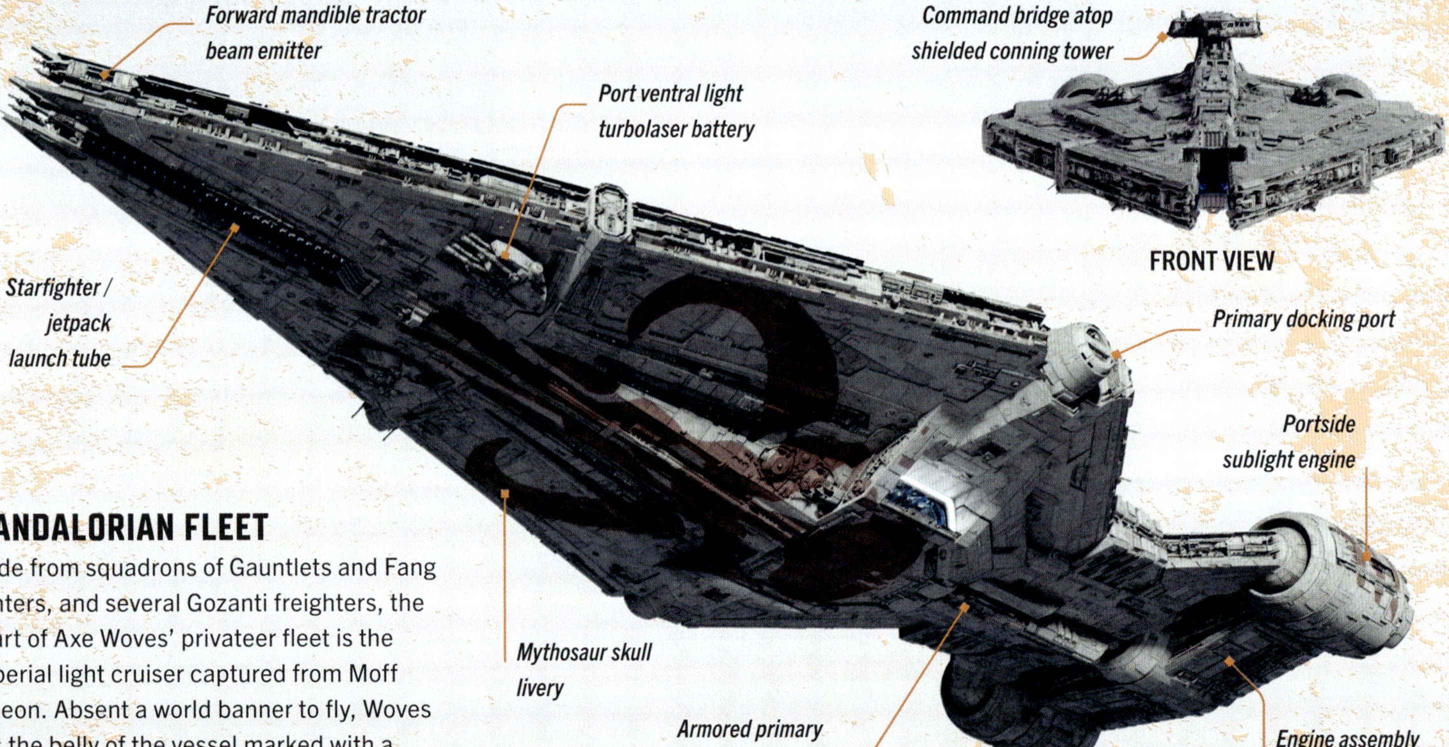

- Polished beskar breastplate
- Belt pouch carries jetpack repair tools

AXE WOVES

KOSKA REEVES

- Forward mandible tractor beam emitter
- Port ventral light turbolaser battery
- Command bridge atop shielded conning tower
- Starfighter / jetpack launch tube
- Mythosaur skull livery
- Armored primary power conduit
- Primary docking port
- Portside sublight engine
- Engine assembly alignment frame

FRONT VIEW

MANDALORIAN FLEET

Aside from squadrons of Gauntlets and Fang fighters, and several Gozanti freighters, the heart of Axe Woves' privateer fleet is the Imperial light cruiser captured from Moff Gideon. Absent a world banner to fly, Woves has the belly of the vessel marked with a giant painted mythosaur skull as a warning.

CAPTAIN SHUGGOTH

- Temporomandibular fin
- Supple facial tentacle
- Quarren merchant fleet captain's uniform
- Finned hands

The commanding officer of the Quarren freighter *Hydroid Traveler*, Shuggoth hauls cargo from the oceans of her homeworld to various Mon Calamari and Quarren colonies and outposts. As befits her station, she commands her ship from a capsule filled with Mon Cala seawater.

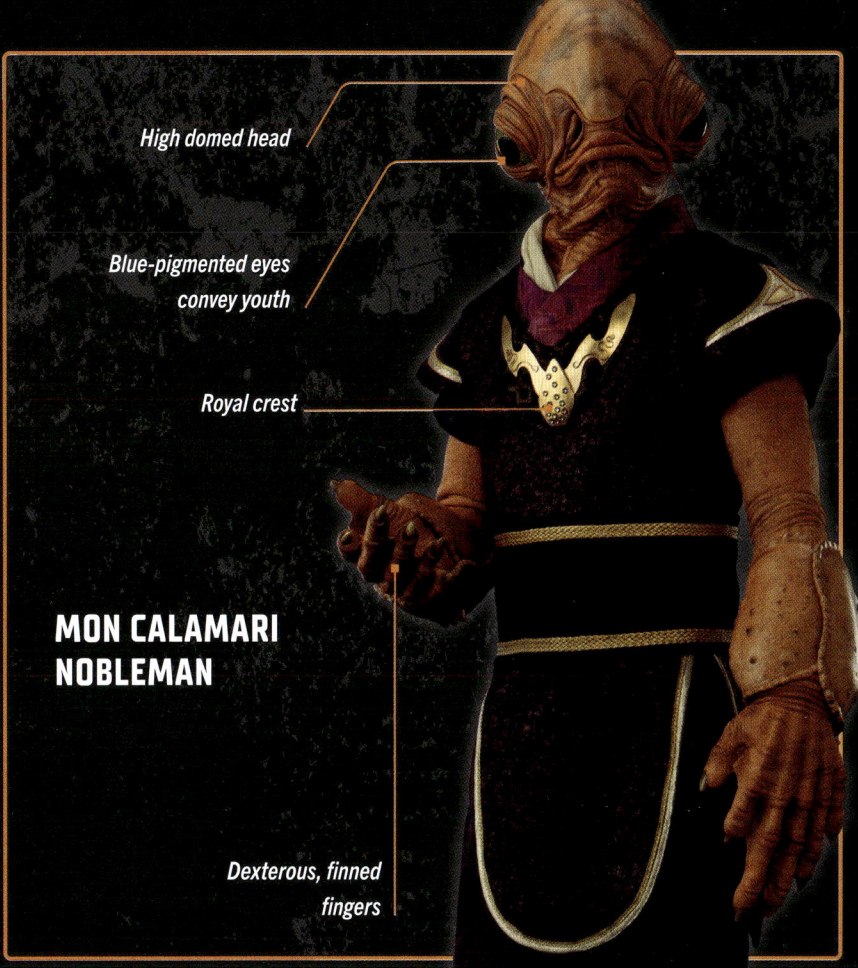

MON CALAMARI NOBLEMAN

- High domed head
- Blue-pigmented eyes convey youth
- Royal crest
- Dexterous, finned fingers

HYDROID TRAVELER

- Upper loading hatch
- Starboard cargo blister
- Communications antenna
- Engine cluster signature shroud
- Diamond configuration sublight engines
- Fuel pod
- Flight deck viewport
- Crew quarters portholes
- Engineering systems service access

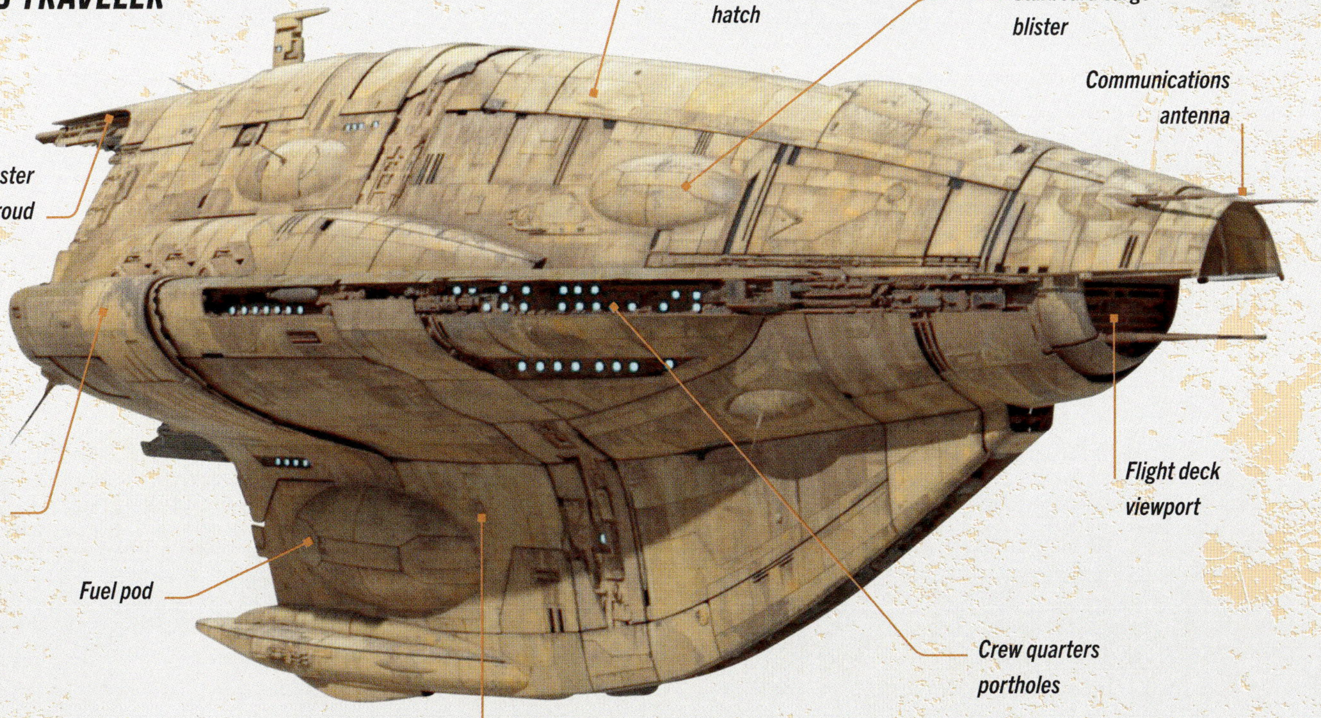

PART III: A NEW HOME

PLAZIR-15

A pleasant and modern world that has recovered capably from harsh Imperial rule, Plazir-15 lauds itself as the Outer Rim's only remaining direct democracy. Its citizenry votes via automated systems on all matters, large and small, requiring no overarching governmental bodies. Plazir-15 is not on the New Republic registry, and as such must rely on its own resources for defense, the nature of which is tightly restricted by the will of its pacifistic people.

Bow textured with stylized city plan

KEY TO PLAZIR
An intricately crafted curio, this honorary—and oversized—symbol of goodwill and alliance is bestowed by the nobility of the planet.

NOBLE RULERS
The Duchess of Plazir comes from a long line of nobility. Though she and her former-Imperial husband serve important diplomatic functions, they have little governmental authority beyond their direct votes, equal to any citizen's. They welcome Din Djarin and Bo-Katan Kryze.

- Holographic halo
- Epaulets of command
- Mighty and well coifed beard
- Sequined sleeves
- Antique Ghorman silk
- Amnesty Program uniform

THE DUCHESS OF PLAZIR

CAPTAIN BOMBARDIER

Their hands tied by procedure, the nobles discreetly ask the visiting Mandalorians for help.

> "YOU WILL ALWAYS BE WELCOMED IN OUR DOMED PARADISE."
> – THE DUCHESS

A PEACE-LOVING PEOPLE
By Plazir law, there are no armed forces within the limits of the population centers. The mercenary army of Mandalorians hired to protect the world cannot police the cities. But a series of alarming droid malfunctions requires action, and as de facto diplomatic envoys and guests of the Duchess, Bo-Katan and Din can carry it out.

Bo-Katan Kryze's Gauntlet is overridden by automated planetary traffic control

Freshwater marshes

UGNAUGHT LABORERS

The city populace has voted for lives of leisure, relying on a huge droid labor pool for all menial tasks. Maintaining the droids is the job of Ugnaught workers in the industrial sub-levels. During their investigation of the rash of droid malfunctions, Kryze and Djarin meet with Saifir, the forewoman, and her crew. They insist nothing is wrong with their refurbishment and maintenance work.

Djarin's experience with Kuiil is of great advantage when navigating prickly Ugnaught pride.

DROID CONSPIRACY

The droid malfunctions are not mechanical, but programming based and can be traced to a contaminated lot of Nepenthé lubricant distributed through the Resistor all-droid bar. The droid bartender is helpful to Djarin and Kryze, despite their anti-droid sentiments. The droids of Plazir-15 are being used as pawns by an unknown saboteur; the automatons wish no harm to befall their organic neighbors.

Barkeep M0 defies Mando's expectations by putting up little obstacle to his investigation, instead offering clues.

Security station complex sub-dome

Royal Hall sub-dome

Weather-controlled dome has conditions voted upon daily

Power-generation complex

Hyper-loop terminal junction

Commercial sector

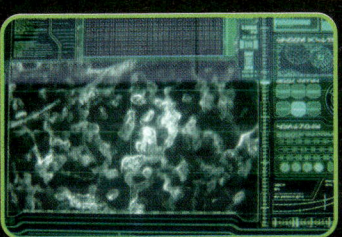

ENHANCE...
A nanometric magnification of the contaminated Nepenthé fuel batch reveals more than just congealed polyolefins or crystallized impurities. Lurking within the mixture are machined nano-droids capable of hijacking data pathways and altering deep core programming. Further proof surfaces that these forbidden droids were imported by a Plazir official.

COMMISSIONER HELGAIT

A forensic examination of the nano-contaminants reveals evidence that Security Commissioner Helgait took possession of Techno Union-era contraband to create chaos on Plazir-15. A man of stern work ethic, Helgait is disgusted by the lazy frivolity of his fellow citizens. At heart, Helgait is a staunch believer in Count Dooku's old rhetoric of self-determination and independence.

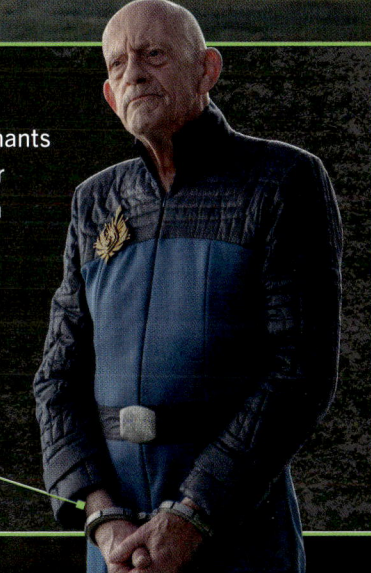

Electronic binders

PART III: A NEW HOME

SHADOW COUNCIL

> The Empire is a shadow of its former self; within that shadow, evil grows. Since the destruction of the second Death Star over Endor, and the capitulation of the Empire that followed, military and political leaders vied for control in the resultant power vacuum. Intense rivalries hastened the collapse of these fragile efforts, but staggered attempts by a few firebrands pushed back against the New Republic.

The years after Endor saw continued efforts by the New Republic to stomp out these cinders of resistance, an ironic reversal of the dynamics of the Galactic Civil War. By five years after Endor, what is recognized as the Imperial remnant is thought to be a diffuse patchwork of stalwart warlords unable to coordinate any concerted challenge to New Republic rule. But it is far more cohesive than New Republic Intelligence imagines.

GATHERING OF SHADOWS
In Moff Gideon's lair he convenes a holographic conference of surviving Imperial warlords and potentates, each transmitting from their own hidden strongholds. These conspirators plot the downfall of the New Republic. Some specialize in military strategies centered on exotic technologies, while others have expertise in political influence and commercial manipulation.

GILAD PELLAEON
A veteran of the Imperial Navy and its antecedent Clone Wars-era Republic fleet, Pellaeon carries the authority of five decades of service. Pellaeon served with Grand Admiral Thrawn and personally witnessed his strategic brilliance. The seasoned captain eagerly awaits word from Morgan Elsbeth on her efforts to ensure Thrawn's return.

Officer's cap
Navy captain's rank badge
Coded data cylinder
Officer's belt
Flared trousers

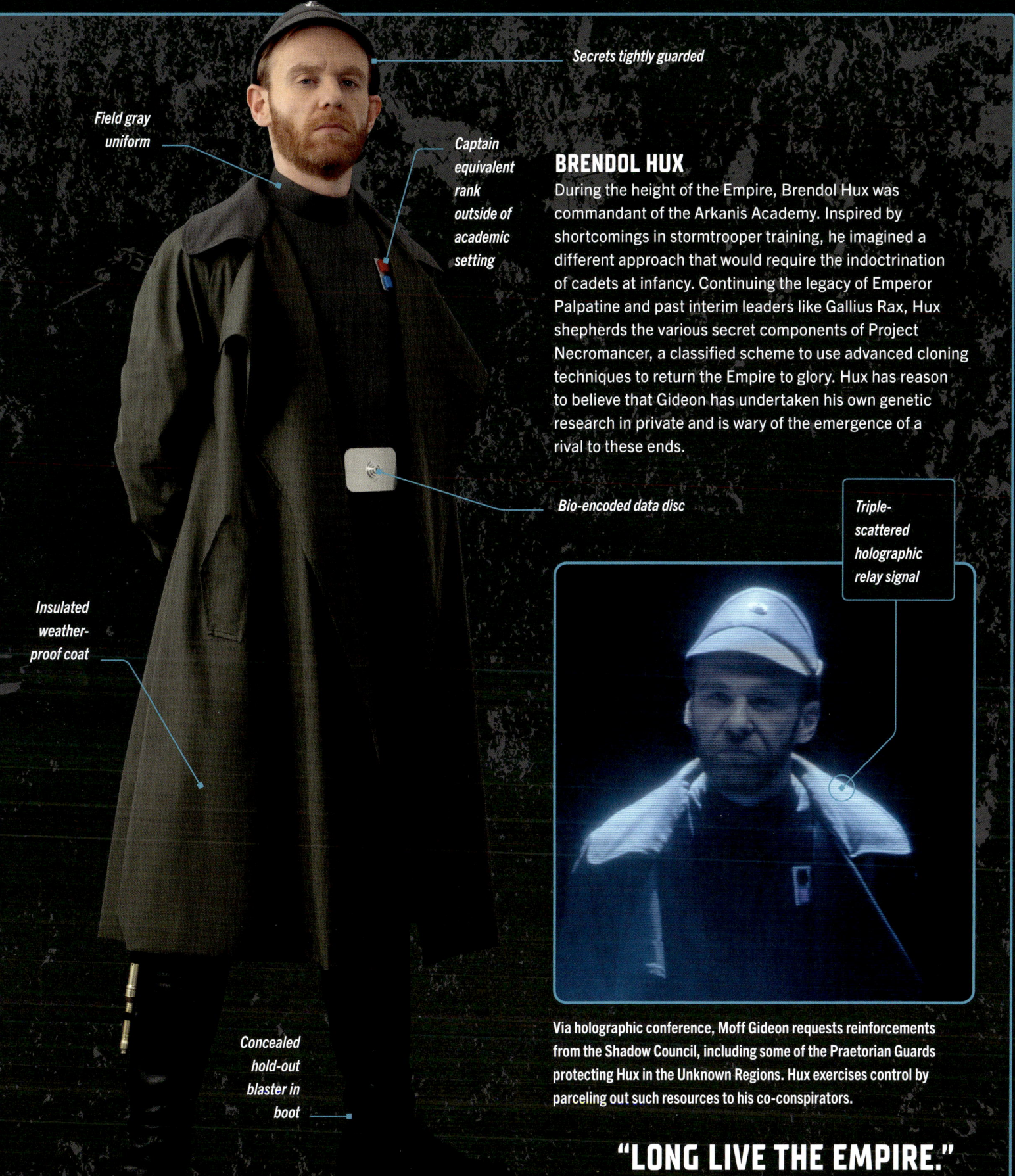

- Secrets tightly guarded
- Field gray uniform
- Captain equivalent rank outside of academic setting
- Insulated weather-proof coat
- Concealed hold-out blaster in boot
- Bio-encoded data disc
- Triple-scattered holographic relay signal

BRENDOL HUX

During the height of the Empire, Brendol Hux was commandant of the Arkanis Academy. Inspired by shortcomings in stormtrooper training, he imagined a different approach that would require the indoctrination of cadets at infancy. Continuing the legacy of Emperor Palpatine and past interim leaders like Gallius Rax, Hux shepherds the various secret components of Project Necromancer, a classified scheme to use advanced cloning techniques to return the Empire to glory. Hux has reason to believe that Gideon has undertaken his own genetic research in private and is wary of the emergence of a rival to these ends.

Via holographic conference, Moff Gideon requests reinforcements from the Shadow Council, including some of the Praetorian Guards protecting Hux in the Unknown Regions. Hux exercises control by parceling out such resources to his co-conspirators.

"LONG LIVE THE EMPIRE."
– SHADOW COUNCIL WARLORDS

PART III: A NEW HOME

MANDALORIAN SURVIVORS

Despite the relentless bombardment that fused Mandalore's surface into glass, small pockets of survivors escaped the ruination. These stragglers emerged from the depths and abandoned their differences of clan and house, banding together as the last of the Mandalorians. Trapped on the ravaged world without communications with the rest of the galaxy, they were unaware of those who had escaped, or the diaspora that followed.

The survivors, or *cuyane*, nomadically scour the surface for other holdouts, or indeed any signs of life, as they hope to find a way forward beyond the Night of a Thousand Tears. A trio of survivors greets the envoy of returning off-world Mandalorians. They continue swearing fealty to Bo-Katan Kryze, believing her return is a harbinger of a long-awaited turn of fortune.

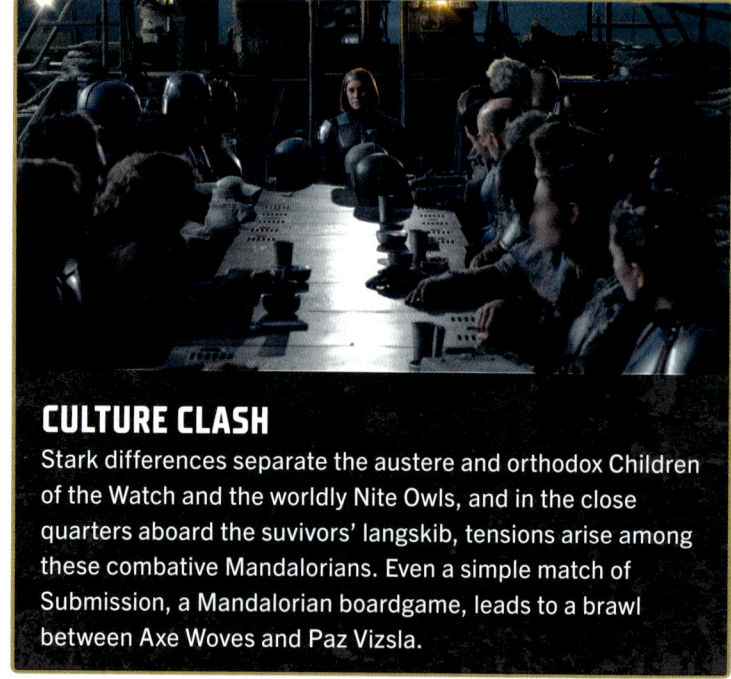

CULTURE CLASH
Stark differences separate the austere and orthodox Children of the Watch and the worldly Nite Owls, and in the close quarters aboard the suvivors' langskib, tensions arise among these combative Mandalorians. Even a simple match of Submission, a Mandalorian boardgame, leads to a brawl between Axe Woves and Paz Vizsla.

MANDALORIAN LANGSKIB
The Mandalorian survivors skate the smooth glass plains of Mandalore atop a massive langskib.

The weathered craft is torn apart by a massive trinitaur, whose lumbering tail strike detonates carried jetpack fuel stores and spelunking explosives.

- Secondary starboard solar sail
- Solar gather sail extended
- Secondary port solar sail
- Tattered canvas weather tarps
- Angled prow
- Aft repulsorlift radiator bank
- Starboard outrigger repulsorlift boom and skid
- Power storage cell
- Forward skid

MANDALORIAN SURVIVORS

A patchwork clan of ragged survivors scrapes out an existence on Mandalore's surface, led by an elder warrior, captain, and scout. Following them are a dozen other veterans, maintaining the langskib and several safe hollows they can count upon for shelter. They've attempted to recreate the pillars of Mandalorian society from within their small and dwindling number.

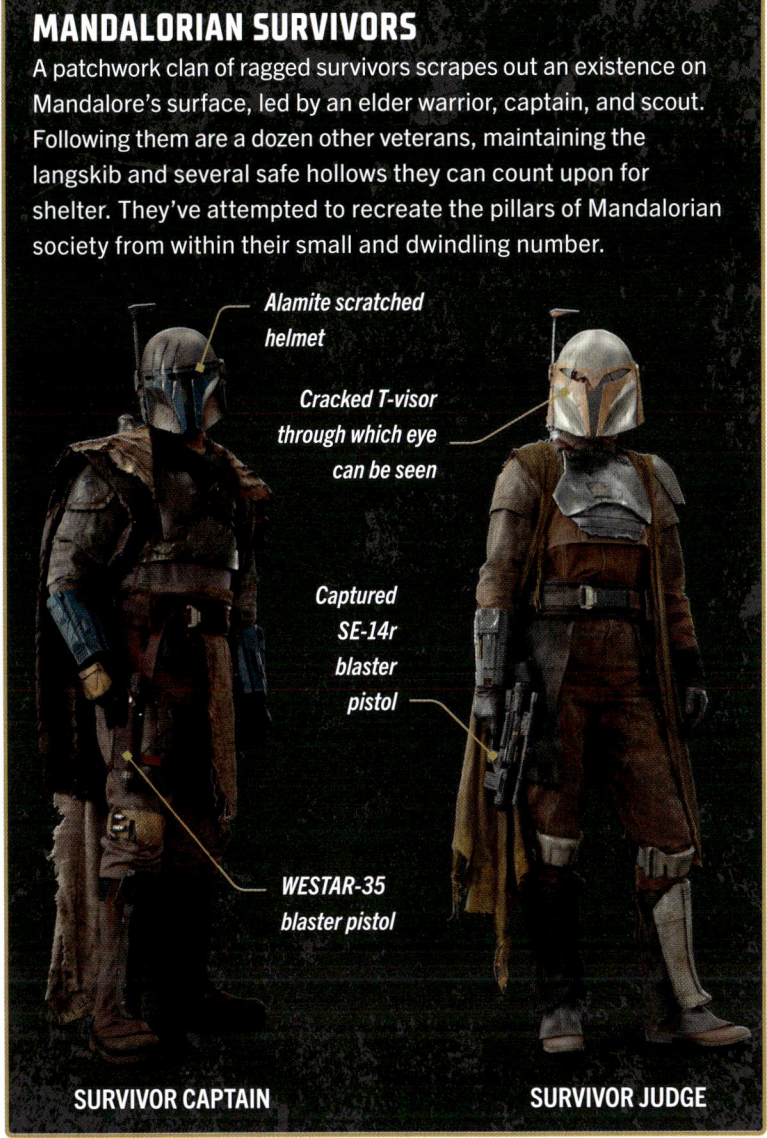

- Alamite scratched helmet
- Cracked T-visor through which eye can be seen
- Captured SE-14r blaster pistol
- WESTAR-35 blaster pistol

SURVIVOR CAPTAIN   SURVIVOR JUDGE

- Bo-Katan Kryze marvels at the greenery
- Nutrient-rich vulp-lichen
- Medicinal cassiusroot to create poultices

UNDERGROUND GREENHOUSES

Among the survivor hollows are sacred anthodite-lined caverns wherein the Mandalorians have collected the rare specimens of plant life that have weathered the chain of cataclysms marking their history. Aquifers and natural solaria made of thinned glass nurture these persistent gardens into viable farms hidden among the wastes. These promise a future for Mandalore that aligns perfectly with their cultural tenets.

TRINITAUR

An enormous subterranean beast awakened in the Purge, the trinitaur's tough hide has become fused with immense shards of trinitite, the source of its unofficial name. Whatever taxonomy this leviathan once had is lost alongside all zoological records obliterated in the cities. These beasts sleep until bothered by intruders to their territory. The largest specimen known is nearly 200 meters (650 feet) in length.

- Fused trinitite shards
- Major osteoderm club tail
- Lateral spikes
- Sturdy burrowing limbs
- Unarmored underbelly surface
- Sharp glass-shattering teeth

A titanic trinitaur erupts from the wasteland surface, maddened by the langskib's approaching electromagnetic signature.

PART III: A NEW HOME
MOFF GIDEON'S FORCES

To protect his headquarters deep underneath Mandalore, Moff Gideon unleashes his most elite forces. Scores of super commandos fill the air. TIE interceptors take to the sky to target the orbiting light cruiser. And guarding the very nucleus of his redoubt, Gideon employs a trio of Praetorian Guards, dispatched from the dark heart of the Imperial remnant's most secret bastion. It is a furious defense against resolute Mandalorian warriors attempting to retake their world, and the cultural legacy that Gideon is determined to wrest from them.

Interceptor in "ready one" scramble position

Articulated wings partially compress to maximize storage

TIE INTERCEPTOR HANGAR
Suspended above the hangar deck in eerie bat-like fashion are squadrons of TIE interceptors ready to launch. It is from here that the earlier attack on Kalevala originated, and these fully fueled starfighters are once again combat ready.

Charged electro-bisento

PRAETORIANS
An evolution of the Imperial Royal Guards who once protected the Emperor, these elite sentinels are trained in a mix of unarmed combat forms. These three warriors specialize in the precise use of edged weaponry, defending the deepest sanctuaries where stray blaster-fire is too grave a risk.

Helmet with kinetic-predictor overlay visor-plate

Bilari electro-chain whip (rigid configuration)

Polished betaplast composite armor

Power cell

Energized vibro-arbir

VIBRO-ARBIR HEAD
Tempered blade surface
Connection point
VIBRO-DAGGER BASE

PRAETORIAN WEAPONS
The Praetorian Guards brandish edged weaponry bolstered with modern alloys and energetic electro-plasma filaments that increase their deflection and cutting power.

Greaves protect lower leg

Flexible boots with mag-soles

IMPERIAL SUPER COMMANDOS

Gideon's armored protectors are the latest iteration of an elite force that first occupied Mandalore prior to the outbreak of the Galactic Civil War. Whereas in the past their ranks comprised turncoat Mandalorians who backed the Empire, these new super commandos are Imperial remnant troops.

Armored fuel tankage

NJP-350 JETPACK

Graphite thruster nozzle

SUPER COMMANDO HELMET

Beskar/betaplast laminate finish

Composite ballistic riot shield

Energized contact vanes

T-visor macrobinocular viewplate

Lightweight greaves

SC-3144

Beskar/betaplast composite cuirass

Red color indicates captain rank

Flexible flight boots

SC-0014 (CAPTAIN)

Magnetic adhesion grip

Power cell service port

T4 RIOT BATON

Entrance to landing bay, where an ambush awaits

EF-11D blaster rifle in low ready position

GIDEON TRIUMPHANT

With the Children of the Watch, Nite Owls, and Mandalorian survivors drawn to his lair, Gideon unleashes his forces. The Moff genuinely admires Mandalorian tenacity and martial prowess, but as he cannot control these attributes, he must destroy them.

Without the Armorer's skills, Gideon must refine beskar using Imperial metallurgic methods. Though far stronger than plastoid, it cannot compare to authentic Mandalorian craftwork.

PART III: A NEW HOME

CONFRONTING GIDEON

Favored DDC D-16 blaster pistol

The Imperial Shadow Council is, by definition, a vague entity. Confirming its membership beyond a handful of known Imperial veterans is of prime importance to the New Republic and its rangers carrying out intelligence missions. Moff Gideon is a leading member, petitioning for reinforcements to his fiefdom to deal with the resurgent Mandalorian threat. Gideon convinces the council to back his move, though they are not aware of the depths of his plans.

Gideon employed his ISB expertise to craft and spread the tales of Mandalore being cursed and poisoned, for he wanted no survivors rallying to reclaim their world. These lies have afforded him cover, for Gideon bases his secret operations out of a lair deep beneath the sundered surface of Mandalore. Here, far from the prying eyes of the Shadow Council he carries out unauthorized experimentations to create a regime worthy of the Empire of old.

At long last, the clues revealing his plot are gathered, as are the scattered Mandalorian clans eager to retake their planet. Gideon launches his Imperial super commandos to ambush and reduce the Mandalorian numbers.

The Mandalorian crumples after a pummeling from Moff Gideon's servo-enhanced strength and beskar crushgaunts.

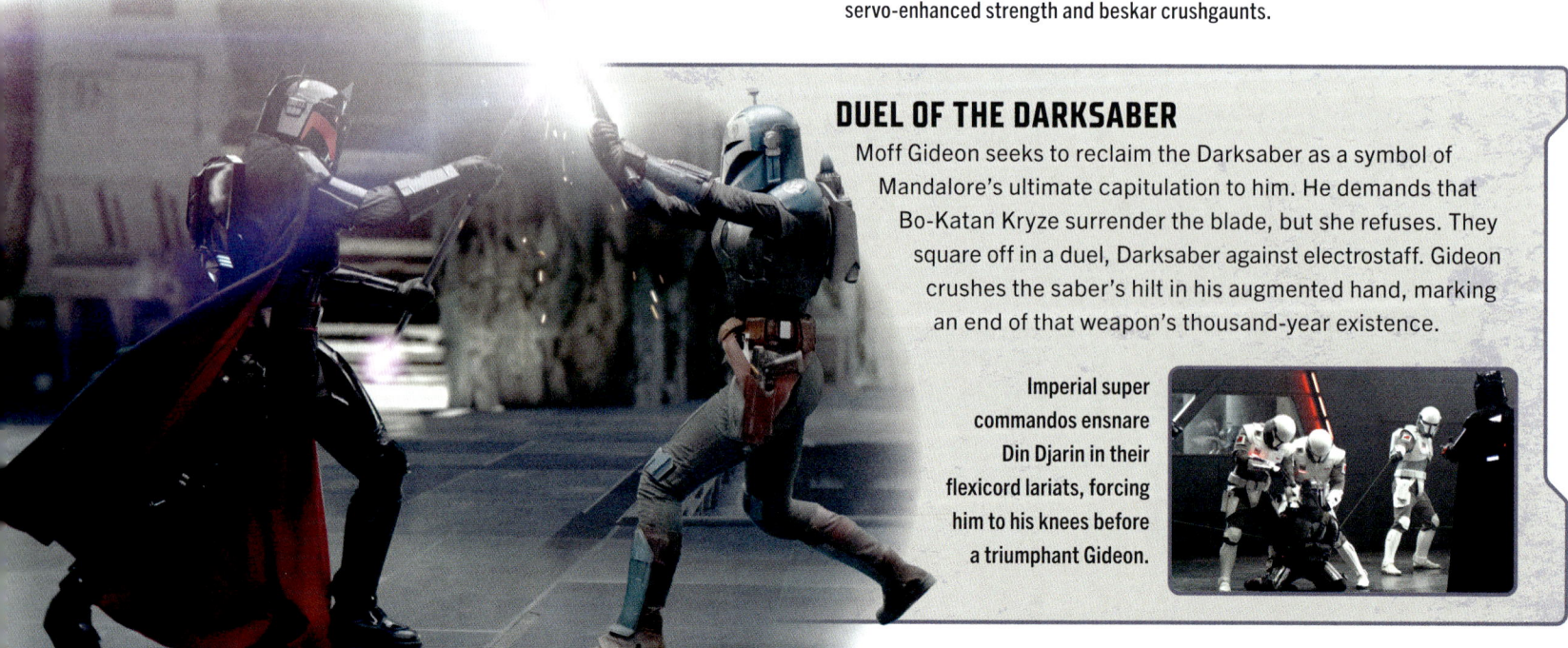

DUEL OF THE DARKSABER
Moff Gideon seeks to reclaim the Darksaber as a symbol of Mandalore's ultimate capitulation to him. He demands that Bo-Katan Kryze surrender the blade, but she refuses. They square off in a duel, Darksaber against electrostaff. Gideon crushes the saber's hilt in his augmented hand, marking an end of that weapon's thousand-year existence.

Imperial super commandos ensnare Din Djarin in their flexicord lariats, forcing him to his knees before a triumphant Gideon.

217

- **Reinforced helmet with horned crown reminiscent of Clone Wars-era super commandos**
- **Multifrequency / multispectral macrobinocular viewplate**
- **Power systems status indicators**
- **Triple folded kyberous-weave plastron**
- **Amplifier sheet-flex servomotor substructure**
- **Excess heat-radiating belt**
- **Servo-flex crushgaunt**
- **Wrist-launched missile**
- **Sensor-absorbent stygian triprismatic polymer coating**

As is to be expected from a design appropriated from Mandalorian culture, Gideon's armor is loaded with hidden weaponry.

FINAL-PHASE DARK TROOPER

Gideon wears a beskar-reinforced, strength-augmenting power armor, the next generation of dark trooper technology. It is the Phase IV incarnation, the first three being autonomous droid constructs. This latest iteration is the culmination of research gleaned from disposable automated soldiers serving as valuable testbeds against enemy weapons. While so armored, Gideon is practically undefeatable in direct combat.

PART III: A NEW HOME

SHOWDOWN ON MANDALORE

Gideon's calculated immersion into—and appropriation of—sacred Mandalorian culture to subjugate the survivors has instead focused their resolve. The disparate bands of Mandalorians unite in a push into the heart of Gideon's subterranean lair, with a confrontation pitting Bo-Katan Kryze, Din Djarin, and little Grogu against the power-armored Moff. Gideon's plans unravel as Djarin destroys his incubating clones, the jetpack battles decimate his super commandos, and Axe Woves brings the orbiting light cruiser crashing down.

Abandoned point-defense stations

NOBLE SACRIFICE

It is a coordinated effort to rid Mandalore of its Imperial intruders; despite his disagreements with them, Paz Vizsla works alongside the Kalevalan Mandalorians. His repeating blaster lays waste to many super commandos, but the Praetorian Guards prove a true challenge. Though Vizsla's brawn lets him last long in the engagement with these elite warriors, their swift strikes overwhelm him and he falters.

Paz Vizsla dies while reclaiming Mandalore; his name is added to the growing ballad of fallen heroes.

TIE bomber on an attack run

TIE interceptor upper starboard laser cannon

Smoldering point-defense emplacement

FIRE IN THE SKIES

Above the turbulent clouds wreathing Mandalore, the skies erupt in laserfire as TIE craft strafe the Mandalorian fleet. Swarms of bombers and interceptors tangle with Gauntlets and Fang fighters. Axe Woves takes command of the light cruiser, ordering its evacuation so he can use it as a decoy. In a last-ditch effort to defeat Gideon, Woves brings the cruiser crashing down into the canyon that holds the Moff's hidden base.

Reinforced conning tower superstructure

GIDEON'S END
The resultant fireball from the cruiser's collision engulfs and consumes Gideon, while Mando and Bo-Katan shelter within a barrier of protective Force energy wielded by Grogu.

Proton-bombed burning hull

Forward launch bay tractor control

The fires of the Great Forge are rekindled deep beneath the ruins of Keldabe, the ancient capital of Mandalore. This was once the very heart of Mandalorian society.

DIN GROGU
Din Djarin formally adopts Grogu as his son in accordance with the Way, speaking for the wordless Child in acceptance of the Creed. Grogu will follow his father as an apprentice. The Armorer consecrates the act with a baptism of the Living Waters.

Baptismal font

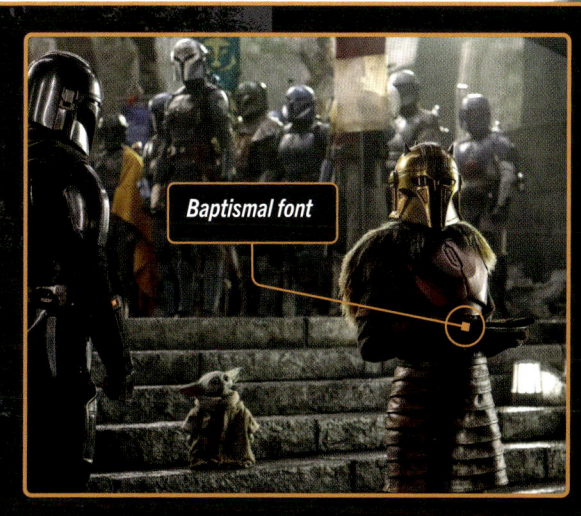

PART III: A NEW HOME

NEVARRO HOMESTEAD

Prior to the departure of the Mandalorian fleet to retake their homeworld, High Magistrate Greef Karga made a heartfelt promise. As a show of gratitude for the Mandalorian assistance in ridding Nevarro of the pirate menace, Karga extended an invitation to resettle on his planet. The lands from the western lava flats to the former Imperial Canyon could serve as a new home for the displaced Mandalorians. With the recapture of Mandalore, many have decided to try to rebuild there. But not all.

Din Djarin relaxes, earning a well-earned respite from adventure at his new home on the reclaimed lava flats. Grogu practices Force abilities under his watchful eye.

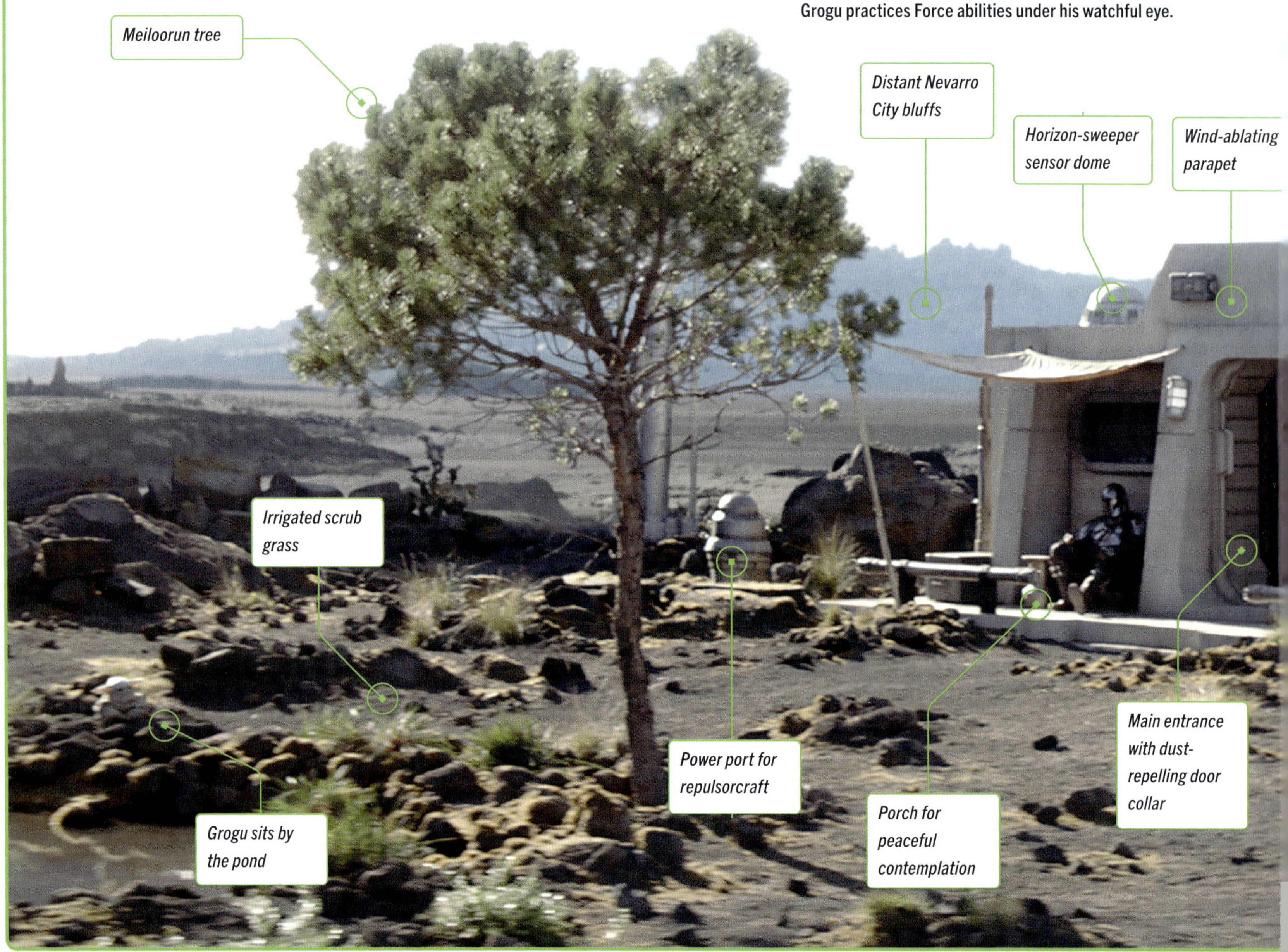

- Meiloorun tree
- Distant Nevarro City bluffs
- Horizon-sweeper sensor dome
- Wind-ablating parapet
- Irrigated scrub grass
- Power port for repulsorcraft
- Porch for peaceful contemplation
- Main entrance with dust-repelling door collar
- Grogu sits by the pond

A CABIN TO CALL HOME

High Magistrate Greef Karga hands over a datacard with the deed to Mando's new cabin, a tranquil place to call home between adventures. As Djarin has agreed to track down the wanted Imperial fugitives for the New Republic, such sanctuary is especially welcome. Mando has a gift as well, presenting Karga with a refurbished IG-11 droid that will serve as marshal of Nevarro.

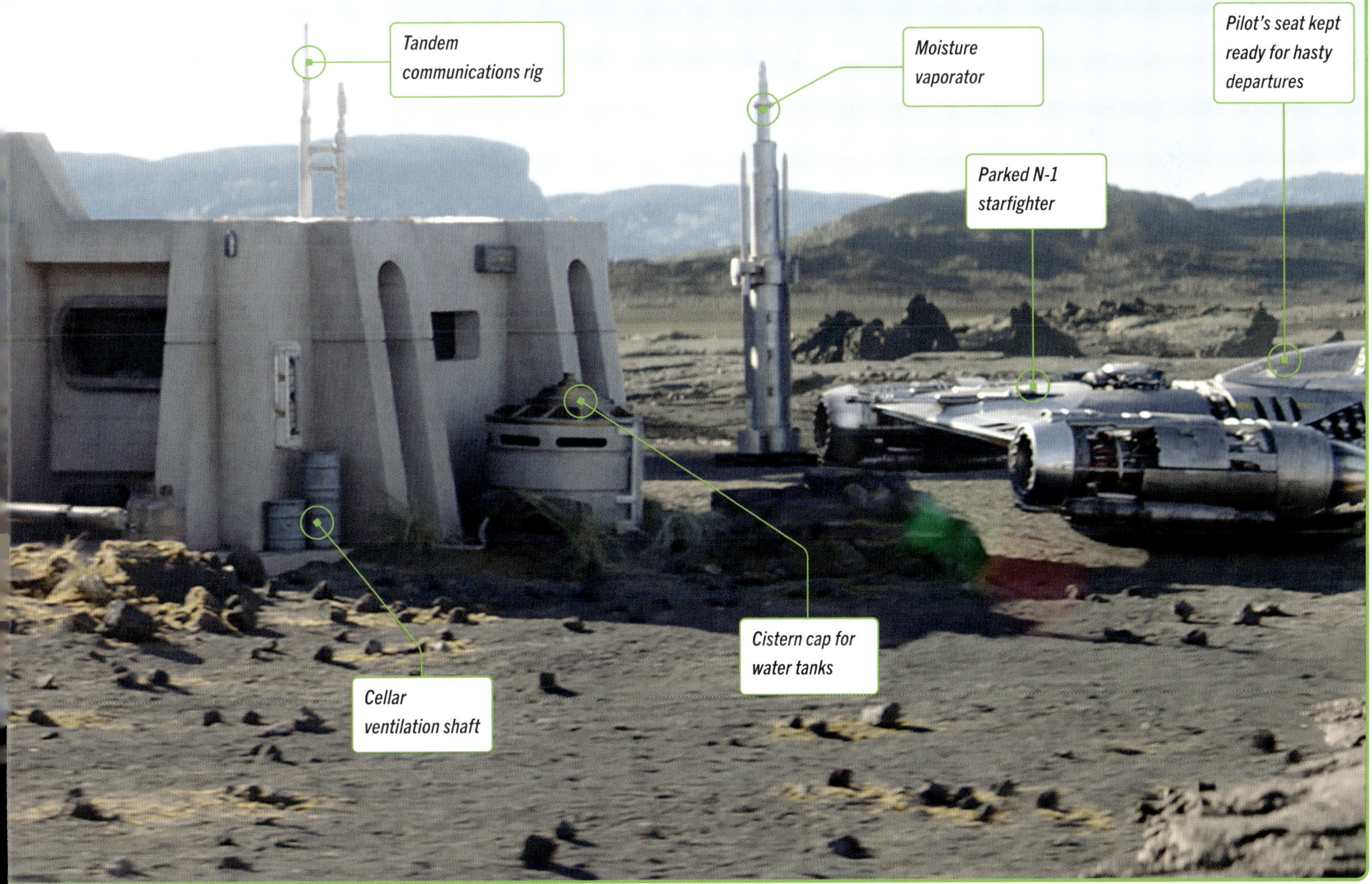

- Exchange of chain code-imprinted datacard
- High magistrate's raiments
- Grateful Din Djarin settling on Nevarro
- Newly adopted Din Grogu
- Tandem communications rig
- Moisture vaporator
- Parked N-1 starfighter
- Pilot's seat kept ready for hasty departures
- Cellar ventilation shaft
- Cistern cap for water tanks

CHASING THE REMNANT
The Mandalorian and Grogu track a group of snowtroopers to a snowy planet where an Imperial remnant base is located. The snowtroopers ride inside four-legged All Terrain Armored Transports (AT-ATs), used by Imperial ground forces. The pair fight the AT-ATs from an All Terrain Reconnaissance Transport (AT-RT), which they commandeer from an Imperial driver.

AT-AT DRIVER

Walker pilots often consider themselves the elite of Imperial combat driver personnel, as they literally tower over their cohorts on the battlefield while at the helm of some of the largest armored vehicles in the army. The reinforced plating that encases the walker cockpits contributes to their air of untouchable superiority.

- Temperature control air exchange ports
- Compressed atmospheric tankage
- Insulated driving gauntlet
- Stowed service SE-14R blaster pistol
- Insulated jumpsuit with ample pockets
- Insulated boot with plastoid-reinforced toe

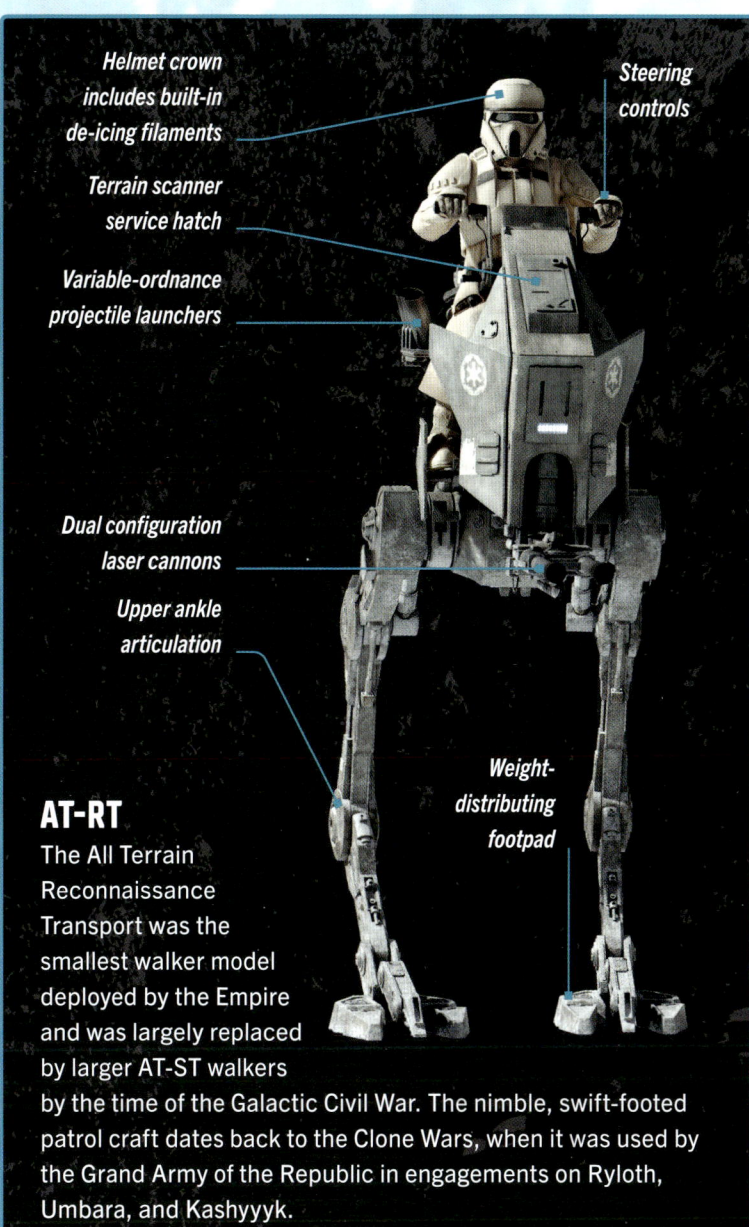

- Helmet crown includes built-in de-icing filaments
- Steering controls
- Terrain scanner service hatch
- Variable-ordnance projectile launchers
- Dual configuration laser cannons
- Upper ankle articulation
- Weight-distributing footpad

AT-RT

The All Terrain Reconnaissance Transport was the smallest walker model deployed by the Empire and was largely replaced by larger AT-ST walkers by the time of the Galactic Civil War. The nimble, swift-footed patrol craft dates back to the Clone Wars, when it was used by the Grand Army of the Republic in engagements on Ryloth, Umbara, and Kashyyyk.

WELCOME TO THE NEIGHBORHOOD
Din Djarin and Grogu have made a life for themselves on Nevarro, and among their neighbors in town are the resident droidsmiths, a helpful group of Anzellans—tiny beings who were especially good at fixing machinery.

HOMESTEAD AND HEADQUARTERS
Mando and Grogu have grown quite comfortable on Nevarro between assignments.

REPUBLIC BUSINESS

Though Moff Gideon was defeated, the power he wielded at his demise was a sobering reminder of the danger that the Imperial remnant still poses. The Senate and bureaucrats in the Core Worlds try to emphasize the New Republic's strengths and successes in reestablishing trade and commerce, but those on the galaxy's fringe face a starker reality. With little fanfare, the understaffed New Republic works to root out Imperial holdouts.

COLONEL WARD

- Officer's rank plaque
- Officer's belt with stowage loops
- Light jacket suited to Adelphi climate

BDX DROID

- Integral comlink antenna
- Neck articulation
- Gyro-balanced feet

THE OFFER
Colonel Ward has a new assignment for Djarin and his apprentice.

INDEX

3R5-D3 55
74-Z speeder bike 99
712 AvA speeder bike 76

A

Adelphi 120, 121, 204–205
aircraft see vehicles
alamites 189
Alderaan 66
Amban rifle 22
Andasala 69
Anzellan droidsmiths 180–81, 202
Aphra, Dr. Chelli 50
Aq Vetina 16
Aqualish 172
armor, beskar 12, 23, 39, 40, 174, 188, 215
    beskar'gam buy'ce 16
    Boba Fett's armor 105, 110, 144, 145, 146
    Grogu's armor 195
    the Mandalorian's armor 16, 17, 22, 60–61, 108, 111, 124, 154, 159
    Moff Gideon's armor 217
the Armorer 40–41, 58, 61, 100
    Armorer's ritual 177
    Glavis Ringworld 165
    and Grogu 105, 195
    and the Mandalorian 102
    and Paz Vizsla 58
    relocation of the Mandalorian Covert 176, 177
    Rising Phoenix 102, 103
    workshop 42–43, 176, 195
Arquitens-class warship 158
artillery stormtroopers 150
Arvala-7 32, 36, 44–45, 46–61
    Jawas on 54–55
    mudhorns 45, 56–57
assassin droids 46, 138, 178
    IG-11 50–51, 101, 102, 180, 221
    notable IG units 50
astromech droids 55, 101, 160
    R2-D2 186
    R5-D4 186–87
AT-ST (All Terrain Scout Transport) 68, 69

B

Baiz, Kaba 164
ballista 113
Bane, Cad 50, 173
bantha 112, 113, 114
BARC recon speeder bikes 198, 199
Barlidan 28
BD-72 74
Behold-Urward Droid Concepts explorer unit 74
Beq, Kelleran 196, 198–99
beskar 36, 189, 190
    the Armorer 40, 41, 42
    beskar armor 12, 16, 23, 39, 40, 60, 61, 105, 144, 145, 146, 174, 188, 195, 215
    beskar spear 139
    beskar'gam 171
    forging 42, 43, 188
    Grogu's armor 195
    whistling birds 61
BlasTech 1B-94 blaster pistol 23
BlasTech KA74 blaster rifle 111
blurrgs 47, 48–49
Botajef Shipyard 18
Bothan-5 84, 86, 88–89, 118
    crew 90–91
bounties, guild 32
Bounty Hunters Guild 16, 36
    carbon-freezing 26
    Greef Karga 16, 32, 33
    Grogu 86, 108
    IG-11 50, 51
    and the Mandalorian 14, 32, 52, 76, 86, 103, 108
    Toro Calican 76
Bralor, Kort 39
Burg 85, 86
Burnin Konn 155

C

Calican, Toro 76–77
    and Fennec Shand 76, 77, 80, 81
    and the Mandalorian 76, 77, 78, 80, 81
Calodan 137, 138
camtonos 37
canyon raptors 200, 201
carbon-freezing 26
Charon River 100
Chihdo 16
the Child see Grogu
Children of the Watch 126, 206, 212, 215
    relocation of 165, 176
    training 194–95
    the Way 58
the Client 32, 36, 37
    death 93, 98
    Grogu 52, 53
    and the Mandalorian 34, 35, 36, 60
    Nevarro safe house 34–35
clone troopers, 501st Legion 197, 198, 199
Clone Wars 10, 12, 196, 197
Coruscant 141, 192–93, 196–99
Corvus 105, 136–41
Crossroads Common House 31, 32, 133, 134
    assault on 98–101
cryoflux 43
CU-28 178
Cumulus-class corsairs 183
cyborg mech 189

D

Dala, Hewitt 38
dark troopers 150, 151
Darksaber 12, 94–95, 165, 206
    Bo-Katan Kryze 95, 126, 127, 128, 185, 216
    Moff Gideon 94, 95, 128, 157, 159, 216
Davan, Lant 90
DDC D-16 blaster pistol 93
Death Star II 155, 210
death troopers 98
Death Watch 12, 38, 102, 103, 126
Deeves, Taur 67
Delrian 91
Desta, Idalia 39
dewbacks 78–79, 114
Djarin, Din see Mandalorian
DL-75 heavy blaster pistol 76
Docking Bay 3–5, Mos Eisley Spaceport 72
Dragon's Pelt 49
droids
    Anzellan droidsmiths 180–81, 202
    assassin droids 46, 50–51, 101, 102, 138, 178, 180
    astromech droids 55, 101, 160, 186–87
    BD-72 74
    CU-28 178
    foot droids 179, 180, 184
    IG-11 178, 221
    IG-12 202–203
    interrogator droid 37
    MA-13 ferry droid 101
    N5 sentry droid 91
    Peli Motto's droids 74–75
    pit droids 75
    Plazir-15 209
    protocol droids 87, 133, 178
    R1 security droid 91
    R2-D2 160
    scorpenek droid 173
    spelunking droid 186
    Treadwell 75
    TT-87 gatekeeper droid 35
Droppers 66, 67
Dune, Cara 66–67, 154, 156
    Crossroads Common House attack 92, 100
    and Grogu 157
    and Moff Gideon 92
    on Nevarro 132, 133, 135
Dune Sea 76, 78, 79, 80, 112, 142
Duripan Plains 45, 48

E

E-Web 15 98
EE-3 blaster carbine 147
electrobinoculars 77
Elsbeth, Morgan 139, 171, 210
    and Ahsoka Tano 138, 139
    Corvus 136, 137, 138–39
Embeggu 69
the Empire 36, 91, 159, 161, 197
    Mandalore 38, 40, 58, 100, 188
    on Nevarro 30, 31
    Order of Six-Spoked Roundel 36
    see also Imperial remnant
Endor 210
    Battle of Endor 66
    Blurrgs 48, 49

F

Fedall 125
ferry droids 101
Ferryman's Reach, Pagodon 25, 28
Fett, Boba 74, 105, 110, 144–45
    armor and equipment 144, 145, 146–47, 149
    assault on Tython 150
    attack on Gideon's cruiser 156, 157
    Battle of Mos Espa 172
    and Bib Fortuna 163
    and Cad Bane 173
    and Fennec Shand 142, 157, 172
    and the Mandalorian 163, 172
    starship 148–49, 154, 156
Fett, Jango 102, 144, 145, 146, 148
Firespray-class pursuit ship 148–49
foot droids 179, 180, 184
the Force
    Ahsoka Tano 140
    Grogu 52, 57, 160, 173, 220
    Ossus 170
    Tython 142, 143
Forest Moon of Endor see Endor
Fortuna, Bib 163
foundlings 39, 41, 52, 103, 144
Frog Lady 116–17
Frog Man 116
Fulcrum 140

G

gaderffii 113, 147
Galactic Civil War 18, 66, 96, 123, 205, 210
Galactic Empire see Empire
Galactic Republic see Republic
the Galaxy, map of the 10–13
gauntlets 23
Gentes 46

Gideon, Moff 14, 92–93, 108, 130
   armor 217
   assault on Tython 150
   attack on Gideon's cruiser 156–57
   Crossroads Common House assault 98–101
   Darksaber 94, 95, 128, 157, 159, 216
   death 219
   forces 214–15
   and Grogu 98, 135, 150, 152, 156–57, 159, 218
   Imperial light cruiser 158–59, 160, 206, 217, 218, 219
   and the Mandalorian 96, 133, 216, 218, 219
   on Nevarro 134
   threat to Mandalore 12, 174, 188, 203, 210, 211, 214–19
   TIE fighter 96
Glavis Ringworld 164–65
Gorbah 155
gorvin snu 44
Gozanti freighters 128, 129, 130–31
Great Purge of Mandalore 16, 36, 38, 58, 60, 92, 127, 174, 189
grinjer 64
Grogu (the Child) 52–53, 119, 133, 180
   and Ahsoka Tano 141, 142
   armor 195
   blood 135, 216
   and the Bounty Hunters Guild 86, 108
   capture of 151, 152, 156–57, 159
   the Force 52, 57, 160, 173, 220
   IG-12 202, 203
   and Kuiil 47
   and Luke Skywalker 160, 171
   and the Mandalorian 14, 65, 72, 92, 103, 105, 123, 136, 137, 141, 143, 152, 163, 166, 168, 171, 174, 194, 203, 219
   and Moff Gideon 92, 93, 98, 135, 150, 218, 219
   Mos Pelgo 108, 109
   Order 66 196–97, 198
   and Peli Motto 72, 166
   on Tython 141, 143
   the Way 194

H

Helgait, Security Commissioner 209
helmets 16, 177, 188
   Armorer *buy'ce* 40
Hess, Valin 155
HK-87 assassin droids 138
holopuck 32
Holowan Laboratories 50
hover pram 52, 124, 196

Hutt, Jabba the 148, 172
   carbon-freezing 26
   death of 68, 72, 74, 110, 163, 173
Hutt Clan 68, 69, 80
Hutt Twins 172
Hux, Brendol 211, 217
Hydroid Traveler 207

I

ice spiders 117, 119
IG-11 50–51, 101, 102, 178, 180, 221
IG-12 202–03
Ilum 95
Imperial light cruiser 158–59, 160, 206, 217, 218, 219
Imperial remnant 10, 105, 133
   and Bo-Katan Kryze 128, 187
   and Boba Fett 145, 156
   cloning 135
   forces 98, 99, 145, 214, 215
   Imperial light cruiser 158–59, 160, 206, 217, 218, 219
   Moff Gideon 92, 93, 98, 158, 214
   Morak Imperial base 152, 153, 154–55
   Nevarro 34–35, 42, 92, 98
   Nevarro safe house 34–35
   Shadow Council 210–11, 216
   Trask 122, 130
Imperial Security Bureau 154, 216
Imperial Space Ministry 19
incinerator troopers 98
Industrial Automaton 91
InterGalactic Banking Clan 50, 89
interrogator droid 37
ITT (Imperial Troop Transport) 99

J

Jawas 20, 146, 186
   and Kuiil the Ugnaught 46
   mudhorn eggs 57
   offworld Jawas 45, 54–55
   and Peli Motto 74
   Razor Crest 20, 46
   silicax oxalate 110
Jedi Order 160
   Grogu 196
   Order 66 197, 198
   Ossus 170, 171
   trials 199
   Tython 142, 143
   see also individual Jedi
Jedi Temple, Coruscant 141
   Order 66 196, 197, 198
Jedi Temple, Ilum 95
jetpacks 58
   Rising Phoenix 102–103, 126, 194, 201
Joth, Rosh 16
the Judge 194, 195

Juggernauts 153, 154, 155

K

Kalevala 184–85
   Kalevalan Mandalorians 218
Kane, Elia 193
Karga, Greef 32–33, 36, 92, 181
   Anzellan droidsmiths 180
   and Gorian Shard 182
   IG-11 221
   IG-12 202
   and the Mandalorian 16, 32, 86, 221
   on Nevarro 32, 33, 132, 134, 135, 178–79, 220, 221
Karthon Chop Fields 85, 89, 91, 152, 155
Kelborn, Emast 38
Keldabe 219
Keldau, Clan 190
Kenobi, Obi-Wan 160
Kessler DB-41 blaster pistol 147
Klatooinian raiders 63, 68–69
Klatooinians 172
Kol Iben 122
Kom'rk Gauntlet fighter 157
Koresh, Gor 106, 107
krayt dragons 113, 114–15
Krrsantan 172, 173
Kryze, Bo-Katan 94, 95, 126–27, 206
   allies 128–29, 130
   Darksaber 95, 126, 127, 128, 185, 216
   Gozanti-class freighter attack 128, 129, 130
   and Grogu 194
   Mandalore 159, 212
   and the Mandalorian 105, 157, 184
   and Moff Gideon 218, 219
   mythosaurs 191
   on Plazir-15 208, 209
   Ragnar rescue 200, 201
   ship 157, 158, 185
Kryze, Duchess Satine 12, 38, 58, 126, 185
Kryze Fortress 184, 185
Kuiil the Ugnaught 45, 46–47, 180
   blurrgs 48, 49
   and IG-11 46, 50, 51, 180
kyr'bes 190

L

L-s7.2 laser cannons 97
Lambda-class shuttle 156, 158
Lang, Captain 138
langskib 212
Lars, Beru 160
Lars, Owen 160, 186
lava meerkats 101

lava punt 100
leviathan krayt dragons 114–15
lightsabers
   Ahsoka Tano's lightsabers 140
   Darksaber 12, 94–95, 126, 127, 157, 159, 165, 185, 206
Living Waters of Mandalore 174, 176–77, 191, 194, 200, 219
Loomis, Jird 78

M

M-32 light repeating blaster rifle 66
M-335 speeder 29
MA-13 ferry droid 101
Mainos, Jorad 156
Maldo Kreis 116, 117, 118–19, 120
Malk, Ranzar 82, 83, 84, 88
   crew 84, 85, 86–87, 88
mamacore 125
Mandalore 126, 184, 188–91, 194–95
   Darksaber 94–95
   and the Empire 38
   foundlings 39, 41, 52, 103, 144
   Great Purge of Mandalore 16, 36, 38, 58, 60, 92, 127, 174, 189
   history of 12
   Living Waters of Mandalore 174, 176–77, 191, 194, 200, 219
   Mandalorian Covert 16, 31, 38–39, 40, 42–43, 58, 60, 100, 165, 176–77
   Mandalorian Creed 103, 105, 171, 177, 194, 219
   Mandalorian *kyr'bes* 190
   Mandalorians 10
   Mines of Mandalore 189
   Night of a Thousand Tears 12, 174, 212
   showdown on 218–19
   survivors (*cuyane*) 212–13
   the Way 16, 39, 40, 41, 42, 58, 60, 126, 177, 194, 219
the Mandalorian (Din Djarin/Mando) 16–17
   Aq Vetina 16
   armor 16, 17, 22, 60–61, 108, 111, 124, 154, 159
   and the Armorer 102
   blurrgs 47, 49
   and Bo-Katan Kryze 105, 126, 157, 184
   and Boba Fett 163, 172
   Bothan-5 86, 87, 88, 90
   and the Bounty Hunters Guild 14, 32, 52, 76, 86, 103, 108
   and Captain Carson Teva 120, 121
   capture of Grogu 152, 156–57, 159
   and the Client 34, 35, 36, 60

on Glavis Ringworld 165
and Gor Koresh 106
and Greef Karga 16, 32, 221
and Grogu 14, 52, 53, 65, 72, 92, 103, 105, 123, 136, 137, 141, 143, 152, 163, 166, 168, 171, 174, 194, 203, 219
IG-11 50, 51, 102, 180, 221
IG-12 202
and the Jawas 46, 57
krayt dragons 115
and Migs Mayfeld 84, 85
and Moff Gideon 96, 133, 216, 218, 219
and the Mythrol 26, 27
N-1 Starfighter 166–69, 185
on Nevarro 220, 221
Nevarro Imperial base 134, 135
and Paz Vizsla 58, 59
and Peli Motto 166
on Plazir-15 208, 209
Ragnar rescue 200
Razor Crest 16, 18–21, 86
return to the Way 174
Rising Phoenix 102–103
on Tatooine 72, 74, 105
and Toro Calican 76, 77, 78, 80, 81
on Trask 122–23
Tuskens 112
on Tython 150
weapons 22–23, 97
Mandalorian Covert 31, 38–39, 40, 58, 60, 100, 165
the Armorer's workshop 42–43
relocation of 176–77
Mandible, Doctor 72
massiffs 113
Maul, Lord 126
Mayfeld, Migs 84–85, 86, 152, 154, 155
Merr-Sonn Munitions 785MK Firepuncher-X Sniper Rifle 80
Merr-Sonn Munitions HF-94 heavy blaster pistol 111
Midani 69
Mining Collective 108, 110, 111
Miv'rah 48
Mods 172
Momonth's Public House, Pagodon 25
Mon Cala 122, 207
Mon Calamari 122, 123
Morak 152–53
Imperial base 154–55
Mos Eisley Cantina 72
Mos Eisley Spaceport 74
Docking Bay 3–5 72
Mos Espa, Battle of 172–73
Mos Pelgo (Freetown) 108–11
krayt dragons 114, 115

Mott 156
Motto, Peli 72–73, 77
droids 74–75
and Grogu 72, 166
and the Mandalorian 166
N-1 Starfighter 166, 167, 168
R5-D4 186, 187
mud yaks 170
mudhorns 45, 56–57, 60, 103
mythosaur 42, 190–91, 206
Mythrol 89, 132
"The Mythrol" 26–27
Nevarro Imperial base 134, 135

N

N-1 starfighter 74, 166–69, 185
N5 sentry droid 91
Na'al, Voren 186
nau'ur kad beskar'gam 40
Nevarro 30–43, 54
Anzellan droidsmiths 180
Crossroads Common House 31, 32, 98–101, 133, 134
and the Empire 30, 31, 34–35, 42
Gorian Shard's desires on 182
Greef Karga on 32, 33, 132, 134, 178–79
Imperial base 134–35
Imperial safe house 34–35
lava banks 100–101
Mandalorian Covert 16, 31, 38–39, 40, 58, 60, 100, 165
Nevarro homestead 220–21
revitalization of 132–33
Nevarro City 31, 92, 178
New Republic 10, 14, 36
Adelphi 204–205
Bothan-5 84, 86, 88–91, 118
Cara Dune 66, 67, 133
Coruscant 192, 193
droids 91
Fennec Shand 91
Imperial Shadow Council 210–11, 216
Karthon Chop Fields 85, 89, 91, 152, 155
Migs Mayfeld 84
Moff Gideon 92, 216
New Republic Academies 205
New Republic Amnesty Program 193
New Republic Correctional Corps 91
New Republic Defense Force 118, 120–21, 167, 182
New Republic Intelligence 183
and the Shadow Council 210
Night of a Thousand Tears 12, 174, 212
Nightsisters 139
Nikto 45, 50, 68

Nimbus-class V-wings 197
Nite Owls 105, 206–207, 212, 215

O

Ohnaka, Hondo 148
Omera 65
Order 66 140, 197, 198
Order of Six-Spoked Roundel 36
Orrelios, Garazeb 205
Organa, Leia 161
Ossus 170–71

P

Pagodon 24–29
the boardwalks 25, 27
Ferryman's Reach 25, 28
landing yards 25
Momonth's Public House 25
threats of the ice 28–29
Palpatine, Emperor 159, 211
pauldrons 60, 103
Pellaeon, Gilad 210
Pershing, Doctor Penn 37, 193
capture of 156
and Grogu 35, 37, 53, 135, 156, 216
New Republic Amnesty Program 193
Phase IV dark trooper 217
Phoenix Squadron 140
"Pilots' Rest" Quonset hut 205
Pirate Nation 182–83
pit droids 75
Plazir, Duchess of 208
Plazir-15 208–209
Praetorian Guard 203, 211, 214, 218
Project Necromancer 211
Project Phlutdroid 50
protocol droids 87, 133, 178
Pyke Syndicate 163, 172, 173

Q

Q9-0 86, 87, 116
qartuums 30
Qin (Prisoner X-6-9-11) 86, 88, 89
Quarren 122, 124, 129, 206, 207
Querm eggs 116, 117

R

R1 security droid 91
R2-D2 160, 186
R5-D4 186–87
rancors 172, 173
ravinaks 25, 29
Rax, Gallius 211
Razor Crest 16, 18–21, 72, 133
and *Bothan-5* 83, 86, 88, 118
destruction of 163, 166
Frog Lady 116, 117
interior 20–21, 22

the Jawas strip 20, 46, 57
on Maldo Kreis 117, 118
on Sorgan 63
Rebel Alliance 120, 121, 123, 205
Red Key Raiders 110
Reepayto 72
Reeves, Koska 128, 129, 157, 206
Republic 10, 94, 126, 197
Clone Wars 12, 50, 158
conflict with the Mandalorians 14
Ugnaughts 46
vehicles 158, 159
Reseeta, Senni 16
Reuss VIII 69
rhydonium 154
Rising Phoenix 102–103, 126, 194, 201
The Roost 82–83
Royal Guards 198, 214
RTK111 106–107
Rybets 116, 117
Ryloth blurrgs 48, 49

S

sabacc 72
Saifir 209
sandcrawlers 45, 54–55
Sanyassan Marauders 49
Sarlacc 114, 144
Sastos 68, 69
Saxon, Gar 127
scorpenek droid 173
scout guards 139
scout troopers 99
security droid 91
Seeing Stone temple, Tython 143, 150, 160
sentry droids 91
Shadow Council 210–11, 216
Shaiz, Mok 172
Shand, Fennec 78, 80–81, 163
and Boba Fett 142, 157, 172
and Toro Calican 76, 77, 80, 81, 142
on Tython 150
Shard, Gorian 182–83
flagship 183
shoretroopers 154
Shriek-Hawks 200, 201
Shuggoth, Captain 207
silicax oxalate 108, 110, 146
Sing, Aurra 148
Skywalker, Anakin 140, 160
Skywalker, Luke 160–61
and Boba Fett 144, 147
and Grogu 160, 171
Ossus 170
R2-D2 and C-3PO 186
Solo, Han 26
Sorgan 62–69
krill farming 62, 63, 64, 68

Sorgan Common House 63
Sorgan Village 64–65
Spectres 140
speeder bikes
   74-Z speeder bike 99
   712 AvA speeder bike 76
   BARC recon speeder bikes 198, 199
   Zephyr-J speeder bike 79
speeders
   Cobb Vanth's swoop 110
   M-335 speeder 29
   Trexler Marauder 135
spelunking droid 186
spotchka 62, 63, 64, 69
squawkfowl 64
starfighters 120
   N-1 starfighter 74, 166–69, 185
   Rogue-class Porax-38 starfighter 83
   T-65 X-wing 121
stormtroopers 99, 128, 130, 211
   501st Legion 197, 198, 199
   artillery stormtroopers 150
   captains 150
   dark troopers 150, 151
   death troopers 98
   incinerator troopers 98
   on Nevarro 32, 34, 35, 42
   Order 66 197, 198
   Phase IV dark trooper 217
   scout troopers 99
   shoretroopers 154
   super commandos 215, 216
   tank troopers 154
   TK-4610 34
   TK-6717 34
   on Tython 145, 146
Sugi 147
Sundari 188, 189
Sunspot 91
super commandos 215, 216
Svivren 69

T

T-65 X-wing see X-wings
Taanti 109
Tallon, Adar 50
tank troopers 154
Tano, Ahsoka 126, 140–41
   and Grogu 105, 141, 142, 171
   and Morgan Elsbeth 138, 139
Tatooine 72–83, 147, 160
   Battle of Mos Espa 172–73
   dewbacks 78
   krayt dragons 113, 114–15
   Mos Pelgo (Freetown) 108–11
   Pyke Syndicate 163
   Tuskens 112–13
Tenau, Amot 38
Teva, Captain Carson 120, 183, 205

and Cara Dune 133
and the Mandalorian 120, 121
R5-D4 186, 187
and Trapper Wolf 118, 121
Thrawn, Grand Admiral 138, 139, 210
tibidons 114
TIE fighters 158
   Gideon's TIE fighter 92, 94, 96–97
TIE interceptors 185, 214
TK-4610 34
TK-6717 34
tracking beacons 90
tracking fobs 32
training darts 194, 195
Trandoshans 172
Trask 105, 116, 122–23, 128, 130
trawlers 25, 26
Treadwell 75
Trexler Marauder 135
trinitaur 213
TT-87 gatekeeper droid 35
Tuskens 112–13, 147
   krayt dragons 113, 114, 115
Tuttle, Colonel 183
Twi'lek 86, 89, 106
Tython 142–47
   assault on 150–51

U, V

Ugnaughts 46–47, 209
V-82 dropship 150
V-wing 197, 198
Vader, Darth 198
Valfin 91
Vanth, Cobb 110–11
   Boba Fett's armor 145, 146
Varad, Pen 39
vehicles
   74-Z speeder bike 99
   712 AvA speeder bike 76
   Arquitens-class warship 158
   AT-ST (All Terrain Scout Transport) 68, 69
   Axe Woves' privateer fleet 206
   BARC recon speeder bikes 198, 199
   Boba Fett's starship 148–49
   Bothan-5 84, 86, 88–91, 118
   Cobb Vanth's speeders 110
   Cumulus-class corsairs 183
   Gozanti freighters 128, 129, 130–31
   Imperial light cruiser 158–59, 160, 206, 217, 218, 219
   ITT (Imperial Troop Transport) 99
   Juggernauts 153, 154, 155
   Kom'rk Gauntlet fighter 157
   Lambda-class shuttle 156, 158
   langskib 212
   M-335 speeder 29
   N-1 starfighter 166–69

Pirate vessels 183
Razor Crest 16, 18–21, 22, 46, 57, 63, 72, 83, 86, 88, 116, 117, 118, 133, 163, 166
Rogue-class Porax-38 starfighter 83
T-65 X-wing 121
TIE fighters 96–97, 134, 135, 158
TIE interceptors 185, 214
Trexler Marauder 135
V-82 dropship 150
V-wing 197, 198
Zephyr-J speeder bike 79
Vestar 155
Vish 64
Vizsla, Paz 58–59, 165, 212
   death 218
   Ragnar rescue 200
Vizsla, Pre 58
Vizsla, Ragnar
   darts challenge with Grogu 194
   rescue of 200–201
Vizsla, Tarre 12, 95
Vizsla clan 95
Vodran 68

W

weapons
   Ahsoka Tano's lightsabers 140
   Amban rifle 22
   beskar spear 139
   Blastech 1B-94 blaster pistol 23
   Bo-Katan Kryze's 126, 127
   Boba Fett's starship 149
   Cobb Vanth's 111
   Darksaber 12, 94–95, 126, 127, 128, 157, 159, 165, 185, 206, 216
   DDC D-16 blaster pistol 93
   DL-75 heavy blaster pistol 76
   E-Web 15 98
   EE-3 blaster carbine 147
   Kessler DB-41 blaster pistol 147
   L-s7.2 laser cannons 97
   M-32 light repeating blaster rifle 66
   the Mandalorian's 22–23, 97
   Merr-Sonn Munitions 785MK Firepuncher-X Sniper Rifle 80
   Paz Vizsla's 58, 59
   Praetorian Guards' 214
   Tusken weaponry 113
   whistling birds 61
whistling birds 61
Wing 136, 138
Winta 65
Wobani 91
Wolf, Trapper 118, 121
Woves, Axe 128, 206, 212, 217, 218
Wren, Sabine 94

X

X-6-9-11 (Qin) 86, 88, 89
X-wings 159, 160, 186
   patrol 84, 88, 90, 118, 167
   T-65 X-wing 121
Xi'an 85, 86

Z

Zephyr-J speeder bike 79
Zygerrians 46

Senior Editors Matt Jones and David Fentiman
Project Art Editor Chris Gould
Production Editor Marc Staples
Senior Production Controller Mary Slater
Managing Editor Emma Grange
Managing Art Editor Vicky Short
Publisher Paula Regan
Art Director Charlotte Coulais
Managing Director Mark Searle

Designed for DK by Robert Perry

For Lucasfilm
Senior Editors Brett Rector and Robert Simpson
Creative Director Michael Siglain
Art Director Troy Alders
Story Group Leland Chee, Phil Szostak, Kate Izquierdo
Associate Technical Director Cameron Beck
Asset Management Chris Argyropoulos, Jackey Cabrera, Elinor De La Torre, Gabrielle Levenson, Tim Mapp, Bryce Pinkos, Erik Sanchez, Newell Todd

First published in Great Britain in 2026 by
Dorling Kindersley Limited
20 Vauxhall Bridge Road,
London SW1V 2SA

The authorised representative in the EEA is
Dorling Kindersley Verlag GmbH. Arnulfstr. 124,
80636 Munich, Germany

Page Design Copyright © 2026 Dorling Kindersley Limited
A Penguin Random House Company
10 9 8 7 6 5 4 3 2 1
001–356327–Apr/2026

© & TM 2026 Lucasfilm Ltd.

All rights reserved.
No part of this publication may be reproduced, stored in or introduced into a retrieval system, or transmitted, in any form, or by any means (electronic, mechanical, photocopying, recording, or otherwise), without the prior written permission of the copyright owner.

DK values and supports copyright. Thank you for respecting intellectual property laws by not reproducing, scanning or distributing any part of this publication by any means without permission. By purchasing an authorised edition, you are supporting writers and artists and enabling DK to continue to publish books that inform and inspire readers. No part of this publication may be used or reproduced in any manner for the purpose of training artificial intelligence technologies or systems. In accordance with Article 4(3) of the DSM Directive 2019/790, DK expressly reserves this work from the text and data mining exception.

A CIP catalogue record for this book
is available from the British Library.
ISBN: 978-0-2417-9129-5

Printed and bound in Italy

www.dk.com

This book was made with Forest Stewardship Council™ certified paper – one small step in DK's commitment to a sustainable future. Learn more at www.dk.com/uk/information/sustainability

ACKNOWLEDGMENTS

Pablo Hidalgo: Thank you to Jon Favreau, Dave Filoni, John Bartnicki, Karen Gilchrist, Carrie Beck, and Noah Kloor for their generous time and feedback on this project. Special thanks to Josh Roth, Phil Szostak, Gabrielle Levenson, Bryce Pinkos, David Marsh, Dan Lobl, Hal Hickel, Richard Bluff, Ryan Church, Cameron Neilson, Dylan Firshein, Abby Keller, Kristen Schreck, Joseph Shirley and Gina Hermosillo for their expertise and access. Thanks to James Waugh and Mike Siglain for shepherding this project's journey, and David Fentiman, Matt Jones, and everyone at DK for making it real. And to Kristen for being there.

John R. Mullaney: Huge thanks to Chris Gould, Matt Jones, Clive Savage, and Vicky Short at DK for all their help, meeting every conceivable reference request and being such a pleasure to work with. Additional thanks to Pablo Hidalgo, Leland Chee, and Jim Piszar for their generous feedback and expertise; to the filmmakers for crafting such an awesome show; my brother James for his IT assistance; and to Hans Jenssen, Richard Chasemore, and Kemp Remillard whose cutaway art remains a constant inspiration. Finally to Clare and my boys for their support and being with me every step of... the Way.

DK Publishing: We would like to thank Kathleen Kennedy, Jon Favreau, Dave Filoni, Michael Siglain, Brett Rector, Robert Simpson, Pablo Hidalgo, Leland Chee, Emily Shkoukani, Josh Roth, Bryce Pinkos, Sarah Williams, Crew Parker, and Elinor De La Torre at Lucasfilm for their assistance with the creation of this book. Additional thanks to John R. Mullaney for his cross-section artwork; Brian Rood for the cover artwork; Chelsea Alon at Disney; David McDonald, Clive Savage, and Stefan Georgiou for design work; Emma Grange for editorial help; and Rajdeep Singh, Satish Guar, and Anurag Trivedi for DTP design work.

Concept Artists:
John Park (page 1)
Nick Gindraux (pages 2–3)
Anton Grandert (pages 4–5)
Christian Alzmann (pages 8–9, 12–13)
Brian Matyas (pages 104–105)
Anton Grandert (pages 162–163)
Richard Lim (pages 174–175)

Standard Imperial uniform

Lieutenant rank plaque